D1458478

THE CELTIC WAY
a long-distance walk through Western Britain

Val Saunders Evans

Published by Sigma Leisure – an imprint of
Sigma Press, 1 South Oak Lane, Wilmslow, Cheshire SK9 6AR, England.
British Library Cataloguing in Publication Data
A CIP record for this book is available from the British Library.

ISBN: 1-85058-618-7

Typesetting and Design by: Sigma Press, Wilmslow, Cheshire.

Cover illustration: Ken Johnston

Text illustrations: Louisa Frears

Maps: Alan Bradley

Photos: Val Saunders Evans unless otherwise credited

Printed by: MFP Design and Print

Preface

The Celtic Way is the walking guide to a new 722-mile route through Western Britain. It is also the name given to the new long-distance footpath through the ancient sites in this area.

There are various ways of approaching the route and the guide. Within the guide, the walking is divided into eighteen sections, each representing anything from two to five days' walking. Each section has some geographical and historic feature that makes it a unit. It is possible to begin with the Megalithic Sites section and do four days' walking in the Stonehenge area. Or one can begin with the Arthurian Centre section and spend two or three days doing the linear route linking Glastonbury and Cadbury Castle. One could begin at the beginning in Pembrokeshire, or the end at the tip of Cornwall. One could go straight to the sections on less-frequented areas such as Gwent or Carmarthen, or to the challenges of Dartmoor and Exmoor, or the high level walking on the Black Mountain. Most people will probably walk a section at a time over a long weekend, or perhaps two linking sections over a week. There is a lot to be said for dipping into sections and walking a day here and there.

Someone local – and knowledgeable about the area – has written the walking notes for a section. As well as local knowledge, each of the guide-writers has a particular perspective to offer. Therefore, the aim in compiling and editing this guide has been to achieve reasonable consistency of information and format without losing the individuality of written material or style.

Sections are divided into stages: these reflect how, from the writer's experience, the route should be set out most effectively and walked most naturally. Generally, few recommendations about walk length have been made because needs differ too widely. When planning, it is generally wise to play safe and over-estimate the difficulty and under-estimate your ability, and allow time for finding paths.

The Celtic Way is a linear route (with circular options in two areas), so public transport connections may be more relevant than car parks. Some basic sources of information about transport and accommodation are given at the beginning of each section. Car owners may choose to leave their vehicles adjacent to overnight accommodation. Taxis – especially shared – are a useful way of beginning and ending a walking stretch, but if you plan your walking carefully, you can get from the start to the finish of the day's journey completely on foot.

Safety is an important consideration. No walking route is without its challenges and surprises and the Celtic Way is no exception. Comments about terrain and other safety factors are given by the writer of each section. Basic safety information is in the introduction. Proper planning, preparation, and realistic appraisal of each person's pace and stamina are key factors in safe walking. Sound equipment helps, too.

One other aspect of preparation needs emphasis. The guide has an array of sketch maps, but do not rely on these alone. It may sometimes be possible to walk using only the walking descriptions and maps, but at other times it will not. Do not depend only on the guide. This is a new route; it has no waymarking yet. You will need the relevant Ordnance Survey map, and details are given in each section. Grid references are given in areas where it aids direction finding. Very occasionally you will need to be confident with taking a compass bearing. This is a new guide: although we have tried hard to eliminate them, you may occasionally find ambiguities and problems. Let us know where they are.

Walking some of the less-frequented sections has revealed that prime historical sites are not confined to the more well-known areas featured in this guide. Carmarthenshire was the most difficult county to take the route through, yet anyone who walks this section will come across an uncommon place, at times like walking through a mythic landscape: no wonder legend attributes this county to Merlin. South-east Wales had so many surprises that we extended the length of the description through the area. Choosing from the abundant walking opportunities from Glastonbury to Devon proved to be too difficult a decision to make – so we offer two routes, north to Exmoor, or south to the old kingdom of Wessex. Let us know what you think of the walking in these areas.

When you are walking the route, within each section you will see the Celtic Way symbol displayed somewhere along the path through the area – perhaps in a shop or pub window. This will be a place where, if you like, you can pick up a question sheet or leave any route comments you want to make. You are also invited to write to the address below. Your feedback is vital to assist in the successful revision of the Celtic Way. In time, it may be possible to bring connections to it from Ireland, Brittany, and perhaps the North and East of Britain. If you have ideas for a route to extend or connect with the Celtic Way, get in touch. Be warned though: a lot of people have been involved with the work on this route and guide, but not for the money – there has been none. If they are lucky, their share of the royalties – when it eventually arrives – might reimburse the cost of a few maps. Everyone concerned has been giving his or her free labours to an idea which reflects a certain affection for the land and its ancient sites.

On a less material note: the land makes mystics of some of us. There isn't a section in this guide which doesn't throw up more questions than answers. At the end of the guide there is a bibliography for anyone interested in the ideas and features they have come across on a part of the route.

Finally, one of the guiding principles when putting together the Celtic Way has been to avoid adding new routes to an area where something already exists. Instead, we have linked with them. In addition to the 722 miles of the Celtic Way, sixteen are on the Jubilee Way at the Severn Crossing, and seven are on the Cotswold Way. If you take the Wessex route over to Dartmoor, from the Axe Crossing it links with the South-West Coastal Path and the Templer Way (although there is a proposed walking route from Beer to Dartmoor by way of Woodbury which we hope to have up and running soon – see Appendix Two). If you take the Exmoor option, from Withypool to Grimspound, it runs to Dartmoor on the Two Moors Way. Then from Tavistock to Hayle there are 111 miles on the Land's End Trail team's tremendous spine route through Cornwall. So, of the 722 miles, 611 is new Celtic Way walking! With the exception of the Land's End Trail, the linked paths are not described because they are well-established routes, with guides and waymarking, and they appear on the Ordnance Survey maps for the area.

Now it is time to cancel the milk, dust off the boots, and make for the counterpart environment which – like Tolkien's Middle Earth or the realm of fable – runs within and yet separate from our day-to-day world. Walk safely and sensitively, and, as the Celtic humorist Dave Allen used to say: may your God go with you.

Correspondence to: The Celtic Way Project. P O Box 111, Bridgend, CF33 4YF.

Acknowledgements

I should like to acknowledge the key elements of support and encouragement contributed by the following during the project.

The Guardian 'Volunteers' Page – Two adverts were placed, asking for walkers and researchers for an innovative walking guide. Over 90 people responded. This gave impetus to the project over the winter of 96/97. In time the numbers hardened down to the people whose work is in the guide. Without this low-cost facility to reach large numbers of predisposed people we would never have got started. **The South Wales Evening Post, Rambling Today and The Great Outdoors** – Gary Spinks wrote an item in the 'Post'about the project which brought people to help with the Welsh sections. Both walking magazines ran features asking for test-walkers. **Archaeology Cymru** – Karl-James Langford has brought his expertise and that of other members of the organisation to the sections of the route through south-east Wales. **Cornish Ramblers** and the **Land's End Trail Team** – some way into the project, Brian Stringer discovered the Land's End Trail Team working on a route from Avebury to Land's End. Their route in Cornwall covers much of the ground we intended so – with their permission – we have incorporated the part of the Land's End Trail between Tavistock and Trencom Hill, near Hayle, into the guide and acknowledge it here and in the appropriate section. **The Ramblers' Association** – Many aspects of the Association's work are invaluable. In this case, in particular, their advice, their network of contacts and their map library service. In the future, this route will benefit from the energy and efforts of local Ramblers' Association Groups to walk it and improve it. **Footpath Officers** – For their knowledge, advice and constructive criticism. **The Celtic Way Volunteer Contributors** – the guide would not exist without the following: their initial response to the idea; their voluntary efforts; their persistence in getting out onto the hills and into the lanes, tracks and fields to make the route work, in spite of the frustrations of blocked footpaths, then writing it up and meeting the deadline. My thanks also to travelling companions, friends and families.

On a personal basis, I thank my husband for his practical and financial support, my daughter for her help and constant encouragement, and my son for his belief in the idea.

Artwork

Louisa Frears

Louisa was born and brought up in Bath. She moved to Plymouth to undertake a Geography degree and has lived there since. She spent one year in Aberdeen taking a Masters degree in Rural Resources Planning. She currently works as a tutor on a post-graduate distance learning degree in Environmental Management at Bath University. She spends much of her spare time drawing and doing freelance design work specialising in countryside interpretation.

Ken Johnston

Ken Johnston spent his childhood in Yorkshire where he developed a love of nature and exploring on foot. He enjoys all sorts of walks; from day walks in the lowlands to backpacking with a tent through the highlands. He has a special interest in ancient tracks and woodland and is indebted to writers such as Jacquetta Hawkes, W.G. Hoskins and Oliver Rackham. In recent years he has drawn sketch maps for books and magazines including *The Great Outdoors*, *Dalesman*, and *Rambling Today*.

Dedication: Ann Beaumont, neé Kent-Smith, 1947-1994.

It is unusual to put a dedication in a walking guide, but this is a unusual guide. Ann was a special friend, and first walking companion. Her sense of fun and zest for life will be remembered by the many people who knew and loved her.

Huccaby Bridge, Dartmoor

Contents

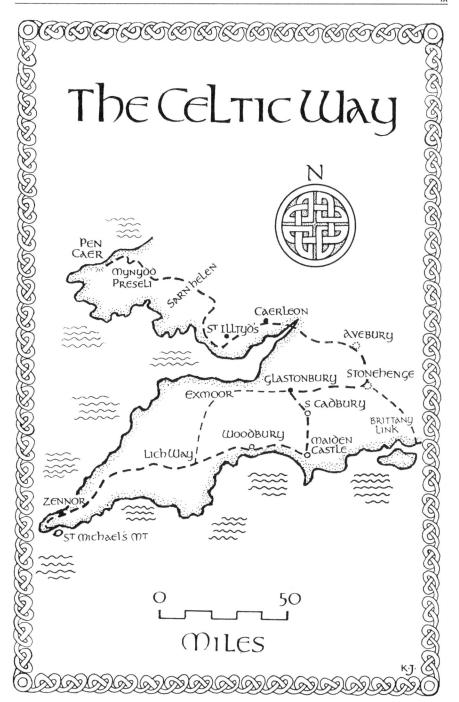

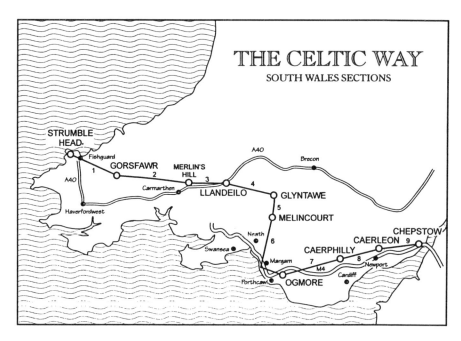

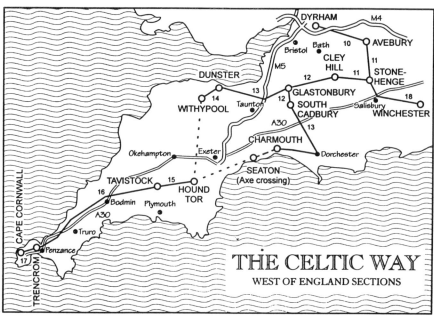

Introduction

This introduction gives some background to the guide. Its most essential part is the section on safety. The rest can be read at leisure, perhaps when relaxing at the end of a day's walking.

What is The Celtic Way?

It is a project, in three stages, to provide a walk through the ancient sites of Western Britain. It came about because we were looking for a route that would take in the legacy left on the land from the time before Britain developed a written history. Production of the guide has been the first stage of the project, getting it walked is the second. Getting it signed will be the third.

So, The Celtic Way is about the marks left upon the land by its earliest travellers and settlers: paths and tracks, homes and fortifications, barrows, sacred sites, stones and circles. It includes remains, monuments and sites from 3000BC up to and after the Roman presence. Historically, it extends to the 6th century: the time of the travels of the early Celtic Christian saints and of the beginning of the Arthurian legend. The Celtic Way, as a historical walking route, is an undertaking to hold on to our remaining ancient sites and paths.

Most of us know relatively little about our prehistory. Evidence from contemporary accounts: a few marks on stone, the remains of homes, these are all we have to go on. Interpretations of the evidence frequently alter as later scholarship delivers new theories. Walking the Celtic Way not only exposes us to the remains left by the earlier inhabitants of this island, but allows us to reflect on our ideas about the past: for example, to experience the legacy of the early Celtic saints while walking this route leads one to ponder the aptness of the term 'Dark Ages' to describe the period in which they were active.

Although walking the Celtic Way is a robust physical experience, it can have its mystical moments. No-one wanted to create some fey, twilight walking zone, but there are qualities about this route which make it exceptional. In walking the path, the walker is taken to ancient sites with their distinct magnetism and mystery. Visually – let's not pull any poetic punches – the route has a rain-drenched, wind-blasted, sun-spread, limestoned, flower-graced, lark-sung and quartz-sparkling quality which the illustrations and photos, but not the prose, attempt to communicate.

The Guide

This first edition of the Celtic Way is a pioneering one. The guide has been written by volunteers and all parts of the route have been walked in the year of writing. Each person writing for the guide has worked on the part of the route which passes through his or her area, bringing local knowledge and experience to the guide. It was a deliberate decision to work in such a way. How else could we realistically and credibly cover such a long route? Because of the amount of walking description necessary, our walking notes are, where possible, concise. We do not include much anecdotal or personal reflection. Some of you will be relieved about that; others will miss it. When actually on a guided walk, the personality and competence of our human guide are important factors. You get less of the personality of your guides here because of the sheer scale of the task. As to competence: all volunteers are qualified by experience and interest, but we are fallible. If you find errors, let me know.

When working on something like The Celtic Way, the route becomes bigger than the individuals. How often do we know the names of the people who built the things which make up our past? Who created the hill fort sites? Who placed the standing stones? Many of us would have preferred anonymity. However, it is also necessary to stand by our walking directions. An individual, possibly assisted by friends, family and walking companions, has put in the experience, time and enthusiasm to create the walking details for each section. The brief biographies included in the guide show the diversity of the people involved.

Feedback

The feedback about the route we get from walkers will be indispensable to the aim of getting the Celtic Way established. Without it, problems will not be solved, improvements will not be made, errors will not be rectified. Each walker is integral to the project. Please use one of the feedback mechanisms: on route stops where the feedback sheets can be picked up and returned, or use the PO Box address. From now on, the walking experiences which matter are not ours but yours. It is your walking which will make The Celtic Way become a present-day reality upon the land. The path is not yet set in stone so your ideas, thoughts and comments on the route and the walking will be welcome. Write to the address at the back of this guide and please let us know what you think.

Access

That there are still so many walking possibilities open to us is very much due to the determined efforts of organisations like the Ramblers' Association and others who act as guardians of the freedom to walk. It is due also to the efforts of those who have maintained the land and the footpaths. I respect, too, the work of those who live off the land: while I am there for a leisure activity, they are earning a livelihood. In a sense, many of us living in the new towns, cities and suburbs are displaced: generations ago our ancestors left the land to find work in the great industrial areas. Perhaps that is why the zest for outdoor activities is strong – as a sort of homecoming. It is good to return to the land, but we remain visitors, with homes to go back to at the end of our walking, and the balance between the walker and those whose only home is the countryside requires some sensitivity and consideration.

All the walking has been checked for right of access, and on many parts of the route it is clear-cut because you are on a waymarked or signed path, or a track across open common, or a stony or metal lane. Unsigned walking across farmland and through farm building complexes is the time when we are less confident. If you are confronted by an owner who challenges access, give way, and let us know and we will check it out. Most importantly, let the local Ramblers' or Footpaths Officer know. Although we have checked these things already, owners change, perspectives alter. Most of the time this will not be a problem.

The other access issue is one of access for people who have some restriction on mobility. There is no information to help make judgements about this, particularly as circumstances differ very widely. By the time we reach the stage of signing The Celtic Way, we hope to have produced information about the parts of the route which are more accessible.

The Country Code

There is a countryside code which is based on common sense and courtesy. All walkers will be aware of the need to respect the property, safety and living of the land they cross. It takes only one careless or stupid person to leave a gate ajar and cause stock to wander. Dogs have a great capacity for getting us into trouble. We all think the problems lie with other people and other dogs. Not so. Much of the walking on the Celtic Way, once it moves into the countryside, is not dog-friendly. Although most of you will be familiar with The Country Code, it is repeated below.

• Guard against all risk of fire.

• Fasten all gates.

• Keep dogs under proper control.

• Keep to paths across farmland.

• Avoid damaging fences, hedges and walls.

• Leave no litter.

• Safeguard water supplies.

• Protect wildlife, wild plants and trees.

• Go carefully on country roads.

• Respect the life of the country.

Safety

Most of you reading this guide will have done some walking before. Basic safety information is included below because it bears repeating no matter how experienced a walker one may become. Two things are worth stressing:

• This is a new route and you must expect to have to look for the gate, or sign or indication that you have followed the directions correctly. **Allow more time to cover the distance** than if you were walking an established long-distance path. By walking the Celtic Way, you are helping to bring it to the point where it is an established path but please allow more time to get between points.

• We have taken an initiative in creating a route between these ancient sites. We have walked the route, and checked it and described it carefully. We put our names to the walking directions as an indication that we stand by them. However, the responsibility for how and when you walk is yours. If you choose to walk a high route in mist, if you choose to go out on exposed places when it is cold and wet, if you choose to walk part of the route without an Ordnance Survey map to back up the walking descriptions, the responsibility for those choices is yours.

Basic safety:

Inform someone: Whether going for a half-day walk or backpacking for several days, let someone know your starting point, finishing point, route and estimated time of arrival at the end of the day's walking. If you are using cars to do a day's walking, then leaving these details in a plastic envelope under the windscreen wiper can be useful. If you are a lone female walker – as I have been for considerable stretches of the walking – you will already have strategies for feeling comfortable. There is no doubt that a lone female walker attracts attention – usually polite concern and mild curiosity – in a way that a man walking alone does not. Attitude and presentation are the key factors. Lone walkers, male and female, need to let someone know where they are heading and when they expect to arrive. Leaving this sort of information is a sound safety practice for all walkers, and absolutely essential when walking the more exposed parts of the route.

Plan: Even a half-day or day's walking needs some planning regarding route, equipment, refreshments and transport. The days of wandering off at whim in a light jacket with sandwiches in the pocket are part of a simpler and vanished past. We are expected to prepare responsibly: no-one wants to be the cause of an emergency.

• Be well-shod, in boots which support, grip, and are broken-in properly.

• Be well covered, with wet-weather gear that works, and wind-proofing in the form of a spare top (for example), hat and gloves.

• Walkers need to be protected from the violence of the sun, especially on hills with no shade. Sun-block and sunscreen need to be carried and renewed as sweating will remove them. Sun hats are commonly worn now, and carrying a loose, light, long-sleeved shirt can be a barrier against burning on exposed arms and necks.

• Carry the right equipment for the length and level of walking you are undertaking. Some items will feature in the well-equipped rucksack on all occasions, some are variable. The perennial items are a rucksack liner, rucksack stiffener (also used to sit on) and a first aid kit with the recommended treatment for bites, burns, cuts, stings, blisters, sprains and breaks. You will also need food, liquid, your maps, a compass, a whistle (for emergency use – six long blasts), a spare top and possibly bottoms. A head torch is a possibility if you plan to be out late. I have never found them helpful for seeing the path, but they are essential for ease of map-reading and wayfinding once light has fallen. Walking after dark is one of those pleasures possibly best reserved for the brief balmy periods of the year.

Longer walking journeys bring in the business of getting overnight accommodation or taking a tent. The Celtic Way lends itself to backpacking with B&B or hostels. True back-packing, with everything aboard, is best undertaken only by those who have previous experience and some training. Self-sufficient backpackers will already be experts on the paring down of equipment to essentials and the merits of one kind of stove over another.

And finally, the name of the route

The project started as an idea for a route linking the Arthurian sites of South Wales. It quickly moved beyond the Arthurian and South Wales to include much of Western Britain and many prehistoric sites. It became 'Celtic' because this was a word which expressed the essence of what we were about very quickly and simply. 'The Celtic Way' could be questionable as a name because the word Celt has not only a historical definition which is obviously much narrower than the scope of prehistory we allude to, but also the word has acquired connotations of a passionate, hard-drinking, self-destructive poetic people. I would say that the Celts I met on the route were generally an enduring, hard-thinking, practical people. In spite of the range of meanings and connotations, we hope the word 'Celtic' succeeds in communicating the idea of the footpath's characteristics of location and historical emphasis simply and well.

Setting the route began with poring over recent and old maps for a mixture of overview and detail to see where the ancient sites, standing stones, names, and prevailing direction of movement indicated by paths suggested the route should be. Then it was a question of going to an area and surveying its footpath access, quality of the prehistoric sites, and atmosphere.

Certain common features emerged as representative of a Celtic Way landscape: a high ridge; valleys with strip lynchets; apple orchards; a small church in its protective 'llan' or circular churchyard walls; shapely hills which would catch the eye and hold it; fast-moving water; historical relevance and legendary significance. Some areas retain a sense of the past, the ancient past, not recent past. It is these qualities which argued for inclusion on the route. Of necessity, modern roads and building have affected the route. Some of the best old tracks have become main roads so could not be used. We have rarely avoided motorways or industry if the route needed to pass them. The juxtaposition can be a useful contrast. However, some of you will know of an improvement to the route at some point. So please write and tell us. Write to The Celtic Way Project - using the Feedback sheet at the end of the book.

The Beginning
Strumble Head (Ynys Meicel) to Fishguard
9 miles

Ynys Meicel from Garn Gilfach

Val Saunders Evans

Born into an Army family who pitched camp for a time in the West Country, Val spent much of her teenage years getting lost on Dartmoor. Curiosity led her to try everything. This gave lots of excuses for taking groups wherever she and they wanted to go in Britain and overseas. She pursued her own learning by doing research in Eastern Europe. Since returning to Wales, walking the hills has been a revelation from which came the idea for the Celtic Way. Val has been responsible for development and co-ordination of the project. She is planning to walk the full route during the summer of publication (1998).

Maps: OS Outdoor Leisure 35 (covers this and all the Pembroke section and extends about 10 miles into the Carmarthen section) or Landranger 157.

Highlights: Garn Fawr hill fort, Garn Gilfach burial chamber, Garn Folch and Garn Gelli. Ffynnon Druidion is a short diversion. Goodwick Brook footpath

Starting point: Ynys Meicel (Strumble Head) Car Park. GR 895 412.

Refreshments: Carry enough for your needs. Youth hostel (self-catering with a few food items), otherwise nothing till Fishguard.

Accommodation: Plenty of B&B in and around Fishguard. I've stayed at Pwll Deri Hostel, Hamilton Backpackers' Hostel and Brynawel Country House, but you really are spoilt for choice in the area.

Information: Fishguard Harbour at Goodwick (station and ferry) – 01348 872037, Fishguard Town Centre – 01348 873484.

Introduction

There are at least four islands around the Celtic coastline named after Saint Michael. Two lie within the area covered by the Celtic Way: St Michael's Mount off the Cornish coast, where the Celtic Way ends, and Ynys Meicel (Michael's Isle) at the tip of the Strumble Headland, where the Celtic Way begins. The other two, Mont St Michel and Skellig Michael, lie off the coasts of Brittany and Ireland respectively. Anyone interested in the St Michael Line might find *The Sun and the Serpent,* an investigation into earth energies, by Hamish Miller and Paul Broadhurst (Pendragon Press) helpful. It gives an account of their exploration of the St Michael Line by dowsing from the tip of Cornwall up to Stonehenge and beyond.

Entry into Pembrokeshire is most direct by way of Fishguard because of its combined rail and ferry links. Its position as a terminus makes it, like Penzance at the other end of the route, a natural place to begin or end a journey. In addition, anyone who drives along the A40 to Fishguard past the lair of Wolf's Castle and the Treffgarne Rocks will see how even the landscape creates a sense of entry at this point. On arrival at Fishguard it may be more practical for most people to start the walking from there. However, the Celtic Way route begins with the hill forts and burial chambers which run over Strumble Head, and for those with the time and enthusiasm it provides a perfect introduction to the area and the walking.

On your arrival in Fishguard, if you decide to walk the beginning of the Celtic Way and have plenty of time free in which to walk then it is possible to follow the waymarked Pembrokeshire Coastal Footpath along the coast for 6 miles from Goodwick to Strumble Head. (The guide I used was 'The Pembrokeshire Coastal Footpath' by Dennis R. Kelsall.) Here you will find the start of the Celtic Way at Ynys Meicel, a small island with its white lighthouse. If you have less time for walking, take a bus or taxi through the lanes for 4 miles to the car park at Ynys Meicel. Ask the driver for the car park at Strumble Head.

When walking any part of the coastal footpath you will be exposed to the full impact of the weather and you need to be prepared for this. The coastal

Strumble Head

path is exceptionally beautiful but is quite demanding in its ascents and descents to bays and coves. Way-finding is not a problem, but you need to exercise appropriate caution when walking along a cliff's edge, especially in strong winds or wet conditions. This is a remote area and there will be nowhere to get refreshment on route. The youth hostel is self-catering and carries a small stock of basic items.

The Celtic Way walking starts from Ynys Meicel and makes for Pwll Deri which is 3 miles along the coastal path. There is a simple and attractive youth hostel at Pwll Deri, a good place to spend the first night, especially if you have walked from Fishguard on the Pembrokeshire Coastal Footpath. The next six miles begin on a stony ridge then follow a bridleway and lanes. This is a gentle exploration of a route less than 200 feet above sea level yet full of views. The walking brings you into contact with the atmosphere of this remote part of Pembrokeshire and includes several sites of interest.

The Route

On the cliff top – whether having walked from Fishguard by the Pembrokeshire Coastal Footpath or taken a bus or taxi to this point – stand and enjoy the fresh, clean air. This is a good time to feel anticipation of the walking ahead. In clear weather the views are inspiring.

Facing the sea, turn left and follow the Pembrokeshire Coastal Path signs for three miles eastwards. The walking is beautiful and isolated. It crosses a cwm and stream at Pwll Arian (Silver Bay) before reaching Porth Maesmelyn and the small stony isles of Tri Maen-trai and Ynys Ddu. After something over two miles comes another isle, Ynys Melyn, and the site of a fort on the hill slope. If, like me, you approach it as light is fading, the lights of the youth hostel and a few nearby cottages signal the welcome approach of Pwll Deri.

Pwll Deri is famous for its views and vivid sunsets. The hill fort rising up behind you is Garn Fawr. Keep a look out for grey seals here and elsewhere along the coast.

From the youth hostel buildings, cross the road and follow the signs past Swn y Mor Cottage to the stile. Apparently, there is a clochan-type hut behind Swn y Mor Cottage which might have been a hermit's cell, a pigsty or a hut such as those found in Western Ireland which are used for drying fish. I have not investigated. Crossing the stile brings you onto the open hillside of Garn Fawr hill fort. There is no path to the top so choose your way sensitively. There is a path which goes to the right and will bring you round the hillside to the car park. Use this if you prefer. Once on the summit there is a ridge path.

Garn Fawr is part of the volcanic eruptions which give Strumble Head its distinctive, dragon's back crest. (If you look to the south-east you can see another dramatic outline of hills on St David's Head). Garn Fawr was an Iron Age hill fort and on the summit it is possible to get a sense of its defensive enclosures.

Follow the summit path over and down into the car park (the path round the hillside comes out close to the same point). There are two very simple cottages to the right below – looking as though they were part of the hill themselves – one belonged to John Piper, the artist.

From the car park turn left. Follow the lane to the west and down the hill passing the entrance to Tan y Mynydd Farm on the left. (Garn Fechan is the crest on the right.) Go 100 metres past the farm to a sign, on the right, for a track and bridleway onto the hillside over to Garn Gilfach and Garn Folch. Take it.

The path runs between two drystone walls. It was rich in wild flowers when walked in June. Gradually, Garn Gilfach, to your right, rises above you. It has a distinctive atmosphere. There is definitely one burial chamber and it might have been a burial ground. After the bright openness of the rest of the walking, I found it dour when walking in June; revisiting it in December I am not so sure.

Go through a gate onto open moor (note the stone gatepost). Follow the path under the ridge unless you want to climb to explore the top. Continue on the path under Garn Folch, going right as a path joins from the left. On approaching two hillside cottages, go through the aluminium gate. The path becomes a track going downhill. Follow it to come out opposite Penysgwarne. You are joining a quiet lane. Turn left and follow the lane to the first right signed Rhosycaerau. Follow the lane uphill towards Garn Gelli.

Garn Gelli stands out in all directions. It is only a couple of rock formations at less than 200 metres but its characteristic appearance draws the eye. It creates a strong visual link between the dragon-back hills you have just walked over and leads the eye on to the Gwaun Valley, to Mynydd Dinas, and ultimately Carn Ingli. Footpaths exist in theory but not in practice at the time of walking on this next stretch, but the lanes used instead are unfrequented. The hedgerows are bursting with wildlife. These and the views lift the spirits.

From the lane there is a footpath sign for the Garn Gelli footpath, but the undergrowth was 5 feet high in the summer. Use it to visit the top if possible, but be warned that the path down was indistinguishable in muddy, cattle-filled fields when last walked. It may be best to keep to the lane. It is possible to take a detour to Rhosycaerau to see the church and churchyard if you wish.

Continue along and down the lane, passing the entrance to Fron Haul on the left, and on to the crossroads. From here you have a choice. The route goes left for two thirds of a mile along a belvedere lane with outstanding views of Pembrokeshire's hills, valleys and amazing coastline. However, if you have time, it is well worth making the diversion to see the burial chamber, spring, and standing stone at Ffynnon Druidion by going right for half a mile.

For the diversion to Ffynnon Druidion (921 365), go right for nearly half a mile to the complex of farm buildings. Turn downhill and the burial chamber is just off the road in a field to the right. The standing stone is alongside the road on the right, a little further down the hill. It is an attractive spot. There are various suggestions as to the origins of the name: "Ffynnon" refers to the spring and "Drudion", or "Druidion", spelling dependent on which source used, could refer to several legendary figures. Interestingly, the older name for the site of the well was Fonnan Pedrykaun, then later Fynnon Pendrigion – the well at the head or end of Drigion's land would be one interpretation. (Information from 'Sacred Stones' by Terry Jones, Gomer Press.) It is tempting if not misleading to see the word Pendragon. Retrace your steps back to the crossroads to rejoin the route.

Continue along the lane. Rocky outcrops from Garn Gelli come close to the road – enjoy the view, you have a ringside seat. Take the next turning right and follow a steep lane downhill for three-quarters of a mile, passing Ty Newydd. When the road turns to the right by Trefwrgi, continue going downhill. Pass Glanmor B&B and cross the A487 with care. Continue down past the Ivybridge B&B and under the old tunnel to come out on a forked track. Take the left fork and go uphill past some cottages. You will pass a meadow with goalposts on your left. Follow the path down and round, approaching reed beds and the Goodwick Brook. The path becomes a Dyfed Nature Walk with waymark signs of a blue house on a yellow background, not that you need them as the path is the only one possible across the reeds. You are walking close to the brook and reeds on a narrow, stony path, edged with small, gnarled trees. This is one of two points on the Celtic Way when one gets a sense of being on an ancient Way. Look back up the valley to a small cottage on the hill. You could be looking at a view from anytime in the past – the present does not intrude apart from a piece of rusty farm equipment and a notice about SSI status. I disturbed a heron fishing.

Cross the small footbridge over the brook and turn left at the junction of tracks. The path then rises to come out by the Seaview Hotel. Cross the road to the Strumble Art Gallery. On your right is the commemorative plaque for the Fishguard Marine Walk. Before continuing, spend a moment at the Goodwick Parrog. Enjoy the tide flows, cloud scenes, sea colours and cormorants. The Strumble Art Gallery has paintings by three fine and very different local artists.

The Marine Walk is delightful. Coast-hugging and often shaded by trees, it avoids traffic and reinforces the contact with the sea which is this area's hallmark. However, it is worth going up to The Square in Fishguard. My ventures into the town took me to the very helpful Tourist Information Centre, and the Bird in Hand Coffee Shop and the Hamilton Backpackers' Hostel, both of which I enjoyed for their friendliness and character.

Looking Ahead: *The route now goes from Fishguard to Newport, taking in Carn Ingli, Pentre, Ifan, and the famous Preselis.*

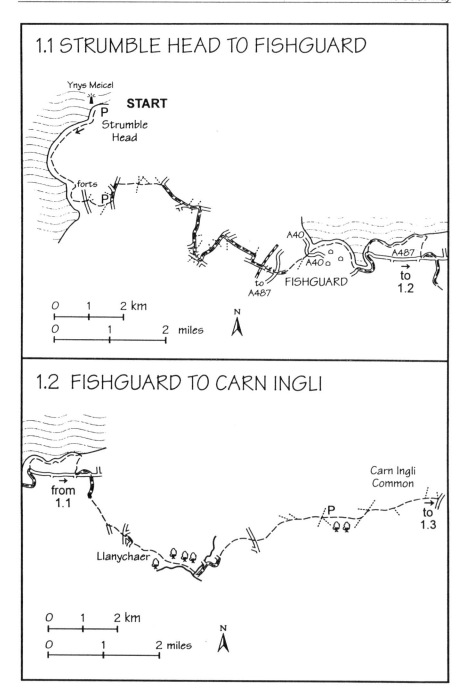

1.1 STRUMBLE HEAD TO FISHGUARD

Ynys Meicel

START

P

Strumble
Head

forts

P

A40

A40

A40

A487

to
A487

FISHGUARD

→
to
1.2

0   1   2 km

0   1   2 miles

N

1.2 FISHGUARD TO CARN INGLI

→
from
1.1

Carn Ingli
Common

P

→
to
1.3

Llanychaer

0   1   2 km

0   1   2 miles

N

Section One
Preseli Mountains: Fishguard to Gors Fawr

20½ miles

View from Carn Gelli to Mynydd Dinas

Wayne Lewis and Dave Puddy

Wayne Lewis has lived in the area for close on the last 10 years. His walking experience is mainly local to the area in which he happens to live although he enjoyed a 'once in a lifetime' dash around Pakistan, Afghanistan and China a few years ago. Dave Puddy lives on a smallholding in Carmarthenshire and is employed as a social worker. When not tending to the needs of wife, goats and sheep, he is to be found walking anywhere in Wales – Offa's Dyke and the Pembrokeshire coast are favourites. Buddhism, jazz and playing the guitar occupy the winter evenings, together with planning the next walk.

Stages:
Fishguard to Castell Henllys – 12½ miles
Castell Henllys to Gors Fawr – 8 miles

Maps: OS Outdoor Leisure 35 and Landrangers 157 and 145.

Highlights: Fishguard, Tre-Llan Holy Well, Mynydd Dinas, Carn Ingli, Castell Henllys Iron Age village reconstruction, Pentre Ifan burial chamber, the Preselis Mountains and Gors Fawr stone circle.

Starting point: Fishguard ferry port and railway station (947 382), or continue from previous route as indicated.

Refreshments: Not easy to find after leaving Fishguard. Possible at Castell Henllys and Crosswell (in season) on the next section.

Accommodation: Easy in Newport – YHA and B&B available. Ask at TIC about accommodation later in the route. Camping may be an option near Gors Fawr. An alternative to stopping overnight in Newport might be to take accommodation in the Eglwyswrw or Felindre Farchog areas. Booking ahead and careful planning is essential on this part of the route.

Public transport: Apart from the railway at Fishguard, enquire at TIC about local bus companies and timetables. Local taxis can be an economic option if shared (TIC will have names and numbers). Some B&B owners will offer a pick-up service if you are staying with them. Enquire at time of booking.

Tourist Information: Fishguard TIC – 01348 873484, Fax 875246; Fishguard Harbour TIC – 01348 872037, Fax 875125; Newport TIC – Tel/Fax 012339 820912; Newcastle Emlyn TIC – 01239 711333.

Introduction

The route ahead has so many highlights that, although the distances are not great, it is worth allowing plenty of time to appreciate the ancient sites. Pembrokeshire displays its past to the open skies for all to see. The many sites of prehistoric interest – old routes, burial chambers and standing stones – argue the significance of Pembrokeshire, almost as if it were once the beginning of a route and not the end, as it is seen today. The emphasis given to localities may have changed throughout our history, but the sites remain. The link between Carn Meini Bluestones and Stonehenge supports the idea of Pembrokeshire's prehistoric importance. However Pembrokeshire has not only coastline and mountains: the solitary Gwaun Valley is an important feature of this section of the walking.

Leaving Old Fishguard harbour by foot is a challenge. The section along the A487 is, fortunately, brief. Entering the Gwaun Valley is a huge contrast: stepping back in time may be a cliché but in the Gwaun Valley there are places where it is a reality. The route passes a holy well and close to the Parc y Meirw megalithic alignment before moving onto open hilltops and an old track over to Bedd Morus and Carn Ingli. The walking is undulating, with wonderful views on a good day but very exposed on the hills in rough weather. After Newport it is important to plan carefully and give some thought to where to stop overnight.

It is possible to break the journey anywhere before the Preseli mountains, but after that there are few other overnight stopping places available.

Stage 1: Fishguard to Castell Henllys

On leaving the ferry or station, proceed to the port gates. Turn left and walk along the newly paved area which follows the sea's edge. On leaving the paved area, walk for about 100 metres along the edge of the beach before rejoining the newly paved area. At this point you will see a mosaic depicting the French invasion of Fishguard in 1797, the last invasion force to land on British soil. More details are available in town.

On leaving the footpath, pass to the landward side of a number of flagpoles at Goodwick Parrog and follow the old road (now disused) for approximately 50 metres behind some renovated cottages where you will see a blue footpath sign heading to your left. **This is where the route from Strumble joins with this section.** The current A40, with the Seaview Hotel, doglegs to your right. Proceed up a flight of steps and follow the well-marked Marine Walk around the headland until Old Fishguard Harbour emerges into view on your left. Proceed along the footpath, which then drops downhill.

Approaching the old harbour, almost opposite an old bus shelter-type building, take the smaller path which drops away to your left. Shortly the path joins a metalled road near some cottages (finger-post) and drops sharply back to the left, emerging at sea level. Cross the river at the road bridge and enter quayside car park. Opposite the exit is a grey, corrugated iron building. Follow the path to the left and round the back of this building. Cross the road into Old Newport Road and climb the hill until you reach the A487. Here turn right, and in 50 metres right again along a footpath and through a gate. Go left at a stile to reach the main road. Walk along the grass verge for 400 metres to the Cilshafe track (979 374). Turn right down the metalled track marked as a bridleway at the entrance to Cilshafe Uchaf. Pass through the gates and continue to Cilshafe Uchaf Farm.

There appears to be a nesting box for barn owls in a tin-covered Dutch barn in the farmyard. The farm, whilst a working unit, apparently has some of the buildings given over to holiday accommodation. Carry on through the farmyard and at the farm pond go straight through a metal gate and follow the bridleway uphill. At the top of the short rise, keep the high point of the field (gorse-covered) to your left and carry straight on towards a gateway. Here follow the bridleway downhill.

At the bottom of the hill, cross a small stream through a gate mounted on a piece of old railway track and head uphill again. Having reached the top of the hill, pass through a gateway with stone posts and head through the farmyard immediately ahead.

In the farmyard, bear left and pass a whitewashed farm building on your right as you head up through a gateway with a stone post (Dutch barn on left). Proceed uphill, over a stile and turn right along a concrete road. After 50 metres, at the end of the concrete road, go straight on, ignoring the gate on the left. On cresting the top of the field there is a small standing stone in front of you, and directly ahead of that, a semi-derelict church. This is Tre Llan (982 362).

The spring at Tre-llan

There is a Holy Well in the field to the left of the church. Mynydd Dinas can be seen clearly in front and slightly to the left.

The next part of the walking goes to the Parc y Meirw megalithic alignment and through the Gwaun Valley.

Exit the field through the gate. Cross the metalled road and head up the lane in front of you for about 10 metres before turning right through a gateway and down a farm track. After 50 metres pass a small pond on the left and continue through a farm gate to pass farm buildings on the right, followed shortly afterwards by newer farm buildings also on the right. Head slightly uphill through a gate, following an obvious track. Continue to climb at the end of the track, keeping a fence on your right. At the end of the field pass through a gateway. There should be a wire fence on your right and a stone wall heading uphill, 90 degrees to your left.

On passing through the gateway, note the standing stone on the brow of the hill in the field on the left. This is one of a series of standing stones that are clearly marked on the maps and stand to the left of the path we are taking. The stones of Parc y Meirw (998 359) formed an alignment. One of the fallen stones may have been decorated. The name – Field of the Dead – may give some clue as to the original function of the stones. To the right there are views of Cwm Gwaun and the valleys of the Gwaun's tributaries.

There is no stile at the bottom corner of this field so you have to climb a wall which appears to have been built across an original gateway. This can be done without too much trouble for someone with full mobility. Now head diagonally across the field to your right, passing a standing stone on your left (999 353). By line of eye, the path runs from the wall straight across the top of the standing stone to the bottom corner of the field. At the corner of the field you will need to negotiate a fence as no stile exists, then descend through a wooded area on a fairly obvious path. The path proceeds downhill.

At the time of writing (January) the area is covered in the leaves of bluebells and should be beautiful in the spring. The woodland itself largely consists of small sessile oaks which are very typical of this area.

At the end of a woodland path, turn left onto a small path. This is a new footpath as the valley floor path is no longer in use. Proceed up the valley with Afon Gwaun on your right. After about 125 metres, go diagonally left to the stile at the bottom of the wood. Follow the path at the bottom of the wood for approximately three-quarters of a mile, until it meets a track by a building. Follow this track and cross a small stream by a concrete bridge (006 349). Beware of the dog (usually chained) at the farm by the road.

Pass a house on the right, and immediately turn left up an obvious track heading at 90 degrees to the road. A beautiful stream runs downhill parallel to the road for a few hundred metres before the road doglegs back to the right. Carry on uphill crossing a main track which goes off to the left. The track narrows to a footpath with banks on both sides. Pass a white-painted, old farmhouse with green, tin barns. The house is a traditional design for this area. Note the small, almost round, walled garden with traditional stone steps leading into it from the track. Follow the track bearing uphill to the right until you reach the metalled road at (021 358).

Follow the track which goes along the bottom hedgerow to your right and then turns 90 degrees left again, keeping the hedgerow on your right. (The footpath, whilst marked on the map as going straight ahead from this field, is, in fact, blocked off.) Leave the field through the gateway and take the obvious track, again leading right.

At this point you notice that you have gained considerable height and there are views back down Cwm Gwaun towards Fishguard, although the town is obscured. Follow the track which leads from the farm all the way to the main metalled road (021 358).

It is always worth stopping to look back over your shoulder – you'll be pleased with the views and also able to appreciate the distinct contrast between the Gwaun Valley and the upland area you are now approaching. As a point of interest, one of the main airline routes from London to North America passes overhead so, if all else fails, in bad weather you can find a shady nook and plan your next sunny holiday making use of public transport. My more academic colleague points out that the aeroplane vapour trails will also give you some orientation as regards east/west – a man of very little soul!

On reaching the metal road, cross it and enter the field directly in front of you through a gate. Keep the wire fence immediately on your right and proceed straight ahead. (At the time of writing, you immediately pass an old, metal-wheeled plough, which is, without doubt, destined for the front of some suburban house and a coat of inappropriately bright paint.) At this point, ahead of you and to the right you will notice the Preseli Range rising somewhat gently. It was from these hills that the lintel stones for Stonehenge were originally quarried. How they were transported remains a matter for conjecture, although at the time of writing an underwater archaeologist claims to have found evidence of similar stones on a sea bed at Milford Haven, suggesting they may have been taken by boat.

Leave the field through a gate and head diagonally left through the centre of another field, rising very gently as you go. When you reach the other side of the field, follow the wire fence uphill. As you start gently descending and the sea is directly in front of you, exit the field through an iron gate with two railway sleepers as gate posts. (Ignore the first iron gate in the fence.)

(At this point a diversion to Mynydd Melyn (029 364) is possible. Instead of leaving the field, head back north-west and visit the impressive carn on the summit before returning to the gate.)

From the gate, head north-east. You are now leaving cultivated field areas and moving on to open common land which is gorse and heather-covered. Follow the path directly across open common land, to your right there are remnants of old hut circles.

In clear weather, but probably not in summer, if you look to your left it is possible to see the Lleyn Peninsula of North Wales with Bardsey Island lighthouse flashing at night. The bay which is in evidence is Newport Bay and Parrog, with Dinas Head back to your left and towards the south. Leave this rough grazing land through a small, iron gate and carry on straight ahead through a quite narrow strip field. There is an old stone wall topped by a barbed wire fence on your left.

Head out of the strip field and proceed directly ahead, following a stone wall on your left. As you crest the top of this field, there is a small car park (038 365) ahead of you. Here, on the mountain road which crosses from Gwaun Valley to Newport, is the Bedd Morris (Morus) standing stone. According to Terry Jones (*Sacred Stones*, Gomer Press) there is a relatively recent inscription on the stone to indicate that it shows the junction of two parishes. The maenhir is a beautiful, tall, mottled stone, and its name indicates that it once had some memorial function in its high spot at the roadside.

Directly beyond the maenhir, about one and a half miles away, is the summit of Carn Ingli (carn of angels). In the car park, you will notice a wooden finger-post which highlights the directions of Nevern/Nanyhfer, Castell Henllys (a reconstruction of an Iron Age fort) and Moylegrove. Although not on the main route, it may be worth considering a detour to visit the old church at Nevern, which has one of the few existing standing stones with Ogham inscriptions. There is also a 'bleeding yew' oozing red sap, plus an interesting Celtic Cross.

If you wish to either visit Newport or perhaps stay overnight, on reaching the tarmacked road, Ffordd Bedd Morys, turn left and start to head gently downhill. At this point there is a large boundary stone, the inscription on which is now almost totally indecipherable. However, at the time of writing (December 1997), the local authority had recently affixed a public notice indicating that Carn Ingli has recently been designated as a Site of Special Scientific Interest, a welcome development.

The road at this point has a field wall to your left and open, unfenced land to your right. There are beautiful views out over the sea and estuary around Newport and Parrog from this point and almost the whole way down into the town itself. You meet the first house on this road on the right after exactly one mile, with houses (including B&Bs) becoming more frequent as you progress down the lane.

Carn Ingli

After a further half mile and opposite a house called Blaenpant, there is an interesting old pig sty with six or eight huge stone slabs used as roofing material. Cross a cattle grid. Ffordd Bedd Morys meets the main coast road almost exactly two miles from the point at which you joined it near Bedd Morys. Turn right and enter Newport via West Street in approximately half a mile. The track into Newport runs down and off the hillside. It joins a track from the right and becomes a deep lane passing Castle Hill House. Ignore all tracks leading off the lane, which will come out to the right of the castle and into Newport by St Mary's Church.

There are some lovely local walks, especially along the coastal path in this area. More particularly, however, there is some fine food to be had in the town, so it is worth stopping over. For further information, you could contact the Pembrokeshire National Park Tourist Information Centre in the town, where their staff are always very helpful. If you make Newport the end of your walk for the day, there is a particularly good restaurant, Cnapan, which, for a price, provides excellent food backed up by some superb wine (if it is available, try the Lebanese red wine – recommended).

(You can reach Carn Ingli from Newport by walking up Castle Hill and taking the signed steep track up past some cottages. At the end of the cottages leave the track and go left on to the open hillside. Climb the track to the summit and pick up the directions from there.)

To begin your journey to Carn Ingli (065 373), leave the car park, following the finger post in the direction of Castell Henllys. An obvious path goes gently uphill, keeping the carn on your left and a wire fence on your right. The path runs over and round large boulders. Follow it gently downhill to a stile, keeping woodland on your right. Ignore the stile and turn left, following the wire fence parallel to you on your right for approximately 200 metres. You are heading gently uphill and towards the coast. There are good views out to sea.

Follow the fence which turns at right angles to the right, and the obvious path that runs parallel with the fence. Proceed gently uphill for a quarter of a mile. Pass Carn Edward (055 365) and its stile access on your right. Carn Ingli now comes into view in front of you and to your left. At the end of the fence, pass to the left of a small spring and to the right of Carn Ingli. Start to head downhill. Note the sheep gate next to the gateway near the end of the fence.

If you now decide to make Newport the end of your walk for the day, the track into Newport runs down and off the hillside. It joins a track from the right and becomes a deep lane which passes Castle Hill House. Ignore all tracks leading off the lane and you will come out to the right of the castle and enter Newport by St Mary's Church. To rejoin the route you can return up the Carn Ingli track to where you left it, or take the Cilgwyn road out of Newport for a mile, then take the right fork on to a no through road and follow this along the lee of the hillside to meet up with the route at the junction of tracks at 069 370.

The countryside in the distance ahead of you becomes more gently rolling as you leave the Preselis on the right and behind. Keeping Carn Ingli to your left, head downhill to the point where the path again meets the fence at a field corner. The fence runs along the top of the stone wall. The path runs across the side of the hill for approximately 25 metres in a small ditch between banks. Leave the ditch after 25 metres and again head downhill and to the right, keeping the stone wall to your right.

At the metalled road (finger-post to Cwm Gwaun, Nevern and Newport), turn left and proceed 50 metres to a telegraph pole. Leave the road to head diagonally right and down, across open ground towards a house. At a track, turn left through the farm gate and walk down the track to a metalled road. Turn right for 200 metres, then left at a road junction.

Proceed down the track to a stile and finger-post. Continue straight on down the track, ignoring the stile. Pass through a ford and uphill to a metalled road (081 369). Turn left after approximately a quarter of a mile, passing over a small bridge and turn right up a farm track to Fachongle Ganol (083 371). There is an iron drain cover at the beginning of the track. **Take care here as signposts are scarce**.

Pass Fachongle Ganol on your right and proceed to Fachongle Uchaf. Pass some farm buildings on your right and go through the farm gates (there is, or was, a small finger-post in the hedge at this point, but it's difficult to see until you look back having passed through the gate). The farmhouse is in front of you and down on your right. Do not go down to the house, but pass into the field through the gate in front of you and slightly to your left.

On entering the field, immediately head to your right towards the stile under the large oak tree. Cross the stile and head diagonally uphill to your left towards the fence and edge of woodland. Follow the fence up to the next stile and enter the wood (the stile is slightly hidden behind a set of fire beaters).

Having crossed the stile, enter the nature reserve and follow the waymarked 'Path through the Woodland'. This part of the walk is absolutely enchanting with the woodland being made up of old oak and ash trees. Follow the gently rising path for approximately a quarter of a mile through the wood, with a steep-sided small valley on your right. The path splits at the head of the small valley. Turn left and immediately climb a little bank to where the house Ty Canol, becomes visible (093 368).

At this point the obvious path seems to take you straight ahead and slightly to your right, but you need to turn left. Follow the marked path out past the front of the house (facing west) and proceed down the track towards Pentre Ifan. Follow the track, with views behind to the estuary at Newport, to a met- alled road (098 367) and turn left. There are views of Pentre Ifan to your left across two fields. (At the junction of the track and metalled road there is a small green lane to your right which will take you up to Carnedd Meibion Owen for a mile-long diversion which enjoys good views.)

Proceed down the metalled road for about three-quarters of a mile to where Pentre Ifan is to be found on your left (100 370). It is clearly signposted. This ex- ample of a burial chamber is worth a visit for many reasons, not least of which, as I can testify, is that in the teeth of a westerly gale it provides some shelter for lunch! Follow the metalled road gently downhill for approximately another mile, past Iet-wen to a T-junction (105 379). Here, turn right and proceed for about 100 metres before taking the marked path to your left. After about 200 metres you arrive at a gate and finger-post. Proceed through the farm gate (Ysgwboran is an attractive house up to the left) and go gently downhill along the edge of a wood for three-quarters of a mile (105 383). This path is marked as a bridleway and the lower part can be very wet underfoot. At the end of the path go through the gates and further down the track towards the house at Wenallt. Go through the gate into the yard of the house. At the far end of the house, turn right and head down a short path to cross the river via a footbridge with hand rails. At the end of the footbridge turn left and exit to the main road through the entrance to the garden of a family house, Pen y Bont (105 388).

At the main road (A487), turn right and follow the road uphill for about 250 metres (there is a public toilet at this point). At the lay-by enter the field on the left via a stile (108 386) and head diagonally right to another stile. Cross the next field to a gate below a house and then cross the following field to a stile (slightly to your left). Cross the next field and proceed into Glanduad-fawr farmyard through a gate. In the yard go left and exit through another gate. Head slightly downhill to a stream crossed by a footbridge (115 389).

After the footbridge, go to a metalled road and head right, uphill, past the boundary fence of Castell Henllys. Continue uphill before descending to a stile on the right. Cross the stile and enter woodland. This path skirts round the base of the hillock on which Castell Henllys has been reconstructed and on this part of the path you will often find examples of rebuilt items and craft-type artworks displayed within the woodland. Follow the obvious path and take the route over a stream by the side of the house. During the tourist season there are toilets, a café and various artworks. An entrance fee is charged to view Castell Henllys.

Go uphill, following the main track past Mammoth – yes, honestly!. On leaving the track there, turn right onto a metalled lane and pass in front of Eglwys Meline Church (118 387). Leave the lane to take a farm track. Follow the track to its junction with the main farm track from Glanduad Fawr Farm (which you have now looped) down to your right. Turn left and walk uphill to the main Cardigan to Fishguard road (115 384). At this point you are well placed to get a taxi, public transport or to walk into Newport or to accommodation in the more immediate area. The next stage over the Preselis begins from here.

Stage Two: Castell Henllys (115 385) to Gors Fawr stone circle (135 294)

Cross the main road and follow the farm track directly opposite. At Pen y Benglog Farm pass the first farm buildings on your right and then, after about 100 metres, take the bridleway to your left (just before the track swings 90 degrees to the right) (113 381). Follow the bridleway as it ascends and descends. Pass through a small gate (Castell Llwyd marked on the right) (114 375). Proceed gently downhill.

You can hear the river on your right as the path bottoms out and passes through a fairly ornate gate. Carry on and exit through a farmyard, crossing over the river via a bridge at Troed y Rhiw (114 374). At the metalled road, turn left and proceed uphill slightly for 150 metres, past a house on your right. Take a stile on the right at the finger-post. On entering the field, follow the marked path downhill towards Afon Bryberian. Pass the ruin of an old house. Walk along the riverside (it's very beautiful and quiet) for approximately three-quarters of a mile. Exit the field through a gate by the ford and footbridge (the water level is marked on the bridge) and turn left onto a tarmacked road.

Proceed uphill to the main road and turn left. At the T-junction (120 363) turn left and follow the B4329 down into the village of Crosswell/Ffynnongroes. At the crossroads, turn right and after about 20 metres turn right again up a track through a farm gate. (At the time of writing, a black and white footpath sign in the shape of a boot has been placed on the farm gatepost, but it is only visible if doing the walk from east to west.) After approximately 250 metres the track is blocked by two farm gates, entering two separate fields, separated by a very old gate post. Take the right gate and proceed directly ahead for the length of the field, keeping the old, now overgrown track route to your left.

Rejoin the track at the top left corner of the field, passing through a farm gate set between two stone posts, so typical of this area. The track proceeds directly ahead, slightly sunken below field level with trees meeting over your head, producing, at the time of writing, a beautiful dappled sunlight. The track can be very wet, even in summer. Cross a more clearly defined farm lane which merges from the right and proceed directly ahead up your original track. The track remains in what my two-year-old son would call a 'tunnel of trees'.

Arrive at a small, isolated cottage. Pass to the rear of the building and then immediately to the right past pine end of building, through a small gate and

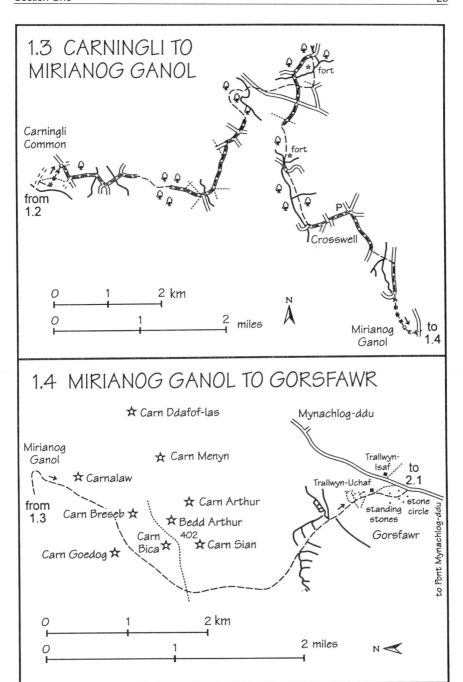

1.3 CARNINGLI TO MIRIANOG GANOL

fort

Carningli Common

fort

from 1.2

Crosswell

P

0   1   2 km

0   1   2 miles

N

Mirianog Ganol

to 1.4

1.4 MIRIANOG GANOL TO GORSFAWR

☆ Carn Ddafof-las

Mynachlog-ddu

Mirianog Ganol

☆ Carn Menyn

Trallwyn-Isaf

to 2.1

☆ Carnalaw

Trallwyn-Uchaf

from 1.3

Carn Breseb ☆

☆ Carn Arthur

standing stones

stone circle

☆ Bedd Arthur

Carn Bica ☆

402

Gorsfawr

☆ Carn Sian

Carn Goedog ☆

to Pont Mynachlog-ddu

0   1   2 km

0   1   2 miles

N

down to a stream which is crossed by a footbridge. Proceed, with the stream to your right, until the path meets a track to the house. Turn left and go to a metalled road.

Here turn right and head gently uphill. Follow the road to its end, adjacent to farm buildings of Mirianog-fach on your left (133 350). Pass over the stream and continue to a fork in the road. Take the left fork and continue to rise gently to a cattle grid. Head upwards again on the tarmacked road.

Note: At this point various Carnedds are visible on Mynydd Preseli in front of you and it is worth planning the route you intend to take across the open moorland from here, prior to following the road on to Mirianog Ganol.

You are now going to cross the Preseli Mountains. Take account of distance, weather, stamina levels and proximity of overnight accommodation. This section is best attempted on a reasonably clear day. For the next two miles the paths are not clear over the Preselis, so refer closely to the map for this section.

At the end of the metalled track (139 345) you are facing the Preseli Hills. Follow the footpath sign to the right going gently uphill towards an outcrop of rocks which is Carnalw, on your left (139 337).

Pass below Carnalw and then a second crop of rocks on your left which is Carn Breseb (135 333). Keep Carn Goedog (128 332) close to your right. Head diagonally left to a saddle in the hills (122 342). Proceed down the saddle on the other side an indistinct path crosses your way at this point. Head south on the rough path towards a house with a barn in the distance on the left of the open valley in front of you. The path gradually becomes clearer as you descend to the road at (127 307), where there is a sheep fold.

Turn left and continue on the road for $1\frac{1}{2}$ miles to where the road bears left (132 304). At this point turn right and join a track. After 50 metres bear left on to a track leading towards farm buildings at Llain-wen. Keep to the right of this farm and the collection of scrap implements. Go through a gate and keeping farm fields to your left, cross rather boggy land for another 150 metres. Ignore the gate to an old green lane on your left and continue ahead and then half-right towards a standing stone. Continue to Gors Fawr stone circle (135 294).

Looking Ahead: The next section begins at Gors Fawr where this route ends. It takes the route into Carmarthenshire as far as Merlin's Hill, just outside Carmarthen. It runs through hilly farming country and includes some interesting villages and a burial chamber.

Section Two
Secret Carmarthenshire:
Gors Fawr to Merlin's Hill
32¼ miles

Sheep gate

Stephen Edwards

Dr. Stephen Edwards took on the challenges and frustrations of the route through rural Carmarthenshire. His meticulous directions make it possible to walk through an obscure, yet lovely, section of the route.

Stages:
1. Gors Fawr to Gors Fach – 3¼ miles
2. Gors Fach to Login – 5¼ miles
3. Login to Llanboidy – 3½ miles
4. Llanboidy to Maesllwyd Inn – 3½ miles
5. Maesllwyd Inn to Abernant – 7¼ miles
6. Abernant to Newchurch – 2½ miles
7. Newchurch to Afon Gwili – 3½ miles
8. Afon-Gwili to Merlin's Hill – 3½ miles

Maps: It is strongly recommended that 1:25 000 scale OS maps are used to follow this part of the Celtic Way. You will require Outdoor Leisure 24 (North Pembrokeshire), and Pathfinders 1058 (Llanboidy & Cynwel Elfed) and 1059 (Carmarthen). The equivalent 1:50 000 scale OS maps are Landrangers 145 (Cardigan & Mynydd Preseli) and 159 (Swansea, Gower & surrounding area).

Highlights: Gwal y Filiast burial chamber, Castell Mawr, Merlin's Hill.

Starting Point: The stone circle at Gors Fawr (135 294).

Additional Information: Cadw, Brunel House, 2 Fitzalan Road, Cardiff (01222 465511), Carmarthenshire County Museum, The Old Palace, Abergwili (01267 231691), Lamb Inn, Llanboidy (01994 448243), Trefach Manor Caravan Park (01994 419225).

Tourist Information: Carmarthen – 01267 231557 (open all year), Llandeilo – 01558 824226 (Easter to September), Newcastle Emlyn – 01239 711333 (Easter to September), Llandovery – 01550 720693 (all year – jointly operated with the Brecon Beacons National Park Authority).

Introduction

The next part of the walk takes us through rural western Carmarthenshire to Merlin's Hill, situated just to the east of the county town itself. This is farming country, and all walkers should show sensitivity to the agricultural importance of the area by keeping to footpaths, shutting all gates, and, of course, following the country code at all times. Unfortunately, while many farmers are happy to have walkers crossing their land so long as they keep to the rights of way, others are less welcoming, and a significant number of the rights of way marked on the OS maps are blocked. Thus, in some sections it is necessary to keep to country lanes even when it may appear from the OS maps that other rights of way may provide better walking. This chapter is broken down into eight sections, allowing the walker to plan each day's journey as required. Overnight accommodation around this area is sparse. Unless you can persuade a farmer to allow you to camp in a field (which is unlikely, in my experience), Llanboidy offers the best bet for an overnight stop, with accommodation available in the Lamb Inn. There is little else, however, before Carmarthen itself.

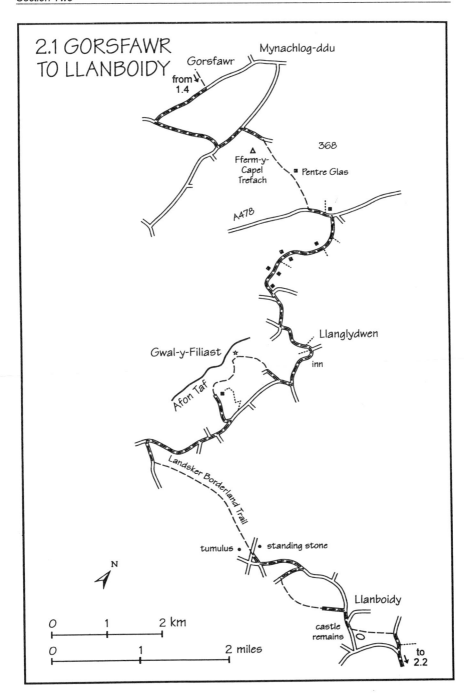

2.1 GORSFAWR
TO LLANBOIDY

from
1.4

Gorsfawr

Mynachlog-ddu

368

△
Fferm-y-
Capel
Trefach

■ Pentre Glas

AA78

Llanglydwen

Gwal-y-Filiast   ★

inn

Afon Taf

Landsker Borderland Trail

tumulus ●   ● standing stone

Llanboidy

N

castle
remains

to
2.2

0   1   2 km

0   1   2 miles

Stage 1: Gors Fawr-Gors-Fach – 3¼ miles

The stone circle at Gors Fawr is thought to be of Bronze Age origin (c2000 BC), and consists of 16 stones with two outlying standing stones clearly visible just east of north. The functions of circles such as this are not entirely clear, though it seems likely they may have had some ritual significance. A number of contemporary theories have suggested that they may also have had some astronomical function relating to the calendar, perhaps allowing Bronze Age people to plan their agricultural activities according to the seasons.

From the stone circle at Gors Fawr, head south-east to the white building of Pen-rhos Farm. Pass through the kissing gate to the road, then turn right and follow the lane down to the junction at 132 282. Turn left here and continue past Allt-y-gog Farm to the junction at 144 286.

Turn left again and head north towards the entrance to Trefach Caravan Park (there is also a pub and other amenities here) at (145 290). Continue north along the lane for about 150 metres, then turn right uphill onto the bridle path leading to Fferm-y-Capel. After about 500 metres, follow the main track round to the right towards the farm buildings. Just before the white buildings, follow the grassy track off to the left.

Keep following this track just south of east through several gates until you arrive at a series of pylons. At the pylon with a yellow waymark sign pointing back the way you have just come, you will see a green lane just to the right, following more or less the direction in which you have been walking. Follow this green lane in a generally easterly direction to a gate, beyond which is a stony track running left to right. Turn right downhill, then past Iet Goch Farm and over a small bridge. This marks your passage out of the Pembrokeshire Coast National Park and into Carmarthenshire. Continue on the main path uphill to the A478, just west of Gors-Fach.

Stage 2: Gors-Fach to Login – 5¼ miles

The spectacular burial chamber, or cromlech, at Gwal y Filiast ("Lair of the Greyhound") – which is also known as Dolwilym or Bwrdd Arthur ("Arthur's Table") – lies on private land, though since it is immediately adjacent to the right of way it is very easy to visit. It is Neolithic in origin, probably dating from about 3500-2500BC, and consists of four side stones and a capstone, although there may once have been more than four side stones. A 19th-century description of the cromlech suggests that it may once have been surrounded by a stone circle and covered by a barrow, though no evidence of this exists now. There are, however, two small stones a little way uphill from the tomb, which has led to suggestions that this may once have been a passage tomb, though since it has not yet been excavated this cannot be proved. The cromlech is protected by Cadw, the Welsh historical monuments organisation.

Head north-east up the A478 for about 100 metres, then turn right at the first road junction (169 289). Turn right, tending south, to the road junction at 169 271. Turn right here, then left, to emerge at the road junction at 173 267. Turn left, and follow the road over the Taf into Llanglydwen (passing a telephone on the left).

Gwal y Filiast burial chamber

Continue along the main road, heading in a generally southerly direction up Rose Hill to the junction at 182 260. Turn right, then, after about 150 metres, right again onto the obvious track signposted for Penpontbren Farm. Proceed west to the farm, taking the right fork down a green lane and keeping the buildings to your left. Continue to a gate where the path forks. Take the left fork uphill past an old, stone gatepost to the Neolithic Gwal y Filiast burial chamber (170 257).

Continue along the main track to a clearing at 172 255. On the far side of the clearing, to the right, the main track continues before bending to the right and coming to a fork. Take the left fork uphill, and proceed to the sharp bend to the left at 170 250. Head on uphill in a roughly south-easterly direction. You pass a farm before reaching the road at 177 247. Turn right, and follow this road south-west into Login. (Note that at the junction at 177 244, bed and breakfast facilities are signposted left at Maencochyrwyn, a detour of about 750 metres.)

Stage 3: Login to Llanboidy – 3½ miles

This section follows the course of the Landsker Borderlands Trail, which is well waymarked for most of the way, though a little confusing around Cilgynydd Farm. Although the word Landsker is most likely of Viking origin, the name refers to a colony of Flemings that was established under English patronage in southern Pembrokeshire in the Middle Ages. Almost from the beginning, the Flemish immigrants resisted Welsh influence, and remained loyal to the English crown to the extent that they fought on the side of the English against the forces of Owain Glyndwr in the fifteenth century. In fact, the colonists resisted Welsh language and culture so strongly that even today the Landsker is widely known within Wales as "Little England Beyond Wales", and southern Pembrokeshire remains a curious part of the nation: apparently slap-bang in the middle of some of the most traditional areas of all, yet almost devoid of the unmistakable stamp of Welshness that pervades even the most easterly border-lands of the Marches.

At the junction at 167 233, turn left uphill, ignoring the overgrown path to the left (which appears to be the correct route for the Landsker Borderlands Trail according to the 1:25000 map) until you reach the Login village sign. A few metres past, on the left, the correct path is waymarked. Follow this way-marked path through the woodlands (copious with Devil's-bit scabious, in flower June-October) to a wooden bridge. Cross the bridge, and follow the path almost due east to a stile at the edge of the woods at 177 236. Cross the stile, and proceed just north of east, uphill across the field until a "standing stone" (actu-ally the remnant of an old fence post or gatepost) comes into view, then head for this stone. From the stone, head roughly north-east to the corner of the field, then follow the waymarked track along the side of the field to Cilgynydd Farm.

At the end of the track at the farm, there are metal gates left and right. Pass through the left-hand gate then around the north side of the farm to another metal gate on the right. Pass through this gate, and then proceed south through a small enclosure and through more gates to the track on the south-east side of the farm. Continue uphill, south-east, to the road junction at 194 231. There are Bronze Age tumuli to the south of the junction, though these may be difficult to see when the hedgerow is dense (a series of tumuli leads north-north-east for about seven miles from Cross Hands). Cross the road and proceed just south of east to another junction at 198 230.

Turn left and head north-east, past Rose Villa, to the part-metalled track on the righ, at 203 234, leading to Maesgwyn Isaf. Turn right up this track until a waymarked stile on the left. Cross the stile, and follow the waymarked direc-tion across the fields, bearing east. Keep heading east, tending downhill to re-join the track at about 209 229. Follow this track, rich in willowherb, north of east into Llanboidy.

Stage 4: Llanboidy to Maenllwyd Inn – 3½ miles

Llanboidy is well supplied with both historical references and facilities for the walker. The Lamb Inn provides food and accommodation, as well as the more traditional forms of refreshment (if muddy, which is highly likely given the na-ture of the farmland you have just crossed, keep to the public bar, where walk-ers appear welcome). There is also a grocery store that opens seven days a week, together with post office and telephone facilities, public conveniences and tourist information. There is evidence of human settlement in this area from Neolithic times (c3000BC), although the earliest remaining structure is the hill fort at Hafod (218 225), just to the south of the village, which is thought to date from the late Bronze Age or early Iron Age (800BC – AD100). (A round detour of about a mile would allow you to visit it.) The discovery of Roman coins here suggests that the site later developed into a Romano-Celtic settlement. Other Bronze Age burial grounds (2000-1400BC) and Iron Age defended enclosures

2.2 LLANBOIDY TO CILCRUG

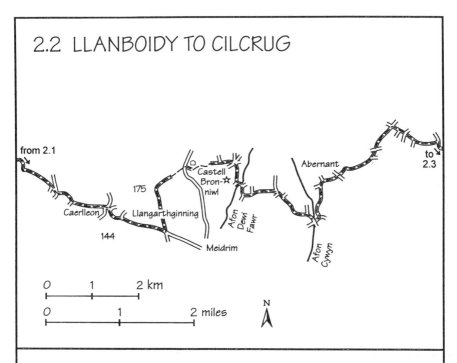

from 2.1

Castell
Bron-☆
niwl

Abernant

to
2.3

175

Caerlleon · Llangarthginning

Afon Dewi Fawr

144

Meidrim

Afon Cywyn

```
0       1       2 km
├───────┼───────┤

0               1               2 miles
├───────────────┼───────────────┤
```

N
ᐱ

2.3 CILCRUG TO
LLANFIHANGEL UWCH GWILLI

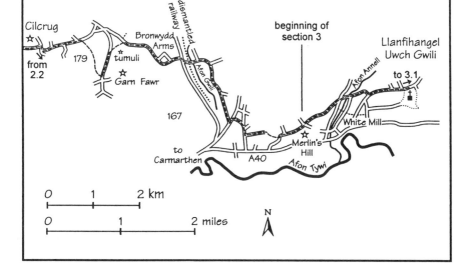

Cilcrug
☆

dismantled railway

Bronwydd
Arms

beginning of
section 3

Llanfihangel
Uwch Gwili

from
2.2

179

☆
tumuli

Afon Gwili

Afon Annell

to 3.1

☆
Garn Fawr

167

White Mill

to
Carmarthen

A40

☆
Merlin's
Hill

Afon Tywi

```
0       1       2 km
├───────┼───────┤

0               1               2 miles
├───────────────┼───────────────┤
```

N
ᐱ

(circa 700BC) have been found in the area. The motte and bailey castle – Castell Mawr – at the east end of the village would have consisted of an earthen mound topped with a wooden tower. It may be of Norman origin, built in the early to mid-12th century as part of the lordship of St Clears, or may be of Welsh origin, built by Rhys ap Gruffudd in his re-conquest of the area in the late 12th century. The castle certainly hints at a strategic importance for the area in the 12th century, and it is possible that the village, which is thought to have grown up around this time, may have evolved around the road between the castle and the church of St Brynach, which is thought to have been of late 10th or early 11th century origin. However, two 5th or 6th-century stones – one of which was built into the church and the other of which was lost – suggest that the site of St Brynach's may also previously have been the site of a Christian cemetery considerably pre-dating the church.

Emerging into the village of Llanboidy between the school and the pub, turn right onto the main road through the village and continue past the Lamb Inn. Follow the road left and then right, passing St Brynach's Church on the left, to the car park at the eastern end of the village, where public conveniences and local tourist information can be found. Opposite the car park, the path is way-marked through a kissing gate next to a metal farm gate. Immediately apparent on the right is the residual mound of Castell Mawr at 219 231.

Follow the right of way, keeping the field boundary to your left, to a stile and a wooden walkway over a bog. Cross these and continue north-east, crossing two more stiles, to a metal gate. Ahead in the field is an upright stone. Pass this and continue in the same direction across the field to the farm buildings. On the far side of the field is a sharp dip down to the stream. A wooden stile leads down to a bridge over the stream and into another field. On the far side is a metal gate leading to the lane at about 226 235. Turn right past Ddol Farm, then south to the road junction at 227 234.

Turn left at the junction and proceed in a roughly south-easterly direction to the crossroads at 239 225. Continue in this direction to a second crossroads at 257 219 and a third at the Maenllwyd Inn at 277 212.

Stage 5: Maenllwyd Inn to Abernant – 7¼ miles

Turn left here onto a smaller lane heading north up to Bwlchgwynt Farm at 276 227. Before the farm, cross the cattle grid and turn left uphill along a farm track to head roughly north-east towards Waun-oleu-fach. **When the track ends at about 281231, continue in the same direction through a field, keeping the field boundary to your left.**

On reaching the road at 284 232, head straight on for about 150 metres, just past the Gellywen road on the left, before turning right onto the farm track. At the far side of the farm the path diverges. The main path heads to the right, but to the left there is a rusty metal gate leading to a reasonably obvious grassy track through the field. Cross the gate and turn left to head north-east down this grassy track, which weaves its way to the road at Plas-paun Farm (293 234). Go through the gate here, past the houses, then turn right and follow the road down to Cenllaith Farm at 302 228.

Follow the road down to the junction at 304 224, then turn left to head in a generally easterly direction past Dyffryn Farm. At the T-junction (telephone and post box here), turn right (signposted Abernant) and follow the road down, enjoying the views of the Cywyn Valley, to a second T-junction at 330 215. Turn left here, then bear left again at the junction just over the hump-backed bridge crossing the river (again signposted for Abernant), and into Abernant.

Stage 6: Abernant to Newchurch – 2½ miles

Walk through Abernant, passing Cottage Farm, to the road junction at 349 236. Turn left, signposted for Carmarthen, (there is a post box here), and walk to the crossroads at 356 246.Turn right, and proceed to the junction at 373 242 (you may be able to catch a glimpse through the hedgerow of a tumulus to the left at 360 247). Turn right at the junction, past the old post office, then left again (signposted for Newchurch), and walk into Newchurch.

Stage 7: Newchurch to Afon Gwili – 3½ miles

Continue on the road through Newchurch, then after the last house on the right at 385 243 turn right onto a waymarked bridle path. Continue just east of south, following the obvious path through several gates to Nant Hir at 389 238 **(it is steep in parts, here, and care must be taken)**. Continue to follow the path, taking the main path south at the fork, through more gates to the road at 391 231.

Turn left onto the road and continue just east of north, past Breezy-bank, to a waymarked footpath on the right at 394 241, just opposite Ffoshelig Farm. Turn right here, then at Garnfawr Farm turn left over a stile and follow the right of way north-east along the fence. At the end of that field, pass through the right-hand gate, continuing north-east and with the field boundary to your left. At the end of this field there is another stile and waymark. Cross the stile and follow the waymark to the road, noting the Bronze Age tumulus to your right.

Turn right onto the road and follow it all the way down to the junction with the A484 at 417 237. Turn right and follow the main road for 150 metres to the junction with the B4301. Turn sharp left (signposted for the steam railway), then immediately right onto the smaller road to cross the railway line and the river. (Straight on after the sharp left turn, is the main terminus of the Gwili Steam Railway, which is a pleasant diversion if you are into that sort of thing, and food and conveniences are also available here.)

Stage 8: Afon-Gwili to Merlin's Hill – 3½ miles

Surprisingly, the hill fort atop Merlin's Hill was discovered only recently, and little is known about it. Presumably Iron Age in origin, it may have been a defensive structure of the Demetae, the local Celtic tribe for whom Carmarthen was the capital at the time of the Roman invasion. The fort covers about four hectares and was designed to withstand attack, having massive ramparts with a well-defended entrance to the north-east. It would seem, however, that the Romans were not deterred for long as Carmarthen became the important Roman town of Moridunum. Interestingly, the Welsh name for Carmarthen – Caerfyrddin – literally means "Merlin's Castle", although it seems unlikely that there is a link between this and the Celtic hillfort of Merlin's Hill. The walk description below includes a possible detour to visit Carmarthen Museum in Abergwili.

From the bridge over the Gwili, follow the road round to the left to the junction at 421 238. Bear right uphill, then after about 500 metres turn right to head south past Awelfryn Farm and Upper Lodge. Continue to the fork at 428 227, and bear right, proceeding east of south through Glangwili to the A485 at 432 219. Turn left, then quickly right onto a road marked "Private Drive" which is waymarked for walkers. Follow this drive for about 125 metres to red signs proclaiming no public access. Immediately before the signs there is a kissing gate on the right hand side leading through to a well-defined path. Pass through the gate and follow this path south-east until you emerge at the road at 436 218. Turn right and follow the road past the rugby ground to the junction at 436 214.

For a diversion to visit the excellent Carmarthen Museum at Abergwili, turn right here and head south to the A40. Turn left onto the main road into Abergwili. The museum is signposted just off the main road (address in the information panel at the beginning of this section). It contains a rich variety of exhibits from the Paleolithic to the Romano-Celtic eras, including Paleolithic and Neolithic tools, early Christian inscribed stones, and a collection of Roman coins found in the area. To rejoin the walk, continue east along the A40 for about 350 metres to a junction at 444 210. Turn left and head uphill to rejoin the walk at **Pen-y-gadair Farm** (see below).

Continuing from the junction at 436 214, turn left to follow the waymarked metalled track in a roughly north-easterly direction until it veers away to the left after about 100 metres. Keep straight on uphill (just north of east) to a gate at the end of the track. The main track now leads off to the left, but there is a waymarked path leading south of east across some fields. Merlin's Hill is now in full view straight ahead.

Across the first field there is a gate and stile – use the stile – then across the next field there is a stone stile some way to the right of the obvious gate. Go over it, and you will see the white building of **Pen-y-gadair Farm**. The right of way passes to the left of this, and over a stile onto the road. Head east uphill, to a house on the left called Porth Myrddin. On the right hand side of the road there is a stile and a waymark. Cross the stile and follow the waymark to another stile and waymark ahead.

Beyond that stile, the path proceeds into woodland. It becomes indistinct for a few metres, but soon on the left you can see a set of wooden steps. Climb the steps to a green lane and cross it to reach more steps. These are **very steep**, but the Llanelli Ramblers have helpfully provided a piece of rope to help you up. Follow the path at the top through the woodland to another wooden, waymarked stile on the left. Cross the stile and head right, tending uphill, to a dead tree trunk. Here, the path continues round along the contour, but there is a clearing to the left which will take you right to the summit of Merlin's Hill.

Looking Ahead: The next part of the route runs from Merlin's Hill to Llandeilo through the Tywi Valley area known as Golden Grove. There are similar problems to those faced by Dr Edwards with some of the footpaths. However it is remarkable countryside which offers some interesting walking on tracks, field paths and unfrequented lanes across an historic landscape.

Section Three
Golden Grove – Bryn Myrddin
(Merlin's Hill) to Llandeilo

17½ miles

Fortified farmhouse

Val Saunders Evans

See "The Beginning" for author details.

Stages:
1. Bryn Myrddin to Llanfihangel-uwch-Gwili – 3 miles
2. Llanfihangel-uwch-Gwili to Llanegwad – 3 miles
3. Llanegwad to Dryslwyn – 6 miles
4. Dryslwyn to Llandeilo – 5½ miles

Maps: Landranger 159, Pathfinder 1059

Highlights: Bryn Myrddin (Merlin's Hill), Llanfihangel-uwch-Gwili church, Pen-y-cnap, Llanegwad church, Dryslwyn Castle remains, Gron gaer hill fort, Dinefawr Castle.

Starting Point: Merlin's Hill (455 215).

Additional Information: Gelli Aur Country Park (2 miles west of Llandeilo) – 01558 668885, Carmarthen Heritage Centre (displays of the area's history from AD75 to the present) – 01267 223788, South Wales and West Railway (runs from Swansea, stops at Llandeilo – 0345 484950, Llanelli Ramblers' Festival of Walks (Spring bank holiday) – 01554 770077

Youth Hostels: Regional Office, Cardiff – 01222 222122. Llandeusant – 01550 740619, Ystradfellte – 01639 720301.

Tourist Information: Carmarthen – 01267 231 557 (open all year), Llandeilo – 01558 824226 (Easter to September), Llanelli – 01554 772020 (open all year),

Llandovery – 01550 720693 (open all year), Pont Abraham (M4 Services) – 01792 883838.

Introduction

There are frustrations in bringing a route along the Tywi Valley – poor signing of public footpaths, the dominance of the A40, and finding crossings for the loops of the river and its tributaries to mention just a few. A further problem for the Celtic Way Project was that for this section we could not find a local guide. However, I was convinced that here, of all places, the Celtic Way should be represented. Consequently, I have devised the route which is described here, but would still welcome suggestions from any knowledgeable local expert.

I have a soft spot for the Tywi Valley. It is the home of the legendary Merlin. It figured memorably during the actions by Owain Glyndwr to raze Carmarthen and take Dryslwn castle as part of his campaign for Welsh independence. It has at least two memorably located churches – one, at Llanfihangel-uwch-Gwili, is tucked away above the folds of the hills; Llanegwad stands proud in the heart of the valley; Llangathen dominates the eastern ridges. Golden Grove is the name by which I came to know the valley, although Golden Grove itself (Gelli Aur in Welsh) is a small spot on the southern valley slopes.

The route runs through a delightful west/east valley, with rich water meadows and a generously curving river snaking its way through. The hills which line the sides of the valley are strongly defined. At Llandeilo the hills fall away to reveal the vista of the Black Mountains and Carmarthenshire Fans ahead. In between are the landmarks of Merlin's Hill; Pen-y-cnap and Llanegwad; and Dryslwyn and Gron-gaer, then the Dinefawr estate, just before Llandeilo.

There is plenty of B&B in the area, and the village of Pont-ar-Cothi has inns and hotels. Llandeilo, at the end of this section, is a historic market town where Welsh is the first language. There is a cosmopolitan variety and character about the town. It attracts many incomers and visitors, and is a good place to end this part before moving on to the high-level walking of the next section.

Stage 1: Bryn Myrddin to Llanfihangel-uwch-Gwili – 3 miles

Take in the views across 3 counties from the top of Merlin's Hill. It is also possible to see the lane we shall be taking. It looks as though it could be reached by striking across the fields towards it, but the correct way down is to retrace your steps the way you came, back to Porth Myrddin. On the way down through the woods take time to admire the spring in its basin, the surrounding plant growth kept carefully at bay by some guardian of the area. At the green lane, look to your left for the steps down into the second part of the woods.

On reaching the lane, turn right and follow it downhill for one mile to a T junction (465 225). (Diversion. If you want refreshments go right and follow the lane for ¾ mile into White Mill. White Mill, with its two pubs – the White Mill Inn and the Adams Arms – is ½ mile to the right. Close to White Mill, on the A40 main road, is the High Noon Café, famous for its good food).

The route to Llanfihangel-uwch-Gwili is over an extended crossroads by going right then immediately left. After turning left, follow the lane down the side of the Annell valley for ½ mile to a T junction. Here you turn left and follow the

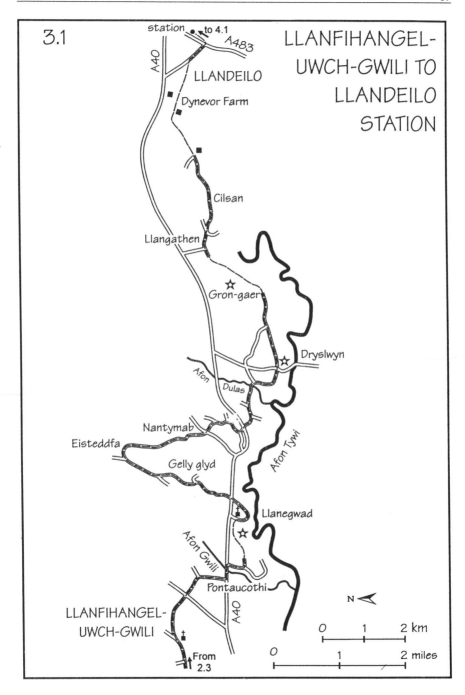

3.1

station • to 4.1
A483

A40

LLANDEILO

Dynevor Farm

Cilsan

Llangathen

☆
Gron-gaer

Dryslwyn ☆

Afon
Dulas

Nantymab

Eisteddfa

Gelly glyd

Afon Tywi

Llanegwad
☆

Afon Gwili

Pontaucothi

LLANFIHANGEL-
UWCH-GWILI

A40

From
2.3

LLANFIHANGEL-
UWCH-GWILI TO
LLANDEILO
STATION

N ◄

0   1   2 km

0   1   2 miles

lane for 1 mile to **Llanfihangel-uwch-Gwili** (Church of St Michael above the Gwili). This is a very quiet spot – a place for reflection.

Stage Two: Llanfihangel-uwch-Gwili to Llanegwad – 3 miles

There is a beautiful path here which would take us to Nantgaredig with its standing stones. Unfortunately, the old, dismantled railway line along the valley floor from Nantgaredig cannot be walked so our route has to leave out Nantgaredig and make for Pont-ar-gothi.

Continue along the lane, past the studio, for just over a mile. At the crossroads, go straight across – **take care** as the road you are crossing, unlike the lanes, carries regular traffic. Follow the lane as it moves downhill towards the Cothi Valley, with some good views of the way ahead. Turn right at the junction and follow the lane, which brings you through the back of the village and into Pont-ar-gothi. Turn left at the A40, opposite Cothi House, to follow the road for 100 metres and over the Afon Cothi. Turn right by the Cothi Bridge Hotel.

You are now on a no through road alongside the River Cothi. Ahead is a long, large hill covered with trees. At the fork in the lane turn left and head uphill on a stony track. Follow the track, which rises quickly and passes Kincoed Farm. Go through the gate and continue on the track through the hill pastures on a scenic path. This track has the atmosphere and position of an ancient way: close to the hill fort of Pen-y-cnap above, and with a good view of the surrounding countryside. Carry on through a rusty gate. As you walk this section, you will begin to get changing views of the valley and the hills ahead. By the next aluminium gate you can see the lovely top of Pen Arthur, which we walk in the next section of the Celtic Way. Later, as you get closer, you will not see it so well.

Go down the stony track, enjoying the views, and come to a junction at Pen-y-garn. It is possible to go left here, but take the right-hand lane which curves round to the small village of Llanegwad with its ancient church. The church ground, with its curved walls, is a llan – an old sacred site. Inside the church is an indecipherable drawing or symbol on its south wall. Outside the church is a stricken tree with steps alongside and a holly bush growing out of the trunk.

Stage Three: Llanegwad to Dryslwyn – 6 miles

After the mystery of Llanegwad and the vigour of the old track, we now have the most frustrating part of the route. No one in their right mind would want to walk alongside the A40 and the footpaths in this section are not signed or acknowledged where I have enquired. So we need to walk for 3 miles on unused lanes to get to the road crossing for Felindre. If you can find a bus or taxi and want to avoid this bit – good luck to you. For the future, I hope that we will be able to establish an improved footpath route.

From Llanegwad follow the road out of the village to its junction with the A40. Cross with care to the other side and follow the verge for 30 metres then enter the lane on your left. Pass Llwynfortune Farm – where a footpath is shown on the map, but is not known of when enquiries were made.(I have since walked it but it involves detours and crossing barbed wire fences. We also frightened a farm resident who had never seen anyone on the path before. It cannot be used yet). Continue on this quiet lane as it rises. Go past Coed-saithpren and descend into the Cothi Valley, where you join a wider road for almost a mile before turning off right towards Eisteddfa. You are on a rarely-used lane which soon rises and goes through trees to come out on high ground. Continue along the lane, passing the entrance to Nant-y-mab Ganol. The road goes down to Nant-y mab – where the public footpath should have brought us, and saved two miles of lane walking!

Go down to a crossroads. Take the unsigned track opposite, which goes uphill. Follow it between two hedges as it curves around, until it comes out on a lane which has been widened at this point. Go right for a quarter of a mile, then right at the next turning. Follow this for a further quarter of a mile until you reach a lane to the left which runs downhill to a crossing of the A40. Cross and take the lane to Felindre, about a mile away along the valley floor. You have been able to see the hill and dramatic ruins of Dryslwn Castle ahead of you for some time. At Felindre there is a junction just before the telephone box. Take the right-hand lane and follow this to its junction with a wider road.

(This road runs past Dryslwn and gives access to the site. It is worth a diversion to visit. The site can be entered opposite the picnic area by the river.)

Stage Four: Dryslwyn to Llandeilo – 5 ½ miles

This involves walking some fine tracks and footpaths, plus quiet lanes. I Have spoken to the Ramblers and Carmarthen Footpaths Officers about some of the paths and the route described reflects the current state of affairs.

From Felindre, enter the quiet lane which runs under the heights of Castle Hill. After three-quarters of a mile the lane doglegs (563 208). Go straight ahead along the road which gives off to Cwmagol and Pentre Davies farms until you approach the huge complex at Alltygaer Farm. The old Pathfinder route sends you through the farm building towards the steeply wooded hillside. However there is a well signed diversion. I am told that the diversion order has been applied for and may be allowed or contested. I followed the signed route and it is described below.

Look for the yellow waymark sign in the left-hand hedge as you approach Alltygaer Farm. It is by the last field on the left before the farm complex. It indicates the route across the field. Cross this into a narrow steep strip of field bordering the mixed woodland. The next stile crossing may be masked by low trees. Aim just to your left to find the stile (by some sessile oaks and a holly tree) which gives access into the woodland.

Follow the track through wood's margin along the slope above the farm complex. It is clearly waymarked and fenced. After ½ mile you reach a new wooden footbridge with stiles at each end. Cross these into a steeply sloping hillside field. There are wonderful views of the river and hills. Continue along this field keeping to the bottom by the overgrown hedge. After 200 metres aim slightly uphill avoiding the track downhill. Keep above the large trees. Ahead is a fence and more yellow waymarking. Cross the stile and go through the bramble area coming out onto a hillside with very young tree-planting. It is difficult to pick out the path. Aim slightly uphill through the young trees. Llangathen Church is ahead on the skyline. An attractive farm house is below. It is tussocky underfoot. As you draw level with the farmhouse there is a post with a yellow waymark sign in the hedge. Go through what remains of the hedge. There are more young trees and lots of old undergrowth. Aim at about 10 o clock and into the hillside. Don't go down. Go for the field's edge to where the land rises among small beech planting. Cross brambles to the next waymarked stile. Cross into the top of a small field for 50 metres to the final waymarked stile and come out on a track on open hillside. Llangathen Church is still straight ahead. 200 yards along the sloping hillside you see the track ahead. Go and pick it up by the power line poles. Go just above the rutted bit and pick up the grassy track. Follow the track for 200 metres passing a cottage being renovated. You join up with the farm track down from Grongar Farm as it reaches the main farm gate.

Go through the gate and carry on downhill to come to some cottages on the right. This is Aberglasney, an estate where renovation is taking place with the help of lottery funds. It will be interesting to see what emerges. There is a sense of peace around here and this stage will be beautiful walking in summer.

Continue along the lane to the road. Turn right and then left to go steeply up into Llangathen. Turn right into Church Lane and explore the churchyard with its fine yews. At the other end of the churchyard turn left onto a quiet lane and go uphill. The road from the village joins from the left. Continue to the Y Junction and go right. Follow the lane with its panorama and fine shade trees for almost a mile down to the hamlet of Cilsan. Here you cross the river on a large footbridge and continue past Cilsan Mill along the lane for ½ mile until you reach Pen-y-banc Farm (604 227). This white building has two new wooden gates to the right of it. Go through the right hand one of these, which leads onto rising hillside. Aim straight uphill at first, then tend over to the right towards a large gap in the hedge. Turn immediately right and follow the right hand hedge for 200 metres to a new stile. There is woodland to your left and a high old estate wall to your left. Cross the stile. At the time of writing (February) it was surrounded by snowdrops. Keeping the estate perimeter wall on your right go through the field, passing a single tree on your left until you reach a rusty gate. Negotiate this. Carry on through this next field. The wall is still on your right, but it has gaps. You pass a fairly new barn and come to an aluminium gate with waymark arrows. Go through the gate and come onto a stony track. This becomes a terrace track with fine views to the north-east. It passes an estate stone house (Pen Parc) and begins to slope downhill.

Dynevor Farm is below but you do not go down to it. At a clump of trees there is a waymark arrow to the right through an aluminium gate. Take this and make for the brow of the hill and shortly afterwards go through another aluminium gate to the large field ahead of you. Aim for the single tree in the middle of the field, then for the visible entrance to the field at its other side. Once you reach this entrance you have the opportunity to divert by taking the track to the right which will bring you out in Dinefwr Estate – under National Trust management. The route however goes straight across the track and continues into the field opposite (no gate). After 300 metres you will find a rusty kissing gate on your right. Go through this and pass through the small plantation up the hill.

Pass the waymarking on the fence and make for the conspicuous parallel lines of trees in the middle of the field, or alternatively, keep to the right hand hedge. Both options last for about 300 metres and bring you up to an aluminium gate. Go through this and make for the nearby kissing gate which leads onto the main road into Lladeilo. Follow the main road right and around and on into the centre of this attractive small market town.

Looking Ahead: *Llandelio lends itself to an overnight stop with its impressive choice of accommodation and wealth of historical features to explore. The route continues from the centre of Llandelio up to the hills leading to the Black Mountain and Fan Brycheiniog. This next stage is wonderful walking, but also challenging. It needs careful preparation in order to get the most out of it.*

Section Four
The Black Mountain
– from the Towy Valley to the
Swansea Valley

24 miles

Fan Hir - View from Sarn Helen

Peter Thomas

A mixed Welsh/Irish parentage gives Peter plenty of Celtic 'street cred.' Started walking at an early age in Ammanford, Carmarthenshire. Continued in University College, Swansea, then Sheffield and the Midlands as an electrical engineer before returning to South Wales in 1970. More walking and running for about 15 years followed in Saudi Arabia from 1980. Currently Footpaths Officer for the Gower Society and the West Glamorgan group of the Ramblers Association. Other outdoor activities include orienteering and road running.

Stages:
1. Llandeilo Railway Station to Carn Goch Hillfort – 5 miles
2. Carn Goch to Hen Bont (via Capel Gwynfe and Pont Newydd) – 6 miles
3. Hen Bont to Llanddeusant – 3 miles
4. Llanddeusant to Dan yr Ogof – fair-weather route – 10 miles. Optional foul-weather route, keeping to lower ground – 7½ miles.

Maps: OS Outdoor Leisure 12 for the high-level part of the route, and Landrangers 159 and 160 (Brecon Beacons).

Highlights: Carn Goch hill fort, Fan Brycheinihog ridge, Llyn y Fan Fach and Llyn Y Fan Fawr. Stone circles at Cerrig Duon and Cerrig Duon (852258).

Starting Point: Llandeilo Railway Station (634 226).

Additional Information: Nearby Roman camps at Arosfa Garreg lwyd (804263) and Y Pigwyn (828313). Stone avenues at Saith Maen (832154) and Godre'r Garn las (820258). Dan-yr-Ogof Cave Complex – 01639 730284, Craig y Nos Country Park – 01639 730395.

Accommodation: Camping at Capel Gwynfe, B&B at Gwynfe, Llangadog – 01550 740686. Youth hostels: regional office (Cardiff) – 01222 222122, Llanddeusant – 01550 740619, Ystradfellte – 01639 720301.

Transport: South Wales and West Railway – the line runs from Swansea through the heart of Wales and stops at Llandeilo – 0345 484950.

Tourist Information: Carmarthen – 01267 231557 (open all year), Llandeilo – 01558 824226 (Easter to September), Llanelli – 01554 772020 (open all year), Llandovery – 01550 720693 (open all year).

Introduction

This section of the Celtic Way starts in the wide and richly fertile Towy Valley and climbs up into the Black Mountain area, which contains some of the most remote hill country in South Wales, before descending into the upper reaches of the valley of the River Tawe. The highest of the Black Mountain hills – Fan Brycheiniog – is just over 2630 feet (800 metres) so it is important not to under-estimate the effects of bad weather. **Check weather forecasts and seek local advice** if at all doubtful. The general safety advice given at the beginning of this book is vital here. Navigation on the ridges is straightforward in fair weather, but avoid the ridges in wet and windy weather. You won't be able to appreciate the views and you might get blown off! You will need to plan each stage carefully and allow plenty of time for the walking. Overnight stops are possible in a variety of places at the start and finish, and the route is written with the possibility of an overnight break in either Llandeusant, where there is a youth hostel, or at Capel Gwynfe. Tourist Information at Llandeilo will be able to give more information about accommodation possibilities.

In Neolithic times, as well as rich farmland for settlements, the Towy Valley would have provided a convenient migration route westward towards the coastal plain. The revolution in agriculture which had begun in the river valleys of the Nile, the Euphrates and the Tigris eventually reached into the river valleys of Wales over a period of about 2000 years.

A number of burial cairns dating from the late Neolithic and early Bronze Age periods have been identified in the area. There is evidence that there were links with the people settling in what is now Ireland. Later, at around the time that the "Blue Stones" were being taken from the Preselli Hills to Stonehenge, there were incursions by people from Brittany by way of the Severn-Cotswolds area. Towards the end of the Bronze Age, at around 2000BC, other groups of immigrants originating from Eastern Europe were making their way into the area. These are known as the Beaker People, and it is recorded that the superior weapons of the invaders enabled them to win a major victory over the indigenous tribes. However, the pressure on land caused by the increase in population was eased somewhat by a change to a warmer, drier climate which permitted more settlement and cultivation in the upland areas. From this period we begin to find evidence of ritual that is not based only on funerary rites and located around burial mounds. Stone circles now appear in the record, and two of these will be mentioned later, in the walks.

Evidence of the need to protect the settlements growing up in the good agricultural land of the Towy Valley can be found in the many hill forts in the area. The largest of these, Carn Goch, was built on the site of a much older stone cairn which is thought to date from around 4000BC. Later Celtic tribes added banks for defence in pre-Roman times. The Romans themselves made good use of the Towy Valley, building roads across from their base at Brecon towards the gold mines at Dolaucothi, villas on the valley floor and marching camps in the hills around. The Romans never colonised Wales, they established military stations and built roads mainly to exploit the mineral wealth of the country. The villa sites were probably those of wealthy, romanised Britons. The bulk of the local population continued to live their lives much as before but in a peaceful way facilitated by the pax romana. Initially, however, the Roman advance into the area was bitterly but vainly opposed by the Celtic Silurian tribes, and it was not until AD74-78 that they were finally subdued. The proliferation of Roman camps and roads is evidence of the serious view which the Romans took of the military threat. On the other hand it appears from the absence of major military ruins that the Demetae peoples further west, whose tribal capital was Carmarthen, presented less of a military threat to the Romans. The Silures were still sufficiently strong when the Romans left to be able to mount a vigorous defence of their lands against invasion by marauders seeking rich pickings from the remains of the Roman Empire.

Many leaders of the Celts emerged in this period. The most well known is Arthur Pendragon. The location of his famous Battle of Mount Badon against the Saxons in 516 is unknown, but one legend places it at Mynydd Baedon near Bridgend. His magician, Merlin, hailed from Carmarthen, and Arthur himself, together with his trusty companions, is said to be asleep in a cave under Dinas Rock, near Pont-Nedd-Fechan, awaiting a call to defend the homeland! Over 200 years later, at Dinefwr Castle in the Towy Valley, another leader, Rhodri Mawr, having reduced the Viking menace, arranged for his lands to be governed after his death by the three strongest of his six sons, giving the country a unity which it enjoyed for many years until the death of Hywel Dda in 950 A.D.

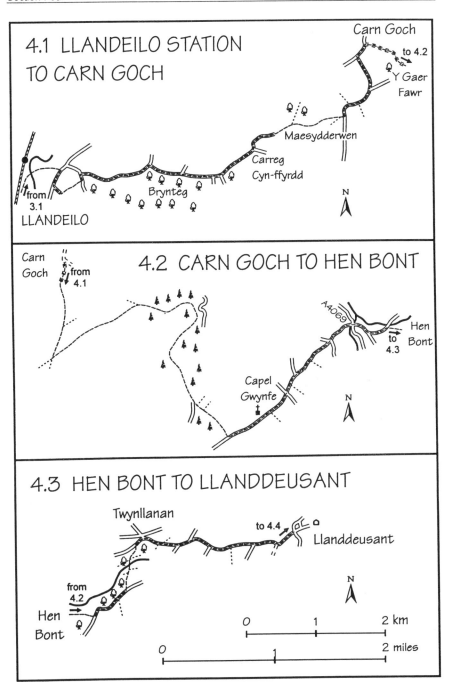

4.1 LLANDEILO STATION TO CARN GOCH

Carn Goch

to 4.2

Y Gaer
Fawr

Maesydderwen

Carreg
Cyn-ffyrdd

Brynteg

N

from
3.1

LLANDEILO

4.2 CARN GOCH TO HEN BONT

Carn
Goch

from
4.1

A4069

Hen
Bont

to
4.3

Capel
Gwynfe

N

4.3 HEN BONT TO LLANDDEUSANT

Twynllanan

to 4.4

Llanddeusant

N

from
4.2

Hen
Bont

0   1   2 km

0   1   2 miles

Stage 1: Llandeilo Railway Station to Carn Goch Hill Fort – 5 miles

Take a moment to stop at the seat in Claredon Road on the approach to the station. Many of the features of the next section of the walk will, weather permitting, be visible from here. On your left is Maes-y-Dderwen Hill with the bulk of Trichrug rising up to its right. To the left of Maes-y-Dderwen are the twin mounds of the hill forts of Carn Goch. The smooth, grass-covered mounds in front, across the valley, mark the site of old quarry workings. The River Towy flows down from the hills away to your left and meanders across the valley floor beneath you. Your way ahead after the station is over the suspension bridge to the right and along the path across the meadow to the Bethlehem road, which is the boundary of the Brecon Beacons National Park.

At Llandeilo Station, cross the line with care and take the footpath to the right, passing over stiles to reach the suspension bridge. Feel the bridge swinging as you cross over to the concrete path which leads you through gates to the Bethlehem road. Bethlehem is the famous village where the young and not so young send or hand in their Christmas mail in order for it to have the distinctive postmark. Go right along the Bethlehem road. **Take care:** although traffic is light, walkers are rare and speeds often high. After approximately 300 metres take the waymarked footpath on the left over a cattle grid and up a driveway.

Turn right immediately after the cattlegrid and pass through a small gap in an electric fence. Follow a sunken track, keeping a line of tress on your right. At a stream near a ruin, turn left to go through a gate, keeping the stream to your right. From here, the path is not very distinct but goes straight ahead to a waymarked stile in a hedgerow. Cross the stile into a lane and turn left.

Pass a disused, old well in a red brick enclosure at the foot of a mound on the left before reaching a country road. Turn right up the hill for a gradual climb of about 2 miles. As you climb the hill, the telegraph line crosses over to your right and the poles are numbered. Near the top of the climb look back over the hedge between poles 5 and 8 for views over the Towy Valley, west of Llandeilo. Beyond the bridge is Dynevor Castle on its mound high above the river. On the left bank is the mansion of Gelli Aur and in the distance, high on the left, is Paxton's Folly, also known as the Nelson Tower (a National Trust property).

Ysgubor-Wen Farm is passed on your right and then, on a bend, the road leading to Pantyfynnon and Highfield goes off to the left. Start to climb again past Troed-y-Rhiw ("The Foot of the Slope") Farm (652 225). The road follows a ravine where the stream has cut down into a deep valley. Pen-y-Cae Farm is on the left, and a little way ahead an old milk churn stand marks the turn off on the right to Brynteg Farm. The long lane and waymarked footpath leading to Pen-y-Garn and Tir-y-Lan comes next on the right, but stay on the road a little longer, passing Waun Hir (664 227) on your left. You come to a sharp right-hand bend in the road, 2½ miles from Llandeilo. Here, go left to take the main route to Carn Goch and proceed towards Maesydderwen Hall. Go right for the optional detour to the standing stone, then return to this fork and go left.

If you wish to make the detour to visit the standing stone, take the right fork and continue for another 700 metres around the left-hand bend in the road, going up the slope and passing the track to Ty'r garn Farm. The standing stone is approximately 2 metres (6ft) high and stands at the right-hand side of the road, near a metal gate and next to a wooden telegraph pole. Further on up the slope is Cennen Tower woodland. In the woodland are the ruins of Cennen Tower, possibly a lookout tower for Carreg Cennen Castle. The tower was still standing in the late 1950s. Legend links it with the nearby mansion of Glyn Hir, at one time the home of a Huguenot family, and with tales of a Frenchman living in the tower with a number of "wives"! From the top of the tower it was possible to see as far as Penlle'r Castell, about 6 miles away on Bettws Mountain.

After the detour the walk continues by taking the left fork and continuing towards Maesydderwen Hall. In approximately 200 metres, at the end of the drive to Dderwen Deg, go right, following the road towards Maesydderwen Hall. Do not bear left at the main gateway but go straight on towards farm buildings. Pass through a metal gate on the right of the main building. At the far end of the building, turn left and cross over a waymarked stile and then a second stile, also on your left, about 50 metres up the slope. Continue up the slope, keeping the wire fence on your right, to reach another waymarked stile.

Cross this stile and follow the waymark to the right, keeping the old quarry workings on your left. The track leads to a waymarked wicket gate set in the stone wall ahead, about half way down the slope. Follow the waymarks down the slope with the stone wall on your right until you reach a gap for a gateway in the wall. At this point go left for 50 metres to another wicket gate and pass through to cross a muddy field, keeping an earth bank and fence to your right. Near a waymarked post, you reach a gate giving access to a quiet, country road.

Turn left in the road and walk down, passing Gors Cottage on your left then another house on your right. When you reach Cwmdu the road turns sharply left, downhill to a stream then rises to a road junction At the junction turn right, signposted Bethlehem. Keep straight on until the sign for Carn Goch hill fort is reached on the right. There is a plaque with a pictorial map and brief description of the Iron Age fort.

Follow the well-defined path (682 243) up the slope behind the descriptive plaque, passing through Y Gaer Fach with extensive views up the Towy Valley. Keep to the path into the dip between the two forts. At a fork in the path a right turn will take you around the outside of Y Gaer Fach, showing the impressive fortification and opening up views down the Towy Valley past Dynevor Castle. Return to the main path and continue up to Y Gaer Fawr. Pass the 4000 year old cairn and keep following the path out over the north wall of the hill fort.

The remains of an ancient cairn lie in the bracken below on the right and the plain alongside the river ahead contains the site of a roman villa at 705 255 as well as Llysbrychan Farm. This farm stands at 705 254, near the site of a Roman villa. The name translates as "The Court of Brychan". The Welsh name "Brycheiniog" for Breconshire is derived from "Brychan". Brychan ruled over the area in the second half of the fifth century. According to Giraldus Cambensis, Brychan had 24 daughters. Among these were Tydfil the Martyr (from whom we get Merthyr Tydfil); Gwladys, commemorated in the name of the waterfall Sgwd Gwladys near Ystradfellte (in the next section); and Eluned or Adwenhelye with a chapel near Brecon. Brychan was an early convert to Christianity and many of his daughters suffered martyrdom for their faith.

Nearer to Llangadog town are the remains of Castell Meurig (709 276), which can be reached by a public footpath from the main road.

Stage Two: Carn Goch to Hen Bont (via Capel Gwynfe and Pont Newydd) – 6 miles

The path now drops down the bracken-covered hillside to a farm road. Go right on the road and pass a track on your left which leads off to Tan-y-Lan Farm (696 242). Continue on the farm road towards Garn-wen Farm (696 239). Trichrug now looms above you to your left. Pass through a gate and bear to the left towards an iron gate at the beginning of an enclosed track. Follow the track uphill past a ruined cottage. The slope now gets steeper, but gives more open views back over the Towy Valley. Pass through a gate at the top of the slope, turn left then cross a stile on your right (696 234). Follow the track south-west, with the mass of Trichrug getting closer on your left. The track climbs even more steeply to reach another stile and gate (695 229). You are now at Bwlch-y-Gors.

Climb over the stile and turn left along the waymarked footpath. The route follows an old trackway below the crest of Trichrug towards Llandeilo Forest at Pen Arthur. Enjoy the panoramic views over the Towy Valley. Keep the fence on your left hand side until, in 500 metres, there is a gate and stile in front of you, at the end of a stone wall. Cross the stile and continue ahead with the fence on your left until you reach another stile and gate, at the end of a wire fence. Cross over the stile and continue ahead with a fence still on your left. A wire fence remains on your left as you keep straight ahead at the next stile and gate.

The path now drops down to cross a rivulet and continues up the slope in front with a wire fence on each side. At a gate and stile, cross the stile and continue with a fence now on your right through an area of reeds. Go through the next stile and gate then continue downhill with the fence still on your right. When the ground rises, keep ahead until you reach a metal gate in front. Cross the stile at the right of the gate and, almost immediately, cross over the next stile on the right into an area of forest which, in 1997, had been clear felled.

Follow the waymarked public footpath which goes off half-left (towards the SE) from the stile. The path becomes easier to find as you proceed, keeping the stream gully on the right hand side. In front now is a panoramic view over the valley of the Gwenllan towards the Black Mountain. In the felled area the width of the path is indicated by a row of tree stumps on each side. Follow the path as it bears left just before the boundary fence and continue round to the left, past where a rough track joins from the left, until the path widens into a grass-covered track. Continue on the grass track with a hill slope rising up on the left. The path now turns downhill through the trees and becomes more distinct. Pass through a gate and turn right and then left to follow a stream downhill to the white-painted building of Lletty Farm.

Cross over the track coming from the left and head towards the farmhouse building. Turn right through a wooden gate before you reach the farmhouse and enter a lane. Follow the lane downhill with banks on each side. The lane tuns sharply right and continues downhill to join a wide forest road (715 232). Turn right (towards the West) on joining the froest road. In approx. 100 metres go through a metal gate on the right hand side and turn left along a grassy track to another metal gate. Pass through onto a grass track rising up through trees with a stream on your left hand side. Follow the grass track for approx. 0.5 km to reach a wooden gate with a building above and to the left (711 229). After the gate, turn left on another track and over a culverted stream to another wooden gate in 100 metres. After this gate follow the track as it rises and swings right to a metal gate. Proceed, with the gate on your right, and continue to another metal gate and waymarked stile. Over the stile, follow the track downhill to a wooden gate. Follow the waymarked track ahead, passing Llwyn-y-neuadd Farm on your right (713 226).

The track is now tree-lined and comes to two gates. Take the waymarked wooden gate on the left hand side into forestry, and pass a large ruin on your right hand side. The old trackway rises up to your right to pass the ruin, but you take the newer track downhill on your left to pass through a gate in about 100 metres. Rejoin the route of the old trackway downhill to a footbridge beside another ruin (714 223).

The track rises up to a junction on the other side of the bridge. At the junction turn right and walk up the hill for 25 metres to a wooden gate into woodland on your left. After the gate, turn left and then follow a broad path on the right uphill, crossing first a stream culvert and then a wider stream. Continue uphill with a stream on your left. After passing through a wooden gate, proceed as before, but now with a clearing on your right. The ground becomes boggy but keep the stream, and now also a boundary fence, on your left until you come out of the trees and reach a hedgerow in front of you. Pass through a metal kissing gate at the right hand end of the hedgerow and cross straight over the field in front, with a hedge on your right. Pass through a metal gate to reach the road. Gwynfe School is opposite to your right (717 217).

Turn left on the road for 800 metres, and you come to All Saints Church, Gwynfe, where there is a postbox and public telephone box. Pass the church and continue along the road, passing Ysgybor-lan Cottage on your right and with distant views of the Black Mountain further away on your right.

Go straight on at the road junction (727 224) at Bryn Clydach. Descend for approximately one mile to pass Crud-yr-Awel and join the main road (A4069) at Pont Newydd (the "new bridge"). Cross the bridge over the River Clydach, and take the minor road opposite. In about 400 metres, fork left towards Llanddeusant along a road marked "unsuitable for long vehicles". Pass Glasfryn on your left and drop down to the River Sawdde at Hen Bont (the "old bridge"). Immediately before the bridge cross the waymarked stile on your right (742 233).

In his book *Wild Wales*, George Borrow ("Romany Rye") writes of coming to a beautifully wooded glen some three hours after leaving Llangadog. To his left a river called "Sawdde" or "Southey" roared down from the hills in the southeast. He then came to a village standing in a semi-circle (Pont Newydd?) and later, along the same road towards "Gutter Fawr" (the present day Brynamman), was a "pandy" or fulling mill driven by the waters of the river which he calls "Lleidach" (this may have been the Clydach). The present road between Pont Newydd and Pen-y-Cae could not have been cut because he then reaches Capel Gwynfe, which he translates as 7the Chapel of the place of bliss". The rest of his journey to Brynamman was past a toll-bar and along the roadway past the Pantyfynnon Quarries, which had been cut to bring coal from the Amman Valley to the farms of the Towy Valley.

Stage 3: Hen Bont to Llanddeusant – 3 miles

Cross the stile at Hen Bont and follow a waymarked path through trees with the river on your left. The path is muddy in places but passable. Continue alongside the river until another waymarked stile is reached straight ahead of you. Cross the stile and drop down to a tributary stream in a deep gully. Follow the stream left to reach a crossing place, and then cross a ruined wall to follow the path winding steeply up to your right to reach another stile. Windblown trees can often be encountered across the path in this area. After the stile, cross the field ahead, keeping near to the fence on your right and passing a wooden gate to reach a hedgerow. Continue with the hedgerow now on your right to a metal gate, with a stone barn visible across the valley to your left. Pass through the gate and cross diagonally across the field ahead to reach another metal gate into the yard of Wern-fawr Farm (747 233).

Go to the right, around the yard, to a short driveway leading to another metal gate and a country road with a footpath sign opposite. Turn left on the road for about 600 metres towards the abandoned Acheth farmhouse (752 237). Cross the stile on the left before the farm and follow the path around, keeping the farm buildings on your right. Cross a muddy track and continue across a gully. Do not go through the gateway ahead but keep to the left, where the ground is very boggy in places. Go down the field to a causeway track leading to the right to a stile in a wire fence. Cross the stile and go right to cross a small stream. Go left around an area of bracken and through a gap in an earth bank to pass by the ruin of Ynys-wen Farm and reach the footbridge beyond (753 240).

After the footbridge, go left towards a tree-covered hillside, following a worn path through undergrowth to where waymarks begin to lead up the hill, alongside a small stream, to a wicket gate. Cross straight across the field ahead towards a white cottage. Opposite the cottage pass through another wicket gate. Come out onto a quiet country road and turn right to walk on the road to the youth hostel at Llanddeusant. At the next road junction follow signs to Llanddeusant Youth Hostel.

Keep straight ahead at Aber Llechach. Bear right at the fork (760243), keeping to the road. Cross the river at Pont Felin-fach (762 244), and continue on the road as it rises steeply. Pass the entrance to Tredomen (770 243) and Bwlchyfedwen (774 243). The youth hostel (777 245) is beside the church and was formerly the Red Lion Inn at Llanddeusant.

Stage Four:
Llanddeusant to Dan yr Ogof, fair-weather route – 10 miles;
optional foul-weather route, keeping to lower ground – 7½ miles.

Before starting out, check the warnings given about safety and weather conditions. Take the lane opposite Llanddeusant church, passing with the churchyard on your left. Descend a very steep hill past the entrance to Cwmsawdde Farm (776 242) to reach a road bridge over the Sawdde. The bridge has a commemorative stone dated 1929. Climb for a short distance to a fork in the road. For the fair-weather route bear left towards Blaensawdde, for the lower level, foul-weather route bear right towards Gellygron.

The Fair-Weather Route

Turn left at the junction to cross another bridge and pass through a wooden gate. Follow the lane up the slope and continue as the lane becomes a track leading to Blaensawdde Farm and open country. The old farmstead, Blaensawdde Farm, is situated at the head of the River Sawdde (784 239) and is closely associated with the legend of the Lady of Llyn-y-Fan, and thus with the story of the Physicians of Myddfai.

The son of Blaensawdde Farm, whilst grazing his mother's cattle on the slopes around Llyn-y-Fan Fach, saw a beautiful girl sitting on the surface of the lake. After a lengthy courtship she agreed to marry him, but only after warning him that she was no ordinary mortal and that she would return to the lake if ever he struck her three times. They wed and she bore him three sons. One day, after many years, he forgot about the warning and teasingly tapped her on the shoulder. He later did this twice more, and on the third occasion she left the house and vanished under the waters of Llyn-y-Fan Fach. The three sons, grieving for their mother, often sat gazing into the depths of the mountain lake. One day their mother reappeared and gave the eldest son, Rhiwallon, a leather container saying, "The mission of you and your brothers shall be to heal the sick. In this bag are the healing secrets of the Other World." After showing them the different herbs growing on the mountain and explaining their use as cures, she returned to the lake and the brothers went down from the mountain full of their new mission. For generation after generation all the sons of the Myddfai family practised medicine and their last-known descendant, Dr C. Rice Davies, practised in Aberystwyth in 1881. A manuscript containing details of all the remedies can be seen at the National Library in that town.

From Blaensawdde Farm the steep escarpment of Fan Brycheiniog is visible directly ahead. To continue our route, go into the farmyard with the house on your right. Pass through two metal gates to reach a lane between a wire fence and a hedge which leads down to a waymarked stile and gate. After the stile follow an enclosed lane between hedgerows to reach Gorsddu Farm (788 241).

Pass through a metal gate and bear left to the continuation of the footpath. Unfortunately, the footbridge over the river to the country road no longer exists and the road cannot be reached from this footpath A farm road leads around the buildings and down to a metal gate which opens onto a lane. The lane swings left over a bridge. The land ahead through another metal gate is subject to an access agreement under the Countryside Council for Wales's Tir Cymen Scheme. You are permitted to go through the gate and follow a bridleway alongside the River Sawdde to see some typical upland valley scenery before returning to the bridge. After the bridge, the lane rises steeply to join the county road (792 242).

Turn right and follow the road. It quickly becomes the vehicle track towards the lake Llyn-y-Fan Fach. The track passes Blaenau Farm and makes a sharp turn to the right at the **Mountain Rescue Post** at 797 239. Cross over a cattle grid and enter open country on Welsh Water land. The track proceeds alongside the

Fan Brycheiniog

river to reach the lake in another mile. After the point where the track crosses the river (804 228), climb up the slope on the right to reach a well-marked path leading onto the ridge of Bannau Sir Gaer, and continue above and to the south of Llyn-y-fan Fach.

On Fan Brycheiniog, above the next lake, Llyn-y-Fan Fawr, a triangulation pillar at 825 218 marks the spot height of 2630 feet (802 metres). Approximately 300 metres further on is the steeply dropping pass of Bwlch y Giedd.

Escape Route from Bwlch y Giedd 828 215

Above Llyn-y-fan Fawr, it is possible to abandon the ridge walk if the weather deteriorates and take a steep but easily followed route of nearly 2 miles, passing waterfalls and a stone circle, to join the road at 853 202. There is then a road walk of about 2 miles to reach Tafarn-y-Garreg public house at 849 171.

To follow this escape route, pass the end of a wire fence on your left, then follow the path down to the left off the ridge towards the lake. The path descends very steeply and **care is needed in wet weather** as the rocks can be slippery. Walk ahead with the lake on your left to reach a small stream (Nant-y-Llyn) emerging from the lake. Cross the stream and bear right where the path forks to follow the stream down towards the road.

Keeping the stream on your right, follow a steep track downhill and pass a series of increasingly dramatic waterfalls until the path swings to the left, away from the stream. A standing stone should be visible below and to the left. Follow the path down to the standing stone, Maen Mawr, at 851 207. There is a cir-

4.4 LLANDDEUSANT TO GLYNTAWE

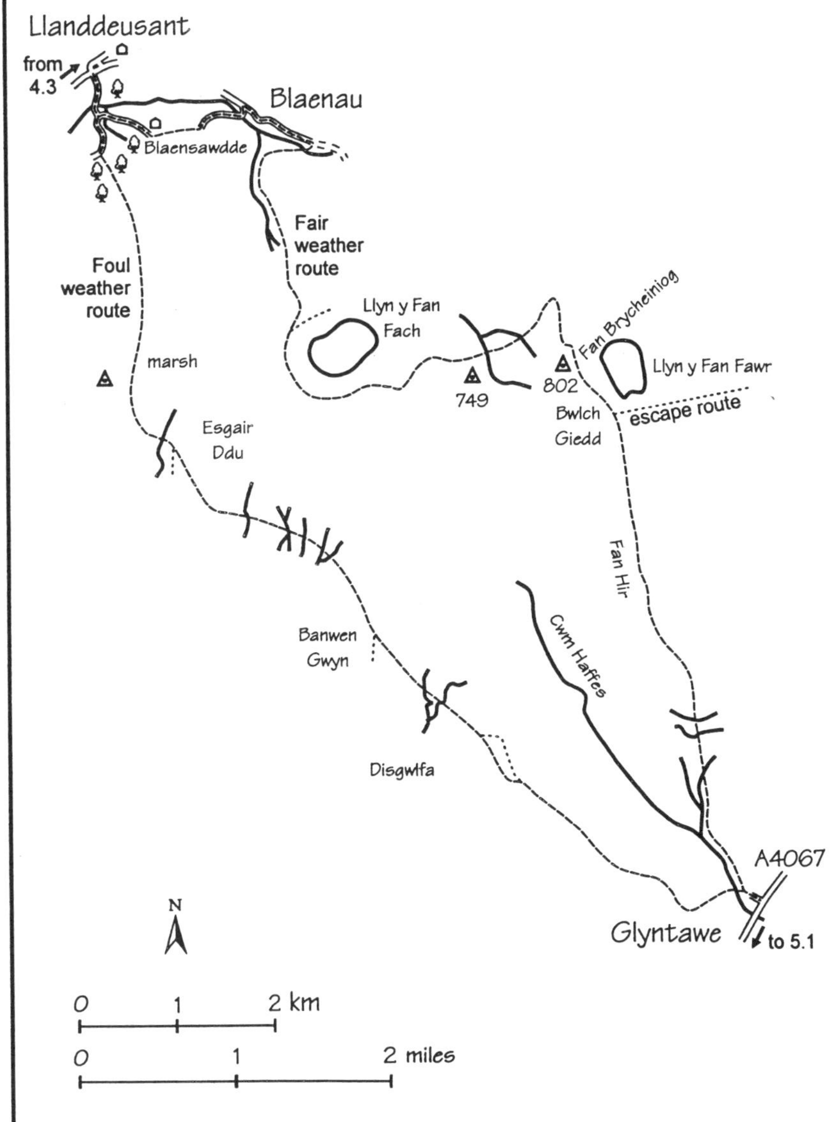

Llanddeusant

from
4.3

Blaenau

Blaensawdde

Fair
weather
route

Foul
weather
route

Llyn y Fan
Fach

Fan Brycheiniog

marsh

Llyn y Fan Fawr

749

802

Bwlch
Giedd

escape route

Esgair
Ddu

Fan Hir

Banwen
Gwyn

Cwm Haffes

Disgwlfa

A4067

N

Glyntawe

to 5.1

0   1   2 km

0   1   2 miles

cle of much smaller stones alongside which is known as Cerrig-Duon. The road ahead is reached by crossing the narrow River Tawe at any one of a number of crossing places. Turn right on the road and walk down in the direction of Tafarn-y-Garreg.

(Cerrig-Duon is attributed to the Beaker Folk and is similar in origin to Stonehenge and Avebury. It is one of only 8 of its type known in South Wales. An avenue of stones reported nearby is not now visible, but Maen Mawr itself can still be shown to influence the direction of a compass needle.)

Continuing the Fair-Weather Route

If not descending at Bwlch y Giedd, follow on up the slope ahead. The lake, Llyn-y-Fan Fawr, is now below on your left. The path ahead is not very clear at this point but gradually becomes more distinct as you ascend, keeping the steep drop to Llyn-y-Fan Fawr on your left. Continue along the hill slopes of Waun Hir, passing lichen-covered outcrops of old red sandstone, until the steep slopes of Allt Fach are reached. Head south along the line of the slope towards the field boundaries below. Descend to the boulder-strewn valley of the River Haffes and follow the river down to meet the waymarked footpath which leads down past a riding school to reach the main road at 845 165.

The Lower Level or Foul-Weather Route

Turn right (signposted Gellygron) at the junction after Cwmsawdde Farm and the River Sawdde bridge. Follow the lane past the entrance to Gellygron. Bear right to follow the waymarked bridleway as you begin the long ascent to Carreg yr Ogof. At the junction of the bridleway keep straight ahead and descend towards the River Twrch.

After fording the river, proceed with the bog of Banwen Gws on your right. Look out for the ruins of some very old limekilns. Keep straight ahead at the next junction to reach the ford where the River Giedd meanders between deeply cut banks. The track, also known as the Coffin Road, continues all the way to Craig y Nos, passing old quarries and limekilns above the Dan yr Ogof Caves complex. On reaching the main road, pass The Shire Horse Centre where, in addition to shire horses, Highland cattle and even alpacas(!) can be seen grazing the fields.

This is a good place to break your journey if you are continuing on to the next section. If not, it is possible to get to Swansea or Neath – both with bus and rail stations – by public transport.

Looking Ahead: The next section gradually makes the transition from high ground to the river valleys. The walking is matchless in this area so we have included two routes from Dan yr Ogof. The intention is to provide a circular walk from Dan yr Ogof to Ystradfellte and Pontneddfechan which returns to Sarn Helen to pick up Ron Elliot's linear route from Dan yr Ogof to Melincourt. It allows an opportunity to spend an extra day exploring the area.

Section Five
Waterfall Country: Dan yr Ogof to Melincourt

20 or 15 miles

Henrhydd Falls

Mike Collins and Ron Elliot

Mike Collins was born halfway up a valley mountainside in the town of Blaina, Gwent. He now lives in Swansea. An Outward Bound course of one month in the Lake District in 1966 fuelled his interests in mountain walking. He has climbed Snowden, Scafell and Ben Nevis and trudged the Brecon Beacons. He will try any walk, anywhere, anytime, especially if there is good company and sound liquid refreshment at the end. Ron Elliot is married with four daughters and lives in Glamorgan. He was brought up in South Wales and commenced walking in earnest on his retirement in 1994. A natural love of the great outdoors and an interest in local history led, inevitably, to his present affection for the delights of the Welsh countryside. He is a member of the Ramblers' Association and also walks regularly in the company of a group of friends.

Routes: There are two routes available for this section, both beginning at Dan-yr-Ogof. There is a circuit route to Ystradfellte and Pontneddfechan, which then joins the linear route at Sarn Helen to continue to Melincourt. The linear route goes to Cribarth, Henrhydd Falls, Sarn Helen and then to Melincourt in one stage.

Stages: circuit route

1. Dan-yr-Ogof to Ystradfellte – 9 miles
2. Ystradfellte to Pontneddfechan – 6 miles
3. Pontneddfechan to Sarn Helen at Banwen – 5 miles

Linear route

1. Dan Yr Ogof to Melincourt – 15 miles

Maps: OS Outdoor Leisure 12 – Brecon Beacons National Park (West and Central areas). This is a double-sided map giving full cover of the section. Landrangers 160 and 170.

Highlights: Circuit – Scwd yr Eira waterfall, Sgwd Gwladys and Sarn Helen. Linear – Cribarth, Henrhyd Falls and Sarn Helen.

Starting Point: Dan-yr-Ogof Caves Complex car park (839 161)

Transport: SWT, local bus information – 01792 580580

Outdoor Centres: Afan Argoed Country Park – 01639 850564, Pelenna Mountain Centre – 01639 636227, Dan-yr-Ogof Cave Complex – 01639 730284 and Craig y Nos Country park – 01639 730395.

Tourist Information: Swansea – 01792 468321, Fax 01792 464602 (open all year), Pontneddfechan, near Glynneath – 01639 721795 (open weekends only out of season), Llandarcy, Neath – 01792 813030 (open all year).

Introduction – The Circuit Route

The move from high ground to the river valleys crosses some uncommon countryside. From the exposed tops of the previous section, the route comes down into the wooded valleys of the rivers Tawe, Nant Llech, Pyrddin and Nedd. The section from Dan-yr-Ogof to Pontneddfechan offers the walker a variety of terrain ranging from the gentle riverside walk to the vast open spaces above Penwyllt and over to Ystradfellte, and on to the ruggedness of the climb down to the waterfall between Ystradfellte and Pontneddfechan. The intention of this route option is to provide a circuit walk from Dan yr Ogof to Ystradfellte and Pontneddfechan, then back along the Pyrddin river valley to join up with the linear route for Banwen and Sarn Helen.

There are no public transport services from Pontneddfechan to Ystradfellte, which is about six miles. Both Dan Yr Ogof and Pontneddfechan can be reached reasonably easily by bus from the centres of Swansea or Neath. The bus journeys in themselves are scenic and a good introduction to the localities.

The beginning of the walk is sheltered and has the impressive Dan-yr-Ogof Cave Complex at its start. This complex has a large car park and a café which welcomes walkers. Accommodation is available. Within half a mile of the caves there are also two public houses: The Gwyn Arms, which has an extensive menu and excellent facilities; and the Tafarn-y Garreg, which is a traditional old-style pub with much character and a basic menu. The landlord, Keith Morgan (01639 730267), has access to a field opposite the pub for camping.

The walking from the Caving Club at Penwyllt to the Farm at Blaen-neddisaf is excellent on a good, dry day, but if contemplating doing this section on a wet day bear in mind that there is little if any shelter on the open mountain and there are few signs. In the driving rain on the top, visibility can be down to a few metres.

The walking from Ystradfellte is mainly above and through the Mellte Valley with its succession of waterfalls. It is not particularly exposed, but there is no way off the route until arrival at Pontneddfechan.

Stage One: Dan yr Ogof to Ystradfellte – 9 miles

The start of the walk is in the car park of the Dan-yr-Ogof Caves Complex (839 161). The path leads directly from the car park through the field down onto the A4067, the main Ystradgynlais to Brecon road. On reaching the road, immediately on the opposite side can be seen a stile and a footpath sign. This leads into a field with a duck pond and picnic area which is owned by the Dan-yr-Ogof Caves Complex. Walk to the right of the pond to the gate with a footpath sign, keeping the river on your right. Proceed to the wooden bridge leading over the river. There are also large stepping stones to the right of the bridge for the more adventurous. This is the River Tawe.

On crossing the river do not turn right as this leads into the Craig-y nos Country Park. Follow the bridleway sign, climbing slightly to a gate. Pass through the gate and turn right onto the bridleway which now takes you between fields. The bridleway at this point is about four metres wide. In the wet this area can be extremely muddy but is easy walking. You pass a large, three-storey, stone house with a gate across the path. Exit onto the unclassified road and walk 100 metres, passing a small brick-built bungalow (846 154) and keeping it to your left. Now on the left is a gate with a footpath sign. Enter into the woodland, where the path now climbs quite steeply and unevenly to a gate which brings you out onto the road.

Turn left and walk up the hill on the road for about 200 metres before arriving at a disused railway crossing and the Penwyllt Quarry. (This point is about 45 minutes from Dan-yr-Ogof.) After walking over the railway crossing and cattle grid, follow the rough stone road to your right for about 300 metres. Here you will see a long, stone-built building which was at one time several workmen's cottages. This is the South Wales Caving Club Headquarters (856 154). Some 30 metres before the club there is a footpath sign (indicating a legally diverted footpath). Follow this to the left onto a grass path, and continue bearing left along a clear path for 400 metres to a drystone wall and a stile.

The sign here indicates Ogof Ffynnon Ddu Nature Reserve. Cross the stile, and after 20 metres take the right-hand fork, still on the grass path. This takes you uphill to a disused tramway. Where the path meets this tramway, walk straight over the tramway to the path where some old stone steps can be seen (861 157). **There are no signs** at this point, and for quite a distance from here.

Follow the steps and the path ahead as it bears left and climbs gradually for about 300 metres. There are no signs, but there is a single tree on the left with an old, tumbledown stone wall behind it. Twenty metres before the tree, turn right onto the faint path and walk uphill to the right of the limestone outcrop, climbing to meet a farm vehicle track.

Bear left onto this path and follow for 200 metres until a fenced section of land comes into view (866 159). Take the path to the right of the fence, which follows the line of the fence. On the right of the path is a steel post with yellow and red markings. Walk 200 metres and you will see another post like this. Continue with the fence on your left. On reaching the end of the fence, follow the path immediately in front. Walking between two rocky outcrops, you reach the brow of the rise in about 400 metres. Immediately in front can be seen a wooden pole on the right of the path and a large mound with a cairn of stones on top.

Follow the path to the cairn (882 163) and then go to its left. On the OS map the path is shown to the right of the cairn but it disappears in 20 metres and I could not pick it up. This point is 40 minutes from the Caving Club. Some 30 metres past the cairn, the path bears slightly right over very uneven ground.

There is a long drystone wall about 175 metres to your left. Keep it that distance on your left, and after about 400 metres see a small stone cairn two feet in height on the right of the path. There is an excellent view over the Brecon Beacons, and Pen-y Fan can be seen on the horizon to the front left. The path is undulating and very narrow with deep shake holes on the right. Next to the path, on the left, is a boarded cave entrance. (Railway sleepers are used as the covering.) The path goes between two rock mounds, it is narrow with deep heather on both sides.

The path crosses the brow and drops gently down to a drystone wall and a stile. There is a sign here to show that you are leaving the Ogof Ffynnon Ddu Nature Reserve. (This point is one hour, about two and a half miles, from the Caving Club.) Climb the stile out of the nature reserve. The path goes straight in front and drops down a gentle gradient – in the distance and to the left can be seen a long drystone wall. Whilst still descending, the path bears to the right and widens as you begin to move more to the right. There are no signs.

Half a mile ahead and to your left can be seen a small stone cairn on a rocky outcrop. Keep it well to your left and follow the path, which is still wide, to the brow of the ridge ahead. On the ridge, about one and a half miles ahead and slightly to the right can be seen a forestry plantation. Follow the path in this direction. Two trees will come into view directly ahead – walk towards them. On nearing the trees you will see a derelict farmhouse on the left of the path, a signpost in the middle and an old railway wagon (sheep shelter) on the right (902 149).

Follow the path sign straight ahead for half to three-quarters of a mile, where you meet a signpost and the old tramway (road) (905 145). Turn right onto the tramway and follow it to the two gates, 500 metres away. Go over the stile at the first gate then 25 metres to the next gate, which is to the front and left. Go through this gate and immediately over the stile on your right. There is a signpost marked Blaen-nedd-isaf. This point is 40 minutes from the Ogof

5.1 WATERFALL COUNTRY: DAN-YR-OGOF TO SARN HELEN
LINEAR AND CIRCUIT ROUTE

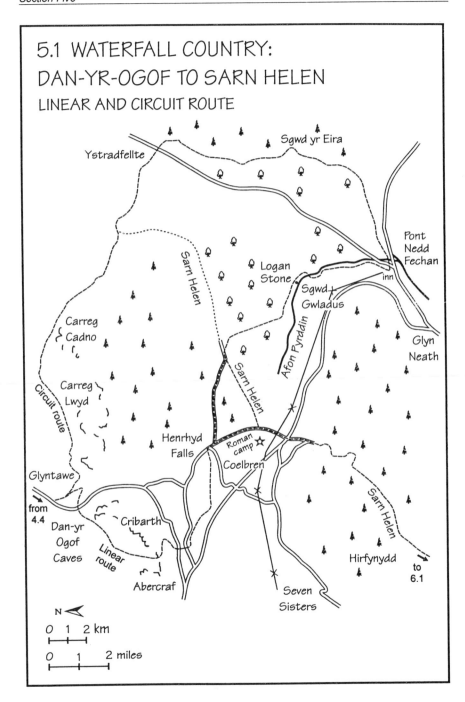

Ffynnon Ddu Nature Reserve. After crossing the stile into the field follow the path, keeping the fence on your right. Stay close to the fence as there are usually sheep or cows in the field. At the other end of the field, go through the gate and follow the sign to Blaen-nedd-isaf, again keeping the fence on your right.

The path descends to another gate. Go through the gate and the path is now **very steep**, rough and can be very muddy and **slippery in the wet**. Descend 30 metres to the concrete bridge over the stream, which is quite deep in wet weather. Cross the bridge to the rear of the barn, and keeping the barn on your left, cross the stile into the farmyard and walk around the farmhouse, keeping it on your right. On meeting the road, walk to your right in front of the farmhouse. There are usually several farm dogs, noisy at the most, and a large flock of geese, which are more frightening than the dogs. The farmer, Mr Morgan Lewis, is friendly and if asked allows parking on the grass verge 30 metres from the farm. (This point is 50 minutes from leaving the nature reserve.) Follow the road away from the farm in the direction of Ystradfellte.

About 300 metres along the road there is a signpost marked Ystradfellte (913 142). Cross the stile into the field and proceed to the stile on the opposite side. Climbing gradually up to the ridge, you will pass through a newly-made gate and a Public Bridleway sign on the fence. Follow the arrow and 200 metres in front you will meet another signpost and direction arrow. Follow the path through the gap in the damaged stone wall and bear right. The path is now barely visible, descending slightly then climbing gradually to the top of the ridge. Here you will see another signpost marked Public Bridleway. Follow the path to the group of large, square stone blocks which are on the right of the path. One hundred metres ahead is another stile and gate with a further sign.

Continue to follow the path, descending for about 300 metres. At this point the path completely disappears, but there is a deep shake hole, circular in shape and fenced. Keep this shake hole to your right and walk alongside it to the top of the brow of the hill in front. Here you meet a 10 feet wide grassy path (920 139). Turn right onto the path and continue along to the rusty gate in the corner where two walls meet (200 metres). Go through the gate into the green lane, it takes you between two fields and has fences or walls either side. Follow to the next gate, pass through and straight on, still descending. There is a sign (Tyle Farm) nailed to a tree on the left as you meet a lane (926 136).

Go straight on, now on a tarmac road, descending to a gate in about 200 metres. Go through the gate into a cul-de-sac where there is a large car park on the right. Walk along the road towards Ystradfellte church and the New Inn pub. This pub serves meals and hot and cold drinks, but does not welcome the eating of one's own food on the premises. There are several bed and breakfast facilities in the village and a youth hostel about 600 metres along the road. The journey from Blaen-nedd-isaf to Ystradfellte takes about 45 minutes.

Stage 2: Ystradfellte to Pontneddfechan – 6 miles

From the New Inn walk to the right of the church, passing the public toilet on your right, and on down the road to the bridge. Cross the bridge. There is a sign on the right indicating that the path is 400 metres up the hill. Walk up to the path entrance and cross the stile at this point into the woodland on your right

(932 130). Follow the path, keeping the river on your right. It is a very good path, which you remain on, passing through several stiles, to the cave car park at Porth-yr-ogof. Pass through the car park and see the sign for Blue Pool and Clun gwyn. Follow this path – not the one for the caves unless you intend to visit them. If you do, you have to return to this point to continue the walk.

After 50 metres go through the kissing gate, keeping the river on your right. You emerge on to a grassy area – pass through to the path which is ahead. The river is on your right and you come to a bridge. Do not cross the bridge. Continue along the path with the river on your right. The path bears left and goes uphill for 50 metres. Turn right onto the path where you come to a high point above the river (926 111). You can detour down to the river but must return to this point to continue the walk.

At this high point there is a sign for Sgwd Isaf Clun gwyn, Scwd-y-Pannwr. Follow this path, climbing to the right to meet another path with pine trees immediately in front of you. Turn right here, you are reaching the top of the walk with the river far below you in a deep valley and can hear the sound of the waterfall.

Follow the path to the sign to Scwd Eira pointing to the right (928 100). Follow this path – a set of **steep steps** made from wood and earth, with some wooden handrails. At this point **take care** if it is wet as it can be very slippery. The steps descend about 200 feet to the river, and this is when all the effort seems worthwhile. The view of the waterfall is tremendous; when there has been rain the flow of water is very powerful. The falls are about 30 feet in height and well worth seeing. Walk along the river's edge, keeping the river to your right. You are actually walking on large rocks and boulders. This brings you up to the base of the falls and the path takes you under the flow of water *behind* the falls to emerge on the other side of the river. How wet you get will depend on the type of gear you are wearing, but **you will get wet**.

There is only one route out and it's a steep climb up the side of the river bank with excellent views behind you. At the top of the steps and path you meet another path and a large boulder. Turn right onto the level path, walking along to the signs marked Silica Mines and Dinas Rock. Follow this path bearing right and going down to the Dinas Rock car park, named Craig y Ddinas. In this car park you will also see a large rock face used by climbers for abseiling, this is on your left as you enter the car park.

Dinas Rock – or Craig y Dinas – has a variety of legends associated with it. Janet and Colin Bond's book *Mysterious Britain* refers to claims that it is the last spot in Wales to be visited by fairies, and to a more common claim that it is the home of a band of sleeping warriors who will reawaken when the country is once again in need of their services. The identity of the warrior band is claimed to be either that of Arthur and his knights or Owen Lawgoch, a Welsh chieftain. The name of the rock – city or king's town – is interesting, too.

At the end of the car park turn right and cross the bridge, walking into a small housing estate. Now bear left onto the road, and walk for about one mile, passing the Graig y Ddinas Hotel, until you reach the post office at Pontneddfechan. Here you will find The Angel pub, which serves food and welcomes walkers and tourists in general.

Stage Three: Pontneddfechan to Banwen – 5 miles *(Val Saunders Evans)*

The Afon Pyrddin river valley, because of its inaccessibility, becomes more of a time warp the deeper one travels. Clear paths exist along the Pyrddin as far as the Logan Rock, then it is a question of getting back on the hills to pick up Sarn Helen. The walking is atmospheric in this area.

A wonderful beginning to this stretch, along a clear path through the Pyrdein river valley to the Logan Stone, is followed by walking mainly through old forest, with some wet areas and paths made difficult by fallen trees. Bro Nedd Walk waymarking helps the direction finding. The next part of the walking moves through forestry onto open hill tracks with a final stretch along a quiet lane. The rewards of this section are the landscape and natural features, the sense of history, and the unique atmosphere.

From the car park at The Angel Inn, opposite the Tourist Information Centre, turn left and immediately left again, down a lane with a few properties. You will see ahead of you wrought iron gates with the words *Sgwd Gwladys* – Lady Waterfall, and a kissing gate entrance. Go through these and follow the clear path alongside the left bank of the River Nedd.

You are in a deep gorge which will widen out. Iron ore was mined from this area and you will notice a blocked mine entrance tucked away into the hillside adjacent to the path. It is a good reminder of the rich mineral wealth and the difficulties in reaching it. There is reputedly a chalybeate spring nearby. You will also pass the ruins of a flour mill. When you reach the junction of two rivers, take the left fork and follow the Afon Pyrddin. You will then cross a footbridge to the right bank of the Pyrddin.

After almost half a mile, at a point where the path rises, you can keep by the river and come out by the falls, or take the rising path to come out above the falls on a natural stone pavement. (My walking companion and I have argued over whether this is limestone or millstone grit.) 'Sgwd Gwladys' translates as 'the cascade of Gwladys'. You may remember Gwladys from the legend of Brychan of Brycheinog referred to in the Black Mountain section. Gwladys was one of his daughters and the mother of St Cadoc.

This is an excellent point to take a break and take in the many views and the ancient atmosphere of this area.

There is a distinctive triangular stone in the middle of the river above the falls. To the right of this area there is a clearing with a larger rectangular stone – the Logan Stone – set in the middle. This is a logan, or rocking stone – one of the 20 or so reputedly placed in the landscape thousands of years ago. A theory has linked these stones to ley lines, suggesting that stones were originally positioned so that they could easily be rocked, with the intention of renewing the forces travelling on the ley lines. Tourist information offices may still have copies of the old West Glamorgan leaflet which explains the history of this Logan Stone. The stone weighs 17 tonnes and apparently could once be moved with one finger's pressure upon it. It was overturned by mineral railway workers in the 19th century. Although it no longer rocks, it has a strong presence and commands respect in its clearing setting.

Take the path up the hill and bear left when there is a choice. You are climbing quickly through mixed oak and birch woodland, well-populated by birds. Soon you have good views back up the valley and of the opposite hillside. The path continues upwards and curves around a little to the right. You now start to pick up Bro Nedd waymark signs. The Bro Nedd route starts and finishes on the coast, coming all the way up the valleys to Sarn Helen. We shall be coming across parts of it for the next mile.

The woodland is still deciduous but edged by pines and larches. The path becomes blocked in places by fallen trees and because of these walkers have to take diversions so the path itself is less distinct. Follow the waymarking along the edge of a field and the woodland until you reach ruined farm buildings – Cilfach Bronwydd. Keep this to your left and head for the metalled road just beyond the stile and trees. As you come out onto the road you will see the finger-post for Sgwd Gwladys pointing back the way you have just come.

Turn right and go past the entrances on your right to Bronwydd Farm. Continue for 500 metres to where this quiet metalled lane turns sharply right. You will see a path left through the trees, then a signed bridleway. Take the bridleway. It can be muddy in wet weather and winter. Follow it for about half a mile to where it crosses the Nant Hir.

It continues for another half mile through open forestry land to a cattle grid, where it meets with a track from the right. This is Sarn Helen. Where the two tracks join becomes a metalled track. Go left along it, passing a small reservoir, and continue on what is now a metalled road, passing through the open gates of Cefngwaunhynog Farm. Sarn Helen goes off to the left across farm land before this, but it is worth staying on the metalled road – it is a no through road and serves only the adjacent farms. The road crosses the head waters of the Fedwen and Bryn streams, and after just over a mile comes out close to Henrhydd Falls. Here you can turn right and follow the road for 500 metres to the falls or go left and follow Camnant Road around to the A4109 and cross it into Banwen. In other words, you are now on the linear route over to Melincourt and need to follow the walking directions for that stage of the route. You will find them below.

Introduction – The Linear Route

The route includes a fascinating conglomerate of caves with displays of Palaeolithic life in the area, a country park, two memorable hills, delightful woodland and farmland and two spectacular waterfalls. This walk really does have something for everyone. **Much of the route is strenuous,** but the views from Cribarth and Sarn Helen reward the climbing. The first part of the walking includes the famous Henrhyd Waterfall. The route then climbs onto Hirfynydd, picking up Sarn Helen Roman road. Then it drops down to Abergarwed, crossing the River Neath, goes under the new A465 and comes up into Melincourt.

From the Dan yr Ogof (839 161) car park, follow the finger-post, crossing the A4067 to Craig y Nos Country Park. The castle around which the park was created was once the home of world-famous opera singer, Adelina Patti, who, in the later years of the nineteenth century, entertained the rich and famous in a most opulent manner.

Opposite the castle, cross the main road again. Then cross a series of stiles alongside a farm and follow the path just to the right. Go left up the steep-sided Cribarth (828 142). Beyond a farm gate take a left fork and continue until you meet a wall on the left. At this point leave the track and climb the hill on the right to admire the glorious views of the Swansea Valley and the Black Mountain from the trig point.

Return to the track and follow the wall where it turns to the left down a rocky trail to a stile. Across the stile, turn right and follow the path as it meanders down to another stile. Ignore this one and turn left to go through a farm gate then a second one. Finally, go through a third gate, on the right, and take the right-hand path through Abercrave Wood (830 133).

At the bottom, enter the extremely well-kept Abercrave Farm via two farm gates. Exit alongside a stream onto a metalled road to the right down to Abercrave Inn. Here turn sharp left, then right to cross a road bridge over the River Tawe (825 127). Immediately across the bridge, go through a kissing gate on the left alongside a house, then a further two kissing gates under a major road and across a field to a small wooded area alongside the river.

Follow the waymark to the left, then fork upward to the right to a stile. Cross another stile in the far right corner of the field onto a metalled road. Turn left and follow the lane down a steep hill to cross Llech Bridge. Climb a stile on the right to begin almost two miles of the most enchanting woodland walking alongside the river to Henrhyd Falls (854 119). These are the highest in South Wales at 30 metres.

From the falls take the steep path uphill to a car park. Go through the car park and turn right, crossing Pont Henrhyd. Follow the very quiet road south for just over a mile. When you reach the A4109, take the local access road immediately opposite to enter the village of Banwen Pyrddin (856 095). Walk through the main street of the small village. At time of writing the colourful local inn was up for sale and not in operation so refreshments cannot be guaranteed in this area.

You are heading straight uphill to the forestry area ahead which will eventually lead to Sarn Helen. Cross the cattle grid and enter the forest. At the junction of Forestry Enterprise roads with numerous waymark signs take the steep hill track which bears southerly. On reaching a monument, The Gnoll Stones, a pause for breath will be welcome if not essential.

Refreshed, continue the climb to Sarn Helen (831 070). The track, the old Roman road, will be enjoyed for the next hour or so as you journey south-west with Rheola Forest on the left and spectacular views over the Swansea Valley and the Black Mountain and Brecon Beacons beyond.

At this point you should begin to use **Landranger 170** – Vale of Glamorgan and Rhondda. Eventually you again emerge onto a forestry road and here turn left through a vehicle barrier. Next go right and proceed until a wire fence enclosing a quarry is reached. Immediately the fence becomes parallel with the road, seek a rather obscure path on the left slanting down the hillside through

Scwd yr Eira Waterfall (Angela Rowe)

the heath. After the first 10 metres or so the path is well-defined as a woodland track. On emerging on a lower road continue directly ahead down a wide forestry road.

At a Y-junction turn right, following a stream. A dead tree stands as sentry on the road immediately before a lay-by or turning area. At the end of the lay-by, near a clump of buddleia on the left, is an ill-defined path dropping steeply to the valley floor.

Having negotiated the path, you will find, at the bottom, a St Illtyd's Walk waymark directing you to the left. Follow this pleasant woodland path over a babbling brook down to a major curve in a forestry road. Pause here to marvel at the view across the valley and the next stage of the walk to Afan Argoed. Take the down curve, ignore the next waymark (a sadly overgrown path) and continue to a cluster of rocks guarding the entry to a path which turns very abruptly to the right. After about 30 metres or so follow a waymark directing sharp left, a most pleasant downhill walk through the woods. Cross another path and at a Y-junction turn sharp right onto an ancient tramway. Turn left on a concrete path to enter the village of Abergarwed, where you will find pubs and refreshment.

Cross the road and follow a public footpath sign down a lane past some buildings. The lane leads to a footbridge over the fast-flowing River Neath. The path then runs under the A465, Heads of the Valley road. Continue to a road, turn right then left to a path which crosses a railway line. Proceed to the quiet car park for the Melincourt Waterfall.

Looking Ahead: *Beginning at Melincourt, the route continues its pattern of crossing successive river valleys to the coast. There are some impressive hills and two river valleys to cross in the next section before coming out at Margam and crossing the coastal plain to the sand dunes at Kenfig.*

Section Six
The Iron Hills of Afan: Melincourt to the Heritage Coast at Ogmore

36 miles

The Bodvic Stone

Ron Elliott and Val Saunders Evans

See Section Five for details of Ron Elliott and
"The Beginning" for details of Val Saunders Evans.

Stages:
1. Melincourt to Afan Argoed Country Park – 10 miles
2. Afan Argoed to Kenfig Castle – 14 miles
3. Kenfig Castle to Newton Church – 6 miles
4. Newton to the Ogmore River Crossing – 6 miles

Maps: Landrangers 160 (Brecon Beacons) and 170 (Vale of Glamorgan and Rhondda)

Highlights: Melincourt Falls, Cwm Blaenpelenna, Cefn yr Argoed, Bodvic Stone and Twmpath Dilith, Cwm Philip, Margam Abbey, Kenfig Castle, Kenfig Nature Reserve and Dunes, Sker House, St David's Well, Tythegston Long Barrow and Ogmore Castle.

Starting Point: The car park at Melincourt (822 019)

Alternative Route: It is possible to take the Ogwr Ridgeway from Margam to Llantrisant to meet up with the Celtic Way route through S.E. Wales. The Ridgeway is signed and marked on OS maps.

Accommodation: B&B, camping and hotels close to the route at Cymmer and Cwmavon (one mile from Afan Argoed); Maesteg and Bryn (one mile from Rhiw Tor Cymry / golf course crossing); and at Mawdlam and Pyle near Kenfig. Abundant camping, B&B and hotels at Porthcawl.

Transport: Nearest rail and bus stations at Bridgend and Port Talbot. Good local bus services to most villages and towns adjacent to the route.

Additional Information: Pelenna Mountain Centre – 01639 636227, Afan Argoed Centre – 01639 850564, Margam Abbey complex – 01639 871184 (includes the Museum of Standing Stones) and Kenfig Nature Reserve Centre – 01656 743386.

Tourist Information: Porthcawl – 01656 786639

Introduction

Moving down from waterfall country, the route traverses the great hills above the coastal plain where the rivers we have been crossing cut their way through to the sea. We leave our last waterfall at Melincourt and cross the hills into the Afan Valley and Afan Argoed Country Park, where we walk part of the Coed Morgannwg Way. The route brings us into Margam Country Park and Cwm Philip before we cross Margam Moors to the coast and the Nature Reserve at Kenfig Dunes. From the dunes the route takes in the local wells on the way to the long barrow at Tythegston and the river crossing at Ogmore.

Evidence from Bronze Age and Iron Age settlements suggests that the early inhabitants of the area moved from the coastal plain to the hills because a climate change, over-farming, population growth or the Roman presence, or all these things made it expedient. Archaeological finds in Margam and Newton give evidence of previous settlement. The Museum of Standing Stones in the Margam Abbey complex houses the original standing stones; replicas have been placed in the sites where they stood.

Walking the Celtic Way through this section is to experience its contrasts and surprises. Industry and husbandry compete for the valley floors. In the valley there may be a sunrise technology site, an open-cast mine or a dairy farm on its oasis of pasture. On the hills 1500 feet above there may be an ancient track, a standing stone or the weather-flattened remains of hill camps. Open, whale-backed tops and slopes covered with mixed woodlands and forestry are the reward for climbing out of the valleys, but there are times when the incentives of

Tree sculpture in the Margam Estate

a pub lunch, a dive into a general store, or the tired stroll past gardens to the B&B make the descent to the valley floor attractive. The villages of the Neath Valley and those adjacent to Afan Argoed, or the towns of Maesteg, Pyle and Porthcawl offer refreshment and accommodation on the route through this section of the Celtic Way.

Stage One: Melincourt to Afan Argoed – 10 miles

On this stage you will encounter a waterfall, woodland, farmland and open moorland: it is a walk of considerable variety and suitable for all. From the car park at Melincourt, cross the road (B4434) and follow the path to the right of the OAP Hall alongside Melincourt Brook to Melincourt Falls. After a rainy period this can be an awe-inspiring experience. Retrace your path as far as a stepped path which zigzags up the side of the valley to a stile onto a farm track. Turn left and continue through a gate to a metalled road. Here, turn right up the hill. At this point, if time allows, the top of the falls provides a splendid place to linger for further exploration or a picnic on the banks of the river.

About 200 metres up the hill, cross a stile on the right, waymarked St Illtyd's Walk, and follow the blue arrow directing left. Take the next left fork up a grassy bank. Immediately after passing through a gap in a wall, turn left and head up through another gap in a wall to the brow of a hill. From this point you will see the next waymark on a gate and stile. Follow this arrow in a southerly direction across open country and you will soon pick up a grassy trail. Where the zigzagging path bends to the right of a wall, pick out rocky outcrops or cairns. The topmost of these is your next point of reference.

At the top of the hill do not enter the farm gate but turn left, and with the wire fence on your right continue to another gate at the corner of a forestry plantation. Go through the gate and follow the line of trees until it turns 90 degrees to the right. At this point enter a single gate and pick up the St Illtyd Walk waymarks again.

An extremely pleasant woodland walk leads to a stile. Over the stile you are on a stony track in open, attractive moorland. Turn right and follow the track as it twists left then turn right to enter forestry again over a cattle grid. After about 150 metres, turn left following a yellow waymark, but ignore the second arrow to your right.

Eventually the road crosses a stream. Just past embankments on both sides of the road and a right-hand bend, look for a footpath to the left. It is not easy to spot, but a recently constructed cairn should help you to locate it. Half a mile through the woodland, cross a stile to Cwm Blaenpelenna, an open, interesting valley with an industrial history. Take the rocky path down to the river, cross by a footbridge and follow the Pelenna on its southern bank until you cross a stile near a single road bridge. Turn left, following a farm road up the hill, and at a farm gate turn right to cross a stile into a woodland of broadleaved trees.

Just below and to the left are the remains of Fforch-dwm Viaduct, once part of a tram road system known locally as Parson's Folly. It was built to convey coal to the Neath Canal, but the rapid growth of the coal industry established the railway before the tram road could be proved commercially viable. Hence, the apparent folly.

The path crosses a footbridge over Nant Fforch-dwm then climbs through a beech wood to a forestry road. Turn right and after about half a mile follow a yellow waymark to the left for a further half mile, along a pleasant grassy track. On emerging onto yet another forestry road, turn right to the Pelenna Mountain Centre and the remains of Gyfylchi Chapel. Turn sharp left then immediately right, following the large indicator to Penrhys Walk. At the bottom, where the track bends to the right, continue straight ahead on a bridleway. Follow the path to the next bridleway arrow, turning sharp right downhill. Just prior to this turning on your left may be seen the bricked up remains of the Gyfylchi Railway tunnel. This was part of the South Wales Mineral Railway from Briton Ferry to Glyncorrwg which was opened in 1861.

At the foot of the short bridleway turn right onto yet another disused railway. A sharp left turn takes you down to the river bridge which leads across to the Afan Argoed Countryside Centre.

Stage Two: Afan Argoed to Newton – 16 miles

Warning: this route crosses the River Kenfig where it comes out into runnels on the beach. Generally there is no problem crossing this here, but, exceptionally, at times of high tides or heavy rain, the beach crossing may not be possible. **Tide tables can be checked at Tourist Information Offices before starting out.**

On this stage you will be walking on broad, open hills, with some forestry climbing from 500 to 1500 feet. The walking starts at Afan Argoed Centre and goes over the hill to Rhiw Tor Cymry then onto the Coed Morgannwg Way into

Margam Forest. The route then comes down into Cwm Philip and skirts the Margam Estate to come out by Margam Abbey with its museum of standing stones. From here the route crosses Margam Moors, passing the British Steel Coking Depot, and runs along the beach and dunes before turning inland to the ruins of Kenfig Castle.

From Afan Argoed (820 950) car park, go up past the museum onto a tarmacked track up to Ty Canol farmhouse on your left. Go through a small gate into a well-fenced green track, which rises quickly. Carry on up the hill. The path is waymarked with brown arrows. Pass fenced off fields, and get a splendid view as the height increases. At the end of the track you come to a gate and should take the uphill path marked with a blue arrow. There is a fence to the right, open hillside to your left and a view to the rear of the river valley cleft you are leaving behind. You are walking in an easterly direction.

Come out onto the top on a path with a blue waymark arrow passing Forestry firs. Swansea can now be seen miles behind you (on an un-Celtic note – the high building is the famous Driver and Vehicle Licensing Centre, DVLC).

The path crosses over a small ravine, there are trees to the right and a hilly bank on the left, then a gate and stile. Turn right onto open hillside. Go through a farm gate. Here you have a choice of four tracks – take the **south-west track,** second from the right, third from the left. You pass a pond with bullrushes. As you go downhill, there is a view of the route ahead, and view of hills to Vale of Glamorgan. This is an ideal place for a swift breather.

Go downhill, leaving Rhiw Tor Cymry behind, and out of the forest by a small car park. Cross the B4282 Bryn to Maesteg road and cross a stile (currently in a poor state of repair) to Maesteg Golf Course. At the entrance to the golf course, take the track through the centre, keeping an eye on low-flying golf balls. Go up onto the forestry hill following the track as it curves up and round to left. There are good views of the Maesteg hills from here.

Cross the cattle grid and follow 200 metres of forest path until you come, on your left, to Coed Morgannwg Way. You will now see signposts with a black footprint on a white background and an arrow pointing in the path's direction. Follow these unless told otherwise. After 10 minutes there is a division of paths – follow the sign and take the middle road. At a corner in a small valley, follow the sign straight on into trees – it is a green lane and very attractive. Contrast this with the next section – a metalled forestry road with a stream and marshy area on the right. At a choice of tracks keep on the main road.

You will pass a memorial stone to Billy Vaughan, forestry commissioner. When we saw the stone it was surrounded by masses of pine cones. At the next division, take the left by the very tall trees. There is no sign at the next junction so look for a small cairn on the left and go straight uphill, passing an enclosed conifer forest then an open, cleared area.

The next waymark is by the Bodvic Stone (this is a replica – the original is in the Museum of Standing Stones). There is a small pool and a diversion to a stile and a path leading across boggy ground to the twmpath diwlith. This was a preaching mound in the last century. It is chastening to imagine the zeal which drew preacher and audience to this exposed hilltop. From the Bodvic Stone,

6.1 SARN HELEN TO AFAN ARGOED

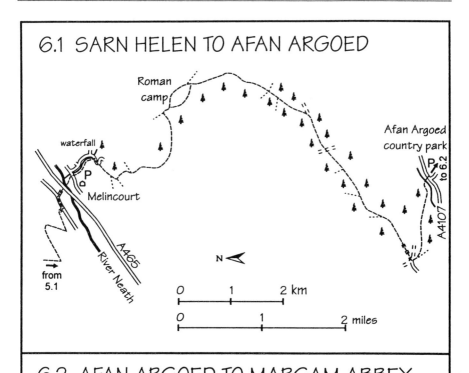

6.2 AFAN ARGOED TO MARGAM ABBEY

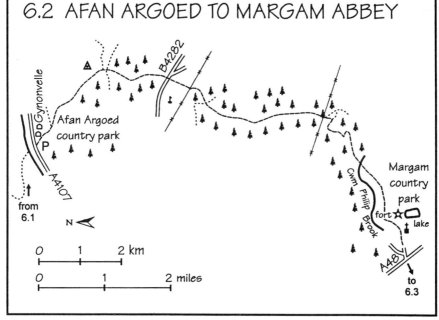

follow the forestry road downhill and south-east to a wide metalled road form-
ing a T-junction. (Here is the point where those who wish to can leave the Celtic
Way and follow the waymarked Ogwr Ridgeway to Llantrisant. Turn left at the
forestry road junction and in 400 metres you will reach the signs for the Ogwr
Ridgeway. Ogwr (Ogmore) was the name of the old borough council. The route
is shown on OS maps and well-signed).

Continuing on the Celtic Way route, take the path downhill into Cwm
Philip by taking a quick left then right to take the route downhill into the valley.
This is not waymarked. It is a distinctive curving track with hairpin bends
which loops down the valley-side. The hill below the track has mixed woodland – predominantly birch, oak and larch. You are entering a small valley, accessible only on foot. Follow the path south-west along the stream. This is Cwm
Philip, the heart of the Welsh part of the walk, and the place where the idea for
the Celtic Way first formed. During the next mile of walking, see if you agree
that the valley has a special atmosphere of its own.

After a mile you will come out at the back of the Margam Estate. Directly
ahead is the slope leading to its dramatic hill fort – Mynydd y Castell. At the
junction by the old iron washeries there is a choice of paths: into the estate, up
to the hill fort or out through the back exit. There is no right of entry to the estate, the castle or the amenities. If you are well prepared you will have asked the
TIC for a leaflet showing you all the features of this place to help you decide if
you want to pay to enter. Unless you are prepared to pay, you should turn right
to leave through the back route out of Margam. Go downhill alongside the ore-
stained River Philip, passing a glade on your right. The path bears left, then
right, and then crosses the river and leaves the estate through a kissing gate. It
continues alongside the remarkably emerald waters of a boating lake, passes a
lodge and comes to a complex of buildings which include Margam Abbey, the
museum of standing stones, and the Abbot's Kitchen.

The Cistercian abbey was established by Robert, Earl of Gloucester in 1147.
However a Celtic monastery was previously there and the site had been re-
garded as sacred for centuries before. Some early crosses are preserved in the
museum. The Museum of Standing Stones is a small collection managed by
CADW. It contains some inscribed Romanesque, Roman and Celtic stones and
crosses, including the great wheel cross of Conbelin. You can find out more
from the *Wales Cymru Tourist Guide. Allow yourself some time in this area before going on to the coastal part of the walking. There will be no places for refreshment for the rest of this stage in the walking.*

Now you move onto something completely different. Leave the abbey complex on the small access lane and walk past several houses and a copse until
you come to the A48. This road used to be the jugular of South Wales before the
M4 was completed. For the moment it is relatively quiet, although I am told that
there are plans to add housing and industry to the Margam Moors and Hirwaun
Woods areas. Cross the A48 and make for the huge roundabout. You are going
to cross this and take an industrial access road to the coast. Keep your wits
about you and take a deep breath: the air is going to alter for the next mile.

Go south down the access road past the playing fields, crematorium, and

BOC. This is about half a mile and should take about 20 minutes. Now you are on Longlands, an attractive open lane with fields either side of you, British Steel's Coking Depot in front of you and some railway lines to cross. Go over the lines for the main Swansea to Paddington rail link, and also for British Steel. Keep going south. You are still on Longlands Lane and passing adjacent to the fragile ecosystem of Margam Moor. You are approaching the beach, fir copses and dunes.

Friendly horses will probably come to greet you as you pass them. As you walk the next few miles it is a good time to make a leap of the imagination to visualise the empty beauty of the coastal plain when small Celtic tribes farmed its soil. Picture the Romans building their roads and marching posts, and the early saints moving all along the coastal plain alongside the Severn Sea, building churches on local sacred sites and bringing their unique vision of Christianity.

If passing on a weekday, you will not be able to take your eyes off the activities of lorry after lorry carrying their black loads on the slope to the right, nor the sweep of the gantries where the coal is unloaded. Walking here, I am struck by the paradox of the creative and destructive potential of the iron, water and coal. The qualities of the land that have drawn us to this coastal strip have also led to its contamination.

Go through the small car park, cross the tarmacked Haul Road and go onto the beach. Now you turn left. Although not easy underfoot, if the tide is going out or still some way from being high, the beach is a good place to walk. **Do not attempt the beach route in heavy weather with a high tide. Go back to the A48 and take Water Street to Mawdlam to connect with the route.**

Walk along the beach for about a mile until you reach the Afon Kenfig (River Kenfig). Cross it on the beach, where it is only a series of runnels. After crossing the river, follow it back upstream for about 100 metres until you come to a Kenfig Dunes Nature Reserve sign. There are the remaining stanchions of what was once a bridge over the Kenfig. Take the long, straight track east for 300 metres. This is a continuation of the British Steel Haul Road, once used to fetch stones from the local quarry to build the deep-water harbour. When you leave it you will be aiming for the green trees alongside the river, and then the church of St Mary Magdelene at Mawdlam so take sightings of the tower to your north-north-east to get familiar with the landscape. **Direction- finding here can be awkward** because the river's reed-beds force you wide and the dunes are full of shifting paths.

Alternative Route to Porthcawl

If, at this stage, you are tired of direction-finding and want an easier time of it, then just follow the beach or the adjacent path all the way into Porthcawl, which is where you are most likely to have reserved your accommodation. It will take a couple of hours. You will pass the ruins of Sker House, a lifeguard hut, and the Royal Porthcawl Golf Club before coming to Rest Bay with the famous 'Rest' convalescent home, associated with Florence Nightingale. You then reach the low cliffs of Locks Common before you stumble onto the revitalised seafront of Porthcawl, with the lights of the harbour and fairground ahead of you. Not very Celtic to look at yet the hills above Porthcawl contain the remains of a round barrow and a long barrow.

Continuing the Main Route

Just after the low grass bank which blocks the track you are on, leave the track. You will see a mere in front. Hit out across the dunes for about half a mile to meet up with the river once the reed-beds are passed. If it is cloudy and you cannot see the church tower, just keep going north. Current markers are a rusted buoy, fencing on the dunes and a lone Scots pine.

After a mile of tracking the river you will meet up with it. The trees which line its banks stand out amongst the dunes you are travelling through. Once you find the riverside path follow it northwards, enjoying the shade if it is a warm day, until you reach the ruins of Kenfig Castle. These few walls are all that remains of the royal borough of Kenfig, once a thriving town, now buried under the sand. The destruction took place in the 15th century. The church was rebuilt and is the one you have been using as a landmark.

You are about half a mile from the very prominent Angel Inn on the eastern skyline, and the less visible Prince of Wales Inn. Both provide refreshment. Alternatively, this is a good time to end your walking with a visit to the Kenfig Nature Reserve and Centre at Kenfig Pool. Buses and taxis to nearby Pyle and Porthcawl are available.

Stage Three: Kenfig Castle (801 827) to Newton Church – 6 miles

From the castle head south-easterly towards the church tower. Cross the road and with the church of St Mary Magdelene on your left, walk into Mawdlam village. Take the first road to the right, Heol Broom, and follow it for about half a mile. It rises slowly and on a bright day gives views back to Swansea Bay and the Gower Peninsula beyond. Take the third footpath sign to the right, 50 metres before the road bends 90 degrees to the left. Cross two fields on the well-defined paths by hedges and enter a metalled road. Continue in the same direction towards the sea, crossing a minor road, and you come to the Kenfig Nature Reserve Centre which is well worth a visit. The seabirds in this area are varied and keen ornithologists will find a hide at Kenfig Pool Nature Reserve.

Now head south, skirting the golf course. Such a mishmash of paths cross the dunes that the best option is to aim for the sea. All paths come out at the Haul Road met in the earlier section.

On reaching this track turn left and approach Sker House. This is the home of Elizabeth, the Maid of Sker, the eponymous subject of R.D. Blackmore's novel. Blackmore's more famous novel is *Lorna Doone*, and the two settings of Exmoor and Sker beach face each other across the Bristol channel. The future of the house has recently been taken on by CADW, the agency responsible for the management of historic buildings in Wales. Reports are that it has been sold and will be developed – in what form has yet to be seen. It would make a terrific hostel for walkers!

Approach the house along a rough farm track and climb three stone steps over a wall to enter the farmyard and then exit onto a wide farm track going

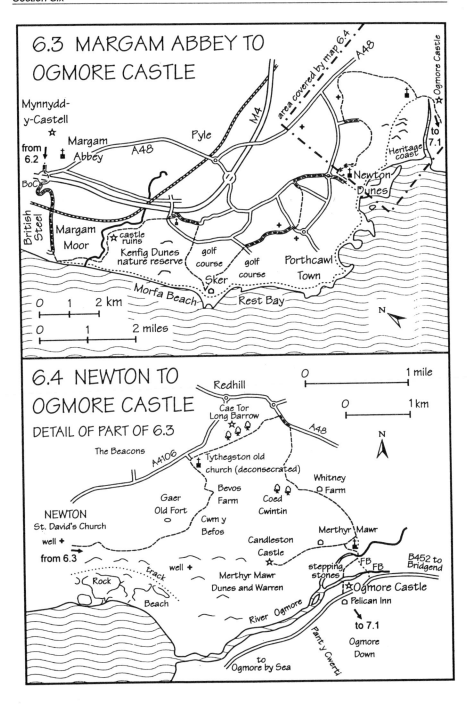

6.3 MARGAM ABBEY TO OGMORE CASTLE

Mynnydd-y-Castell

from 6.2

Margam Abbey

Pyle

M4

area covered by map 6.4

A48

Ogmore Castle

to 7.1

Heritage coast

Newton Dunes

British Steel

BoC

Margam Moor

castle ruins

Kenfig Dunes nature reserve

golf course

golf course

Porthcawl Town

Sker

Morfa Beach

Rest Bay

N

0 1 2 km

0 1 2 miles

6.4 NEWTON TO OGMORE CASTLE

DETAIL OF PART OF 6.3

Redhill

Cae Tor Long Barrow

A48

0   1 mile

0   1 km

N

The Beacons

A4106

Tythegston old church (deconsecrated)

Whitney Farm

NEWTON
St. David's Church

well

from 6.3

Gaer Old Fort

Bevos Farm

Coed Cwintin

Cwm y Befos

Candleston Castle

Merthyr Mawr

Merthyr Mawr Dunes and Warren

stepping stones

FB FB

B452 to Bridgend

Ogmore Castle

Pelican Inn

Rock

track

well

Beach

River Ogmore

Pant y Cwrti

to Ogmore by Sea

to 7.1

Ogmore Down

east. This runs for about a mile before coming to a minor road. Cross it and go into Moor Lane opposite. Walk along this quiet lane and pass under a railway bridge then take the right-hand fork 500 metres or so further on. Here lies St David's Well. Continue along the lane to an enchanting spot, a small green valley to the left known as Dewiscomb – David's Valley. It is a place of peace and soft on the eye. Opposite is what is left of the old Nottage Halt from the days of rail. Continue until reaching a T-junction. Here you have the opportunity to make a short detour by turning right into Nottage Village – with three pubs, shops and a post office, it is an excellent place for refreshment.

To continue, turn left and follow the lane as it runs down towards a main road. Just before the main road you will see a signed, small footpath to your right, edged by trees (ignore the earlier signed path across the field) and running the perimeter of the grounds of Nottage Court. Keep to the footpath and follow it for 400 metres through a tunnel of trees to the well called Ffynnon Fawr.

To move on from the well, return into the tunnel of trees running parallel with, but unseen from, the road. At a pair of stiles take the right-hand one and cross the A4229 to a gate and stile immediately opposite. Cross a field and a lane by means of a further two stiles and then a series of stiles across fields – aiming roughly eastwards where the stiles are not immediately visible. You emerge on a lane with a secondary lane immediately ahead. This is Tyn y Caeau Lane which leads to a roundabout on the Bridgend road.

Cross the roundabout and follow the signs for Newton. Turn second left onto Clevis Hill and follow this to the village green before the ancient church of St John. At the seaward edge of the green is Sandford's Well. Read the legend in verse attached to the well. On the route between the Kenfig and Ogmore rivers we have been close to or passed five wells. If you are spending any time in the area, the local tourist office in Porthcawl will be able to supply leaflets which describe the Wells walk in more detail.

Stage Four: Newton Church to Ogmore – 6 miles

This stage of the route takes in the Long Barrow at Tythegston then the Ogmore river crossing. With Newton church on your right, walk up the hill and follow the road around past the allotments. At the end of the allotments take the track to the left. This crosses two small access roads then you take a left fork into woodland. On approaching a large house, turn right down a sandy trail to a T-junction. Turn left and left again onto a grassy plain. At the next fork go left and then follow a straight path (waymarked) ahead into a woodland in a pleasant valley.

At the next fork go left again to a stile into a narrow field in a shallow valley. Through a gap in the trees, the path bears to the right up the side of a valley to a stile, and then follows the hedge on the left to the next stile onto a metalled road. Follow the road to the left into the village of Tythegston. Just before the main Porthcawl to Bridgend road ahead of you, take a stone stile to the right and cross the centre of a field (currently with a glorious sycamore in the middle) to a stile which crosses onto a farm track and then into another field.

Cross the centre of this field to a gate and continue ahead to a wooded area –

this is pheasant country. To the left of the copse and near a pond is a long barrow, a must for any walker in this area. Cae Tor at Tythegston is one of the six acknowledged chambered tombs in the area once known as Glamorgan, and the most westerly of the long barrows. Two of the others are encountered in the next section. One of the most interesting aspects of the distribution of chambered tombs in Wales is the way they are found around estuaries and on peninsulas. In *A Guide to the Prehistoric and Roman Monuments of England and Wales* by Jacquetta Hawkes, a case is made for an overseas origin for their builders.

After viewing this cromlech, retrace your steps to the path and continue with the copse on your left past an old farm barn to an ancient gateway in the corner of the wood near the wall. Follow the steps down into a ditch and up the other side to a stile into a field. Head towards the busy major road (A48) via a stone stile in the far right-hand corner, and then remain alongside the hedge to a similar one. Immediately ahead is the stone stile which is the entry to the A48. From here it is necessary to walk the A48 footpath, but only for 150 metres.

At a break in the footpath, turn right, taking the left fork through a gateway alongside a sheepfold. Follow the path between two clumps of trees and near the fence enclosure at the bottom, climb an inferior stile to the right. Turn left and cross yet another stile. Follow the line of trees on the left to a stile in the bottom left-hand corner. Turn right, and in the left corner of the field cross a gully. Keep to the hedge on the right to a novel stile made of removable logs. After crossing this head directly up the field to two farm gates. Turn left onto a road which runs through two gates, into and out of Whitney Farmyard, and continue on the road to the delightful village of Merthyr Mawr.

Walk through the village, past the church, then continue for three-quarters of a mile to Candleston Castle. Really a fortified manor house, it is worth adding another hour to the walk to see it. You are also in the vicinity here of the highest sand dunes in Europe. Return to Merthyr Mawr Church and immediately after the village green turn right down a road to a suspension bridge over the River Ogmore. After this a path directs the walker to stepping stones over the River Ewenny to Ogmore Castle. In the event of flooding making a crossing by means of stepping stones impractical, turn left after the suspension bridge across a field to a footbridge to a road (B4524).

Turn right into Ogmore Castle. After exploring the site, go up the hill and cross the road to The Pelican public house opposite, where the next section of the walking, through the Vale of Glamorgan, begins.

Looking Ahead: *You are now crossing a physical and psychological divide between South-West and South-East Wales and entering the area of the Vale of Glamorgan. The area can justifiably be described as the cradle of Celtic Christianity – with the college at Llantwit Major being the training ground for the early Celtic saints. The route will follow the Heritage coast almost to Barry before going inland to two famous long barrows and then on to meet with the Ridgeway at Llantrisant.*

Section Seven
Around the Vale of Glamorgan:
Ogmore to Caerphilly
48½ miles

Llantrisant - the northern Vale hill town

Karl-James Langford and Viv Small

Karl-James Langford has been responsible for the establishment of several organisations over the years, in particular the Barry and Vale Museum Association and the Welsh Archaeological Institute and his work and time is presently dedicated to Archaeology Cymru Ltd. of which he is its present director. Karl-James is an ardent campaigner in archaeology. He has published a book entitled 'The Romans in the Vale of Glamorgan' and is planning a work on the Romans in South Wales.

Viv Small organises walks to the ancient Celtic and Roman sites in South. He is a member of Archaeology Cymru and the Cardiff Storytelling Circle. His interests in these organisations can lead to contradictions so that walks can sometimes stray towards the margins between history and folklore in the legend-haunted hills of Glamorgan.

Stages:

1. Ogmore to Llantwit Major – 13½ miles
2. Llantwit Major to Porthkerry – 12 miles
3. Porthkerry to Llantrisant – 13 miles
4. Llantrisant to Caerphilly – 10 miles

Maps: Landrangers 170 (Vale of Glamorgan and Rhondda) and 171 (Cardiff and Caerphilly)

Highlights: Dunraven hill fort, Llantwit Major church, The Bulwarks, Tinkinswood burial chamber, St Lythan's burial chamber and Garth Mountain.

Starting Point: The Pelican Inn, Ogmore near Ewenny (883 767)

Transport: Cardiff Central Station – 01222 227281

Additional Information: Caerphilly Castle – 01222 883143, Llancaiach Fawr Living History Museum – 01443 412248.

Tourist Information: Caerphilly Visitor Centre, Twyn Square – 01222 880011, Sarn Services – Junction 36, near Bridgend – 01656 654906.

Introduction

Allow enough time to experience this historic area – little-walked except by locals who know how good it is. The route generally follows the Heritage Coastline before turning inland to cross the Vale and approach the defensively placed hill town of Llantrisant. The area is bounded by the Heritage Coast to the south, and the Welsh Ridgeway, which we rejoin in the north. We cross the undulating Vale of Glamorgan, with its prosperous central town of Cowbridge. Llantwit Major, the cradle of Celtic Christianity, lies halfway along the Heritage Coast route, just inland. Unfortunately, the demands of a long-distance route do not allow enough time to properly explore the historical secrets of the Vale, merely give a taste that may whet the appetite. Accommodation is available in the main centres of Llantwit Major, Barry and Llantrisant. Between these it will be limited to occasional inns and B&B. Llantwit Major possesses more old inns per square mile than most places – a reflection, perhaps, of its historical status as a place of religious learning and the pilgrims it attracted. Barry, like Porthcawl, a seaside resort, will have plenty of accommodation. As well as hill fort remains, there are two significant burial chambers on the route: St Lythan's and Tinkinswood. After these the route goes directly north. Karl's route ends just before Llantrisant. Follow the directions to join the next stage of the Celtic Way at Rhiwsaeson for Llantrisant.

Here, we follow the Ridgeway and Viv takes over as the guide. He describes the features you will encounter walking up on the ridges and over the top of the Garth Mountain then down into the Taff Gorge before coming out in the historic town of Caerphilly. The nearest youth hostels are at Llwyn y Pia and Cardiff, both entail a bus journey to get to them from the route. Both Llantrisant and Caerphilly have plenty of B&B and inns.

Walking along the coastline and the Ridgeway offers wonderful views, but can be very exposed in bad weather. The Heritage Coast is a cliff-edge path and subject to erosion. It is generally wide and edges are often screened, but it has some exposed edges and sheer drops. The route through the Vale is likely to be changed by an airport link road and future improvements which will allow for less walking on minor roads.

Stage One: Ogmore Castle to Llantwit Major — 13½ miles

Look around you, this is the start of the beautiful walk around the Vale of Glamorgan – the Vale. As an archaeologist I feel this trip needs to be a trip into the past, which I feel supports the natural beauty of the Vale. Looking north from the inn you can see a flat, frequently flooded plain (in winter and high tides), also the remains of a picturesque castle built by the De Londres family. Take note, too, of the late medieval, so-called ancient, stepping stones.

Let's now move south-west towards Ogmore by Sea. On your right is the River Ewenny, and on your left is a hill. Soon you'll be taking advantage of the peace and quiet that is found behind the hill. The road that you are taking is the B4524 and at a bend in the road, you turn left along a footpath (before the Spires Woodland) into Pant y Cwerti valley. This is surrounded by steep, sandy slopes. There is a small well, part way along the footpath and you can imagine that this would have played an important role in village life years ago.

Continue on until you reach Pant Mari Flanders – an area that until the 19th-century Enclosures Act was an open landscape, with several burial chambers visible. These are no longer visible. Carry on forward into the village of St Brides along a B road. The village of St Brides has two public houses: the Farmer's Arms and the Fox and Hounds. Even though you have walked a modest half an hour or so, sit outside and have a look at the ducks and swans swimming. As St Brides Major is an important village, it also has a pleasant church with an ancient cross nearby, well worth a visit on a future occasion.

Now check that your walking gear is securely laced up and that you have made **somebody aware** that you will be walking along the dangerous Vale of Glamorgan coast. At this point check your map, you should be at 895 743. Fifty metres south along the B4265, you will find a trackway leading past a farm on your right. Follow this until the trackway forks after 50 metres into two public footpaths. Take the one on your left.

Follow the footpath until you reach a woodland, **take care** as you head downhill towards the coast. You will now enter a valley called Pant y Slade. This short valley opens out into a car park at Dunraven Bay. Here you will find the Heritage Coast Centre with toilets and exhibition boards. Turn into the car park and head left through a gate (which closes in late evening).

In front of you and on your left is Dunraven, the remains of a very large hill fort, now partly destroyed but still accessible. This once impressive site still preserves some of its majesty in its banks and ditches. Go to your right heading up a slope, all the time looking down at the banks and ditches. The smaller ones in particular belong to internal divisions and building for storage and habitation. As you head to the crown of the hill, be wary always of the edge of the cliff.

Now head downhill towards several burial mounds, or at least that is what we believe they are. The end of the point here is called Trwyn y Witch. From here you can look south and north along the Heritage Coast. The natural beauty here is awe-inspiring. The natural geology of the rocks shoots out at you as a message from millions of years ago. This can only be matched by a flight over the area in a light plane.

Following the cliff edge around until you are safely on the footpath again, take ten minutes to have a look at this moat of a castle. Once a splendid site, all came to a Bonfire Night end when it as lost in a deliberate fire after the Second World War. Only a tower, some wall, and a well-maintained garden exists, but contemplation here isn't a waste, take a look around at the exotic plants.

Head south-east now, preferably after a break, along a private trackway until you come to Cwm Mawr Lodge. Note the woodland here is reminiscent of a storybook, also the farmland that is the Vale of Glamorgan. Enter a valley called Cwm Mawr that is lightly wooded and proceed until you reach the Sealands Farm. Here you reach another trackway heading east and walk this until you reach the B4265 again.

Carry along this road due south until you reach Monknash, at least one mile south. Monknash once bustled with song and the sound of monks working in the local field. On your right are the remains of a dovecote. You can gain permission to see this after you have asked the publican in the Plough and Harrow Inn.

Around the dovecote there are various buildings of monastic use over 500 years ago. The footpath here is dangerous, and difficult to follow. So take the B road, heading south-west to the coast. As you reach New Mill Farm, over half a mile down along this road on your left you will see a road heading north-west. Follow this until you reach a small bridge over the Nash Brook. There is a footpath stile here on your left – head over this. The valley here hides many secrets, lost buildings amongst others. **Beware of uneven and wet surfaces**. Please take care. The woodland is dark and dull, but suddenly it opens into a sheltered but open, narrow valley called Cwm Nash.

The coast here, as before, is beautiful, and boggy. Head south up a bank onto the cliff-edge path. This heads across eight large fields. Remember the country code, and take heed. Keep safe and stay away from the edge of the cliff. BA safe distance here is between one and two metres. Carry on south for one and a half miles. Look around at the flat landscape which has been home over the centuries to many crops, from the Iron Age emmer wheat to Roman barley and today's oats.

You will now come to another hill fort, namely that of Nash Point. All but an east bank has been destroyed by erosion. The valley here is very well maintained, with a nature trail through the short stretch of woodland, apparently foxes roam here. Next head up the opposing hill to a small café, open for refreshments in season. Directly in front of you there are two lighthouses. You should now be at 917 683. The shorter of the lighthouses is the older, soon it is planned to mechanise the remaining lighthouse (being the taller).

Carry on past the lighthouses. Note the cracking of the ground. This could be due to the undercutting and natural erosion by the sea of the cliff's edge nearby. Now follow the path for over one mile alongside open farmland. One interesting feature about this part of the countryside is the true diversity of the natural environment between modern agriculture, ancient woodland and hedgerows. Crossing a stone stile the footpath enters woodland with steps in places to stop slipping and erosion.

As you reach St Donat's, care must be taken with the beaches, its large boulders and sharp rocks. The small inlet of Cavalry Barracks at St Donat's Bay is reached by steps. Take a brief look at the 19th-century buildings to your left. This is the modern home of the Inshore Rescue Station, at home along this windy coast. In the bay are two Second World War pillboxes, now filled up with pebbles and rubbish. It seems ironic that a so-called smugglers' cave, still accessible along the west side of this cliff, is protected by 20th-century defences. Such is the mixed legacy of the past.

Now continue along the coast into Barracks Wood, a short stretch of dull, dark woodland. Then go on to Tresilian Bay. There is a wonderful hamlet of houses here. Head up some steep steps again to the top of the cliff (948 677). Look over to your left, there is a wonderful, ruined farm building. Once many such sites were the home to semi-independent communities.

From here it is possible to continue walking or to break your journey at Llantwit Major. You will return to the coast for the next stage of the walking. Take the footpath signed to the left across fields into the west end of Llantwit Major (Llanilltud Fawr). Enter the village and make for the church tower.

Llantwit Major church was and is a centre for pilgrimage, being one of the oldest Christian sites in Europe. *The Pilgrim's Guide to St Illtyd's Church* by Vivian Kelly provides an insight into its fascinating history. The church is dedicated to St Illtyd who reputedly came to this area and founded the college from which the saints went to take the gospel to western Britain, Ireland and Brittany. A visit to the church is rewarding. There are local historians who will answer the visitor's questions. There are also some fascinating Celtic crosses in the West Church which stand over 8 feet high. The Houelt Cross is a splendid 9th-century Celtic wheel-cross. One cannot escape comparing them with the standing stones met on the Celtic Way. Although the present building is Norman and medieval, a sense of earlier times is present in the place and the artefacts. There is a recent renewal of the Festival of St Illtyd, which is celebrated on November 5th and involves townspeople, local schoolchildren, arts groups and students from the nearby international college in a torch-lit procession to the hilltop Church Field. With its candle-filled lanterns and paper figures, dancing skeleton and banging drums, it is a dramatic procession. The bonfire and fireworks bring a secular note to the occasion.

Stage Two: Llantwit Major to Porthkerry – 12 miles

To continue the walking, leave Llantwit Major by the signed Beach Road. Follow this for a mile into the Col-Huw Valley and past the car park to rejoin the route. This sheltered valley, protected on one promontory by a hill fort, is Cwm Col-Huw. There is a coffee and tea shop for refreshments, they do a good selection of snacks. Now head up the very steep hill in front on the east. Here is another hill fort. This, like most of the other hill forts along the coast, isn't complete. Local legend has it that the Romans disembarked here in the year

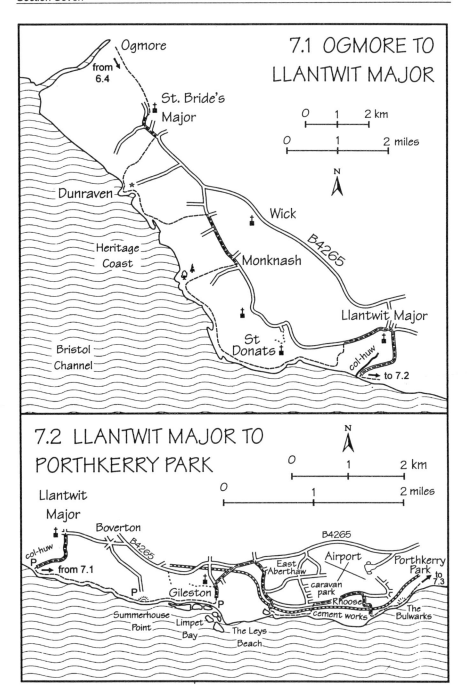

7.1 OGMORE TO LLANTWIT MAJOR

Ogmore

from 6.4

St. Bride's Major

0   1   2 km

0   1   2 miles

N

Dunraven

Heritage Coast

Wick

B4265

Monknash

Bristol Channel

Llantwit Major

St Donats

col-huw

to 7.2

7.2 LLANTWIT MAJOR TO PORTHKERRY PARK

N

0   1   2 km

0   1   2 miles

Llantwit Major

Boverton

B4265

B4265

Airport

Porthkerry Park

col-huw

P

from 7.1

East Aberthaw

caravan park

to 7.3

Gileston

Rhoose

P

Summerhouse Point

Limpet Bay

The Leys Beach

cement works

The Bulwarks

St Illtyd's festival at Llantwit Major

436AD, but there is no archaeological or supporting documentary evidence to prove it. The defences encircle one hectare (over an acre) of land, which is divided into two by an internal defence.

Carry on over the banks and ditches and go east for one mile. The contours go up and down. Here head to Stout Point, and start heading uphill. From this point you can see miles along the coast, a magnificent demonstration of the geological past that has been all around us on this walk. Head east along the coast for one and a half miles until you reach the former coastguard lookout post. This is now called the Seawatch Centre and is used as a centre for study. If it is open the warden will allow you up the ladder to visit the lookout area, explain some of the tasks they do, and show a few of the artefacts which people have brought to them.

Continuing from the centre you will be met by another ditch of a hill fort, this time that at Summerhouse Point. This ditch is one of the deepest to be found at all the sites visited. There are also the remains of a 19th-century summerhouse in the woods, surrounded by the defences of the hill fort. You can either proceed along the cliff edge – less dramatic than before – or along the pebbly beach. Whatever route you take, do take care.

Walk for three-quarters of a mile until you reach a marshy area, which is protected by Second World War tank blocks (large stacks of cement). This area is known as The Walls and Limpet or Limpert Bay. In times past the Aberthaw area was known for being an important harbour. Now that place has been taken by a large power station, ugly by all standards, but the buildings do chart the development man has made in past decades in producing electricity for towns and cities. The power station is very reliant on the energy produced by water power, a circular building (laisson) can be seen off-shore.

Head north into the village of Gileston. Take a look at the interesting church and the remains of a very ancient village. When you enter the village, take the right fork in the road and walk for half a mile. Take the road to the left, that heads under the railway bridge, onto the A4265, and continue east for three-quarters of a mile towards the Aberthaw turning. Before this the countryside is a mix of woodland and marshland. There is a castle and a series of bridges hidden at East Orchard, with the footpath overgrown and blocked (please take note ramblers' groups). Head past the cement works and the old road on your right into East Aberthaw. Aberthaw has a wonderful, old-world public house known as the Blue Anchor – well worth a visit.

Carry on down the road until you come across a turning on your right which heads over the railway, take this and walk down to the large, ruined building. There are many suggestions why this was constructed, but one thing is clear: it is good for exploration! Before we carry on you must find time to look at the large pond here. From time to time it is possible to see a whole variety of birds feeding, or building nests.

Now take the footpath, which is not clearly marked, for about a third of a mile, until you arrive at a set of steps heading up along the cliff. Climb the steps – on your left is the Ffontgari Caravan Park. Continue along the cliff edge until you come across the cement works. **It is dangerous to continue along the foot-path directly in front.** Take the left turning until you come to a railway bridge. Go under this and head into the village of Rhoose. Continue for 300 metres until you reach the main road. Walk east along the road for just under half a mile, until you reach the footpath on your right. Continue on down this until you reach the coast again.

After a track across farmland and going under yet another railway bridge, you should now be in an area rarely visited by anybody. This is a small pocket of farmland yet it looks fallow. Continue on the footpath to your left for a quarter of a mile. The landscape here is truly barren. You will reach a quarry. **Do take care**. After the assault course up and down the quarry, you should now have reached the limekilns. These defunct but proud-looking structures once assisted the quarrying industry in the area. This is a good time to look back and reflect on the scenic views and ideas collated along the coast. The GR now is 076 659.

Head north-east into the caravan park and towards its exit. Before the exit of the caravan park, find a sign for the ancient monument of The Bulwarks. This is yet another hill fort, and the gateway to the last part of the walk. The Bulwarks – nearly complete in defences – allows the walker to appreciate past events. The large, open space that you are met by was once the temporary home of hundreds of Celts. On hot summer's days, when the grass is a few inches high, you can discover the outlines of ancient hut circles, wooden-built structures which once housed grain and people.

Now let's move on. Head east towards Porthkerry Park along a track in the woods, **close to the cliff's edge**. Beware, take light steps or you might slip on the dark mud. Enter the park of Porthkerry, once owned by Romilly Estates. This large park becomes water-logged in winter, a sign that once this large, sheltered valley was an inlet to the sea. You will now be aware of a large viaduct which was built at the end of the last century. The park must be negotiated with care as it is easy to become lost. Head east along the open grassland with great woodland on either side of you. Maybe you will see the ghostly figure of Annie Jenkins, the 18th-century witch of Cliffwood Cottage. Or the ghosts of smugglers may leap out at you and question your presence in their domain.

You will enter the second part of the park under the bridge. Continue for 50 metres until the roadway forks. Head north along the roadway. It soon becomes a track. Go past a house on your left and over a fence. You are still on the footpath. Keep your eye on the ground, wary of outlines of buildings which once belonged to a medieval village of Cwm Ciddy. As you head north several gates block your way – negotiate these. You will see a large complex of newly refurbished buildings on your left, a model farm maybe?

Continue north along a roadway for half a mile until you reach the A4226. This road is the main access route for the airport, but is due to change. Please note that the new airport link road will be developed over the next few years, this description does not take that into account. Follow the road east for just over a quarter of a mile, until you reach a traffic island. Continue on over this into the northern part of Barry. This may be a good point to break your journey for the day. It is possible to walk, get taxi or public transport into the centre of Barry.

Stage Three: Barry to Llantrisant – 12 miles

Leave Barry by the road which brings you out on the north-western edge of the town. You will see Tesco's. Turn here and follow the road along in a northerly direction for a quarter of a mile, until you reach a trackway. Follow this. On your right is Highlight Farm and a skip company. Continue over the gate and along a trackway (also a footpath). You should now be at 099 697. When you reach another gate, head over it and on your left is the church of Highlight. It is now ruined and difficult to imagine it in its medieval state. What is clear is that once a congregation would have fought to enter the small nave.

Head now in a northerly direction. You are on the newly upgraded footpath. Head down a hill, this part of the Vale constantly undulates. There is a golf course on your right. Head down to a bridge, cross this and continue past two farm buildings for about one mile until you reach Duffryn Mill Farm. Duffryn has many secrets: a possible medieval moat and several prehistoric monuments. Carry on along the road until you are forced right, passing a bridge on your left. Pass Home Farm and continue, with a daunting wall on your left. This encircles Duffryn Gardens and house. You will now find yourself surrounded by trees, just as it would have been in Neolithic Britain.

Continue north-east, passing a northern turning on your left. You will find a lay-by and a sign for St Lythan's burial chamber. This stone-built Megalithic site was once buried by a huge mound, which has now weathered away. This is another legacy of prehistoric times. Briefly contemplate the walk, but don't fall

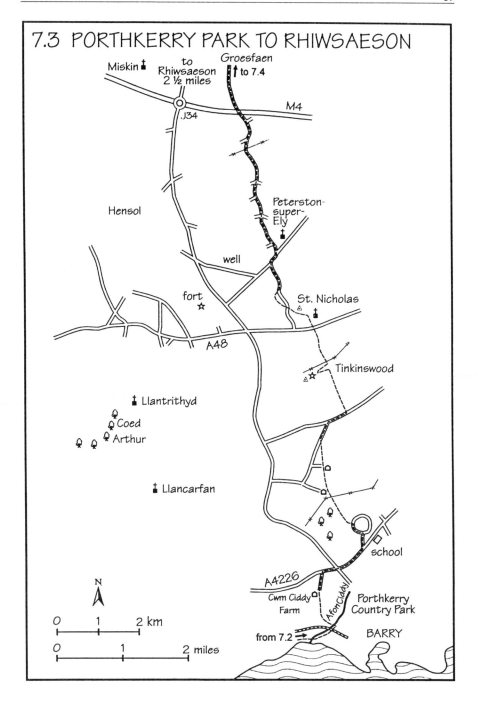

7.3 PORTHKERRY PARK TO RHIWSAESON

asleep as legend has it that, 'one who falls asleep here may turn into a poet, go mad, or simply die'.

Head back along the road that you have just walked until you reach that northern turning again. To avoid any confusion your GR should be 099 723. Head north now with Duffryn House on your left. Note the curious contrast here between nature and geology. Continue for three-quarters of a mile until you reach a sign for St Nicholas Tinkinswood burial chamber. Head through a kissing gate, just time to embrace anybody with you, and head south over a wooden bridge spanning a dry moat.

You will see a gap in the hedge to your right. Head through this and walk forward until you see the long cairn that is St Nicholas burial chamber. An immense capstone is present here: one of the largest in Europe. The complex of stones was constructed in two main phases. The site was first occupied over 4000 years ago. In excavation in 1914, over 40 human remains were found and bones are still being found today. Enough of prehistory for today. Let's head back along to the main road. But I can't resist pointing out the other stones on your right; these people of the past were keen on their dead.

Now that you are back on the road, head north into St Nicholas. The village can be reached if you turn left along the main road, here the A48. In the village is the old church of St Nicholas. No time to stop, however. Let's move north again, past the old school on your left, along a footpath (089 744). This footpath forks into two after 150 metres, take the left-hand fork. Continue along this footpath until you meet a trackway. Continue along this until you see an undulating area. There was once a motte and bailey castle known as Y Gaer here. Access is very difficult. There is also a triangulation station here, used for surveying.

Keep on this trackway and head north for at least one mile. You should now be on a secondary road. Continue along this in a northerly direction, taking the left fork at the road under a further railway bridge. Walk along this road, along flat countryside, for two miles, until you reach the M4 and the end of this section, but I hope that you are encouraged to continue along the Ridgeway.

To reach Llantrisant, continue along this road as it crosses the M4 and follow it for a further two miles until reaching the junction at Rhiwsaeson. This is on the route out of Llantrisant which follows the ridges to Caerphilly, but for now your path will probably be into Llantrisant for accommodation and refreshment. The walking notes continue from the centre of Llantrisant.

Stage Four: Llantrisant to Caerphilly along the Ridgeway Path – 10 miles

The Ridgeway is an established footpath route and waymarked. It is also shown on the OS Landranger map for the area. Following the Ridgeway route from Llantrisant to Caerphilly, the walking is predominantly on hills from 300 to 1000 feet. Walking starts with the path from Llantrisant to Caerau hill fort, then moves on to Rhiwsaeson. From here walking aims for the tumulus which tops the Garth Mountain, a conspicuous destination, although at 307 metres not especially high. From Garth Mountain the route drops down into Gwaelod y Garth and crosses the narrow Taff valley to climb again to the distinctive building of Castell Goch. The route then continues on the Ridgeway over Caerphilly Mountain. I hope that my perspective, as a local historian, will enhance the walking ahead.

Llantrisant, with its ancient church, pubs, castle and common, sits on top of a hill overlooking the Vale of Glamorgan to the south and mountains to its other sides. The town name is dedicated to Illtud, Gwynno and Tyfodwg, three Celtic saints, and although the church is Norman, an earlier church may have occupied the site. The town of Llantrisant was chosen by the Normans in the 12th century to defend their gains in South Wales. The castle was probably fought over and destroyed during the fierce clashes between the Welsh and the Norman conquerors. The bowmen of Llantrisant had given their allegiance to the English and fought bravely at the Battle of Crecy, earning themselves the title 'Black Army' after Edward, the Black Prince, youngest son of Edward the Third. Because of its situation on the top of a hill, it has changed very little in character since the Middle Ages. Llantrisant is unique, charming and unspoilt. The Bullring was named after the sport of bullbaiting, a barbaric game where dogs were set upon a bull roped to an iron ring. The people of Llantrisant were expected to provide entertainment at the markets and fairs at this important mediaeval centre until the Industrial Revolution transformed Britain and turned the town into a sleepy backwater full of curiosity for the traveller and historian.

Our route begins at The Wheatsheaf pub in High Street. Here also is the Erw Hir, a collection of cottages, and where the Ridgeway Walk continues along the slopes of East Caerlan. Here Llantrisant's favourite eccentric, Dr William Price, cremated his young son and created unknowingly the revival of the custom of cremation. Dr Price was a strong individual with a deep sense of social justice, a man who made a considerable impact on Wales.

The Vale and Cardiff stretch to the south as we descend towards the tiny hamlet of Cross Inn, cross the A473 and begin to follow the Ridgeway Walk as it winds its way around the ancient hill fort of Caerau. The history of Caerau is lost in antiquity. Built by the hardy Celts, and probably attacked by the Romans when they conquered South Wales, the ancient banks and ditches are now home to sheep and cattle, which graze among the tangle of defences once designed to trap and destroy the attackers of Caerau.

Following the Ridgeway Path from Caerau, we arrive at the Rhiwsaeson to Efail Isaf road. Rhiwsaeson ('slope of the Saxons') is part of a local tradition which tells of a great battle fought here between the Saxons and the Danes. Just before the old Taff Vale railway bridge, the trail turns into a footpath that follows the valley of the Clun.

From Caesar's Arms, the path begins to climb towards the Garth mountain, passing through mixed woodland that contains remnants of old level mining the shafts were sunk at a gradual gradient into the side of the hill. At the top of Mynydd Y Garth are the tumuli which are visible from practically each point of the compass in Glamorgan. The ancient barrows run in a line that corresponds with sunrise and sunset of the druidic festivals of May Day and Hallowe'en. Iolo Morganwg held a Gorsedd festival at the summit. Unfortunately, as it was during the Napoleonic Wars, the local militia thought he was signalling to a possible French fleet in the Bristol Channel and so they hurriedly dispersed the crowds.

From the tumuli, the view south to the Vale extends across the Bristol Channel to the coast of Somerset and the hills of Devon. Cardiff and the Penarth Head seem laid out like a map, and in the distance are the white columns of the new Severn Bridge. To the north is the valley of the Taff, and beyond that we can see the distant Brecon Beacons. Foreign tourists still visit the Garth, lured by the film *The Englishman who Went Up a Hill and Came Down a Mountain*. The story is a piece of fiction that turned into a legend and then became a fact. Who built these barrows on this windswept summit, empty and silent now except for the grazing sheep, will probably remain a mystery.

After a rest to get our bearings we walk south along a country lane along the slope of the Garth. A winding public footpath will now take us to the footbridge over the Taff and the Edwardian spa of Taff's Well. Following a path between gorse and bracken, we walk towards the Taff Gorge and begin to descend to Taff's Well, taking care to avoid the legendary white horse believed to haunt these slopes. The ground rapidly falls away as we leave the hill to the crickets and swallows that swoop and swerve across the heathland.

The path goes through forestry, silent except for the murmur of the wind, then gradually the sounds of the valley floor drift in with the rumble of traffic, rattle of a train and the barks of a dog. We now reach Gwaeclod y Garth. The village, set at the mouth of a chasm which hems in the River Taff on its journey to the sea, is a collection of middle class houses and villas that probably date back to the turn of the century. There are a few quiet pubs, tennis courts, and a bowling green that suggest that it was created during the affluent days of King Coal, to be a middle class dormitory of Cardiff.

We can either follow the A4054 towards Tongwynlais or follow the Ridgeway where it intersects with the Taff Trail (129 839). At the Taff Trail, we turn South towards Castell Goch. By following the Ridgeway we will avoid all traffic.

The fortunes of the village of Tongwynlais were founded on the Glamorgan Canal and the Melin Griffith iron and tin works. Using local iron and coal, the company forged a reputation for excellence throughout the world from the 1850s until the 1870s, when the local economy suffered a depression. During this period the Marquess of Bute began work on the rebuilding of Castell Coch and a project to create a vineyard, although the industrial village enjoyed a grisly reputation for rowdiness and murder. An international trade depression plus cheaper imported ores led to the liquidation of Melin Griffith in 1878, which in turn led to lower wages and the soup kitchens. The situation was so bad at Pentyrch that people resorted to eating donkeys. With the decline of the canal, the village stagnated to the sleepy hamlet that lies in the shadow of Castell Coch today.

The antiquarian John Leland describes Castell Coch in the 1540s as standing: 'On a high rok of a redde stone or soil a 2 miles from Landaf upper on taue. Castelle Gough no big thing but high.' Although the lands had been owned by the church since the beginning of the 12th century, the bishops of Llandaf

7.4 LLANTRISANT TO CAERPHILLY

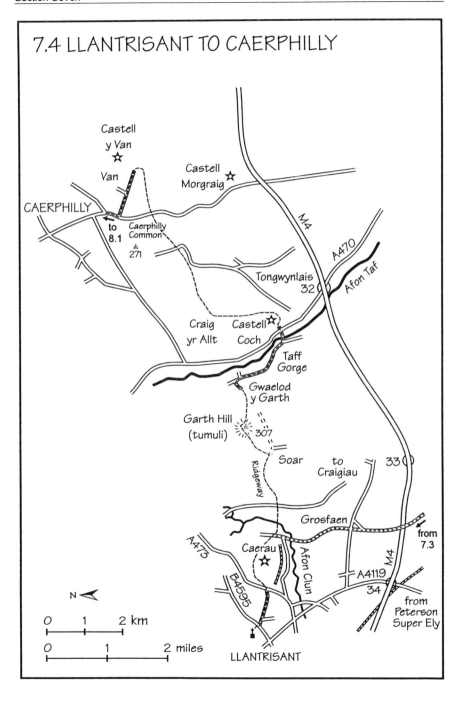

Castell
y Van
☆
Van

Castell
Morgraig ☆

CAERPHILLY

to
8.1

Caerphilly
Common

△
271

M4

A470

Tongwynlais
32

Afon Taf

Craig
yr Allt

Castell ☆
Coch

Taff
Gorge

Gwaelod
y Garth

Garth Hill
(tumuli)

△ 307

Soar

to
Craigiau

33

Ridgeway

Grosfaen

from
7.3

A473

Caerau
☆

Afon Clun

M4

A4119

34

B4595

from
Peterson
Super Ely

N ◄

O   1   2 km

O   1   2 miles

LLANTRISANT

experienced the savagery of the natives and the invasions of the Normans, who began to build Castell Coch around 1256-67 when they came into conflict with the Welsh Lords Of Senghenydd. Nature returned to reclaim the castle. It was soon covered with ivy, then weeds, and brushwood grew thick and fast to cover the courtyard and towers. During the eighteenth century, the castle became popular with the 'romantic' travellers and artists who came to Wales to capture an age that was quickly disappearing. They saw an idyllic landscape of an ivy-covered castle, quaint cottages, a rural tradition of farming and quarrying the iron ore in the surrounding hills to be packed upon donkeys to feed the blast furnaces in the valley. When the Third Marquess of Bute saw Castell Coch he was so dazzled by its picturesque charm that he commissioned William Burges (1827-81) to rebuild and furnish the castle in the gothic style of a Rhinish castle. Burges lavished colour and ornament to turn the medieval structure into a Victorian romantic vision.

Leaving Castell Coch behind, we may follow the footpath that climbs through the trees of Fforest Gand to ascend Caerphilly Mountain. to follow lanes and footpaths until we reach the summit. If we turn right and follow the road to the Travellers Inn, then walk through the car park until we reach a break in the fence, a secret world begins to open. There are trees that grow out of walls, vacant towers, and between the thickly-wooded slopes can be viewed a vista of Cardiff that stretches to the Bristol Channel. Cardiff Castle and the city centre are clearly visible – a tempting prospect to the Welshmen who built Morgraig against the rapacious Normans who began to infiltrate the coastal plain during the 12th century. Morgraig was built to counter the Marcher Lord de Clare with his attempt to build castles at Castell Coch, Caerphilly and Cardiff. The story of Morgraig is one of deceit and murder, treachery and lies, of men and the depths to which they stooped in their quest for land and power. But it all seems so quiet now among these ivy-covered walls and rocky outcrops, with a peaceful view across the leafy suburbs of Cardiff. The main road outside the Travellers Rest pub, the A469, will then take us North and down Caerphilly Mountain and into Caerphilly.

A few words of advice to the intrepid rambler. You *will* get lost as you attempt to chart a course through the maze of brambles, footpaths and forests, but **the tumuli of the Garth will always be framed on some horizon**, acting as a beacon as it did in days of old.

A word of caution: there are many quiet inns on leafy lanes between Llantrisant and Caerphilly to enchant the rambler. There is a tendency after a long period in some timeless public bar to emerge back onto the highways and byeways like Rip Van Winkle – be warned.

Looking Ahead: The next stage of the walking is along the ridges from Caerphilly to the border crossing at Chepstow. It begins in the centre of Caerphilly.

Section Eight
High Ways and Holy Places:
Caerphilly to Caerleon

17 miles

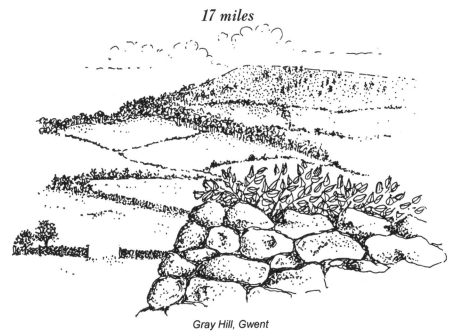

Gray Hill, Gwent

John Owen

J.G. Owen lives in Caerphilly, South Wales, near some of his favourite walks. His interest in landscape and local history was stimulated by his mother who took him from an early age on walks around Caerphilly, and his grandfather, who was a stonemason on the restoration of Caerphilly Castle. He considers walking is the best way to appreciate the relation between a landscape and its history, and on holiday enjoys being a landscape detective. One of his favourite landscapes is the twenty miles each side of the Welsh border, with its wide variety of scenery and history. He dislikes manicured landscape, but is continually delighted by the small English market town.

Stages:

Caerphilly to Rudry – 3 miles

Rudry to Draethen – 2 miles

Draethen to Llandanglws – 2 miles

Llandanglws to Twmbarlwm – 3 miles

Twmbarlwm to Henllys Vale – 3 miles

Henllys Vale to Caerleon – 4 miles

Maps: OS Landranger 171 (Cardiff, Newport).

Highlights: Machen Church, Twmbarlwm, Lodge Word, Caerleon.

Starting Point: Twyn Tourist Information Centre, Caerphilly (156 869)

Transport: Cardiff Central Railway Station – 01222 227281, Valley Lines – 01222 231978 – local rail service which runs between Caerphilly and Cardiff.

Additional Information: Caerphilly Castle – 01222 883143

Tourist Information: Caerphilly Visitor Centre – 01222 880011, Magor Services (Junction 23) – 01633 881122, Caerleon – 01633 430777.

Introduction

Traditionally, Britain is divided into highland Britain and lowland Britain, the divide running from the Severn to the Trent. It is a topographical divide between the less fertile and more fertile areas of Britain. To some extent it is a cultural divide, but not in historical terms a racial one. It is now felt that most of the Romano-British population survived in what is now England, merely changing overlords, language and culture.

One end of this barrier between highland and lowland is anchored on the Severn, and the division is evident in the Caerphilly Caerleon area, where it makes for spectacular scenery on a small scale and an interesting historic record.

The Glamorgan County History describes the ridges between the coastal plain around Cardiff and the valleys to the north as the border ridges. In the Caerphilly area there are three distinctive ridges. To the south we have a ridge of old red sandstone, followed to the north by ridges of Carboniferous limestone and millstone grit.

These ridges are pierced to the west of Caerphilly by the Taff, which cuts a spectacular gorge on its way to the sea. On the east the ridges are pierced by the Rhymney, which breaks out of the hills to the coastal plain at Machen. At Machen the outcrop turns sharply north towards Pontypool and Blaenavon. The southern portion of this is marked by Machen Mountain, which dominates the area. The coalfield rim is well marked topographically, presenting a steep scarp to the Vale of Gwent. The scarp is pierced at Risca by the Ebbw. To the south of the Sirhowy, Machen Mountain dominates the Machen ridge between the Rhymney and the Ebbw. To the north of the the Ebbw, Twmbarlwm dominates the scarp running north to Pontypool. Twmbarlwm, like Machen Mountain, is of tough Pennant sandstone.

From the mountain grasses of Twmbarlwm the ground dips steeply to the east. The outcrop of the coal measures, which were ridges north of Cardiff, appearing as successive terraces running north-south along the scarp. Below these terraces the land sweeps down to the fertile landscape of Gwent. The fertility increases rapidly from Henllys down to the valley of the Afon Llwyd, where the monastery at Llantarnam was established in the 12th century. To the east of the Afon Llwyd, a low ridge of limestone forms a low barrier from the Usk valley. The Afon Llwyd is a tributary of the Usk and joins it at the Roman settlement at Caerleon.

To understand the area we must be aware of the variety of landscape. This ranges from the high moorland of the coalfield plateau in the north-west with hills of 300 to 400 metres, to the undulating landscape of the south-east around Caerleon. Today the coalfield plateau (known as the Valleys) is an area of bleak moorland cut by urbanised river valleys running mainly north to south. As a result of industrialisation from about 1750, the plateau was transformed from an area of low population to one of high urban density in the river valleys, separated from each other by open moorland. The growth of the iron and coal industries transformed the landscape. While much of this occurred to the north of the area, small-scale industrial development occurred in Machen from the 16th century.

After the Second World War the valley of the Afon Llwyd was transformed by the creation of Cwmbran new town, and more recently by the expansion of Newport. In the 1950s the eastern slopes of Mynydd Henllys and Mynydd Maen, its northern extension, were an area of small farms with some industry. Now large housing estates run north and west from Llantarnam Abbey up to Pontypool and up the slopes of Mynydd Maen. To the south, Newport has developed large housing estates at Malpas and Bettws. Despite this urban development there are still large areas of open moorland, woodland and farmland along the route.

The present-day valley communities are the result of intense industrial development and inward migration over the last two hundred years. This was not the pattern in the past. The older theory that Britain saw successive huge waves of migrants is now discounted by modern archaeologists. They tend to deprecate the notion of abrupt change and to emphasise the continuity and development of society. Along the Caerphilly Caerleon interface there are examples of changing cultures from Bronze Age to Iron Age, to Roman and the Dark Ages and to the Norman period and beyond. Despite this, the overall pattern was of continuity and adaptation on both sides.

Early settlement was on the high ground. Areas which today are bleak moorland were far more densely inhabited in the Neolithic and Early and Middle Bronze Ages. This is because the climate was much milder than today. There are major areas of Bronze Age settlement, but they are some miles to the north of our route. Gelligaer Common and the Machen ridge have much evidence of Bronze Age occupation.

After about 1500BC the climate deteriorated, the temperature dropped about five degrees and the Sub-Atlantic climatic period saw an increased rainfall and a change in settlement pattern. Coupled with this climate change, there was a migration of Iron Age peoples into Britain. This migration, which was small but influential, spoke a Celtic language. Professor Sir Ifor Williams has shown that this language did not fully develop into Welsh until about AD700. More recently Peter Stead of the University College of Swansea made the statement that the Welsh were more Romano-British than Celtic.

The area centred on Caerphilly, to the north of Cardiff, was the Lordship of Senghenydd. It had its origin in the post-Roman period and survived under a Welsh lordship until 1270. By 1263 Llewelyn ap Gruffydd, the last native Welsh Prince of Wales, had extended his power from Gwynedd down to Glamorgan, its furthest extension being Caerphilly Mountain. He was now in conflict with Gilbert de Clare, Earl of Gloucester and Lord of Glamorgan. Despite a siege and destruction of the half-built Caerphilly Castle, Llewelyn was driven northwards out of Glamorgan. This emphasises the border nature of the area dictated by the landscape. Gilbert took over Senghenyd and reorganised it under Anglo-Norman control, a state of affairs that lasted until 1536. The Act of Union between England and Wales in that year saw Senghenydd, along with the other autonomous lordships in Wales, being reorganised on a shire basis.

The Rhymney Valley Ridgeway

This is a route developed by the old Rhymney Valley District Council. It runs east-west along the ridge between Cardiff and Caerphilly towards Machen, and then runs north along the Machen ridge. Though the route may be old, the southern portion was not identified as such by the Royal Commission of Ancient Monuments in their Inventory of Glamorgan. In their volumes covering the Iron Age, Roman occupation and the early Christian period, they identify only ridgeways running north-south, for the route used by the Roman road from Cardiff to Brecon. This ran through the Caerphilly basin northwards, with a secondary route over Mynydd Eglwysilian.

Similarly, a route has been identified running from Bassaleg along the Machen ridge. The small collection of round barrows above Bedwas may indicate an early date for this route. All these routes provide access from the coastal plain to the interior.

The Rhymney Valley Ridgeway runs along the border ridges of the coalfield outcrop. There are a number of Iron Age settlements along this route. There is a homestead at Graig y Parc and a small hill fort at Llwynau Du, both near Pentyrch, on the west. side of the Taff. These are connected by pathways, which in some instances are hollow ways, always an indication of age.

East of the Taff there is a small hill fort on the Wenallt, above Rhiwbina, and a large one at Coed Graig Ruperra. Both sites may be on an identifiable route. It is possible to suggest there may have been a route from the west along this ridge and going to the large hill fort at Newport known as the Gaer. This may have crossed the Ebbw at Bassaleg. The later Roman road from Caerleon to Cardiff passed through Bassaleg but ran south along a low ridge to Michaelston y Fedw and then to Cardiff. The Roman priorities were different.

Stage 1: Caerphilly to Rudry – 3 miles

Caerphilly is now a dormitory town, mainly for Cardiff, with some small-scale industry. There was a small Roman fort to the north of the castle. Prior to the construction of the castle in 1270-1278 and the borough in about 1280, Caerphilly has no recorded history. The castle was built by Gilbert de Clare to counter Llywelyn ap Gruffyd, the last native prince of Wales, who had extended his power from Gwynedd down to Glamorgan. Despite being the second biggest castle in Britain, its recorded history is limited. The most significant event was the siege of 1326, which led to the capture and death of Edward the Second.

It is possible to catch a bus from the bus stations at Caerphilly and Cardiff to the Travellers' Rest public house and join the Ridgeway there. The relevant services are 70, 71 and 72. It is also possible to catch a train from Cardiff to Caerphilly for those who want to join the Celtic Way from Caerphilly.

We begin at the Tourist Information Centre, which is on the market site of the medieval borough, to the immediate south of the castle. At the top end of the Twyn, Van Road leads to the Van Mansion at (167 869). This mainly dates from 1583, but there was a house there in 1400. The woodland to the north is known locally as Maerdy Woods. The presence of a 'Maerdy' place name indicates a pre-Norman manorial centre. It is highly likely that it was the centre of an early Welsh estate. The house was enlarged in 1583 by Thomas Lewis, one of the leading local gentry, who claimed descent from Gwaethfod, an eighth-century prince. It has been recently restored and is now a group of private residences.

Return to Van Road and turn left. After about half a mile, take the small lane on the right. This is a pleasant walk between forestry plantations which once were part of the deer park attached to The Van. After about three-quarters of a mile the road forks. The left fork climbs up to the Cefn Onn ridge and is an optional short cut. The right fork carries on up through the woods to the A469, the main Caerphilly to Cardiff road.

On reaching the A469 turn left. The road descends into a small valley between the ridges at Blaen Nofydd Farm (159 845). The Rhymney Valley Ridgeway crosses the road, and the Celtic Way follows the Ridgeway in this area. Turn left onto the Ridgeway, the direction is waymarked.

Optional Site of Interest and Link to the Previous Section

On the ridge to the south of Blaen Nofydd farm is a public house called The Travellers Rest. To the immediate east of the public house is Castell Morgraig (160 843). There is a stile from the pub car park giving access to the castle, which is on private property but access is allowed. (This is where the previous section ended.) The castle is an item of contention. CADW feels it was an Anglo-Norman castle, built by Richard de Clare in the 1240s. Local historians disagree, claiming it was a castle built by the lords of Senghenydd, but financed by Llywelyn ap Gruffydd. The style is not Anglo-Norman. The keep is very similar to Dolbadarn, the Welsh castle in North Wales, and the towers are D-shaped in the Welsh fashion. There is no recorded history, but style and location suggest it was built by the Welsh to guard a ridge crossing and to act as a political statement of their presence on the skyline.

After visiting the castle, return to the Celtic Way at Blaen Nofydd Farm. The Ridgeway is very well defined, running between old hedge lines. It can be muddy after rain. Though it is not confirmed that this route was an ancient ridgeway, it is recorded that in the 18th century the track was used to carry iron ore from Rudry Common to the Pentyrch iron works owned by the Lewis family of New House. The path runs parallel to the ridge, following the side of a clearing long used for grazing. To the north of the path is a ridge of limestone containing conglomerate. You will meet this again on Gray Hill, between Caerleon and Chepstow. The Welsh name for the ridge is Cefn Carnau (the ridge of the small stones). However, local tradition used to claim the meaning was 'ridge of the horseshoes', the horseshoes in question being those of Llywelyn ap Grufyydd who was campaigning locally in 1270.

The area where the Ridgeway crosses the road is known as Thornhill ('Y Ddraenen' in Welsh). However, there are no thorn trees today closer than Cefn Onn Quarry. To the south of the ridge, below The Travellers Rest, is the New House Hotel. It could make a convenient, though expensive, starting point. The core of this is an 18th-century house built by Thomas Lewis, a descendant of the builder of the Van.

At (169 849), the Ridgeway meets a hollow way running north – south over the ridge. This is Heol Hir (the long road), running from Cardiff to the Rhymney Valley. The old name for the area is Bwlch Y Llechfaen (the pass of the standing stone). There is no tradition of a stone on the site. Take the left fork and follow the waymarked path alongside a large group of old beech trees. This leads alongside the old Cefn Onn Quarry and meets a road at 178 852. This is the road you would have followed if you had taken the left fork on the road from the Van up through the woods.

For the next half mile the unmetalled road follows the ridge. Here we have thorn trees and views of Caerphilly to the north and Cardiff to the south. The name Cefn Onn means 'ash ridge', but there are no ash trees. The soil is red because of the eroded old Red Sandstone which forms the ridge to the south. Though pleasant on a summer's day, Cefn Onn can be cold in winter. This is celebrated in a poem in a traditional Glamorgan verse form:

> *Y tri lle oera yng Nghymru*
> *Yw Mynydd Bach Y Rhydri,*
> *Twyn Y fan a Chefn Onn*
> *Lle buo i bron a sythu.*

This translates as:

> *The three coldest places in Wales Are Rudry Mountain,*
> *The Van Heath and Cefn Onn*
> *Where I almost froze to death.*

In the Cefn Onn area, Richard Williams, Oliver Cromwell's grandfather, was born. He later moved to East Anglia and changed his name. Local tradition has it that when Oliver was in the area, he stabled his horse in the local churches.

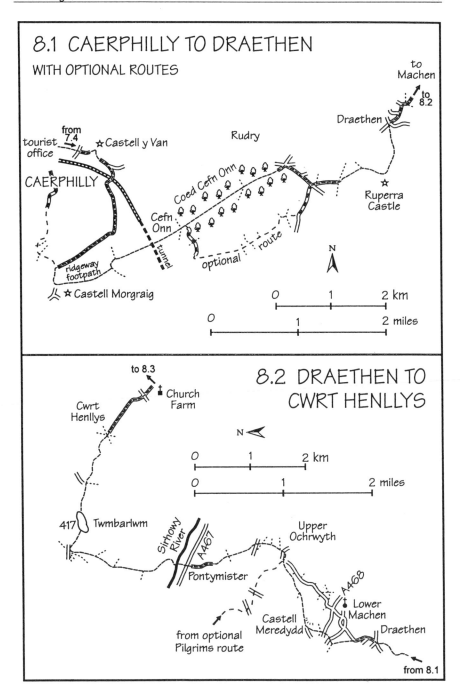

8.1 CAERPHILLY TO DRAETHEN
WITH OPTIONAL ROUTES

to Machen

to 8.2

Draethen

from 7.4

tourist office

☆ Castell y Van

Rudry

CAERPHILLY

Coed Cefn Onn

Cefn Onn

Ruperra Castle

optional   route

ridgeway footpath

tunnel

N

丛 ☆ Castell Morgraig

0   1   2 km

0   1   2 miles

---

to 8.3

Cwrt Henllys

Church Farm

8.2 DRAETHEN TO CWRT HENLLYS

N

0   1   2 km

0   1   2 miles

417 Twmbarlwm

Sirhowy River

A467

Upper Ochrwyth

Pontymister

Castell Meredydd

Lower Machen

Draethen

from optional Pilgrims route

A468

from 8.1

At Cefn Onn Farm (182 854) the route meets another cross ridge road. It is reputed that the farm was once a public house. During the 1939 to 1945 war, a farmer ploughing marginal ground is said to have exposed a Roman coffin lid made of lead. From the Roman period on there has been considerable small-scale lead mining along the ridge. The Ridgeway is waymarked to the right of the farmyard.

There is a choice here: to follow the Ridgeway or turn right. There is a prominent path between hedgerows running through woodland along the ridge. This is waymarked to (201 844), where it meets the road at the Maen Llwyd public house. The name Maen Llwyd (grey or holy stone) may indicate the site of a standing stone.

It is worthwhile making a short detour before reaching the Maenllwyd. At (183 863) there is a path to the left. This leads down to St James's Church, the parish church of Rudry. This small church, with a saddleback tower, is probably an Anglo-Norman foundation, being mentioned in a survey of Llandaff in 1280. Rudry is a parish which has a rural, Welsh-style, dispersed settlement. The church has virtually no buildings around it. The farms which comprise the parish are widely separated. The small village centre is a half a mile north of the church, consisting mainly of two terraces built to serve the Rudry Colliery (1890-1906).

At the side of the church is the Griffin Motel, its core is claimed to be a medieval priest's house. The motel and restaurant, tailored for the Cardiff middle class, supplies food, drink and accommodation. You can retrace your route back to the ridge or walk about a third of a mile on the road to the Maen Llwyd. **Care should be taken on the road.**

If you turn right at Cefn Onn Farm, the road goes steeply down the side of the limestone ridge and climbs up on to the old red sandstone ridge of Craig LLysfaen. Llysfaen (stone court) the modern Cardiff suburb of Lisvane, was an early Welsh manorial centre. Its site may indicate an earlier settlement because there is an Iron Age camp in the parish (205 840).

As the road reaches the ridge above Lisvane, it turns sharply right down the hill. The Celtic Way turns left at this point, along the unmetalled track along Craig Llysfaen. As you turn, there are two mounds of stone in the field facing you. These are the remains of two medieval towers built to control traffic over or along the ridge. The track is well defined along the ridge crest, in the First Edition Ordnance Survey map of 1875 it is marked as Old Road, and may well be an early route.

One advantage of this route is the spectacular view up and down the Bristol Channel. As a result it is popular with walkers. One walker you will not meet, is Diana of Lisvane, who lived in the 17th century. She was traditionally claimed to a be witch, but according to my grandmother was a only a healer collecting herbs on the ridge.

The route is easy to follow, being well signed even through the woods. As you leave the woods, the track to the left will take you down to the valley bottom, from which you can climb up to the Maenllwyd public house. If you turn right a footpath takes you to the Lisvane to Rudry road. Follow this to the next crossroads, at 200 866. Facing you will be the entrance to Ruperra Park, marked as a private road. Any self-satisfaction at having followed the more likely ridge-way may be dampened by the fact that the Maenllwyd public house is the other side of a small valley.

Stage 2: Rudry to Draethen – 2 miles

Outside the Maenllwyd there is a crossroads. Take the road to Lisvane. This goes down to the valley bottom and climbs up to another crossroads. **Care should be taken on this road**. On the left is a private road sign alongside one of the lodges to Ruperra Park. This is the old Caerphilly to Newport Road which ran through Ruperra Park. It is a public right of way along the south of the ridge. It is easy to follow and pleasant walking. The immediate landscape was planned, being part of Ruperra Park. There are lovely views over the coastal plain and the Bristol Channel. As you proceed you get occasional glimpses of Ruperra Castle.

Ruperra Castle (220 863) is a country house, rebuilt in 1626 in a European style on the site of an earlier building. Its architect was Robert Smythyson, also responsible for Lulworth Castle in Dorset. The castle is in the parish of Llanfi-hangell y Vedw, the current parish church of Michaelstone y Vedw is on the other side of the Rhymney. It has been suggested that the earliest church was near the castle and dedicated to a 6th-century Welsh saint, Fedw. The castle, originally owned by relations of the Lewis family of the Van, passed by mar-riage to the Morgan family of Tredegar Park. The building is a good example of a type of house favoured by the 'new men' coming to local eminence at the begin-ning of the 17th century. It is in private hands, but may be viewed from adja-cent footpaths. The house is in an unsafe condition and no attempt should be made to enter the building.

About a hundred metres from the castle entrance the ridgeway climbs steeply to the left off the estate road, it is not well marked. A short but steep climb takes you to the ridge top. The Celtic Way crosses the ridge, but it is worth taking a diversion to the right to climb to the crest of the ridge.

The views alone would make it worthwhile, but in addition the ridge is crowned with an Iron Age hill fort and an eleventh-century motte (222 866). The hill fort, tentatively dated to 250BC, was built by the Silures. According to Tacitus, they were swarthy and curly-haired (the Celts were tall and fair-haired). He also said that, 'Neither punishment nor kindness could turn them from their ways.' Their territory comprised most of South Wales, west of the Usk. They were predominantly a pastoral people,. but the presence of lead mines on Cefn Coed Pwll Du (the wooded ridge of the black pits), just to the north (217 878), may indicate industrial activity on their part.

The presence of the motte, erected over a thousand years later, indicates the military value of the site. The Normans (or the French, as the Welsh chronicles called them) built a motte on the northern end of the hill fort, utilising part as a bailey. There is no known history of the site, but the early Norman advance into the area before 1100 was repulsed by the Welsh by 1150 and they then held the area for another 100 years.

It is best to retrace your steps to the Celtic Way, which follows the Rhymney

Valley Ridgeway down a forest drive through the woods, which are covered with bluebells and foxgloves in early summer. This track can be muddy even in summer. The Rhymney Valley Ridgeway then branches left along a footpath down to the edge of the woods. Where it leaves the woods it runs diagonally down the field to the Holly Bush public house in Draethen (221 873). The right of way runs through the pub grounds. Draethen is a small hamlet, originally built for the Ruperra estate. There are some buildings which pre-date the estate. On the hill to the west there are lead mines that have been worked since at least the Roman period.

At the pub entrance there is a road junction. Take the road through Draethen hamlet marked Lower Machen. This is **a narrow lane to be used with care**. Once over the bridge over the Rhymney, the road is wider and safer.

Stage 3: Draethen to Llandanglws – 2 miles

As you cross the River Rhymney, known as Afon Elyrch (the swan's river), you cross from Senghenydd into what was the lordship of Gwynllwg (sometimes called the lordship of Machen). The river is an old boundary, dating back to the Dark Ages.

The Welsh lordship of Gwynllywg was named after Gwynllyw, a 6th-century ruler who abducted Gwaldys, a daughter of Brychan, king of Brychieniog. They are important in the early Welsh church, both becoming saints. The cathedral at Newport is dedicated to Gwynllwg. Their son, Cadoc, was also a significant figure in the early Welsh church, becoming an important saint and a great teacher. The quality of scholarship in his monastery at Llantwit Major has been described as being of university status.

The arrival of the Normans in the 12th century split Gwynllwg in two, the more fertile southern part becoming the Norman Wentloog and the northern part becoming the Welsh lordship of Machen. One family, the Morgan family, dominated the area for over a thousand years, eventually becoming ennobled as Lord Tredegar. The generosity of the family in bardic patronage was reflected in the words of the poet Gwilym Tew, who, in the fifteenth century, described the then owner, John Morgan, as 'Gwin llydan Gwynllwg' (the bounteous vine of Wentloog).

There are two options here and a section which links the two, so you have plenty of choice. Whichever you choose, you will end this stage at Llandanglws.

Option 1

Continue along the road to the main road at (225 880). You will notice the valley bottom here is wide and flat. The village at (225 880) is Lower Machen. In the 1930s, during road widening, a Roman mining settlement was discovered. The actual lead mines were at Cefn Coed Pwll Du, on the ridge to your left. On your right in the distance you can see Plas Machen. This is mainly a Tudor building, but it was also the medieval manor of Machen. In Lower Machen we can see the development from the Roman period, through the Dark Ages, to a major Welsh pre-Norman estate, which developed into a lordship that lasted until the Act of Union between Wales and England in 1542.

At the road, cross carefully, and turn into Lower Machen. You will come to a crossroads, turn left up to the church. The church is mentioned in 1102, but the site was used at an earlier date. There is reused Roman brick in the tower and there is a Roman gorgon's head built into the vestry inner wall. It is believed it may be the site of a Roman temple.

Leave the church and turn left. It is possible to follow the lane up to the top of the ridge. At the top there is a crossroads, but just before the crosssroads there is a tumulus in the field to your right. At the crossroads (239 890) turn left. You are now on an early ridgeway running from Newport into the hinterland. About a hundred metres up the track is Llandanglws Farm. This is the site of a 6th-century chapel to the Celtic Saint Tanglwst, a sister of Gwynllyw. She was one of the alleged 24 sons and daughters of Brychan, the part Irish, reputedly pagan, almost mythical ruler of Brecon. In reality, they were Christian missionaries, or more probably reforming evangelists, since there is good evidence of the survival of Roman Christianity in the area.

An Alternative Ending to Option 1

Just north of the Machen church, follow the waymarked footpath along the back of the church. Cross the field and make for the large house called the Volland. Here you join the old Caerphilly to Newport road, which is now a lane and effectively the drive to The Volland. On your left you have good views of the hill fort and lead mine area. Where the old road rejoins the existing Caerphilly to Newport road, turn right under the railway arch. You are now joining option two.

Option 2

At the bridge over the River Rhymney, take the footpath to the left and follow the river. At Pandy House (222 883) the path climbs up to the road. Cross the road with care and follow the small lane to the quarry under the railway line. The railway, initially horse-drawn, was opened in 1826 to take iron to Newport. Once under the railway, the quarry road goes left but you go straight ahead over the cattle grid. Follow the track up past Park Farm onto the ridge, where it meets the Ridgeway at Llandanglws. At (225 887)are the much eroded remains of Castell Meredydd, a Welsh castle built about 1150. This was a castle of the Morgan family, the family of the lords of Machen and Caerleon. Though on private property, responsible visitors are welcome. Return to the track and follow it up to the ridge. At the ridge, the path passes Llandanglwys Farm.

Stage 4: Llandanglws to Twmbarlwm – 3 miles

Opposite the farm is a stile. Follow the path down through the fields, where it forks take the left-hand fork to the small hamlet of Upper Ochrwyth (239 894). Here a signposted path leads to Risca. The first section is through the fields, but after it crosses a road it is a well-defined green lane between hedgerows. This lane runs diagonally down the hillside to Danygraig (236 903).

At Danygraig the lane passes the cemetery and passes though a small bungalow estate. At the other end of the estate there is junction, take the left-hand fork and follow the road. The road runs below and alongside the Risca bypass.

After you pass a small factory on your left, the road forks. Take the right-hand fork, which leads to a tunnel under the bypass and a bridge over the River Ebbw (236 911).

This is probably the shortest way to cross Risca – walk down Exchange Street (the one you're facing). At the end of the street, on the main road, is The Exchange public house. At the main road, St Mary Street, cross the road and turn left. You pass St Mary's Church, rebuilt in 1852. During the reconstruction, Roman remains were found, including a floor of tiles stamped with the mark of the Second Augustan Legion.

The name Risca was probably 'Yr Isca'. Isca being originally an early British name for water, in the sense of 'river'. Modern survivals are found in the river names Esk and Usk in the western half of Britain. The name Isca is associated with Roman occupation e.g. Isca Dumnoniorum (now Exeter) and Isca Silurum (now Caerleon). The Second Augustan Legion was present at both Exeter and Caerleon, the presence at Risca may have been to do with lead mining.

Just past the church is the Darren public house (234 913), which provides food, drink and accommodation. Turn sharp right past the Darren, and over the level crossing. The railway was opened by the Monmouthshire Canal Company and now serves Ebbw Vale Steelworks. Turn left after the railway, go past the houses and a track bears right up a lane. As you turn right you pass the remains of the Monmouthshire Canal, opened in 1792. The track you are on is part of a walk called Raven's Path and is signposted. It is a **steep climb** up to Twmbarlwm, and **should be approached with caution if you are unfit**.

Follow the lane up the side of the hill, it leads to a cottage. Do not take any of the paths crossing the lane. Eventually the lane bears left and footpath carries on up the hill. This is signposted and a stile leads to the forestry land. The path is well signed. After about ten minutes a forestry drive cuts across the path. Carry on straight up. As you reach the crest at Pegwn y Bwlch (248 938), you see a signpost pointing to the right, marked Castle Mound. Another signpost, pointing the way you have come, reads Darren Road. The Raven's Path goes left here, but at this point you leave it and turn right.

Immediately to the north are the wooded valleys of two tributaries of the Ebbw. These are now devoted to commercial forestry. On the skyline you can see the Brecon Beacons. To the south, the Severn Estuary is visible.

From Pegwrn y Bwlch, a fairly steep climb of about ten minutes over grassland and whinberry-covered mountain brings you to Twmbarlwm. The path crosses the bank and ditch of an Iron Age hill fort which crowns the summit. At the other end of the fort is a motte, but you cannot see it from the first bank of the hill fort. The path crosses the fort to the motte.

Twmbarlwm (242 926), height 1360 feet (419 metres), **should not be climbed on a wet or misty day**. There is no shelter and you could easily get lost or injured. It is a landmark for miles around and has much legend attached to it. It is rumoured to be the burial site of a giant, and at the end of the last century tradition in Newport claimed the motte was the burial mound of the horse Lord Tredegar rode at the Charge of the Light Brigade. On a clear day the panorama makes the ascent worthwhile. You can see the whole of the Severn Estuary from Devon up to the Severn Bridge, and around through Gloucestershire, and Herefordshire. To the north, the Brecon Beacons are prominent.

It was the view from Twmbarlwm which stimulated W.H. Davies, the Newport-born poet, author of *Autobiography of a Supertramp*. He wrote:

> Can I forget the sweet days that have gone.
> When poetry first began to stir my blood
> And from the hills of Gwent I saw
> The earth torn in two by Severn's silver flood.'

The top of Twmbarlwm is crowned by a hill fort which may be Iron Age, though the current feeling is that some hill forts have their origin in the Late Bronze Age. This may be true, for at Twmbarlwm, there is a small Bronze Age tumulus on the outer lip of the ditch around the motte. Occupation of the area may even pre-date the Bronze Age. About twenty years ago a flint arrowhead was found near Twmbarlwin. It may have come from the hill just to the north. Mynydd Maen has yielded several worked flint items over many years.

As mentioned earlier, at the eastern end of the hill fort is a motte, possibly of the 12th century. There have been suggestions that the hill fort is a large bailey to the motte. Examination of the bank and ditch indicate a style more common to the Iron Age. It is doubtful if the fort was completed. The location is very exposed and would not have been attractive in the deteriorating climate of the Iron Age. The motte is also open to question. At the time of the Domesday book, Caerleon was under Norman control, but by 1150 the native Welsh had reoccupied the area. Some authorities suggest that the motte is 13th-century, dating from the time Gilbert de Clare was in conflict with Llywelyn ap Gruffydd in the 1270s. A motte at this period, and in this location would be anachronistic. The motte can easily be seen from the lowland to the south and east, which would have been Norman-controlled and a this suggests that Twmbarlwm is a Welsh motte, which would have been a constant reminder of their presence to the dwellers in the lowland.

Stage 5: Twmbarlwm to Henlys Vale – 3 miles

From the top of the motte, a path leads eastwards and down a steep slope. A minor road from Rogerstone can be seen which runs to the west of a woodland plantation. Where it enters the plantation (248 926), a forest track turns right off the road and into the wood. Follow this track through the wood. At the other side of the wood the lane becomes almost a hollow way leading down the slopes of Mynydd Henllys. Just above Cwrt Henllys Farm at (257 922), the track becomes metalled. Henllys (old court) takes its name from the dwelling of a Welsh chieftain. There is no positive evidence of the location of the court. Cwrt Henllys Farm from a distance looks like a long house, but is a substantial building modernised in the 18th century. This could be the site of the court. The track from Twmbarlwm past Cwrt Henllys has the feel of an ancient way. There is little motor traffic and it is a pleasant walk.

About a mile from Cwrt Henllys you pass Henllys Church (268 911). The church is dedicated to St Peter, any possible Celtic dedication being unknown. The current building is medieval and has a preaching cross base outside the porch. Henllys and Bettws to the east were chapelries of Bassaleg. Bassaleg was the mother church of a pre-Norman group of chapels, so Henllys may have an early foundation. Today Henllys church is near the edge of the Newport Cwmbran conurbation. It is remarkable to see several Welsh language memorials in the graveyard, one as late as 1925. The language link with the Silures of Twmbarlwm and some of the graves in Henllys are a reminder of continuity of culture.

The ancient way from Twmbarlwrn continues east past Bettws, now a Newport housing estate, to Malpas and possibly Caerleon. However, to follow it would mean a considerable amount of urban walking. So our route takes us over the stile opposite the church and alongside the farm. After the farm bear right. The stiles here have route markers set up by the local authority, and if you follow the direction indicated by the arrows you cannot get lost. You cross a small stream on a footbridge and cross two fields to a road linking Rogerstone and Cwmbran (272 913). The view from the road back to the church, with Twmbdrlwrn in the distance, is spectacular, though daunting if you are walking east to west. The route crosses the road and goes over a stile. **This road, though narrow, is dangerous**.

Stage 6: Henllys Vale to Caerleon – 4 miles

Once over the stile the route crosses a field to Mill Wood. The route through the wood is obvious. Once out of the wood, the route crosses several fields to Henllys Vale Farm. It is hard to believe you are in the middle of urban South Wales. At each stile follow the arrow to the next. The stiles are well made, but in some instances overgrown. On reaching the farm, the route goes through the farmyard out to the road. Turn left at the road and follow the road to Llantarnam.

This may be part of the Pilgrims' Route from Llantarnam Abbey to Penrhys in the Rhondda, where a Marian cult developed in the Middle Ages. This route ran from Llantarnam past Croes y Mwyalch (this may have been a wayside cross and their grange may have been at Pentrebach). It would have continued up past Henllys Vale Farm to Castell y Bwch public house on the Rogerstone to Henllys road. From there a series of footpaths runs to Henllys Court Farm. This could be an alternative route but it would miss Henllys church.

This is a lane with little traffic, but care must be taken. After about a half a mile you pass Pentre Bach Farm. This was a manor house, and prior to the dissolution of the Monasteries was a grange of Llantarnam Abbey. The site was apparently moated at one time. In the house is a Roman sepulchral slab with an inscription to the memory of Vinditus, soldier of the Second Augustan Legion.

A walk of half a mile brings you to Croes Y Mwyalch (the blackbirds' cross) at Llantarnam and the which provides good food. As stated above, this cross may have been a wayside cross on the pilgrims' route. On the way you cross the Monmouthshire Canal and the Cwmbran Driveway. On reaching Llantarnam you may empathise with W.H. Davies, who, lonely and homesick at the sight of the pretty American villages he was trampimg through,

'Wished they were Llantarnam's Green.'

Just past the public house is a crossroads (302 924). At the crossroads go straight across and follow Malthouse Lane. To the left, about half a mile away, is the site of Llantarnam Abbey, a Cistercian foundation established in 1170 by Howell ap Iorwerth, Lord of Machen and Caerleon. Recent urbanisation and road building have succeeded in making the abbey site missable.

Having crossed yet another urban expressway, on the right you see Pen Y Parc cottage. The public right of way runs through the garden on the side of the house. Once in the garden take the right-hand path. The right of way follows the field boundaries up to and past Park Farm. It may be easier to pass Pen Y Parc cottage and take the farm road leading to Park Farm. The park in question is the park that was attached to the Tudor house built on the site of Llantarnam Abbey. The abbey was purchased by William Morgan of Pentrebach at the Dissolution He built a Tudor house from the ruins of the abbey.

Cross the fields beyond Park Farm and you reach Lodge Wood. This is an Iron Age hill fort. The views are quite impressive. This is a large, multivallate fort with an area of 7 hectares (17 acres) dating from about 500BC. Inside the Iron Age hill fort is a smaller structure that appears to be later than the fort. This may be the site of a post-Roman or Dark Age occupation, though none of the Arthurian experts have made the possible link with the literary connection between Arthur and Caerleon.

From the eastern side of the hill fort you walk through a modern housing development down to Caerleon, along The Paddocks, Lodge Hill Road and Lodge Road, passing St Cadoc's Hospital. The centre of Caerleon is a pleasant, small town, much of the which overlies the legionary fortress of the Second Augustan Legion. This dictated the road pattern in the town centre. It is possible to see the amphitheatre, bathhouses, barrack blocks and remains of walls. The excellent museum can do more justice to the site than this short guide.

The town is also famous for its early Christian associations, being the site of the martyrdom of Saints Julius and Aaron at the end of the Roman era. Following the departure of the Romans, the Christian tradition persisted. The church of Llangattock juxta Caerleon is dedicated to St Cadoc. The dedication indicates an early date for the foundation of the church, which is on the site of a Roman temple. It was the seat of the Welsh lords of Caerleon and Machen before and after the Norman arrival. The Welsh were not finally expelled until 1230.

Caerleon is famed for its possible connection with King Arthur. In one of the group of early Welsh traditional stories, known collectively as *Y Mabinogion*, he is holding a court at Caerllion ar Wysg (Caerleon on Usk). The earliest of these stories date from the sixth century, but they were not written down until the Early Middle Ages. *The Mabinogion* gives us the earliest literary mention of Arthur, who may have been a battle leader among the early Welsh.

The transference of his story to a wider world is due mainly to Geoffrey of Monmouth, who was a Breton monk. In his *History of the Kings of Britain*, a work which may possibly be more fiction than fact, he has Arthur hold court at Caerleon. Through Geoffrey's work in Norman French, Arthur became a hero throughout Europe. The myth was used by authors dealing with the new concepts of chivalry and courtly love. He and his knights were intended as role models for the real world. The Welsh scholar T. Gwynn Jones wrote in 1909:

'Tithau a'th ramant weithion a'i meddwaist
Oni liwiaist y byd a'th chwedleuon.'
(Wales may have been conquered by the Normans
But through them it coloured the world with its tales.)

One cannot write of Caerleon without mentioning Arthur Machen. He spent his early life in the town, but went to London as a journalist at the end of the last century. He wrote a number of novels and short stories based on Celtic legends and the stories of Caerleon and district. These are considered to be minor masterpieces of the supernatural.

However, in Caerleon it is King Arthur who is the more important, there is even a small museum devoted to him. He may not have existed, despite the possible Dark Age site on Lodge Farm, but the myth does. The power of the myth atttracted Alfred, Lord Tennyson to Caerleon, where he wrote the masterly Arthurian romance *Idylls of the King* in the Hanbury Arms. The Hanbury Arms is still a public house. It is in an idyllic location on the banks of the Usk. It is quite easy to sit there all day watching the tide rise and fall under the slopes of Wentwood, contemplating the next portion of the Celtic Way.

Looking Ahead: *The next section continues the route through the ancient kingdom of Gwent – an area dominated by Wentwood – to the towns of Caerwent and Chepstow, before leaving Wales on the border crossing of the old Severn Bridge, shown below. As in this section, the wealth of detail given is a reflection of the many sites of significance in this area and their relative obscurity.*

Walking on the Severn Bridge

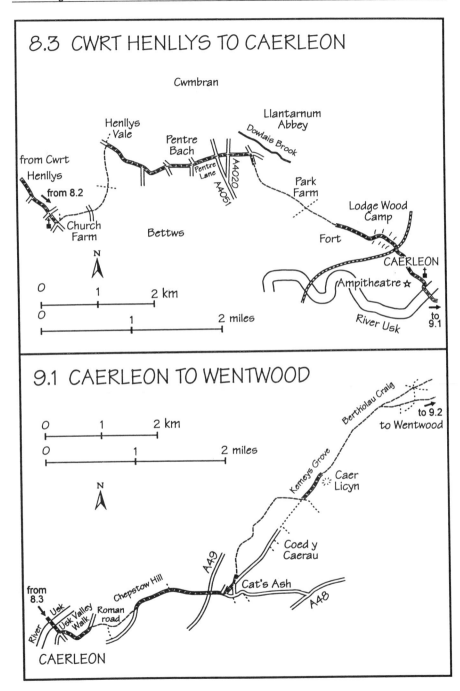

8.3 CWRT HENLLYS TO CAERLEON

Cwmbran

Henllys
Vale

Pentre
Bach

Llantarnum
Abbey

Dowlais Brook

from Cwrt
Henllys

from 8.2

Pentre
Lane

A4020

A4051

Park
Farm

Lodge Wood
Camp

Church
Farm

Bettws

Fort

CAERLEON

N

0   1   2 km

0   1   2 miles

Ampitheatre ☆

River Usk

to
9.1

9.1 CAERLEON TO WENTWOOD

0   1   2 km

0   1   2 miles

N

Bertholau Craig

to 9.2
to Wentwood

Kemeys Grove

Caer
Licyn

Coed y
Caerau

A49

Cat's Ash

Chepstow Hill

A48

from
8.3

River Usk

Usk Valley Walk

Roman
road

CAERLEON

Section Nine
The Gwent Borderlands:
Caerleon to Chepstow
18 miles

The Severn Bridge

John Owen

See Section Eight for author details.

Stages:

1. Caerleon to Gray Hill – 7 miles
2. Gray Hill to Llanmelin – 3 miles
3. Llanmelin to Chepstow – 8 miles

Maps: OS Landrangers 171 (Cardiff, Newport), 172 (Bristol, Bath)

Highlights: Gray Hill, Wentwood, Kemeys Folly, Caer Licyn, Castell Troggy, Llanvair Discoed, the Gwent levels, Chepstow, the Severn Crossing.

Starting Point: The Hanbury Arms, Caerleon (340 905).

Public Transport: Caerleon is accessible by public transport from Newport. Newport has a mainline railway station and a good bus station. Cardiff Central Railway Station – 01222 227281, Valley Lines – 01222 231978 – local rail service which runs between Caerphilly and Cardiff.

Additional Information: Caerphilly Castle – 01222 883143

Tourist Information: Cwmcarn Visitor Centre, Gwent – 01495 272001, Magor Services, Junction 23 – 01633 881122, Caerleon – 01633 430777, Monmouth – 01600 713898 and Chipping Sodbury – 01454 888686.

Introduction

East of the river Usk, you are in the old land of Gwent. This was the post-Roman name for the land between the Usk and the Wye, its name was taken from the town of Caerwent. Caerwent was a town established by the Romans for the Silures. It was known as Venta Silurum, the market place of the Silures. Unlike Caerleon it was essentially a civil settlement. The importance of the site in the post-Roman period was such that it gave its name to the district between the rivers Usk and Wye. Tradition has it that there was a king in Caerwent around AD500.

The old Welsh kingdom of Gwent was broken up by the arrival of the Normans. William I placed some of his most powerful barons on the Welsh border, to contain the Welsh and to conquer part of Wales in their own right. Since Gwent was not in England, the various Norman lordships such as Striguil, based on Chepstow, were virtually independent of England. They seemed to be held not from the English king, but held, as a lord of Caldicot said, 'Per Gladium' (by the sword!).

The lordship of Striguil (Chepstow) covered most of the land between the Wye and the Usk, south of and including much of the Wentwood ridge. The western part of the coastal plain was part of the lordship of Caerleon. The major change introduced by these Norman lordships was the manorial system. Each manor was held by knight service at Chepstow Castle. The two grades of knight service, a standard forty days attendance and a Welsh knight's service of only twenty days, may indicate native Welsh participation in the manorial system from an early date.

In 1536 Henry VIII passed the Act of Union between England and Wales. As a result of that act the County of Monmouthshire was created out of the Norman lordships in Gwent and Gwynllwg. 'From lands in Wales' in the words of the act. For years writers have used the term Gwent in a romantic, literary way to describe the county of Monmouthshire. In 1974, with local government reorganisation, the county of Monmouthshire was renamed Gwent. In 1995 more reorganisation dismembered Gwent and created a new county of Monmouthshire from rural eastern (modern) Gwent, but incorporating the pre-Norman kingdom of Gwent. The rest of the county, being the industrial, urban areas, were made into county boroughs. When I use the term Gwent in this section, I mean the old pre-Norman district.

The area was divided into two by the wooded ridge known as Wentwood.

This is an outlier of the Forest of Dean and forms a prominent ridge, which runs east – west. To the north we have the so-called plain of Gwent, which is, in fact, an area of rounded hills between the coal field and Wentwood. This is the land of the Usk, which meanders through. To the south of the ridge, Carboniferous limestone underlies the coastal fringe, giving rise to fertile soils along the A48. To the south of the A48, which was the Roman road, there is a low range of hills running east to west. Between the hills, bounded by the 50ft contour and the sea, are the Gwent Levels, which were alluvial marshes, and even today lie below the highest tide level.

The topography of Gwent 'has affected its settlement pattern, the lower more fertile land attracting successive waves of migrants from the Neolithic period on'. The areas identified by the late E.G. Bowen as areas of surviving Welsh tenure on the higher ground in Gwent in the Middle Ages were the same areas ignored by the Romans. These are the same areas with a higher percentage of surviving Welsh place names.

By the 8th century there were two distinct areas, Gwent Uwchcoed (Gwent above the Wood) and Gwent Is Coed (Gwent below the Wood). The ridge was a major barrier in earlier periods, its northern slope was steep and the vast number of trees made communication difficult. Even today only minor roads cross the ridge. The wood consisted of a wide range of trees, but oak dominated the landscape.

In the middle of Wentwood, at the head of the valley dominated by the modern reservoir, was an open space at the meeting of several tracks. A grove of trees here was known as Foresters' Oaks and was the area used to hold the Foresters' Court. This was a similar arrangement to the better-known Speech House in the Forest of Dean.

The clearance of Wentwood was carried out over a long period. The monks of Tintern were among some of the most successful in clearing the wood, leaving areas such as Newchurch almost treeless. Similarly, there is a large treeless area called Earlswood to the east of Wentwood. This is now an area of small farms and fields which were cut out of the wood by squatters centuries ago, when the landlords were absentee. Today the wood is a mere shadow of itself, and what remains is mainly replanted coniferous. However, the ridge of Wentwood is useful for the walker because it provides a good path between the Usk and the Wye, generally avoiding urban areas.

Before beginning the route, I should like to record my gratitude to the officers of the Countryside Unit of the Planning Department of the Monmouthshire County Council, for their guidance on the footpaths and rights of way in the county.

Stage 1: Caerleon to Gray Hill – 7 miles

The obvious starting place in Caerleon is The Hanbury Arms. The Roman bridge was to east of the Hanbury, but the modern bridge is a hundred metres to the west. Cross the river using the footbridge alongside the road bridge, on your left is The Ship public house. Turn left just after The Ship into Lulworth Road and then turn right into Isca Road. This was the Roman road access to Caerleon. Turn left again at the end of Isca Road and follow the lane alongside the river.

After a couple of hundred metres, at 348 902, there is footpath to the right, up the hill. This is the route of the Roman road from Caerwent. Follow the curving footpath up the hill, and just after the house called Cock of the North take the left-hand fork up to the Cats Ash Road.

This area has been transformed in the last few years with the creation of several golf courses on both sides of the road. On clear days there are good views up the Usk valley and over the Severn. On your left you pass a group of houses called Mount St Albans. In a field alongside them was the burial place of Julius and Aaron, Christian martyrs during the late Roman period. The site is on private land and there is nothing visible. The road is on the route of the Roman road along the ridge and is pleasant walking but you should be aware of the Golf Club traffic.

After about half a mile you cross the A449 on a bridge at Cats Ash. The name is reputedly derived from Villa Cathonen, Cathonen being, according to tradition, the ruler of the district. Cats Ash Farm incorporates an early chapel in its structure. The Roman road runs downhill to Langstone, where it becomes the A48. Walk down the Roman road for about 50 metres, and at the signpost marked Coed y Caerau turn left up the lane. Continue to Chapel Cottage (375 911). At Chapel Cottage there are spectacular views back over Caerleon with Twmbarlwm and Mynydd Machen to the west. To the south and east you have the coastal plain, the Severn and the English coast.

You have a choice at Chapel Cottage, the first option is to carry straight on up the lane. This runs along the spine of the ridge up into Wentwood. It appears to be old because it is obviously a hollow way. The problem is that because it was a hollow way there is not much room to stand clear of traffic. In the fields on the left are a series of earthworks at (378 913). These are called Pen Toppen Ash and are thought to be Iron Age. Another suggestion is that they were the site of a Roman signal station. Caerleon is in line of sight, and so is Caerwent. Apart from the Ordnance Survey, the best, if not only, plans are in the travel book known as *Coxe's Monmouthshire*, written almost two hundred years ago.

Just after the enclosures is Coed y Caerau Common (wood of the camps) at 382 915. This is not open heath, but a small, coppiced beech wood. There are several paths running parallel to the road and these may be safer. The ground in the wood is heavily disturbed. Much of it may be small-scale quarrying, but there are several banks which could be Dark Age cross-ridge dykes. Cross-ridge dykes were used to control traffic on ridgeways and to delineate tribal boundaries. The possible dykes at Coed y Caerau are not identified as such on the Ordnance Survey Map.

After a few hundred metres there is another earthwork, reputedly on a Roman site. You cross the site opposite Kemeys Folly (385 922). In an old guide to the county of Monmouthshire it says that Kemeys Folly commands a wide and interesting view. That is an understatement: it is claimed eight counties are visible. There are magnificent views along the southern slopes of Wentwood, with Gray Hill a bracken-covered eminence in the distance. At the foot of Wentwood there is the corridor of the A48, separated from the Gwent Levels by a low ridge of hills. Just after Kemeys Folly there is a road junction to the left. At the right a bridleway climbs up from Kemeys House.

The second option from Chapel Cottage follows the Usk Valley Walk along the northern slopes of Wentwood, with views up the Usk Valley. The northern edge of Wentwood slopes steeply down through the woods to the river. There is a collection of farms, a church and an old manor house, Kemeys House, alongside the river. This is probably the Cemeis given to the see of Llandaff and mentioned in the 7th-century *Book of Llandaff*. Another reference speaks of King Ffernwael 'holding his court in the middle of Cemeis'. What we have in Cemeis is an estate traceable back through the medieval period, the Dark Ages, the Roman era and probably into the Iron Age. You rejoin the Ridgeway (and the end of the first option from Chapel Cottage) at the end of this bridleway.

From the junction with the bridle path (387 924), the Ridgeway becomes a road leading to a private house, but is still a right of way. To the left the ground falls away down the wooded slopes of Kemeys Graig. On the right the wood has been cleared, giving panoramic views over the coastal plain and the Severn. Standing out among the landscape to the south is the Llanwern Steelworks, symbol of the Steel Age, while the conical, wooded hill to the east is from the Iron Age, being Wilcrick hill fort.

Soon the Ridgeway passes through a small wood. This is Caer Licyn, another site with disputed origins. The Ordnance Survey calls it a Norman motte and bailey castle, whereas some authorities consider it to be Iron Age, with the mound to one side being a Bronze Age tumulus. If it is a castle, it may well be an early castle of the Kemeys family, one of whom, Stephen Kemeys, held the manor of Kemeys as a sub-lordship of Caerleon in 1234. The Kemeys family were a large half-Norman, half-Welsh family who held extensive estates in South Wales. Kemeys Manor was sold out of the family in 1700.

Soon after the castle the track ends at a house, but the Celtic Way enters the woodland and follows the high ground. The route is well defined, being partially a hollow way or running between low banks. The route here is unmetalled, and in some places is muddy even in summer. For about a mile the Celtic Way runs through the woodland. At 400 941 the path forks and the left-hand fork goes down to Pen Cae Mawr.

Had you been here in 1798, you could have met The Reverend William Coxe and Sir Richard Colte Hoare. They were travelling in the area collecting material for what is known to antiquarians as *Coxe's Monmouthshire*, a guide to the county written by Coxe and illustrated by Colte Hoare. Coxe says of this path, 'The road is a narrow level way, leading through groves of coppice interspersed with oak, beech and other timber. The height commands at one time the view I so much admired from the top of Pen y cae Mawr and at another the southern parts of Monmouthshire, with the Bristol Channel, bordered by the hills of Somerset and Gloucestershire, till they are lost in the expanse of ocean.'

It is a measure of humanity that the sights Coxe saw can fill us with the same emotions two hundred years later. Like Coxe, it took me some time to suspect that I was 'treading the site of an old British way'. The left-hand fork goes down along the northern slope to Pen Y Cae Mawr. The path leaves the woods and runs through a field to a crossroads. This is Pen y Cae Mawr, and the views remain spectacular. I suspect, however, that Coxe actually stood on the hill above for he writes, 'From the middle of the forest scenery I looked down on the rich vales of Monmouthshire, watered by the limpid and winding Usk.'

Near Pen Y Cae Mawr is, in my opinion, one of the most romantic castles in the area. This is Castell Troggy (415 954). It lies in a field opposite the crossroads. A path leads across the field to the other side, and then you follow the hedge line to the right. The castle lies in marshy ground that is the source of the Castroggy Brook. It may have been an outpost of the lordship of Striguil, based on Chepstow. Coxe, in 1798, called it Striguil Castle. In Welsh this may have been Cas Striguil, which could have become corrupted to Castroggy.

The surviving remains date from the 13th century. The surviving masonry consists of a high curtain wall and towers on the eastern side. It was probably built as a hunting lodge by the Bigod family, the Earls of Norfolk, who held Chepstow through marriage. Eventually it became the dwelling of the lord's forester. These overgrown remains show how some castles should be presented, covered in ivy and full of mystery.

On returning to the crossroads take the road marked Llanvair Discoed. After about a quarter of a mile there is a path to the right after a house called Timothy Cottage. This climbs up to the top of the ridge. This, I think, was the Pen y Cae Mawr (top of the great enclosure) where Coxe stood, and the location of two Bronze Age barrows. The name Pen y Cae Mawr probably relates to the enclosure of Wentwood as a hunting preserve.

If you take the right-hand fork at 400 941,the route runs up through the forest along the high ground. The slopes to the left are known as Bertholau Graig. This is best translated as 'the boundary ridge', emphasising the role Wentwood played in the past as a barrier to communication. The nature of this ridge is best appreciated from the Raglan to Newport road, where it looms high above the river. After about a mile, the woodland track crosses a minor road (422 948) which runs between Parc Seymour and Pen y Cae Mawr. The lack of good roads shows how effective a barrier Wentwood is, even today. Long may it be so.

From the point where the track crosses the road, the Celtic Way is on a Forestry Drive. This part of Wentwood is used extensively for recreation and the Forestry Commission has a large car park, barbecue facilities and an adventure playground. Alternatively, **in bad weather**, you can follow the road to the right down to Parc Seymour, and you reach the A48. There is a bus service between Newport and Chepstow which you can catch on the A48.

Assuming the weather is good, we proceed north from the Forestry Commission car park to the Wentwood Round Barrows (416 945), which are in a group of beech trees. These Bronze Age (2000-1000BC) barrows are some 800 feet above sea level on the edge of the northern scarp. They are thought to be outliers of the Gray Hill complex. However, not enough is known of the Bronze Age landscape to be sure if they would have been visible from Gray Hill.

To the north and north-west there is no evidence of Bronze Age settlement, so these barrows may mark the edge of a tribal settlement. Unfortunately, the barrows are not well protected, or even acknowledged as such by the Forestry

Commission. As a result they are damaged by car parking, by off-road vehicles driving over them, people using them as a picnic site and the replanting of the wood. The presence of beech trees around the barrows, possibly a 19th-century planting, relieves the monotony of the conifer.

From the cairns the track carries on eastward through the woodland for about a quarter of a mile until it meets a minor road. This runs from Llanvair Discoed to Pen y Cae Mawr. Turn right on reaching the road and walk down the hill towards the reservoir. The road is a minor one but in summer there is traffic to the picnic site. It is possible to follow woodland tracks down the hill and not use the road. Do not turn off the road until you leave the woods. At the edge of the wood there is a road to the right signposted Llanvaches and going alongside the reservoir: do not take it. Take the path to the left. There is another picnic site on the right, The Foresters' Oaks Picnic Site, just after the crossroads above the reservoir. Here there are public toilets, which are occasionally open.

The path at 428 939 leads to the summit of Gray Hill. The track leads upward on the left in woodland and on the right is a house called Swn y Coed. After the end of the wood, a bridleway goes to the left, passing a house called Casa Mia, and runs along the edge of the wood to Bica Canman.

The Celtic Way track carries on up to the end of the cultivated land. The track forks in two here. One fork runs around the bottom of the hill, giving views over the Gwent Levels and leads eventually to Llanvair Discoed. The other fork is a bridleway at the north of the hill at the edge of the wood. Another track climbs up the steep western edge of Gray Hill. The climb to the bracken-covered summit is well rewarded by the view since Gray Hill stands out from the hills surrounding it. The more extensive view to the south is almost uninterrupted. To the west lies the conical hill of Mynydd Allt Hir (also known as Money Turvey, being a literal English pronunciation of Mynydd Allt Hir). Between Mynydd Allt Hir and Gray Hill is the Wentwood reservoir supplying Newport.

The view is not the main reason for visiting Gray Hill. In Welsh, Gray Hill is called Mynydd Llwyd. One meaning of 'llwyd' is 'gray'. However, there is a meaning best interpreted as 'holy'. Gray Hill is one of the old holy places of Wales. The landscape has changed from the Bronze Age and today's bracken-covered hill would have been far more fertile, with agriculture reaching up to the edges of what must have been a major cultural and religious site.

Gray Hill dominates the surrounding area, being a focal point in the landscape. From the hill there are views of the upland ridges beyond Wentwood, the Gwent Levels and the land to the south of the A48. Although this land would have been marshy, over the last ten years much evidence of Iron Age occupation of the Levels has come to light. In the distance the hills around Bath are visible, as are the Quantocks and Exmoor. Conversely, Gray Hill could also be seen from a wide area and it would dominate the landscape in a similar way to that in which Salisbury Cathedral dominates much of southern Wiltshire.

Gray Hill has a complex of Bronze Age cairns, three standing stones and a stone circle. To reach the circle at (438 935), walk along the path to the top of the hill. After about 300 metres along the hill, the bracken thins and you reach an area of grass. At this point there are a large number of quarry scoops where the exposed conglomerate limestone has been quarried. Here a path runs down right through the bracken to the stone circle. This lies to the south below the summit of the hill. After a few hundred metres a standing stone is seen, and beyond this, partially hidden in the bracken, is the stone circle. This has been described as a ring cairn, containing a cist burial from the second millennium BC, rather than a small version of Stonehenge.

There are also three groups of barrows and cairns on the hill, on the northern, southern and eastern slopes. These may form part of a ritual complex centred on the stone circle. The series of linear earthworks on Gray Hill may be contemporary with the other elements. The site has not been excavated and so the chronological sequence of construction is not known, and we are not sure of the relationships between the various elements in the landscape.

The function of the complex is the subject of much speculation; was it located on a prominent hill to be the religious centre for a wide area to the south? Alternatively, as is normal in such situations, the circles have been variously described as prehistoric observatories with stones aligned to the midwinter sunrise. Another explanation is that the arrangement of circles and barrows had a role connected with funerary ritual.

Much has been written about stone circles and barrows, but it is best to keep an open mind. In the absence of a written record, it is difficult to come to a firm judgement without imposing our cultural values on Bronze Age society. Whatever the explanation, a visit to Gray Hill makes one aware of a sense of place, of a oneness with the land and an echo of humanity down the ages. There is a feeling of being able to empathise with Bronze Age man through the continuity of the landscape.

Stage 2: Gray Hill to Llanmelin – 3 miles

From Gray Hill there are two alternative routes to Llanmelin hill fort. The second option gives the opportunity of a break for refreshments at Llanvair Discoed.

Option 1

Return to the track on the top of Gray Hill and turn right. The path runs eastwards through the bracken and the mass of silver birch which now covers the eastern end of Gray Hill. Turn left where the path makes a T-junction with the bridleway leading to Bica Common. This bridleway, which can be muddy in places, is well defined, but there are tracks leading off it and into the wood, which can be confusing. At (442 939), at a junction of bridleways, turn right to the farm Cil Voynog. This name, which means 'the enclosure of the stony ploughland' is evidence of the process of reclamation of the woodland.

From the farm, a narrow lane leads down to Bica Common. This is a small, bracken-covered common with a maze of tracks. It is best to stay on the road until you approach Pandy Farm, down on the left. Just before the farm entrance, take the road to the right. This leads across the base of the common, above the small valley of the Castroggy Brook. Below in the valley bottom, and spreading up the hill, is the small collection of houses sometimes called Earlswood Bottom.

The road leads to two houses, only one, Rocks Cottage, is shown on the map. The path goes in through the gate and turns sharp left down to the side of the Castroggy Brook, At the end of the garden the path goes into a small, wooded, stone-walled enclosure. The area is filled with a jumble of large rocks, which may be from field clearance, but it has an ancient atmosphere about it. There is what appears to be a well near the southern end of the wood, but it does not appear as such in the standard work on the holy wells of Wales.

Once out of the wood the path follows the Castroggy Brook down the valley. On your left the valley sides are wooded, but you walk through pastureland, which rises steeply to your right. This valley can be wet underfoot and even on a late autumn day is a frost hollow. Despite that, it is a little bit of paradise, hidden from the world. As the valley turns you pass the Cribau Mill complex, and at the end of the field join the lane which runs to Cribau. At this point you join the path taken by Option 2.

Option 2

On a more practical note, if you are hungry or thirsty it may be worth choosing this option and visiting Llanvair Discoed (442 924). This is to the south of Gray Hill and may be reached by walking down the south side of the hill from the stone circle. A path runs down through the bracken to join the minor road that skirts the hill. The road acts as a boundary between the common land on the hill and the fields. Soon, on your left, is the start of the bridleway to Bica Common, but to go to Llanvair Discoed, stay on the road. At the old house Ysgubor Kemeys, which looks 17th-century, the road turns down to the village. Turn left at the main road, to the village centre. Llanvair Discoed (the church of St Mary below the wood) is a charming but small village. Here you will find The Woodland Tavern, which provides food and drink for the weary, but it is closed between 3pm and 7pm.

The village indicates continuity of settlement not in a specific spot, but in a landscape. As mentioned before, it is felt the higher ground remained Celtic Welsh despite several waves of invaders. The very name Llanvair Discoed suggests a Welsh-speaking population. The large proportion of Welsh surnames in the graveyard tends to confirm this cultural continuity. Its cultural identity contrasts with St Brides Nether Went, an Anglicised coastal counterpart.

It would be foolish to suggest the medieval inhabitants of Lamecare, as Llanfair Discoed was recorded in Domesday, were direct descendants of the Bronze Age dwellers. The church is dedicated to St Mary, any earlier Celtic dedication being unknown. Behind the church is a small castle, held by the St John family as a Welsh knight's fee under Chepstow. The presence of the castle records the introduction of the manorial system by the Normans.

If time is short it is possible to walk to Llanmelin along the road. Walk down from the public house about 100 metres and take the left fork. Where the houses end, take the left fork up the lane. At the next junction turn left again under Culhere woods towards Old Cwm Mill. From the mill the road climbs up to the entrance to Llanmelin hill fort, opposite the entrance to Coombe Farm.

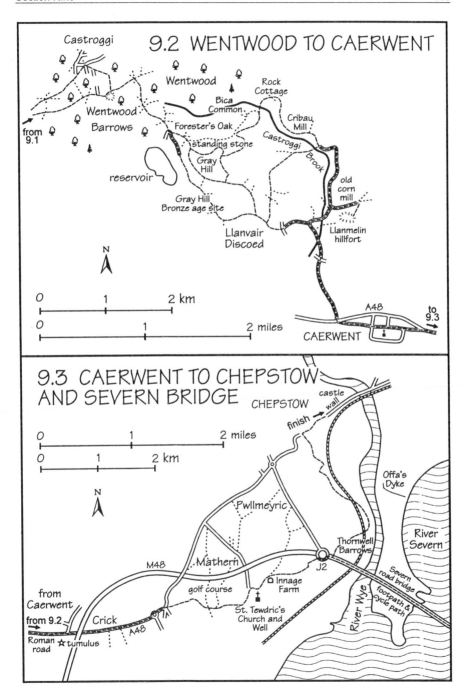

9.2 WENTWOOD TO CAERWENT

Castroggi

Wentwood

Rock Cottage

Bica Common

from 9.1

Wentwood Barrows

Forester's Oak

Cribau Mill

standing stone

Castroggi Brook

Gray Hill

reservoir

Gray Hill Bronze age site

Llanvair Discoed

old corn mill

Llanmelin hillfort

N

0   1   2 km

0   1   2 miles

A48

to 9.3

CAERWENT

9.3 CAERWENT TO CHEPSTOW AND SEVERN BRIDGE

CHEPSTOW

castle wall

finish

0   1   2 miles

0   1   2 km

N

Offa's Dyke

Pwllmeyric

Thornwell Barrows

River Severn

M48

Mathern

J2

Severn road bridge

from Caerwent

golf course

Innage Farm

footpath & cycle path

from 9.2

Crick

A48

St. Tewdric's Church and Well

River Wye

Roman road

tumulus

However, if you have time it is worth taking the scenic route. Starting from the pub take the small lane to the left, back up towards Gray Hill. About a quarter of a mile up the lane is Village Farm. Just before the farm, on the right-hand side of the lane, is Llanfair Discoed well. This is not recorded in the standard work on holy wells. At the farm is a footpath signposted Earlswood, follow it up the field to a stile. You will notice many of the old field boundaries are composed of large blocks of stone. This is conglomerate limestone which, as the name suggests, consists of small quartz pebbles in a matrix of limestone. It is known locally as puddingstone because of its appearance.

At the stile the path crosses a small road, this is the access road to the house Penheim. The path runs through a small wood and re-crosses the Penheim access road. On your right are the remains of old limekilns. The path follows the edge of the Penheim boundary. At the end of the field you go through the gate and turn right through another gate. The path follows the northern edge of the Penheim property, which is marked by an attractive stand of trees. In this area the stiles are well made and bear the sign 'Landowners welcome caring walkers'. It is hoped you will live up to their expectation. At the end of this field you cross the access road to the private dwelling called The Cottage.

You are now on the way down to the valley of the Castroggy, which lies below you. In the distance the patchwork of fields, woods and farms is Earlswood. Once Earlswood was a large wood, it belonged to the detached Shirenewton portion of the Caldicot lordship. At the end of the Middle Ages the owners were absentees. In their absence, and the presence of a succession of weak agents, squatters moved into the wood, cut it down and built small cottages, holdings and farms. This explains the chaotic road and field pattern you see before you.

Having crossed the road leading to The Cottage, the Celtic Way follows the path down across the field to a gate and into a small wood. Once out of the wood the path falls steeply down to the to the valley of the Castroggy. The path comes out on a lane at the entrance to a complex of houses called Cribau Mill. Cribau Mill was, from its name, a woollen mill, the root 'crib' means 'comb' in English, and refers to the habit of combing the finished wool with teasels.

At this point (456 938) Options 1 and 2 merge. There is a right of way down the lane from the start of the Cribau land. The land is basically a long drive to Cribau, and runs along side the Castroggy. We first met the Castroggy as a marsh at Castle Troggy, now we meet it where it has cut its route through Wentwood in a deep, steep-sided valley known as a cwm. The stream was there before Wentwood was formed, and cut its way down as Wentwood was being eroded. Today it runs around Wentwood and this may give another clue to its name. In Welsh the verb 'tro' means 'to turn'. Possibly the Castroggy was so named because of the way it turns around Wentwood. There is just room along the valley floor for the brook and the narrow lane. It is one of Gwent's best-kept secrets. It is particularly attractive in spring with the wild flowers. The Cwm runs for about a mile north – south between wooded slopes and comes out at a cottage called Old Cwm Mill (458 928).

At Old Cwm Mill you join a minor lane. Turn left. **Care must be taken**, it is not a busy road but it is narrow. It climbs up between two wooded slopes. On the crest of the one to the right is the hill fort of Llanmelin, hidden by the trees. Towards the top of the hill you pass the entrance to Coombe Farm, a large building across the fields. Opposite the entrance to Coombe Farm is an over-grown lane (464 928). This is the access to Llanmelin hill fort.

The border nature of the area you are now entering is emphasised by the name Coombe Farm. This is an Anglicisation of the Welsh 'cwm'. Eastern Mon-mouthshire, close to the Wye, has long been exposed to English settlement and influence. You are now leaving the higher ground which was the last refuge of various groups of original populations and are entering a more cosmopolitan world.

As you pass along the overgrown lane, on your left, covered by trees, is an earthwork sometimes known as The Outpost. However, nothing is known of the relationship of this to Llanmelin itself. As you leave the wooded lane you enter a large field. Llanmelin is at the western edge of this field. It is essential you respect the farmer's property and crops. You **must** follow the **western hedgeline**, this helps the farmer and maintains his good relationship with visitors to Llanmelin.

The name Llanmelin is probably fairly modern. Though normally in Welsh the prefix 'Llan' means 'church', occasionally it is a corruption of 'glan' which can mean river valley. 'Melin' is the Welsh for 'mill'. Thus, the location of Old Cwm Mill, situated at the mouth of the valley of the Castroggy, gave the area its name. The name then passed to the much older hill fort.

It was once considered that Llanmelin was the tribal capital of the Silures. This was strengthened by the fact that two miles to the south lies Caerwent, a Roman civil town. However, despite its magnificent location on a south-facing ridge, its double rampart ditch and counterscarp and the annexe to the east, Llanmelin is one of the smaller hill forts. Nash Williams, who excavated it in 1930, thought it dated from the second century BC, but now it is thought to be probably older. Around 170BC it is thought the fort was enlarged and the mas-sive double rampart built. The entrance to the south-east was refashioned in about 50BC.

The annexe to the south-east is the subject of much dispute. It is proposed that it may have formed part of an early fort that was much reshaped. Another suggestion is that it was built as a cattle compound, since the economy of the Iron Age revolved around cattle. Yet again the presence of two medieval huts has lead to the suggestion it may have a medieval origin. There are a total of 29 recognised hill forts in the pre-1974 county of Monmouthshire, Llanmelin, though spectacular, is just one of them.

Stage 3: Llanmelin to Chepstow – 8 miles

Return to the road opposite Coombe Farm and turn left, back down the hill. At Old Cwm Mill turn left. After a few hundred metres, join a footpath that cuts across the field, east of Great Llanmelin Farm. When it rejoins the road, turn left along the road and follow it across a crossroads down to the A48. Regrettably, there is no option but to follow the road. Alongside the road among the trees runs the Castroggy Brook, which by now is an old friend. There are no footpaths running east to west in this area.

The road down is pleasant and tree-lined and runs through good farming country. The land below Wentwood is good agricultural land. The route down the road also has a symbolic significance. Up on Wentwood you were closer to Celtic Wales. Down this road in the first century AD came the Silures of Llanmelin, to become the Romano-British citizens of Caerwent. You are also entering a landscape that was changed by the arrival of the Normans. They transformed the agriculture by the creation of the manorial system. The villages between here and Chepstow were creations of or adoptions to the manorial system, and held by Knight's service from Chepstow Castle.

Eventually, the road ends at the A48,which was the Roman road. You must cross the A48 at the junction – be very careful. Across the A48, the Roman road is the smaller left-hand fork. Take it and walk into Caerwent, in about 500 metres. On your right is the start of one of the best-preserved Roman town walls in northern Europe.

Caerwent was very different from Caerleon. Caerleon was the military base, the legionary centre, with troops from all over the Roman Empire. Caerwent was the Silurian town, built by the Romans for the Silures, once they had accepted the rule of Rome. Not all tribes were treated this way, some were not 'civilised', they were enslaved. The Celtic Silures came here, and over the next three and a half centuries became Romano-Britons with some measure of self-government. As mentioned earlier, the name Caerwent is derived from the Latin 'Venta Silurum', the 'market of the Silures'.

In 1862, George Borrow published *Wild Wales*, a record of his 1854 walk around Wales. He passed through Caerwent and commented that it was 'a poor desolate place consisting of a few old-fashioned houses and a strange-looking, desolate church'. Today, it is a pleasant small village, possibly more English in style than Welsh with an attractive collection of stone buildings gathered around the church. Borrow mentioned in 1854 that, 'No Welsh is spoken in Caerwent, nor to the east of it, nor indeed for two miles to the west.'

The best way to explore Caerwent is to climb up on the western wall, and follow it around the southern edge of the village. The wall and towers survive to a considerable height, overlooking the water meadows of the Castroggy Brook, which here has changed its name to the Nedern Brook. The walls enclose an area of 18 hectares (44 acres), almost the whole modern village. At the eastern end of the southern wall, the Normans built a motte on the corner tower, which survives today. Turn left at the motte and walk up to the east gate of the town.

Turn into the town and walk to St Stephen's Church. As you approach the church you will notice the excavated Roman buildings including a temple, shops, the basilica and the site of the forum. The present church of St Stephen dates mainly from the 13th century, but it is on the site of a church dedicated to the Celtic St Tathan. Tradition says Tathan was granted land here in about AD500 by King Caradoc, who ruled Gwent from Caerwent. Here we see that on the departure of the Romans, it remained a centre of government. The monastery aroused the wrath of Gwynlliw, king of Glywyseg, to the west at Newport. This led to a dispute which was eventually settled amicably. Gwynlliw even sent his son Cadoc to the monastery. He became one of the major saints in the Welsh Church.

The discovery of a silver bowl, dated to about AD500, with the Chi Rho symbol scratched on the base, gives weight to the belief that the Caerwent area has been Christian from the late Roman period. Before coming under the influence of the see of Llandaff, Caerwent was probably the seat of a post-Roman bishop, ministering to the Romano-British who had been Celtic Silures and were now to become the Welsh.

Thus, it is appropriate that St Stephen's consists of much reused Roman material, building on the Roman experience in more ways than one. In the porch are two Roman stones, one called the Silurum Stone is dedicated to the Pro Consul Paulinus on his departure in AD202. The other is the pedestal of a statue to the god Mars. Many relics from the various religions of the Roman period have been exposed in Caerwent. The most interesting, because it was obviously from a non-Roman school of sculpture, was a small Celtic deity, which has been linked to a healing shrine.

Leaving St Stephen's, go north across the crossroads to the site of the north gate of the town. Alongside the gate is the Northgate pub which serves good food and drink during normal opening hours. You may need to visit the Northgate because the next two miles are alongside the A48. The M4 has taken most of the through-traffic from the A48 and walking is relatively easy, the verges are wide with a good footpath. George Borrow wrote, 'the country between Caerwent and Chepstow is delightfully green, but somewhat tame.' The same is true today. It is obvious that you are now in lowland Britain. The landscape could be English, and the domination of arable agriculture is obvious. In the distance you see the higher wooded slopes running from Wentwood to Chepstow, a vista which pleases the eye and lifts the heart.

As you walk along the A48 you are walking through a palimpsest of history: successive layers of history being laid on a pre-Celtic foundation. The road is on the route of a Roman road, but the landscape is older. As you approach the village of Crick, you pass on the left a Bronze Age tumulus, just inside the boundary of RAF Caerwent. This is one of the largest tumuli in Monmouthshire and one of a series of tumuli in the lowlands. Along the ridge to the west are three other barrows overlooking the Gwent levels. It has been proposed that the kerb evident around the circumference of the tumulus may have its origin in a crude, circular structure dating from the Late Neolithic Period. No one has yet drawn the parallel with the ring cairn on Gray Hill.

Margaret Gelling, the renowned authority on place name studies, suggests that place names like Creech, Crich, Crouch and Cricket St Thomas have their origin in the proto-Welsh word 'crug' meaning hill, mound or tumulus. Thus, the village name Crick is probably derived from the tumulus in RAF Caerwent. The importance of the site perhaps having been burned into folk memory. The alternative explanation, that it is a corruption of 'creek', does not bear serious consideration. Locally, creeks are called pills, as in Magor Pill. The word 'pill' comes from the Welsh 'pwll' meaning hollow, inlet or creek.

Passing under the disused branch railway line to the base, you enter Crick.

Architecturally, Crick is a village that would not be out of place in the Cots-wolds. Despite its English appearance, Crick was the site of St Nedyn's chapel (yet another Celtic saint). To the north of the chapel site was a medieval moated grange. In 1250 Sir William Dernford held Crick as half a Welsh knight's fee un-der the lordship of Chepstow. His house, probably at the farm called Ty Mawr (big house), was the manorial centre.

Passing under the M4, you continue along the A48 towards Chepstow. The A48 is not now a busy road and there is an adequate pavement alongside it. The road climbs up from Crick with woods on each side. Just as the woods end, on your left is yet another tumulus, hidden behind some houses. The scenery con-sists of rolling farmland, fringed to the north by the wooded hills which are the south-eastern slopes of the Wentwood ridge and St Pierre Wood.

About a mile from Crick you come to Parkwall roundabout. The A48 takes the left-hand fork to Pwll Meyric and Chepstow. On the roundabout is a restau-rant, this provides overnight accommodation, and food from 7.30 am (1997). To the left of the restaurant, past the garden centre, half-hidden by a boarding, is a footpath signpost to St Pierre Church. Following the sign leads to a large wrought iron gateway, this was the western entrance to St Pierre Park. The offi-cial footpath goes through the gap in the railings to the left of the gate.

Borrow claimed the landscape in this area was tame; extending to 75 hec-tares (200 acres), it is manicured. It is a man-made landscape that has matured. There is a diversity of trees and it contains a large ornamental lake. It is now a famous golf course, but originally was a knight's fee held in the 12th century by Roger de St Pierre, hence the name. By the end of the 15th century it was owned by a branch of the Morgan family of Tredegar Park, near Newport. Their house is now the St Pierre Golf and Country Club. Your fellow traveller Archdeacon Coxe stayed there in 1798. If you have the money or desire you can follow his example because it provides excellent accommodation.

The owners of St Pierre have co-operated with the Monmouthshire County Council over public access to the footpaths through the park. It is expected that their co-operation and understanding are not abused. From the gate the path runs easterly towards the large pond. At the pond it turns right towards the house and church.

The small and ancient church is basically Norman, being the chapel at-tached to the lord's habitation. The church has two early 13th-entury sepul-chral slabs to members of the St Pierre family, as well as to the later Lewis family. From the church the path runs eastwards towards Mathern. There are two ponds to the east of the church, the path goes between them across the course to a wooden kissing gate at the corner of a field (518 906). Crossing the golf course, you should try not to disturb the players.

From the kissing gate the Celtic Way follows the edge of a large, water-filled field boundary. Above the field you can just see Moynes Court on your left. Alongside the three-gabled building are the remains of a partly ditched mound, which may be the site of the castle of Sir Bogo de Knovil who held Mathern in the 13th century. In a booklet on the life of St Tewdric, on sale in Mathern church, it is noted that the ditch is on the inside of the bank. This suggests an alternative origin as a causeway camp of the Neolithic period. The slope of the ground hides the site of the possible moat, and indeed much of Moynes Court. The manor of Moynes Court was created by the Lords of Chepstow, who had cast their eyes on the episcopal property. The manor was in existence in 1254 and eventually passed to the Morgans of Pencoed, who in turn sold it to the Lewis family of St Pierre.

The path follows the Moynes Court boundary around to the left. At the field gate you take the right-hand fork, the path runs towards Mathern church, on your right among a clump of trees. It is best to keep to the path because in wet weather the low ground can be water-logged. The evidence of land drainage is all around. Not far to the south is St Pierre Pill ('pill' is the local name for a creek), which was a large expanse of water. It has been suggested that at one time the pill extended over the water meadows and up to the church.

The footpaths here through the water meadows are well waymarked. At the field end ignore the footpath to Moynes Court and go through the gate into the lane leading to the church. Below the church the lane runs up the hill to the east side of the church. A right-hand fork takes you up some ancient-looking stone steps to the back of the church. The large building behind the church is Mathern Palace, for a long time a residence of the Bishops of Llandaff.

Mathern, according to tradition, became a possession of the see of Llandaff. Llandaff Cathedral is two miles from Cardiff city centre and is the centre of the diocese of the same name. At one time the diocese covered most of south-east Wales. Therefore, it was only natural in the 6th century that Meyric, son of St Tewdric, should grant the church and land to Llandaff. Tewdric had been a king in south Wales, but had given up his throne and had gone to live the life of a hermit at Tintern. His quiet life was shattered by a Saxon invasion. He reluctantly took command of the army and defeated the Saxons in a battle on the banks of the Wye. Mortally wounded, he was brought for cleansing in a holy well, now known as St Tewdric's Well.

He died of his wounds and a church was built on the place he died. It became known as Merthyr Tewdric (the burial place of Tewdric). Tewdric, by virtue of being a Christian and having died in battle against the then heathen English, naturally became a saint of the Welsh Church. It is a tribute to his fame that on the arrival of the Normans, the dedication did not change. In the fullness of time Tewdric was accepted as a saint by the Church of England. By the Middle Ages Merthyr Tewdric became known as Mathern, best translated as 'ma teyrn' (the place of a king). The story begs many questions, but the church and the palace of the bishops of Llandaff exist.

The current church, dedicated to St Tewdric, is probably the fourth on the site. It is beautifully proportioned, and quite large for the area. Its quality and size are due to the fact that the bishops of Llandaff held much of the parish, before and after the Norman conquest, and that the church was built on episcopal land. It has a 13th-century interior. The side aisles and tower are later, probably 15th century. The church survived Victorian 'restoration' and the grave of Tewdric can be seen in the chancel. The church contains the remains of several of the bishops of Llandaff, as well as members of local gentry families.

In its way, Mathern has the same sense of place you feel at Gray Hill. Mathern church and palace sit on a low hill surrounded by trees, separated from Moynes Court by water-meadows. On an autumn morning, with mist covering the water-meadows, you can almost see the barges bringing the body of St Twedric for burial.

At the front gate of the church, turn left towards a road junction, opposite the junction is a farmhouse called Innage. From there take a footpath signposted Bulwark. Just after the farm buildings another path crosses the Bulwark footpath, take the right-hand fork. Follow this well-marked footpath as it runs through the fields to Junction 22 at the Old Severn Bridge.

You may wish to visit St Tewdric's Well before going to Chepstow. At Innage, carry on up the road to the left. Just before the M4, the well is on the left-hand side of the road. Wells were important as religious sites in the pre-Christian period. The Celts venerated many wells and the cult of the holy well can be traced back at least to them. The arrival of Christianity led to a conscious decision by the church to include wells in the process of conversion. In this way many pre-Christian well cults were adapted to suit the new faith. The story of St Tewdric being brought to the well to wash his wounds may hide a process of merging the existing well into the new faith.

On a more mundane level, those in need of modern comfort can walk under the M4 and a hundred metres up the road on the right is the Millers Arms pub. On leaving the pub, retrace your steps back under the motorway. After about fifty metres, you see on the left a finger-post marked Thornwell. You can follow this across the fields to the Severn Bridge.

In this area the footpaths and stiles are particularly well marked and made. As you near the bridge, the landscape becomes grimmer. On your left is the Severn Bridge Industrial Estate. At the end of the footpath is a large underpass under the motorway, leading to the estate. Cross the small road running through the underpass and another path runs along the bottom of the motorway embankment. This leads to the footway over the Severn Bridge.

You now have a serious choice. The walk should not be undertaken without planning: once over the bridge you are a long way from a major town. It may be best to stop overnight in Chepstow and start afresh in the morning.

To get to Chepstow go through the underpass, which is a surreal experience. Once through the underpass you see on your left the abandoned Thornwell farmhouse. Thornwell was a part of Mathern parish but is now a dormitory estate, mainly for Bristol. During the building of the estate in 1990, two burial mounds were discovered, one Neolithic and the other Bronze Age. They are located at (539 917), on the corner of Fountain Way, surrounded by a wooden fence. The spot is marked by a large tree.

They are not on the highest point of the landscape, but are located in a small valley overlooking the Severn Estuary. Their location overlooks the natural crossing point of the Severn. The tomb is alongside the Old Severn Bridge, the New Severn Bridge is visible in the distance. Between the two are the sites of the ferries at Old and New Passage and the pumping station for the Severn Tunnel. It is even reported that in the nineteenth century drovers taking cattle to

London would swim them across at low tide. The Neolithic tomb is an example of the Severn-Cotswold style, which can be found along the Severn and in the Cotswolds, with outliers in the Black Mountains. Until this example was found, the type was unusual in Monmouthshire.

The site may have been important because the location was reused in the Bronze Age. Two Early Bronze Age cist burials were found close to the main chamber. These contained the remains of two men. Alongside, but not excavated, is a mound classified as a Bronze Age cairn. It is tempting to identify continuity of occupation on what was a strategic crossing of the Severn.

To get to Chepstow you can walk up Thornwell Road, which runs through the estate and leads eventually into Chepstow. There is also the Scenic Route, which has the advantage of passing an Iron Age camp. **Portions of this path are lonely.** As you leave the underpass, turn sharp right along a footpath over a rough field. This leads up to a road, turn right and a follow the footpath fingerpost at the. edge of the sports field. This runs up the Wye, along the outside edge of the housing estate. At 542 917, a stile leads down across the fields to the river. This path goes under the railway by an arch. The railway was the South Wales Railway, designed by Brunel. After the arch the path turns left and follows the river. Just at this point it can be wet, even flooded after a high tide. The views on the Wye make it worthwhile. However, soon you climb back up to the path alongside the estate.

The path runs along a back lane to Victoria Road, where you turn left. After about twenty metres a narrow entrance on the right takes the path towards Chepstow. At 538 927 is what appears to be a park. It is, in fact, the Bulwarks, an Iron Age promontory fort high above the Wye. Its banks and ditches are covered in scrubland. Situated in the middle of a housing development, it is one of the larger forts in the county.

The next section, above Beaufort Quarry and alongside an industrial estate, is bleak, but compensated by an occasional glimpse of the Wye. The last portion of the footpath before the road is pleasant and wooded; below, you can see the remains of the old shipyards set up in the First World War to compensate for losses suffered in submarine warfare. Chepstow was an important port and had had a long tradition of shipbuilding going back to the Middle Ages.

The footpath ends at Wye Crescent. At the end of Wye Crescent, turn left into Hardwick Road. This estate, located outside the town walls of Chepstow, around a small valley leading down to the Wye, was built for the shipyard workers. At the end of the estate turn right towards the town wall. This is known as the Port Wall and was built in the 13th century. The road runs down the hill to the town.

Chepstow is a pleasant town which has grown with the opening of the Severn Bridge. It is a quintessential border town: close to Wales's Celtic roots in the Bulwark Fort, established by the Normans, yet it thinks of itself as English, and much of its traditional dialect is similar to that of Gloucestershire. Its picturesque situation on the side of a declivity sloping down to the Wye has made it a popular tourist centre and dormitory town.

The old town is situated inside the port wall. Some of this wall was demolished to build the Chepstow Inner Relief Road, but the sacrifice was worth it because the reduction in traffic has transformed Chepstow town centre. It is a pleasure to walk down the steep main street to the river. The medieval town plan is evident as you walk down through the town, later developments mostly complementing the townscape. Chepstow town centre has a varied range of traditional shops.

It may be unique in Britain in having three names, Its earliest recorded name was the Norman-French Striguil, after the bend in the River Wye. The Welsh name is Cas Gwent (the castle of Gwent) – Chepstow Castle being the first castle in Gwent. 'Chepstow' itself means 'market' in Anglo-Saxon, a role it continues today as a small market town.

The castle presents a picture of a feudal fortress almost unequalled in the country. The best view is from the Gloucester side of the Wye. It hangs off a limestone cliff above the Wye, the masonry is mainly limestone, and it is hard to tell where the cliff ends and the castle begins. The castle was started in 1067 and the keep, built by William Fitz Osbern, is one of the oldest stone buildings in Wales.

Chepstow is a good place to start or finish a section of the Celtic Way. It has a wide range of accommodation from a youth hostel to quality hotels. It is also a good centre for public transport with a bus station and a railway station. George Borrow, in 1854, ended his tour of Wales here. He took advantage of the hotels and the railway. He had dinner in the principal inn, and after which passed his time until his train at ten o'clock at night with his feet placed against the side of the grate, drinking wine and singing Welsh songs. You could do worse than to follow his example. But you might need to catch an earlier train.

Looking Ahead: *Now is the time to cross the Old Severn Bridge and enter England. The bridge crossing is not an unpleasant walk, nor unfrequented. The walkway is also used by cycles. Allow 45 minutes to cross. Immediately upon the other side you will pick up waymarking for the Northavon section of the Jubilee Way, which is the first stage of the route across Wiltshire to Avebury. The Jubilee Way is shown on Ordnance Survey maps and a free leaflet showing the route in more detail is available from the Tourist Information Centre in Chipping Sodbury, where this part of the Jubilee Way ends. The tourist office will also provide an accommodation list for the area. To leave Chepstow in the morning and arrive in Chipping Sodbury in the evening is a good day's walking, where one has moved not only into another country, but also into a different landscape. The Jubilee Way was devised in 1985 to celebrate the 50th anniversary of the Ramblers' Association. It was created to use existing paths to link Britain's long-distance footpaths. The part we use is the Northavon section, which is 16 miles long and links Offa's Dyke to the Cotswold Way. Walks in Northavon, produced by the old Northavon District Council, provides further information.*

Section Ten
Linking the Ways: Dyrham to Avebury

33½ miles

Cherhill White Horse

Val Saunders Evans

See "The Beginning" for author details.

Before beginning this section, there are an additional 23 miles of walking from the Severn Bridge to Dyrham: Severn Bridge to Chipping Sodbury on the Jubilee Way – 16 miles, Chipping Sodbury to Dyrham on the Cotswold Way – 7 miles.

Stages:

1. Dyrham to Castle Coombe – 9 miles
2. Castle Coombe to Kingston St Michael Church – 6 miles
3. Kington St Michael Church to Foxham Church – 6½ miles
4. Foxham Church to Highway Hill – 5½ miles
5. Highway Hill to Avebury – 6½ miles

Maps: Landrangers 172 (Bristol and Bath) and 173 (Swindon and Devizes). Pathfinders 1168 (Chippenham and Castle Coombe) and 1169 (Marlborough Downs).

Highlights: Lugbury long barrow, Castle Coombe, churches at West Kington, Kington St. Michael and Kington Langley, Avon Weir, Spirt Hill, Highway Hill, Windmill Hill and Avebury Great Stone Circle.

Starting Point: Dyrham Village at (741 755)

Accommodation: Youth hostels – Bath – 01225 465674 and Salisbury – 01722 327572

Public Transport: Badgerline Buses – 01179 553231, Dorset/Wiltshire Buses (Salisbury) – 01722 336855. Train Enquiries – 0117 9294255.

Additional Information: Dyrham Park (National Trust) 01179 372501

Tourist Information: Chipping Sodbury – 01454 888687, Thornbury – 01454 281638, Devizes – 01380 729408, Avebury – 01672 539425, Bristol – 01117 9260767, Salisbury – 01722 334956.

Introduction

From the Old Severn Bridge crossing, follow the Jubilee Way – opened to commemorate the anniversary of the founding of the Ramblers' Association – to the centre of Chipping Sodbury. The route then picks up the Cotswold Way to Dyrham. From Dyrham it is possible to leave the Cotswold Way and follow the Celtic Way. It runs directly east across the grain of the land to Castle Coombe and Kington St Michael, then through Foxham over to Hilmarton. The route goes over to Windmill Hill with fine views of the White Horse at Cherhill. This section ends at Avebury to link with the route to Stonehenge.

The Northavon section of the Jubilee Way is described in a leaflet published by the old Northavon District Council and obtainable from Tourist Information in Chipping Sodbury. 'The Cotswold Way' by Mark Richards details the route from Chipping Sodbury to Dyrham. It is also possible to follow both by using the waymarking and the Landranger map 172 for the Bristol and Bath area.

Having left these waymarked and established routes, the walking is on tracks across Wiltshire: byways, bridleways, footpaths, and unfrequented lanes. Paths across fields are generally waymarked near their point of entry and exit. When the path runs through the middle of a ploughed or seeded area, look for the gap in the hedge across the field to see which way to go. The route passes through a well-husbanded part of England, which combines tradition and modernity. Parts of the walking can be exposed in wind and rain, but walkers are rarely more than half an hour from shelter. Although never far from the white noise of the nearby M4, the route touches on beautiful hamlets and includes some peaceful tracks. There are several villages on the route and most offer refreshment at inns. Kington St Michael, Yatton Keynell and Foxham have general stores. Accommodation is available at some inns and B&B close to the route, and the facilities of Chippenham and Calne are a short bus journey away.

Stage 1: Dyrham to Castle Coombe – 9 miles

Leaving the village and the Cotswold Way at the finger-post crossroads, walk up the hill for about half a mile. Go past Sands Farm entrance and keep the Dyrham Estate high stone walls to your left until you reach a signed footpath and stone steps to a stile crossing into the estate. Take the clear path through new tree planting to a strange arrangement of fencing which allows you into the

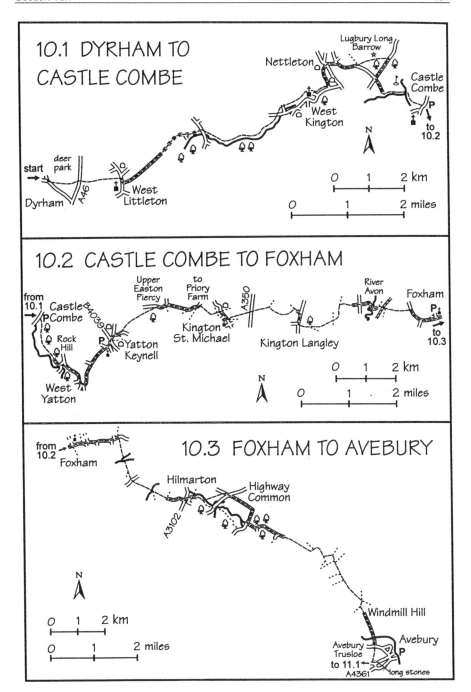

10.1 DYRHAM TO CASTLE COMBE

Lugbury Long Barrow

Nettleton

Castle Combe

West Kington

N

start

deer park

Dyrham

A46

West Littleton

to 10.2

0   1   2 km

0   1   2 miles

10.2 CASTLE COMBE TO FOXHAM

from 10.1

Castle Combe

B4039

Rock Hill

Yatton Keynell

West Yatton

Upper Easton Piercy

to Priory Farm

Kington St. Michael

A350

Kington Langley

River Avon

Foxham

to 10.3

N

0   1   2 km

0   1   2 miles

10.3 FOXHAM TO AVEBURY

from 10.2

Foxham

Hilmarton

Highway Common

A3102

Windmill Hill

Avebury

Avebury Trusloe

to 11.1

A4361

long stones

N

0   1   2 km

0   1   2 miles

field on the right, where the path continues. Follow it until it comes out – by way of a very attractive set of steps in a curved wall – next to the very busy A46 link road to the M4. Cross the road carefully to the footpath sign immediately opposite.

Take the footpath across the field to West Littleton. At the time of walking, the direction was indicated by flattened earth, but the path goes straight across the middle. On reaching the second field, a row of trees and church spire on the skyline ahead show the direction to West Littleton. Cross the second field and then a stone stile into the third field. The footpath is not visible, but aim for the point where two walls meet. Back on a visible path, make for the point in the wall where there is a gap in the middle. Cross the gap and then a wooden stile with a yellow arrow. The route climbs a slope alongside a hedge to the right. There are good views from the top of the hill of a farmhouse and distant hills.

Cross a ladder stile and then go through a gate into a pasture field. Aim for the small gate opposite. This leads to a hollow track lined by stone walls which runs past a garden with a tennis court. The church's spire is an unusual one and surmounted by a cockerel above four balls. A gap in the stone wall leads to the graveyard. The path shortly comes out in West Littleton, onto a road and facing a telephone box.

Turn right and follow the road around until reaching a lane leading off to the left after a letter box. Take the lane, which soon turns into a track of yellow, stony earth. Pass a fortified barn. The route follows a long, open and unbroken trackway for almost two miles. The route is edged by drystone walling and the views are superb. There are pheasants and their feeding stations at points adjacent to the path, and it will be unusual not to startle a few of these noisy birds.

After a mile and a half a large farmhouse comes into view on the right above the track. Walk past the entrance to this, take the metalled path bearing left and follow it downhill. The route now approaches the Broadmead Brook. It is possible to pick up the footpath which follows it here, but it is simpler to follow the metalled track to the point 200 metres ahead where it comes out on a small, unclassified road. Turn right downhill and cross the road where the green sign for the Broadmead Brook footpath points to entry to the field below the road. Take the ladder stile (yellow arrow) down into the field. Take a look back at the stone reinforcements supporting the road wall.

The route follows the Broadmead Brook footpath. Go through an iron gate, you can hear a rush of water on the right hand side. Pass through a field walking alongside the stream. The route continues for over a mile through fine meadow and pasture. At the time of walking there were ewes and tups sharing the field and hillside. The tups can be very protective of their territory and ewes so give them space.

The footpath comes out at the edge of the village of West Kington and cottages can been seen on the hillside to the left. The path goes through an iron gate then passes along a lane by the gardens of the cottages for 200 metres before reaching a metalled, unclassified road. The route does not go into the village so turn right up the hill – signed Drifton Hill higher up the lane – for about

200 metres, until reaching a signed bridleway on the right, just after the yellow sand bunker.

Follow this attractive bridleway, it has good views over the valley as it runs to the right above the road. The bridleway then becomes a narrow path along the edge of a ploughed field. Come to the end of the bridleway and cross a small lane then take the footpath sign ahead This path becomes a proper bridleway again. Walk straight ahead, through some wooden gates then a large field. Some houses are visible to the right. Follow the path around, getting glimpses of the village church tower to the right plus some farm buildings. When reaching a point where there are three gates close together, take the second gate (wooden) to visit the church of West Kington. As this is the halfway point, it is a good place to take a break. To reach the church, cross a small field with a drystone wall. Go through a wooden gate to the church car park.

From the car park, turn right along a track through the stud farm, passing horses and stables on both sides. Walk straight on. Follow the track around. It will veer right towards the road. Go through a gate (sign pointing back to the church). Come out to a small, lodge-type house on the left. Go left onto the metalled lane and follow it around to the left for 400 metres to the sign for Nettleton village. Then take the first turning left.

(It is possible to reach this same point on footpaths through the field by avoiding the gate to the church, then taking the third gate and following the footpath across the fields until it comes out at the same point in Nettleton Green).

Pass some houses, and follow the road as it bears right into Long Leaze and continue until you reach a crossroads. There is a public footpath opposite but there is also a rope barrier all around the field so do not take this. The route takes the Burton road for about 200 metres, until it turns to the left. Do not follow it any further. Instead, continue on an unsigned metalled road which starts straight (ignore footpath signs) then curves to the right past Manor Farm.

Follow the road to a right-angled bend where there are two aluminium gates. This is the route to Lugbury Long Barrow. Take the left-hand gate and pass through another gate in quick succession. Keep to the left of the stone wall and aim for the copse ahead. On reaching the copse go through hunting gates. Pass through the copse and out into a field. Lugbury Long Barrow is on the left – a raised grass mound, 16 metres (50ft) long and with a sarsen stone at the end.

The barrow was excavated in the 19th century. A central burial chamber revealed a single crouched skeleton with a short flint spear. Four additional chambers were found later containing 26 skeletons. It is an evocative site and standing beside the barrow leads the visitor to consider the kind of conflicts which left these remains. There is a cromlech at the eastern end of the barrow: two support stones and a fallen capstone. All three stones are similar to the sarsen stones found at Marlborough, some distance away. Leaving the long barrow, continue on the path eastwards to the edge of the field. The metalled road ahead is the Fosse Way.

(When considering this route we looked at three alternatives here. There is a path through the field opposite, but at the time of walking there was no stile and the gate was tied several times with knotted string. This was checked again in January 1998, and was still the same, although leaning less securely in its gap. To the right, about 200 metres down the road, past the copse on the left is the back entrance to Manor House Golf Club. It is possible – eventually – to pick up the Macmillan Way into Castle Coombe at the far side of the golf course, but although a footpath runs through the golf course, I do not think this is the place to access it. Therefore, the third option is the one chosen and described below.)

Coming out of the long barrow field, turn right on the Fosse Way and follow it for about half a mile. At the time of walking only one car came past, **but be alert and walk to face any possible oncoming traffic.** On the whole, because it is a Roman road, the visibility is good. On approaching the Fosse Way Farm Hotel and Restaurant, where tea shop refreshments are usually available, take the turning to the left down a steep, tree-lined lane. Follow this for about half a mile to the complex of attractive houses at the bottom of the hill, where you are greeted by a no parking or turning sign. Pass the houses and go through a remarkable wrought iron, high, swing gate with its own roof. Cross the Broadmead Brook and continue on the track as it swings around to cross the Bybrook by a beautiful stone bridge. Ornamental signs indicate the way ahead through the golf course. Do not go along the tarmac track alongside the brook. The path rises with the ground to join the Macmillan Way just as it enters some trees. Follow the signs to a stile to the right. Take this and follow the track where it runs past the high stone wall of the Manor House Hotel and offers views of the church. Turn right at the small bridge to take the track which passes under part of the hotel and comes out in the centre of Castle Coombe village at the Market Cross. The village, apart from being a tourist spot in season, has inns and a shop. We enjoyed the cream scones and cider in the Castle Inn.

Stage 2: Castle Coombe to Kingston St Michael – 6 miles

The whole of this section is evidently horse country. On the evidence of the many herds of cattle we met while walking it, this stage is also beef country. It also has a fine terrace walk.

Beginning at the market cross in Castle Coombe village, turn uphill and continue until reaching the museum, an isolated building about 500 metres out of the village. Immediately opposite is a steeply rising, stony bridleway through trees, signed Upper Castle Coombe. Take it and follow the deep path edged with rocky erosion until it comes out alongside first one, then a second barrier on the right hand side of the track. Go through the second right-hand barrier. You are entering a very attractive conservation area and the ledge path above the Bybrook Valley.

Both the Broadmead and Bybrook flow into the Wiltshire Avon, which we join later in the section. Continue for a mile along this beautiful woodland path, which is also part of the Macmillan Way, as it continues, sometimes in mixed woodland and sometimes in open hillside. Other small paths run into and from it but ignore these. Old stone gateposts are passed at various points. One highlight to watch out for is the Loch Ness Monster Tree – a fallen tree which has definitely had some face-lifting tree surgery. The path begins to descend (close to a sewage treatment unit) into Long Dean, where there is a cluster of attractive

Castle Coombe church

houses around a choice of lanes at the bottom. Go left past Rose Cottage for 150 metres and come out on a very quiet lane.

To continue, go right then take the lane up the steep hill, the trees of Chapel Wood on the right. Follow the lane for just over a mile to the hamlet of West Yatton. At the crossroads take the left-hand lane for Yatton Keynell. Take this lane for just over a mile. There is a good view of the valley and hills to the west.

On entering Yatton Keynell, there is a post office store at the road junction, and an inn (The Bell, which was closed when we passed through). Go right in the village, then take the first road right after 100 metres. Ignore the first signed footpath on the right and take Grove Lane, 50 metres later on the right. Follow the lane around past the duck pond – filled with raucous ducks which 'laugh' at pedestrians – and continue as it leaves the houses and becomes the track to Grove Farm. The first waymarked footpath runs straight across the fields to Kington St Michael. Our route, however, does not use this path but takes the next signed footpath 100 metres later on the left.

Take this and cross the stile and the ploughed field, making for the gap in the hedge. At the second field do the same. The third field is pasture at the time of writing, and full of feeding rabbits when walked at dusk. Keep to the hedge to the left of the field and cross the stile into the next field. Keep following this path across three more fields until it comes out across a field and on to the narrow lane to Easton Piercy. Go right and follow the lane around, ignoring all footpath signs, until a left fork signed to Priory Farm. Take this fork and come out in front of the farm after 500 metres. There is a good view of the area from here. There are indications of its previous importance too. The farm is on what was once priory land, and there is the site of a medieval village about a quarter of a mile to the north-west. Whatever the past significance of this village, both Kington St Michael and Kington Langley (long ley) are spread over a large area and possess churches and farms of some substance.

At Priory Farm, facing south-east is a signed footpath to Kington St Michael church. Take this downhill across the field and cross over the small footbridge. Pass through a tiny copse and aim to the right of the football goalpost as you climb the small hill, going towards some grey houses. Cross Grove Lane to the footpath sign and open (if you can) the aluminium gate into the fields. The path goes along the backs of village houses and almshouses by means of stiles and gates to the imposing Church of St Michael and All Angels in the middle of the village. This is a good point to break the journey. There is a shop and inn here (The Jolly Huntsman).

Stage 3: Kington St Michael Church to Foxham Church – 6 miles

This is a relatively straightforward walk across fields and bridleways. The bridleway from Avon Weir is a wide walking passage fit for a king. Leave the village by going to the right along the main road. At the end of the village, pass the last house – Hill House – and, **taking great care because of the traffic**, walk along the main road (**no pavement**) for about 30 metres. Cross to the footpath sign on the left and enter the field.

The way ahead is not clear. Go straight ahead to the gap in the hedge, then follow the right-hand hedge in the next field until level with the farm storage buildings. Then aim for the crest of the rising ground ahead. As you reach the crest the way ahead is clear – go to the wooden open field entrance with the public footpath sign.

Here the route approaches the A350 – the busy dual carriageway to Junction 17 of the M4. There is some B&B close by which is well-placed for the walking. Cross very carefully and head for the signed track directly opposite which is heading east and towards a hill. This is a reasonably pleasant, bridleway-type of path – rutted and hedged. It runs straight then tends around to the left. As it approaches the base of the hill, it swings more to the left and there is a fork, with a small path and old, green-painted, metal gate on your right. Take this gate and aim for the left hedge and gate gap into the left-hand field. This tends to be a cattle field and was very churned up when walked. Follow the right-hand hedge up and as it opens more to the right, go straight up to the stile 50 metres ahead. Continue straight on and up – less steeply now – to the next stile into a meadow-type field. Follow the path to a stile and out on the lane at Newlands Green in Kington Langley. You are on Day's Lane – a long lane. Turn right, not hard right into Ashes Lane, but middle right. Follow this lane, which passes the Hit and Miss Inn if you need a break. On coming out on Church Road, turn left and follow this to Lower Common and the B4122.

Opposite is the Great House, a Cheshire Home. The signed bridleway lies just to the right of it. Cross the road and enter the bridleway flanked by two stone gateposts. Pass a little lodge-type house. At the time of walking – just after the storms of early January '98 – this boggy bridleway was deep in water draining off the crop field to its right. Mercifully, after 400 metres you leave it. There are two more stone gateposts and blue and yellow waymark arrows which point right to the next field. Go to your right and walk along the fenced left edge of the field, passing an ornamental pond in the adjacent gardens and some large pines. Pylons are to your right and they will be with you for most of this part of the walking towards Sutton Lane. Sidney's Wood is off to your right. Spirt Hill is in the far distance.

Here the path on the maps and the route on the land do not seem to agree. The bridleway on the map goes over to the right to the top corner of Sidney's Woods, and doubles back to Bull's Elms, the prominent group of trees to your left. On the ground the gaps in hedges and occasional track lines in fields suggest that the usual route is to follow these and the pylon line over to Bull's Elms on the left skyline. Aim to the right of Bull's Elms. Beyond Bull's Elms there is a farm storage building. The pylons are on your right. Take a line from the last pylon as you go to the right of Bull's Elms. Aim for a gap in the hedge, straight across the field. The path isn't obvious. As you proceed, Bull's Elms and storage building pass to your left.

At about 2 o' clock there is a stile between two trees in the hedge. Cross to the stile by the right of the two trees. It has a white waymark on it. Straight across, directly opposite, is another stile – white waymark arrow again. You come to what appears to my ignorant eyes to be a large warren, with about 20 or 30 holes in the ground. Cross the mini-estate of bunny holes to another way-marked stile and go over this into a roughly square-shaped pasture field with an aluminium gate to the right. (You leave the white waymarking now – that path goes off to a stile in the left corner of the field and towards Sutton Benger.) Cross to the first aluminium gate. There is an obvious line across the next field to another aluminium gate with adjacent wooden fencing but no waymarking. Cross the fencing to enter a bridleway to Sutton Lane. Walk along this pleasant bridleway, which passes under the pylon line and comes out on Sutton Lane, opposite Langley Burrell Farm. The signed bridleway to the weir, Avon and Foxham is straight ahead. The difficult part has been done. The next two miles or so to Foxham is straightforward and extremely pleasant walking.

Take the weir bridleway, passing the farm complex with its dark sheds on your right. Visitors to the weir and River Avon fishers use this bridleway so you may find the occasional car bumping its way along as far as the Avon. After this it is very peaceful. After half a mile you will hear and then see the River Avon. Both the river and then the weir are impressive and beautiful, marred only by the inevitable fly-tipper who seems only to see something lovely to want to spoil it. Cross the Avon Weir and continue along the bridleway as it curls around towards the railway bridge which carries the Great Western high speed trains.

Once under the railway bridge, the walking opens out into a mile of broad bridleway – over 6 metres wide for most of the way, and shaded in parts by the occasional high tree. There is no interruption along this part of the route. To complete it you pass over a stile and, as the bridleway eventually narrows, you come out at the west end of the attractive and meandering village of Foxham.

From Foxham West End to the village centre at the church and Foxham Arms, is about a mile along the very quiet tarmacked road. (As you go along it, about 200 metres after leaving the bridleway, on your left is a footpath sign across a debris-covered field. This footpath exists on the map but I failed to find it. It is not significantly shorter, and, as far as I can see, is not marked at the other end, although another public footpath on the Dauntsey road, which goes over to Christain Malford, is signed and well-marked).

For ease and simplicity, follow the Foxham road, which is very quiet, until it comes out at Foxham church and the Foxham Arms. This is a good place to rest, look around, and get refreshment before the next part of the route over to Spirt Hill, where no refreshment is available, and on to Hilmarton, which has a pub and accommodation.

Stage 4: Foxham Church to Highway Hill – 6 miles

This route uses footpaths across fields, crosses two small valleys and climbs on to Spirt Hill, which rises between them. It is very atmospheric. From the church, go left along the village lane with common land edging it for half a mile. The land begins to rise. You pass the footpath to Foxham Locks. The handsome hill with Melsome and Avon Grove Woods is on your right. Follow the lane past Stockham Marsh Farm on the left, and then Godsell Farm entrance and cottages on the right. On cresting the rise in the road, you will see a footpath sign to the left into a tempting field. Ignore it and take the bridleway sign to the right.

Take the path downhill for 100 metres, across the crop field to a small wooden gate. The handle is hard to find. Pushing works best. There is a clear path on the good left margin of the next field. Keep to the left hedge. The way through the next fields is separated from the rest of the field by posts and electric wire which keeps stock areas clear. Go to the next gate. Cross the flat field, which has drainage equipment on it, to a metal gate. Stockham Marsh Farm is on your right.

Here, there are three tracks. Take the one more or less straight ahead – currently there are arrows, perhaps home-made, indicating the route. Moving between two lines of wire and fence posts, you are coming under the lee of Spirt Hill. Cross the first of three drainage brooks and come to a large, rusty gate. Carry on to the next drainage brook and a hunting gate. You are at the foot of the hill and it is very attractive here. Go through a new hunting gate. You are now climbing. At the next field entrance there is a hunting gate, a white arrow waymark and a 'Beware of the Bull' sign. This is the difficult part!

The path curves to the right, but this is not the route. Head for the thicket. It is full of low-hanging, small trees, more 'Beware' signs and notices about electrified fences. Other walkers have made a route which keeps to the far right of

the thicket and comes out in the right corner of the field above. The correct way
– if you can find it – aims at about 10 o' clock through the thicket to come out at
the stile with a white waymark arrow. Cross this with some difficulty into the
large crop field above. The route goes straight across this field to the gate-gap in
the hedge, then to the next and last field. Continue straight across this last field.
A gate opposite, just to the right of the leylandii garden hedge, leads on to the
lane through Spirt Hill.

Spirt Hill has been a feature on the horizon for some time and is an interesting place – it seems quiet and rarely visited. Our route takes the waymarked
path directly opposite, which will take us on a problem-free route to Hilmarton.

Go into the waymarked track to the right of Leekshedge Farm. There is a
stile and a white double waymark. Take the fairly obvious path across the field
to the aluminium fence and the waymarked stile next to it. These stiles are a bit
overgrown at the time of writing. Continue, with the hedge on the right, to the
next stile, then, in the same way, through the next field and to the third stile.
Cross right into a field. You are moving downhill. The line of direction is very
clear. There is woodland a quarter of a mile to your right, and across the valley
bottom you are aiming for the conspicuous farm building (fairly new or being
restored), which is clearly opposite on the rising hillside. Hilmarton church is
on the skyline immediately ahead and the Windmill Hill plateau beyond.

Go down to the corner of the field, to the point where hedges converge at the
valley bottom. Pass through a small copse area and enter the large field towards
the farm building. There is a track leading off on the left, take this.

Follow the track through continuing on it as it rises and passes some farm
buildings, then private gardens to come out on the southern edge of Hilmarton,
by the main road through the village. Turn left and walk for 300 metres, passing
Manor House Farm. Turn right by the church into Church Road. There is a large
inn opposite which offers refreshment and accommodation. Pass the imposing
church then go left into a no through road. Pass some attractive old cottages. Ignore the bridleway to the left. The Celtic Way route goes straight on and into
Llammas Close past some new, small houses.

At the end of the close is a waymarked path. Cross the ivy-covered stile and
take the path passing some large pines on the right. You come to some poplars
on the left. Continue to a stile. Cross this into a field and follow the left margin.
On the left, after 200 metres, is an impressive new wooden footbridge. Cross
this and enter some woodland. The path is currently well cleared. You pass
through a tunnel of trees for 300 metres before coming out at the corner of an
enormous field.

This was apparently two fields, now merged. Your landmarks for the route
across this huge field are the two tall, conspicuous trees ahead. Walk across the
field – currently seeded grass – aiming for the centre of these two trees. The
field abuts the Highway road, although you cannot see that yet. When reaching
the trees you will see the far corner of the field. Aim for this. There are no
hedges or stiles remaining at the corner. (It looks as if a land-change programme
of some sort is going on here. Further back down the road is an attractive old

farm complex, currently being renovated by the North Wilts Conservation and
Urban Design department, so maybe they know what is happening.)
At the field's edge you meet a straggling crossroads. Go left then right across
the junction at 033 752, and take the open lane across Highway Common to
Highway. In just over a mile the road curves to the right, passing close to what
appears to have been the church at Highway when there was a busy travellers'
route over to Avebury. It now appears to be a private house. Opposite it – on
your left – is Highway Farm, and a signed path onto Highway Hill.

Stage 5: Highway Hill to Avebury – 6½ miles

The walking now leaves the lower farmland to follow a succession of bridleways to the plateau which has Windmill Hill on its southern flank. **You are
away from habitation for about four miles of this route, and it can be exposed
in stormy weather.**

Take the signed path to the left at Highway Farm and go past the farm buildings. Take the metalled track up Highway Hill. The track rises quickly. At a fork
take a concrete road bearing sharply left uphill and into the trees. There is no
confusion – the other option is clearly marked as a private road.

The track continues to rise quickly, and there is a small gorge in the woodland to your left. The track's surface **can be slippery** underfoot in wet weather.
The track becomes a bridleway between two metal fences and a low hedge.
There are views towards Cherhill, with its monument and white horse, on the
right. You will have them with you for much of this part of the walking. You
also pass a raised water tank in the field on your right.

On reaching a fork in the bridleways, ignore the one signed for Cherhill and
take the unsigned track to the left with views of the plateau ahead. The track
stays concrete underfoot for about 700 metres then becomes a bridleway. It
continues in a straight line alongside a hedge coming down off the hill. At a T-
junction of bridleways – there is a blue arrow marker – go left and follow for a
quarter of a mile along the rutted track, called Yatesbury Lane on the relevant
Pathfinder map.

Ignore a bridleway off to the right. Continue on Yatesbury Lane. There is a
straggling copse to your right for about half a mile. You are on this bridleway for
just over a mile altogether. Views are opening out and you come to two large
trees – sessile oaks – opposite a junction to the right. This junction is not very
clear so check you are at the correct point (074 741) by looking out for an old
wooden post on your right and, more visibly, check the oak trees on your left.
One of them, the one opposite the junction, has a small metal square marked
D16. It is also a pleasant place to sit for a break – good views, good trees.

Take the indistinct junction to the right and follow the rutted track for a
quarter of a mile, keeping the field's edge to your right. It leads to another junction. Follow this straight on. In places it forms an attractive tunnel of trees and
could be delightful in summer. You pass a gate and copses to the left. Continue
for nearly half a mile along the obvious bridle path and you come out at a junction of bridleways. Go right on a path which is rutted, it is open to the left and
has a hedge to the right. It bears left after 100 metres. Follow for another 200
metres to an overgrown bridleway to the right. Take this and follow until it

comes out on a yellowish earth trackway. There is waymarking at the next fork, where the yellow track goes right to Yatesbury. Ignore this and follow the white arrow (077 723) into a bridleway, which has fallen trees and undergrowth to negotiate at time of writing.

At the next junction of ways, turn into the bridleway through the gate. There is a copse on the left. Follow the bridleway between two fences. It is tree-lined and has new tree-planting towards its end. Windmill Hill is ahead. At a gate you have a choice. You can go left or right to pick up the path over Wind-

Avebury

mill Hill and to the tumulus on top, or go straight over the stile ahead to cut straight up the hillside.

The path to Avebury is to the right. Follow this to a junction of paths (083 724) facing Cherhill. Turn left and follow the bridleway up the hill. You will pass a stile to the summit. Carry on down the track towards Avebury Trusloe. It is open track for about a quarter of a mile, then becomes metalled. You have unrivalled views of Windmill Hill, the Cherhill Downs, and Avebury.

You are coming towards a farm. Before this there is a footpath through a field to the left directly to Avebury Trusloe, but at the time of writing this was very wet underfoot. Instead, you can continue on the metalled lane as it goes to the left towards the small village. There is B&B available here. From Avebury Trusloe to Avebury village and information complex is another mile. At the junction on Bray Street take the metalled lane to the left. After the village take a tarmacked path with white railings. Follow the path which will bring you out in the churchyard at Avebury. From here you can visit the Tourist Complex, with its shop and café with very wholesome food. The car park is adjacent. The Keiller Museum is well worth a visit – Alexander Keiller, from the marmalade family, bought several of the ancient sites in the area and had them excavated. The complex is well worth a visit, but the main reason for being here is the Stones of Avebury.

Various guidebooks including *The Greatest Stone Circles In The World* – by Michael Pitts (Stones Print) are available on the stones of Avebury, and they all stress that Avebury's Great Stone Circle is one of the most impressive in the world. There is the Great Circle – possibly built around 2500BC – and two other circles within the Great Circle. There are two stone rows (avenues) – Beckhampton and West Kennet – leading to it. At the end of the West Kennet avenue is the Sanctuary – stone and wood rings. Then, alone and utterly outlandish in this English landscape, is the inexplicable huge chalk mound of Silsbury Hill. A British pyramid or what? Compare it with other huge mound hills on the route at Glastonbury, Burrowbridge, and Brent Tor and the Mynde in Caerleon.

Looking Ahead: The walking now enters the heart of the Celtic Way route: megalithic sites. Colin Feltham has described a route from Avebury to Stonehenge which is no small achievement. His route to Stonehenge and then on the Glastonbury is a new experience for us, but the area must once have been one of the most travelled parts of Western Britain. The next section begins at Avebury, where this one ends.

Section Eleven
Megalithic Sites – Avebury to Cley Hill via Stonehenge

60 miles

Beckhampton Avenue, Avebury

Colin Feltham

Colin Feltham is a former senior manager in the NHS. A sportsman who is now restricted to golf and bowls he has, since retiring as a management consultant, taken up walking more extensively, and as a member of the Ramblers Association is keenly interested in keeping rights of way open.

Stages:

1. Avebury to Devizes – 10 miles
2. Devizes to The Lavingtons (Ridgeway) – 11 miles
3. Ridgeway/A30 Junction to Shrewton – 9 miles

4. Shrewton to Stonehenge – 4 miles

5. Stonehenge to Berwick St James – 4 miles

6. Berwick St James to Heytesbury – 12 miles

7. Heytesbury to Arn Hill, Warminster – 5½ miles

8. Arn Hill to Cley Hill – 4½ miles

Maps: Landrangers 173, 183, and 184

Highlights: Avebury, Silsbury Hill, Oldbury Castle, White Barrow, Winterbourne Stoke group of barrows, Wessex Ridgeway, Stonehenge, The Harrow Way, Yarnbury Camp, Scratchbury Camp, Battlesbury Camp, Arn Hill and Cley Hill.

Starting Point: The Red Lion, Avebury (102 699)

PublicTransport: The area is well served by buses. The Avebury to Devizes route is run by Thamesdown Transport – 01793 523700. Services from Devizes to Salisbury and Salisbury to Warminster are run by the Wilts and Dorset Bus Company, with special services to Stonehenge from Salisbury and Shrewton – 01722 336855. The Warminster to Frome service and that from Cley Hill to Warminster are operated by Badgerline – 01225 464446. Sailsbury is on the London – West Country rail route. Rail enquiries – 0117 929 4255.

Additional Information: Museums: Avebury, Devizes, Salisbury and Warminster.

Accommodation: There is plenty of B&B in the area and youth hostels at Salisbury – 01722 327572, Bath – 01225 465674 and Bristol – 01179221659.

Tourist Information: Avebury – 016 723 425, Devizes – 01380 729408, Salisbury – 01722 334956, Warminster – 01747 861211.

Introduction

This is generally easy walking, except on the hard military perimeter roads around Salisbury Plain and over the hill forts near Warminster. From Avebury to West Lavington the route initially follows the Wessex Ridgeway, first across the Vale of Pewsey, then up and around the north-west escarpment of the Salisbury Plain. The route then continues, going south-east down the gap between military ranges to Stonehenge. The direction turns west around the southern edge of the Plain to the distinctively separate hill forts near Warminster, and finally across the Wylye Valley to Cley Hill.

The landscape is generally open, with mainly arable farming land and wide, open spaces on Salisbury Plain, some of which are bleak and exclusively used for military training. However, within these are conservation areas, and the perimeter walks are often alive with an enormous variety of flora and fauna, thriving in the absence of agricultural pesticides.

Its main features are a proliferation of very old prehistoric sites from Old Stone Age (Palaeolithic) to New Stone Age (Neolithic) and Bronze Age. The focal point of this prehistoric area, and of the Celtic Way, is Stonehenge, and as four-ton blue stones from Pembrokeshire were used in the second phase of Stonehenge, it may also have been an early link for subsequent Celtic migration.

Stage 1: Avebury to Devizes – 10 miles

For this stage of the route you should use Landranger 173. Avebury has been a settlement from prehistoric to present times, with the current village situated within the major stone circle of (originally) 100 sarsen (sandstone from chalk areas) stones. At seven and a half hectares (18 acres), Avebury is the largest megalithic ceremonial monument in Europe. This small village, with its museum and Elizabethan manor, is at the centre of a collection of prehistoric sites within a two-mile radius. Windmill Hill is the largest (9 hectares, 21 acres) and best-known Neolithic earthwork of its kind in Britain. It is based on an early settlement in 3000BC. Silbury Hill is the largest earthwork raised by prehistoric man (approximately 2000BC) in Europe. Its base covers two and a quarter hectares ($5\frac{1}{4}$ acres), and it is 130 feet higher than the fields. West Kennet Long Barrow (2500BC) is a remarkable chambered tomb in which visitors can stand upright in a roofed passage. The Stone Avenue leads south-east from Avebury towards the Overton Hill Barrow Sanctuary (a linear cemetery of six round barrows, with associated bell and bowl barrows).

Leave the Red Lion (102 699) in a south-westerly direction down the village street, passing St James' Church. Just before the street stops, take a right turning before the house called The Forge. Go down a lane until a bridge is reached. Just before the bridge, look left for a view of Silbury Hill.

Cross the bridge over the River Kennet and take a left fork, going on through fields towards a thatched cottage. Go through the gate in front of the cottage, and walk up the small road from the cottage to the minor road. Turn right along the road, past the telephone box, and with Avebury Trusloe on the left. Continue along this road until a junction by some barns is reached.

At this point there is a Footpath/Ancient Monument signpost pointing up the road, and in that direction Windmill Hill can be seen (about a 30-minute walk away). At the junction turn left (south-west) along the track between the barns, and follow the track to the end of the field. On the left at the end of the field are the two longstones assumed to be the only remains of a western avenue from Avebury.

Turn right, around the White Gate, and proceed until the A4 is reached. At the A4, turn right up the footpath, on the right of this former major trunk road from London to Bath and Bristol. Continue until the milestone is reached (077 692). (It states 82 miles to London, 5 miles to Calne, 7 miles to Marlborough.) Cross the A4 with care, to the lay-by on the other side, and at the top of the lay-by follow a green track going up towards a copse of trees. Go on through the trees, and on emerging from them, continue along the earthwork ridge towards the monument pillar on the hill ahead. To the left in the valley below racehorse training gallops can be seen.

From the ridge aim for the barn on the side of the hill below the monument, and, in due course, turn left on to the track passing to the right of this barn, and go over the stile. At the next stile there is a National Trust (NT) sign for Cherhill Down and Oldbury Castle. Continue up the track until the Lansdowne Monument is reached, where there are extensive views to the north and west.

At the monument turn left (south) along the ramparts of Oldbury Castle,

keeping the lower fence to the right, and 70 metres before a stile turn right
through a gate. Head downhill until another gate is reached, with a sign marking the other side of the NT property. Go through the gate and downhill towards
a line of trees in the near distance. Just before the line of trees, go through a gate
and turn right up a Roman road towards twin communication towers on top of
Morgan's Hill. This old track goes around the right-hand shoulder of the hill,
and a notice on the third gate identifies Morgan's Hill as a nature reserve. The
track goes through a short, wooded section, and after this there is a further gate
into Morgan's Hill Nature Reserve as the track swings right. Go through this
gate, taking a marked pathway left up a gentle slope.

At the top of this pathway, there is a further gate going into the North Wiltshire Golf Course. Go through the gate and turn immediately left, going around
the course inside the fencing. When the fencing ends, **taking care**, follow the
white posts across the course towards the left-hand side of the clubhouse.

At 022 667, on reaching the road, cross over into a broad green track going
left of the clubhouse. Looking ahead, the line of the route goes up the hill towards the right-hand copse. To the right of this track there is Roundway Down,
the site of a Civil War battle in 1643. It was originally called Runaway Hill to denote the flight of the losing side. At the top of Roundway Hill there is an English
Heritage site on the left, and looking across this, the Vale of Pewsey can be seen
running in a south-westerly direction. To the south is the town of Devizes, and
the escarpment of Salisbury Plain is in the distance.

Continue down the road past the wood on the right until a road branches to
the right. Go up this road until a double gate and adjoining walkers' gap is
reached. At this point, if time is available (about 30 minutes), a detour up the
hill and along to Oliver's Castle, a hill fort, would offer excellent views to the
south-west.

Go through the walkers' gap (011 638) and down the pathway, passing by an
electricity pylon. Bear right across the next field to the far side, where there is a
minor road and a footpath signpost to the left. Go left around the road until another footpath sign on the right indicates a route into the field. Turn left in the
field along the pathway which follows a power line across the centre of the field
to a gateway. Follow the very obvious track bearing slightly right across the
next field towards some houses. At the housing estate road, cross straight over
and go down a pathway through an avenue of trees – called Quaker's Walk –
and go over the canal bridge.

The far side of the bridge (006 617) marks the end of this part of the walk.
Devizes can be reached by walking straight ahead into the centre of the town.
Devizes, founded after the Norman Conquest, has two Norman churches, many
interesting and historical buildings and the Museum of the Wiltshire Archaeological and Natural History Society.

Stage 2: Devizes to The Lavingtons (Ridgeway) – 11 miles

This route has been written with three possible stopping points to fit in with either accommodation or transport requirements. You will need Landrangers
173 and 184. From the Market Square in Devizes, go through the indoor market
and the car park behind. Turn left at the main road, and right into New Park

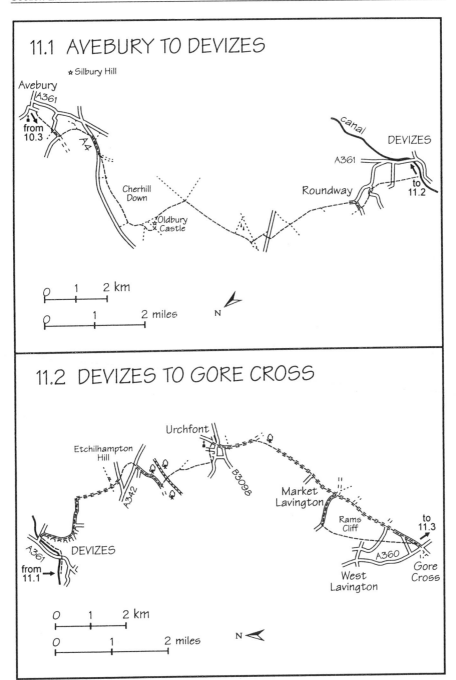

11.1 AVEBURY TO DEVIZES

11.2 DEVIZES TO GORE CROSS

Road, following this road until the canal is reached, just opposite Quaker's Walk. The start of the walk is along the Kennet and Avon towpath (006 617). Leave the canal bridge and walk eastward along the towpath until the third bridge, Coate Bridge, is reached. Go up to the road, and turn right. Continue along this road, which has been built since the latest OS revision, alongside the new housing estate. Go to the end of the road, past the turning right named The Patchway, and walk over the rough ground to meet the byway coming down the hill. Cross this byway, taking a left byway running eastward. Continue along this track, which goes up a small hill, until a byway running north to south is reached. Turn right southward. At this point there are good distant views of the North Wiltshire and Marlborough Down to the north-east. Directly ahead and southward is Etchilhampton Hill, and the Vale of Pewsey runs between them.

The byway continues southward up and around the right-hand shoulder of Etchilhampton Hill. When it reaches a minor road, cross this and go down the pathway to another road, ignoring a crossing pathway. Looking ahead from the far right to the far left there is a high escarpment which is the edge of Salisbury Plain, and the route will climb this escarpment.

When the pathway reaches the A342 (037 594), go straight across and down into the village of Stert. Take the first turning left, which is signposted to Fulloway Farm and Crookwood Mill Farm. As the first farm is passed, there is a good view of the edge of Stert village and church to the right. Continue along this road until a farm gate and cattle grid are reached, marked Crookwood Mill Farm. Just before this point, turn left and go through a small gate into a field. Walk across and down the middle of the field (south-east), passing through a small gap in the hedge and to cross the middle of the next field to a white stile. Cross the stile, go up through the wooded embankment, and climb the steps to the railway. **Taking care**, cross the railway track. Climb down the steps and cross over a stile at the edge of the wooded embankment.

From this stile take a route halfway down the field from the right-hand fence to the bottom left of the field. This route arrives at a double stile and footbridge through the hedge. From here continue straight across the next field. Near the far side turn right, picking up a farm road bearing right, until a gate is reached. Go over the gate and bear left to a stile. Cross the stile and walk up the field, keeping parallel with the farm road. Pass over a stile in the hedge by a power pole. Continue up the hill parallel with the farm road until the top of the field is reached. At this point go straight across the farm road via two stiles, and proceed up the next field to the far end, walking to the left of the right-hand gardens. Climb over the fence by the way markers. Turn right then left along the Urchfont village road. Bear left at the green, pass the Lamb Inn, then bear right at the duck pond. Continue until you reach the B3098.

Urchfont has two shops and two public houses, two B&Bs, a 600-year old church and a William and Mary manor house, once owned by the elder Pitt.

Turn right at the B3098 (041 569). After 150 metres, turn left by a lay-by to go up a track on the lower side of some houses, and start climbing up to the downs. After about half a mile, turn right off the track by some cattle pens, and go straight up the hill away from the track until a stile in a fence is reached.

From this stile go to another stile in line with the right-hand side of a copse. Climb over this stile and walk just to the right of these trees to meet the perimeter road, with 'Danger, Keep Out' signs on the far side. Large parts of the Salisbury Plain are **military ranges and training areas**, with public access either limited or banned. At this point the area ahead is a bleak training area, and the route will go south-westwards around the perimeter path. Generally, the Plain is an open area of gently rolling farmland, with good views, especially from the escarpments. The route ahead, where it follows perimeter roads, is **hard walking and can be noisy due to military exercises.**

Walk along the perimeter road, which follows the Ridgeway until an army vedette post at Lavington Hill is reached (024 534). From this vedette post there are three alternative routes, and each one will be routed to a common point where the Ridgeway meets the A360.

Option 1

Continue straight along the perimeter Ridgeway road, which is now tarmac, going downhill to meet the A360 (009 509). At this point Wilts and Dorset buses to and from Devizes, Shrewton and Salisbury are available.

Option 2

Turn right (north-west) at the vedette post and go straight down to the town of Market Lavington via White Street. Here there are shops, accommodation and buses (Badgerline) to and from Devizes. To continue the route go back up White Street. Just before the last houses on the left, turn right (before the last right-hand house) up a cemented road towards a storage depot, then turn right up a byway. This byway passes between fields, and just after the edge of the left-hand field of strip lynchets, goes into a wooded area. At this point the byway meets one coming up the hill from the right, which leads to West Lavington. This point is the T-junction referred to in Option 3 (012 527). To meet the Ridgeway/A360 junction, continue straight along the byway, which narrows at this point. This shortly meets a road coming up from West Lavington. Turn left, and after just over 100 metres, turn right along a byway which goes along the left-hand side of a wood. This byway goes along a wide strip between two fields to meet the point just after the farm buildings where the Ridgeway meets the A360 (009 509).

Option 3

From the T-junction (012 527) in the wooded area, turn right down to West Lavington, going straight across the first road junction. Continue down Rutts Lane until the main A360 is reached. This is at a point 100 metres south of the Ship Inn. Further north up the A360 there are a number of shops, inns and other accommodation. Wilts and Dorset buses to and from Devizes, Shrewton and Salisbury are also available. To continue the route to the Ridgeway/A36 junction, go back up Rutts Lane to the T-junction, turn right and proceed as in Option 2 to 009 509.

Stage 3: The Ridgeway/A30 Junction to Shrewton – 9 miles

For this stage you will need Landranger 184. From the Ridgeway/A360 junction, turn south towards Tilshead. Proceed for about 200 metres, then turn right along the Imber Range Pathway (IRP), signposted along a road. The IRP is a circular walk all around the Imber Range, which is closed to the general public. After a further 200 metres, go straight along the IRP, which leaves the road as it bends to the right. Go up this pathway to the first corner of the left-hand field, and turn left here as signposted, on a strip between two fields. At the end of the fields, where there are further signposts, carry straight on, parallel with the main road, crossing military roads going down to the main road. Just after a track going down to the road between a double line of bushes, the pathway goes up the hill and starts to meander towards the right-hand side of the long line of trees ahead.

At this point pick out a building partially hidden by the trees. Head for this, keeping a fenced field to the left and tumuli to the right. One of the tumuli is fenced and has star-shaped signs prohibiting digging. This military sign denotes sites of antiquity which should not be damaged in any way. Meeting the minor road, turn left and go downhill to meet the A360 into Tilshead.

At the western end of Tilshead village, just after the garage (031 479), there is a byway to the right which goes behind the Black Horse public house. It is also signposted as the Imber Range Path (IRP). When some small outbuildings are reached, the byway turns left. At this point turn right up the IRP – this is a straight pathway running parallel with the main road (A360).

At the brow of this first part of the pathway look right (south-west). A modern-looking village can be seen on the hill. This is an 'enemy village', used by the military for training purposes. At the end of the first large field there is a byway leading up from the main road. Turn right here, up the IRP towards the top of the hill, ignoring military roads crossing. You will reach the National Trust property – White Barrow. Cut through the right-hand corner of this property using the two stiles. Climb over the second stile and turn left to take a track which runs south-south-east, parallel with the main road.

Continue along this track, ignoring military roads crossing. After about two-thirds of a mile it meets a military road close to the main road. This is at the bottom of a hill that leads up to a farm building on the right-hand side of the main road. At this point go straight over the military road and take the track which goes diagonally up the hill, to the right, and away from the main road and farm building. At the top of the hill there is a pathway crossing away from the 'enemy village', and going towards (ESE) a small communication tower. Turn left here. When a partly-fenced field is reached, go straight on, passing the 'No Entry To Military Vehicles' sign. Head for a clump of fir trees in the distance.

This track leads to the main road. Cross over the road and turn right, walking down the left-hand grass verge for 200 metres until a road off to the left is reached. Turn left into this road, and after a few metres turn right, down a track. This leads down into the north end of Shrewton village.

At the bottom end of this road, in the village, cross over a stream and turn right on to the road from Orcheston. Then turn right again at the George Inn, and continue down through the village until the main A360 is reached by the

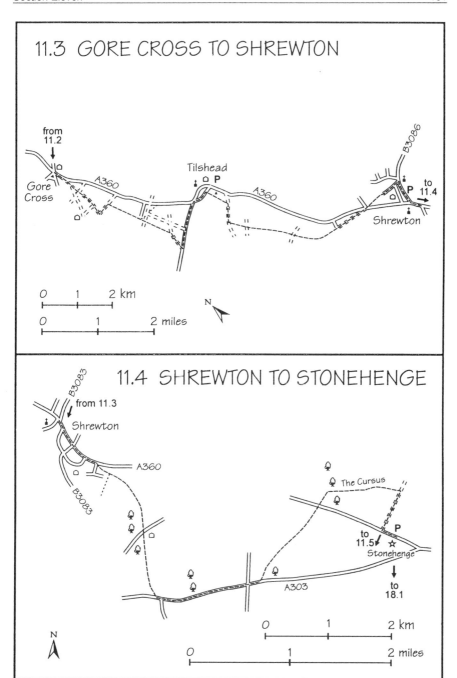

11.3 GORE CROSS TO SHREWTON

from
11.2

Gore
Cross

A360

Tilshead

A360

Shrewton

B3086

to
11.4

0   1   2 km

0   1   2 miles

N

11.4 SHREWTON TO STONEHENGE

B3083

from 11.3

Shrewton

A360

B3083

The Cursus

P

to
11.5
Stonehenge

to
18.1

A303

0   1   2 km

0   1   2 miles

N

Catherine Wheel public house (068 438). Shrewton village is large, has a number of public houses, some with accommodation, other guest houses, a post office and mini stores. There are buses to and from Salisbury and Stonehenge.

Stage 4: Shrewton to Stonehenge – 4 miles

Continue to use Landranger 184 for this stage. From the Catherine Wheel public house (068 438), turn left along the A360, pass the 30 mph de-limit and continue down past the Rolleston road. About two thirds of the way up the next hill, turn right into the rough road, and immediately bear left along the bridleway. After 150 metres, where the bridleway turns right, turn left along a footpath. After a further 200 metres, go through a gate into a field. Bear left up the side of the field, and then follow the field fence downhill. At the bottom end of the field, go straight on through the gate and diagonally up the right-hand shoulder of the hill, going to the right of a number of tumuli surrounded by a shallow ditch.

Proceed around the hill and leave the field by the bottom right-hand corner, near some farm buildings. Go through the gate and farm buildings with the lowest building to the right. Continue along the track running in a southerly direction, which then goes uphill to the A303 (085 412).

Turn left at the A303, going eastward. Unfortunately – at the moment – there is no reasonable alternative to walking for a mile along the grass verges to this busy highway. If English Heritage's plans to re-route or close the A303 and make Stonehenge and its approach the show-piece of Europe go ahead, then this point in the route will alter completely.

Continue along the A303, past the A360 roundabout. Just beyond the roundabout, at the start of a lay-by, there is a National Trust pathway into the wood. Cross the stile and follow this footpath to the other side of the wood where there is a NT information board describing the group of barrows just in front. This is the Winterbourne Stoke group of barrows. They are Neolithic and Bronze Age, and are considered the best in Wessex, containing examples of every type of prehistoric barrow encountered in this region (e.g. long, round, bowl, disc, saucer and pond). Some were being formed when the main part of Stonehenge was erected.

Walk to the right of the first two barrows and climb over the stile into the adjoining field on the right. The footpath follows the left-hand fence of this field in a north-easterly direction. The footpath eventually meets the A334. Looking right (east), a little way along this pathway there is the first intriguing view of Stonehenge.

Climb over a stile (111 427), cross the road and climb over the stile on the other side. Follow the NT footpath through the wood. On emerging from the wood, cross the stile and walk to a small tumulus on the left. At this tumulus there is a NT information board describing The Circus – twin, parallel banks, 110 metres apart and stretching for one and a quarter miles west to east. They were constructed approximately 3000BC, and their purpose was thought to be ceremonial.

Walk up The Circus, keeping to the right, to enjoy further, more dramatic

Stonehenge

views of Stonehenge. Halfway along The Circus there is a byway, turn right here and walk to the Stonehenge car park (123 424). At the top of the car park is the entrance to the English Heritage-managed site of Stonehenge. Members of English Heritage or the National Trust have free entry to the site.

Stonehenge has become one of the most famous prehistoric monuments in Europe, and the most visited in Britain. Most visitors will be aware of this, and the image of a rugged, heavy temple rising from an open site miles from anything else is enduring. However, on approaching the site, especially by foot, many Megalithic remains may have been seen, and closer examination is likely to give rise to marvel and wonder. Stonehenge ranks with the Egyptian pyramids as one of the greatest and most mysterious of all man-made structures: Why it was built, and how, are the questions most often asked. Was it a temple, or an astrological instrument? How were the stones transported or erected?

A Guide to the Prehistoric Remains in Britain, Vol 1: South and East by R. Wainwright describes nearly all the Megalithic sites mentioned in this route, including, of course, Stonehenge. It was built in three phases:

• 2200BC (approximately) – started with the heelstone

• 1700-1600BC (approximately) – erection of the 4-ton 'blue' stones brought from Pembrokeshire in Wales, with the axis of the monument pointing to sunrise on the longest day of the year

• 1600-1200BC (approximately) – rebuilding, using 'blue' stones, and sarsen stones weighing up to 45 tons from Marlborough Downs

The transport of the stones, the careful dressing, erection and fitting of the stones in the awesome second and third phases must have been carried out by powerful and well-organised societies, spanning different civilisations over many hundreds of years.

Stonehenge is surrounded by many sites, eight within two miles, each with many barrow cemeteries. For example, the Normanton site has twenty-four various bowl, bell, disc and saucer barrows. A further twenty-seven are at Winterbourne Stoke. The outlying sites are mainly administered by the National Trust, with English Heritage managing the Stonehenge site. A visit to the site is a must and the hand-held cassette guide provided is recommended.

Stage 5: Stonehenge to Berwick St James – 4 miles

Continuing to use Landranger 184, leave Stonehenge car park (123 424) by its lower west end on to a byway. Cross immediately over the A344 on to the continuation of the byway heading south-west. This is the route of the ancient Harrow Way.

The Harrow Way, or 'Hard Way', runs from the Kentish Coast near Dover, and crosses the Thames in Berkshire. It is one of the oldest roads in Britain and, like the Great Ridgeway, crosses the country East to West. It intermingles with the Ridgeway through Dorset, with both finishing near Axe in Devon. *Ancient Trackways of Wessex* by H.W. Timberley and E. Bell gives more information on this ancient route.

For our route, continue on the byway, which then crosses the A303 and is marked 'Old Sarum 7½ miles' on the other side. After a few hundred metres, there is a footpath on the left to Old Sarum. Ignore this, and continue along the byway in a south-westerly direction. Just past the Old Sarum footpath sign there is a National Trust Information Board describing the adjoining Bronze Age disc barrows on Normanton Down, which archaeologists have determined were for female burials.

At the top of the next hill the byway turns left through a 'No Right Of Way', and at this point the official footpath continues straight on up the track through a field. This track leads up to and through a wood on the brow of the hill. The path through the wood emerges on to a main road (A360) by an old garage (099 394).

Turn left southwards along the road and, by the water tower, cross over the road. Take a small road forking south-west from the main road, passing Druid's Lodge on the right. Keep on this estate road until just before it passes into estate buildings at the top of the hill. At this point carry on to the left of the buildings, following a track which goes around to the far side and drops down into the valley. Continue down the track until it eventually meets the road going into Berwick St James by the Wiltshire Girl Guides buildings. At the main road (B3083) turn right, northwards, up the High Street. Walk up past the church, and just before the bus stop on the left there is a signpost to Steeple Langford (072 393).

Berwick St James is on the regular Wilts and Dorset bus route from Salisbury to Devizes via Shrewton. It has a post office, shop and public house, appropriately called The Boot Inn – a welcome sight if timed with the limited opening hours, frustrating if not!

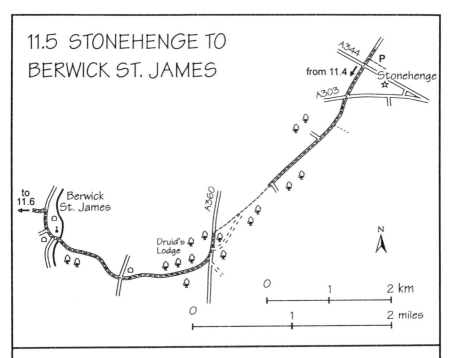

11.5 STONEHENGE TO BERWICK ST. JAMES

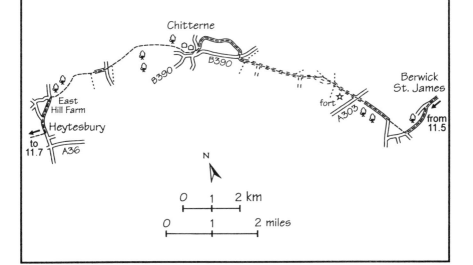

11.6 BERWICK ST. JAMES TO HEYTESBURY

Stage 6: Berwick St James to Near Heytesbury – 12 miles

Continue to use Landranger 184. Go up the rough road (072 393) towards Steeple Langford until it forks just before some farm buildings, and take the lefthand fork up the hill. A little further on the route, the path can be seen going up to two small towers on top of the hill. Just before the first tower (communication), turn right along a crossing byway, keeping the other tower (water) to the left. (Leave the Harrow Way at this point.) Follow the track heading north-west, aiming towards a barn on the edge of a wood near the top of the next hill. Pass the barn, and continue up the track to the A303. Just to the left, on the other side, can be seen the ramparts of Yarnbury Castle. Just before the A303 there is an old milestone which states in Roman numerals, '9 miles from Sarum and 27 miles from Bath'.

At 041 402 cross over the A303 with care, and continue along the byway, going to the right of Yarnbury Castle (167 metres/550ft high). Yarnbury Castle, only partially excavated in 1932, is an impressive hill fort. The first phase is an Early Iron Age enclosure of five hectares (12 acres) and, probably in the first century BC, was doubled in size. There are probable additions from the Roman period. (There is no direct access to the site.)

Carry along this bridleway heading north-west, crossing a bridleway and bearing slightly left. Avoid the track through the private land. The bridleway continues north-west along the right of a field which has 'Private Land, Keep Out' signs. On the right of this bridleway is an area marked with 'Active Airstrip' warning signs. Continue along the bridleway until it reaches the B390. Turn right, and after approximately 100 metres, cross over and turn down a farm road marked to Chitterne village only.

Looking right from this farm road there is a another good view of the modern-looking 'enemy' village built for military training. Just before Chitterne village there is a track marked 'Imber Range Path' (IRP). Cross the farm road, and turn left along this path. The IRP is a recently opened circular pathway around the Imber Range, which is a large military area from which the public are prohibited. The walk will now follow the IRP until the far side of Arn Hill.

On reaching a minor road, turn left down to the village. Turn left on reaching the village road, and just afterwards turn right down the main road (B390), walking adjacent to the stream (follow the sign to Codford). This route then reaches the King's Head (with some accommodation) at the southern end of the village.

Continue from the King's Head (990 438) up the B390. On the first bend there is, on the right hand side, a byway and IRP sign pointing up a track. Follow this track up the hill, crossing a farm road, through the left edge of a copse and towards the right-hand end of a line of trees. A little way past these trees the IRP bears slightly left along the right-hand side of a field with Penang signposts. In this field there are star-shaped signs on the tops of poles. These denote sites of antiquity, which the military must not damage in any way. Continue along the IRP, aiming for the storage tank on the top of the next hill. On reaching the storage tank, carry straight on the IRP, ignoring the byway to the left. There are earthworks just short of the tank, which on the left link to Knook Castle settlement.

On reaching the top of the hill, just past the storage tank, look straight ahead – through a gap in the hills across the valley can be seen the distinctive shape of Cley Hill, with its smaller hill on the right. To the right of these, the hill forts on the edge of the Salisbury Plain can be picked out. The walk travels along these (e.g. Battlesbury, Scratchbury, Arn) before dropping down into the head of the Wylye Valley north of Warminster, and making its way to Cley Hill.

Continue down the hill, ignoring the byway to the left, up over the next hill and halfway down the next, there is an IRP sign pointing diagonally left down the hill. A footpath will probably not be discernible, and the line to aim for is the left-hand end of a wood on the opposite hill, roughly south-west. At the left-hand corner of this wood, continue along the left side of the wood, and at the next corner of these trees aim left towards the left-hand side of the next line of trees. At this corner, turn right and walk along to the farm (East Hill). At the farm, turn left down the road (south-west), again following the IRP sign. The IRP follows the farm road down from East Hill Farm. The road eventually bears left, and at the end of the next field on the right there is an Imber Range Path sign on the road, pointing up through a line of trees.

This point (930 432) is a quarter of a mile from the main A360(T) which bypasses Heytesbury, and just before the entrance to Heytesbury House. This is the nearest point to Heytesbury village, where there is a regular Wilts and Dorset bus service between Salisbury and Warminster. Heytesbury is an interesting village with an old hospital dating from 1449. It was rebuilt in the 18th century and is still in use. There is a Round House (lock-up), and the Angel Inn dates back to the 13th century.

Stage 7: Near Heytesbury to Arn Hill, Warminster – 5½ miles

You will require Landrangers 184 and 183 for this stage. Take the pathway up between the trees from 930 432. On emerging from the trees by a stile, go up the right-hand side of the next hedge and, bearing slightly right, aim for the middle of the trees on the hill. As you reach the wood you will see a track running up through a gap in the wood to the other side. Before entering the wood, take a moment to look back. On the left is the previous route down from the Salisbury Plain and the Imber Range; to the right can be seen Heytesbury House and Heytesbury church.

Pass through the wood and on reaching the far side, bear slightly right across the field, aiming towards the top of the hill (Cotley Hill) and the stile to the right of the tumulus (Bronze Age barrow) at the top (636ft). At this point look north-west to view the route of the walk across a line of individual hill forts (Scratchbury, Battlesbury and Arn) which appear to protect the Salisbury Plain. Warminster nestles underneath the west of the far hills and to its left, and west-north-west from Cotley Hill, is the distinctive shape of Cley Hill arising from the valley (like a humpback whale).

After crossing the stile (920 433), head across the field in a north-westerly direction towards the stile on the far side. Cross this stile and proceed to the next corner of the right-hand field (50 metres), where there is a further IRP sign.

Follow its directions between the side of the right-hand field and the tumulus on the lower side of the path. At the next corner of the field, turn left to the next stile (50 metres). Cross the stile and bear slightly right along the footpath through the next field, heading towards the far side of the field where there is a stile. (located halfway along the hill ahead (Scratchbury). On crossing this next stile, turn right to follow a path which goes all around the hill to the far side, keeping to the lower side of the rampart.

This hill is Scratchbury Hill, or Camp ('Scratch' is an old west country word for 'Devil'). The hill (649ft), with the camp covering 15 hectares (37 acres), has four Bronze Age barrows, artefacts from which reside in Devizes Museum. It also has many Iron Age platforms cut into the north-west slope. It was vulnerable on the south-eastern side, and this weakness led to the fortification at Battlesbury.

On the stile you may note a Wessex Ridgeway sign. *The Wessex Ridgeway*, published by The Ramblers' Association, will tell you more about this 137-mile walk which runs south from Avebury to Lyme Regis on the Dorset/Devon border. It is largely coterminous with the Great Ridgeway walk which starts at Holme, near Hunstanton Norfolk, on the side of the Wash. This part of the Celtic Way follows the same route (in reverse) as the Wessex Ridgeway (and IRP) from near Heytesbury to Arn Hill.

At 911 445, having reached the far side of Scratchbury Hill (ignoring a path halfway around leading down the left-hand side of the field to the farm below), the route ahead can be seen dropping down the hill over a stile (signposted Warminster) to the farm road. It then goes up from the corner of this road (where a track goes to the right) and diagonally up the next hill (Middle Hill) to the right-hand side of a copse. Looking to the right of Middle Hill, strip lynchets can be seen – these are medieval, cultivated terraces formed during a period of acute land shortage. To the left of Middle Hill, below the copse, is the site of the medieval village of Middleton – although only an open space can be seen above Middleton Farm. Middle Hill (590ft) has a barrow on top.

On reaching the copse halfway up Middle Hill, carry on along the path around the right side of the copse and left-hand side (south-west) of the hill, keeping below the tumulus on top, eventually aiming down northwards towards two barns in the valley below. Across the valley is Battlesbury Hill, which also has strip lynchets on its lower side.

Continuing from 907 452, the pathway goes across the farm road (leading to the barns) and up Battlesbury Hill. Keeping to the right-hand side of two fields, cross another track between the fields, aiming towards the right-hand shoulder of the hill. At the top of the second field there is a double stile just below the lowest rampart. Cross the left-hand stile, and go up to the highest rampart and turn left (south-west) to go around the hill to its far side, keeping to the left-hand side of the fenced central grazing area, and above the copse. These hills are not cultivated, and mainly used only for grazing. This encourages wildlife, especially skylarks etc. The above copse is a favourite nesting place for buzzards.

Battlesbury Hill or Camp (682 feet, with a central camp of 10 hectares/24

11.7 HEYTESBURY TO ARN HILL

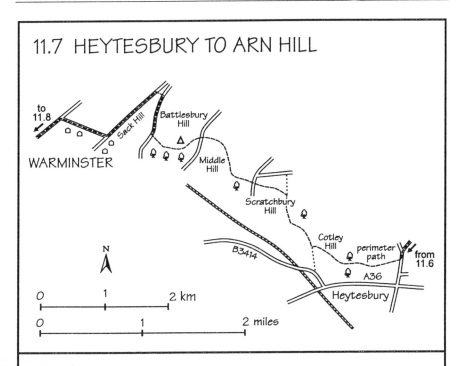

11.8 ARN HILL TO CLEY HILL

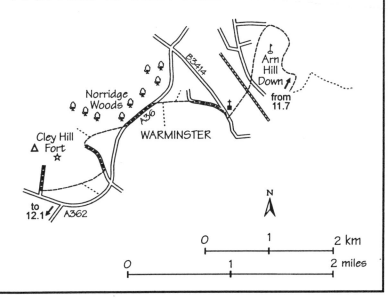

acres) dominates the Wylye Valley, and is one of the finest examples of an Iron Age hill fort in England. It has double ramparts, except on the west side where it has three ramparts. It was built over an earlier occupation site, and is thought to be one of the British 'oppido' stormed by the Roman General Vespasian during the conquest of Wessex. A 'massacre' cemetery was discovered outside the western entrance, and may relate to this event. A refuge during times of stress, it was also a market and meeting place both during the Iron Age and early Saxon periods. Artefacts can be found in Devizes Museum.

Continue around the hill, crossing the stile at the end of the copse. At this point, Arn Hill appears, with its communications tower, behind the golf clubhouse. Down below in the valley is the School of Infantry barracks. The route ahead passes through these barracks to the lower parts of Arn Hill. To the left of, and before Arn Hill (but not on the route), is a small hill, Cop Heap (550 feet), with a Bronze Age burial mound on top. Further left in a westerly direction is Cley Hill.

At the far north corner of Battlesbury Hill there is a farm track from the top of the hill passing through a gap in the ramparts. Turn left here, following the farm track for 100 metres, then bear left down the pathway to the corner of the field, to a stile and IRP signpost. Cross the stile and follow the footpath sign direction around the left-hand side of the field (any unusual smells here probably emanate from the sewage works below) until an underground reservoir, surrounded by a high fence, is reached.

At 897 462 turn left, cross a stile and go down to the main road. Turn left down this road, which runs through the army site. Continue along this road, ignoring any side roads until St Giles Church is reached. Turn right just before the church, and follow the road until the T-junction at the end. At this junction, turn left along the road in the direction of the IRP sign. Walk along this road towards a pair of cottages on a corner on the right. Just past these cottages is a road running up to West Wilts Golf Club and course. There is an IRP sign here that appears to point up the golf course road, but in fact the IRP pathway runs immediately alongside the left-hand side of the garage to the left-hand cottage (878 458).

This is the nearest point to the centre of Warminster, which can be reached in 20 or 30 minutes by either walking down the hill away from the golf club, or taking the footpath on the left just before the cottages, which goes south of Cop Heap and into the centre of town.

Warminster lies at the head of the Wylye Valley, has had a long association with the army and was an important stopping place for stage coaches en route to London, Bristol, Poole and Southampton. Some of the Market Place hotels are former coaching inns, with the Old Bell retaining its colonnaded front. According to Defoe, Warminster was the greatest market for wheat in England, and many houses date back 200 years or more. There is a large free car park which has the new Tourist Information Office and the new library on its Market Street side. Silver Street is the main location for antique shops.

Stage 8: Arn Hill to Cley Hill – 4½ miles

For this stage you will continue to use Landranger 183. From 878 458 follow the

IRP sign (not up the road to the Golf Club) immediately left of the garage (to the left of the two semi-detached cottages). The initial route of this part of the walk goes around three sides of the West Wilts golf course, which covers all of the top of Arn Hill and most of its ancient sites.

Arn Hill, height over 675 feet, has Bronze and Iron Age burial mounds with three types of barrow – long, round and bowl – but some were destroyed in 1911 and 1912 in making the golf course. Artefacts are kept in Devizes Museum. Follow the footpath up and along the first side of the golf course, with the clubhouse to the left, until the corner of the golf course is reached by the sixth tee. At this point, looking east, the Battlesbury and Scratchbury hills can be seen, and to the north-east lies the Imber Military Artillery Range, which is out of bounds to the public.

At this first corner, although the IRP continues north-east, turn left (northwest), following a bridleway sign along the outside of the golf course. At the next corner of the golf course, by an underground reservoir on the right, turn left (southwards) up and alongside the golf course, ignoring the track heading downhill. At this corner there is a tumulus lying underneath the greens and tees. Also, looking south-west, there is a good view of the distinctive Cley Hill. Continue along the third side of the golf course, keeping outside of the white-topped boundary posts, until an isolated stile is reached. The path now continues diagonally downhill in the direction of a small lake in the valley below.

Looking towards Cley Hill, the route will be down across the roads and railway on the edge of Warminster, and after the church, through fields to the A36 bypass. Once over the A36, go across the field to the south of the wood, and take a left-hand route around further fields to the bottom of Cley Hill.

Part-way down the hill, cross a stile and take the track bearing right downhill, ignoring any further tracks to the left, until the main road (A356) is reached (872 462). Cross over the road, turn left and walk along the pathway. Turn down a footpath which runs between houses numbered 20 and 19. This footpath continues over a railway footbridge and meets a residential road. Cross this, going straight down between the houses, taking the pathway at the lower left-hand corner around the houses. Keep left past the small electricity substation. Taking the next pathway to the right, go down to the road with open space on the other side.

On reaching the road, turn right for 30 metres and cross over, taking the pathway marked with a public footpath signpost through the open space. This path goes down through a line of trees, across the recreation ground to a footbridge on the far side. Just before the footbridge, there are seats to the right and left. Pass over the footbridge, going straight ahead along the path which goes past the left-hand side of the cemetery and church grounds. The church of St Denys The Minster originated in Saxon times. The present 14th-century building was extensively rebuilt in the 19th century. The yew tree in front is over 600 years old.

Turn right around the church grounds (869 455) and walk up the footpath alongside the main road going (north-west) out of Warminster. Just outside the 30 mph limit, there is on the left-hand side a house with the name Coldharbour.

Cross over the road by the footpath sign, and take the small road (Coldharbour Lane), up the right-hand side of this house. Walk up this lane, ignoring a turning to the left, and follow the signpost direction 'Cley Hill, 1¾miles'. Walk through the farm buildings, keeping left of the third building, where the lane turns into a grass track. Keep along this track until a stile on the right is reached. Do not cross the stile, but turn immediately left up a track between trees and bushes. At the end of this there is a small field, probably with no apparent footpath across it, however, the official footpath route is straight across to the corner of the copse 50 metres away. On reaching the copse, walk down the left-hand side, straight to the stile by the side of the A36 bypass. Cross the stile and turn left alongside the A36. About 70 metres down there is an information board with maps and information on the local area. After a further 100 metres, cross over the A36 to meet a small road emerging from the wood, and continue alongside the A36 in the direction of the signpost, '2½ miles Corsley'.

On reaching the lay-by (853 454), climb over the stile into an open field with the wood on the right and the bypass on the left. The official footpath line is alongside the road for about 100 metres westwards, then across the field to meet a farm track on the far side. However, if this is obstructed, continue along the side of the field adjacent to the bypass until the farm track from the right is reached by an underpass (849 448).

Do not go through the underpass, but continue straight up the farm road between the highway and a field. At the next corner of the field, cross over a stile into a field (there should be a signpost to Longleat at this point). Keep to the left-hand side of the field with Cley Hill on the right. When you reach the next corner of the field go through a gate and again, keep to the left-hand side of this field. Continue to the next corner of the field, where you cross over the stile. Pass behind some paddocks on the left-hand side of this next field until a stile is reached which leads down into a gully. Cross this stile and turn right up the gully between two lines of trees – a pleasant, cool walk on a hot day.

At the end of the gully a track runs across, going left to a car park by the main road, and right up to Cley Hill (838 443). To visit Cley Hill, turn right, going up to the top as directed by a National Trust Information Board situated part-way up the track. Afterwards, return to this point. There are good views all around from Cley Hill, which at 784 feet is the highest of the local hills. It is an Iron Age fort with two Bronze Age bowl barrows on the highest part. More recently, in the 1960s it became famous as a watch point for UFOs, with many (alleged) sightings.

Looking Ahead: The next section takes us to the Arthurian centre of the route. From Gaer Hill (Gare Hill on some maps), the Celtic Way runs for 40 miles to Glastonbury and then Cadbury Castle before offering the choice of the Exmoor or Hill Forts of Wessex options to move deeper into the West Country.

Section Twelve
The Arthurian Centre: Gaer Hill to Glastonbury and South Cadbury

49 miles

Glastonbury Tor

Richard Henderson

Richard Henderson lives in Bristol and was responsible for the walking section from Cley Hill to South Cadbury. He studied History as an undergraduate and later became a Town Planner. He now works with the Prince's Trust. His interest in the Dark Ages and the Arthurian legends dates back to the time when he took part in the big excavations at South Cadbury in the late 1960s.

Stages:
1. Cley Hill to Gaer Hill – 6 miles
2. Gaer Hill to Bruton – 9½ miles
3. Bruton to Glastonbury – 13½ miles
4. Glastonbury to South Cadbury – 20 miles

Maps: Landranger 183 – Yeovil and Frome
Highlights: Forest of Selwood, The Hard Way, Glastonbury Tor, well and Abbey, Cadbury Castle.
Starting Point: Cley Hill (839 449)
Additional Information: The Chalice Well Trust, Chilwell St., Glastonbury – 01458 831154
Public Transport: Rail Enquiries – 0117 929 4255, Badgerline Buses – 01225 464446, Wilts and Dorset Bus Company – 01722 336855 and Thamesdown Transport – 01793 523700.
Accommodation: B&B is abundant in the area. Youth Hostels: Street – 01458 442961, Salisbury – 01722 327572, Cheddar – 01934 742494.
Tourist Information: Glastonbury – 01485 832954, Street – Clark's Village – 01458 447384

Introduction

By the middle of the 6th century, the Saxons had established themselves over the chalk lands of Wessex, and after the battle of Dyrham in 577 AD they reached the Severn estuary. But west of the open chalk lands lay the Forest of Selwood, known to the British as the Coit Maur or great wood, which acted as a barrier to further Saxon expansion. Consequently, for a hundred years after Dyrham, British rule survived west of Selwood and south of the Bristol Wansdyke – this perhaps constructed after Dyrham to divide the Saxon from the British lands.

The path from Gaer Hill retraces the old 6th-century boundary between the emerging kingdom of Wessex and the British lands – the present boundary between Wiltshire and Somerset. It passes through the surviving woodland of the old forest and, on its way to the Isle of Avalon and the Somerset levels, descends into the valley of the Brue and then crosses the low hills between the Brue and Alham. During Roman times, people carved out for themselves great landed estates, and the memory of these is preserved in the villas that dot the countryside, such as the one near Ditcheat. Towards the end of the Empire, Roman and Celtic ways of looking at life seem to have coalesced – certainly as far as religious observance was concerned – as wealthy citizens built temples on what had been old Celtic sites at Lamyatt and South Cadbury. Such a way of life no doubt survived in some measure when the Empire came to an end.

Dominating the whole area is the great fortress of Cadbury, positioned just behind the Saxon frontier. In the middle of the old marshlands is the enigmatic cult centre of Glastonbury.

Stage 1: Cley Hill to Gaer Hill 780 402 – 6 miles

Descend from Cley Hill to the A362. Turn left, and then right at a roundabout. Proceed along the straight road ahead, which follows the line of an ancient trackway through the Forest of Selwood – now part of the Longleat estate.

After one and a half miles the road leaves the wood. Take the signed foot-

12.1 CLEY HILL TO GARE HILL

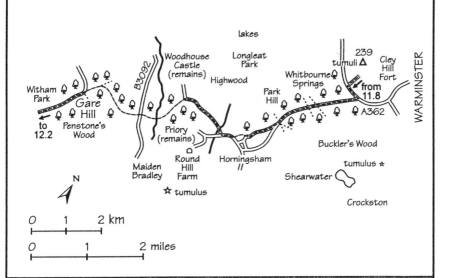

12.2 GARE HILL TO BRUTON

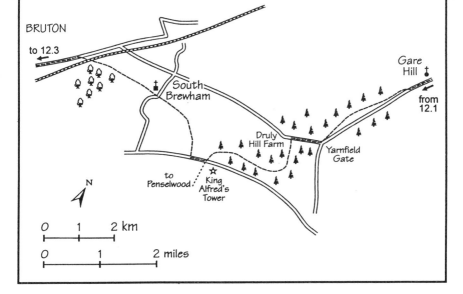

path right, which descends to a metalled lane. Follow the lane to a T-junction. Pass through the gate opposite and cross the field. Emerge onto a road and turn left along the road, which climbs sharply to the church at Horningsham. Turn right and follow the road around to the Bath Arms. Continue straight on. After three-quarters of a mile, where the road bends sharply to the right, take the signed footpath through woods. After about 200 metres, take the right fork in the track, to descend gently through forest. Eventually, emerge through a gate into a field.

Follow the track on the right of the field, passing a pond on the left. Follow a metalled lane straight ahead. When you reach a road, cross it and follow the signed footpath. After half a mile take the fork right. The path descends gently through the wood. At the next major fork, a path joins from the left. Carry straight on to Gaer Hill (Gare Hill on some maps).

Stage 2: Gaer Hill to Bruton 685 350 – 9½ miles

This is generally an easy, well-waymarked route along a ridge to Bruton, but paths through fields are not always obvious. Keep your eyes peeled for stiles and gates, and sometimes for **bulls in fields**. There are no facilities on the ridge, but you will find a pub at South Brewham (not open all day) plus pubs, cafés and shops at Bruton.

From Gaer Hill, take the road to South Brewham. Beyond some cottages take the public footpath signed to Witham Friary. Enter a wood and follow a footpath until it emerges onto a road behind a house at Yarnfield Gate. Take a right fork along the road towards South Brewham. The road soon descends sharply. Opposite Druly Hill Farm is a gate on the left leading to a well-waymarked track through a plantation, eventually emerging onto a metalled road.

Before turning right notice a footpath opposite which leads to the hill fort near Penselwood where, in AD658, Cenwalh of Wessex decisively defeated the Britons and established Saxon rule over all of Somerset east of the Parrett.

To visit Jack's Castle, a round barrow, and King Alfred's Tower, turn left uphill. King Alfred's Tower was constructed by Henry Hoare, creator of the Stourhead estate, in 1769, on a hill known as Kingsettle Hill. It is the supposed location of the Egbert Stone where, after his exile at Athelney amid the marshes along the River Parrett, King Alfred mustered forces from Wiltshire, Somerset, and Hampshire. After collecting his troops at the Egbert Stone, Alfred moved to Iley Oak near Warminster and thence to Edington near Westbury, where Guthrum the Danish leader was decisively defeated. The Danish threat to Wessex was removed.

To rejoin the Celtic Way retrace your steps down the road which winds off the ridge to the plain of the Brue. Pass Hilcombe Farm on the right. You are now travelling along The Hardway, an ancient trackway from Devon to Dover and the likely route of retreat of the Britons after the Battle of Penselwood. In Saxon times this was one of the Herepaths – military means of communication. This one would have been used by Alfred when advancing from Athelney on the Parrett to Egbert's stone.

About 100 metres beyond are farm buildings. Take the footpath to the right, signed to North Brewham. The path leads into a large field. Follow a track to the diagonally opposite corner of the field. Cross into the next field by the stile and pass by Holland Farm on your left. Join the road leading to South Brewham. Follow the road to a T-junction. Turn left and climb to the church. Pass the village hall and school house, then turn right over a stile. Cross the field to a gap in the hedge. Turn left and follow the hedge to a stile, and then cross a bridge over a brook. Follow the hedge to a large field. The footpath runs diagonally right across this field (which may be obstructed by planting), crossing a track from the left, and descends through pasture to a waymarked stile.

Cross the stile into a meadow. Cross the meadow, keeping woodland on your left and a manor house on your right. The path meets and then follows a railway line. Keep railway on your right until path passes under the railway. Follow path and then follow signpost left. From here, the footpath is well waymarked to Bruton.

Stage 3: Bruton to Glastonbury 500 390 – 13½ miles

The route runs over hills behind Bruton then down to the valley of the Alham. It then rises onto higher ground at Pennard Hill, before descending to the Somerset Levels beyond West Pennard. Waymarking and signposting are erratic, and the line of the footpath not always obvious. Pubs and shops at Ditcheat and West Pennard, a café at Evercreech Junction and a farm shop at Havyatt.

Leave Bruton by Coombe Lane and go left at a fork signposted to Evercreech. Continue to the signpost indicating a footpath on the right to Snakelake Hill and Greencombe Farm. Take this path through a field and enter a tree-lined lane which descends to a stream. Cross the stream and carry on straight across the next field for about 100 yards. Bear left and cross to a gate leading onto a metalled road. Turn right along the road and then cross into a field on the left at the next gate. The field gives access to a new dedicated bridleway (**not shown on OS maps**). The path descends to a stream and then bears right and climbs sharply to the gate giving access to Creech Hill (creech comes from cruc, the old Welsh word for hill).

Cross the road and take the signposted bridleway into the field opposite (at the time of writing it was planted with corn, but the farmer had left paths). Look for a gate at the edge of a wood on the left (the designated path proceeds straight ahead and then doubles back to this gate). Go through this gate into the next field. Turn right along the edge of a wood to the next gate, then bear right to the top of the ridge of Lamyatt Beacon.

The wood at Lamyatt Beacon is the site of a Roman temple (remains not visible). The hill to the north-west is the site of some kind of Iron Age enclosure 50 a small hill fort or cattle enclosure. There is a possibility of military use preserved in local stories of a battle on the hill. The temple site is dated to the end of the second century, and it survived until at least the early fifth century. It was dedicated to Mars and possibly Cernunnos, a Celtic horned god 'adopted' by the Romans. Excavators also found burials adjacent to the temple (almost entirely of female graves) dating from the late sixth to the early eighth century, indicating a continued sacred significance of site up to the Saxon conquest.

The temple may have had regional significance since there is some evidence that a special Roman road was built to link the site with the Fosse Way at

Pylle Hill through Lamyatt and Ditcheat. The road may have passed through the present south-west entrance to the wood and descended to Lamyatt along the path of the bridleway followed by the Celtic Way. Creech Hill has a local reputation of being haunted. Old stories speak of people seeing grey apparitions. This tradition is reflected in a tapestry in Lamyatt church.

The footpath to Lamyatt is well waymarked to a farm on the road. Here, turn right and descend into the village. At the T-junction in the village, turn right. After about 20 metres there is a gateway on the left with a public footpath sign. Enter the field and keep to the left, following the stream to a footbridge. Cross the stream and follow the well-waymarked route through fields to an old railway embankment.

Your path now follows the dead straight line of local parish boundaries – leading to speculation that they were following some straight linear feature – possibly a Roman road to Lamyatt Beacon. Look for an iron gate leading to a passage under the embankment. Pass under the embankment and then turn right. Cross the River Alham by a waymarked bridge, and cross the next field to the A371. Cross the road and follow the waymark over a stile into a field. Cross a bridge over a stream into the next field, and then follow the direction of a waymark to the road. Turn right along the road which leads to Ditcheat.

Follow the road around to the church. At the next junction take the road marked East Pennard and continue for about 500 yards to the end of the houses on the right. Enter the field on the right through a gate. The path climbs steeply up Ditcheat Hill. Go through the field gate and then diagonally left across the next field. Go through another gate and follow the field boundary on left (on edge of sharp slope) to a metalled road. If the path is blocked at this point, follow the boundary between field and road to the right until you come to an iron gate leading directly onto the road.

Turn left and continue to the junction with Fosse Way. Fosse Way is the Roman road from Newark to Illchester. Constructed in the first century, it marks the boundary at that time between areas fully absorbed into the Empire and those as yet to be conquered. We cross it in a later section of the walking, too.

Cross the Fosse Way – beware of restricted sight lines – and continue on East Pennard Road. Turn left at the next junction, then pass a cottage to the left. About 100 yards from the cottage a public footpath leads through a gate into a small enclosure. Go over the fence into a field and cross the field diagonally to the right. Descend the hill and cross a stream. Now climb a hill and bear right. There is a school ahead. Leave the field by a partly concealed access by a fence to the right, then turn right into East Pennard.

Follow the road through the village to the church. Take a turning to the left, passing the church on your left, and take the paved footpath which leads onto a lane. Turn right and then left onto the road. Follow this road until you reach steps into a field on the right, and a signpost marking a footpath on the right to Worthy Lane. Enter the field and cross to the next stile (waymarked), and then walk towards a large farm on the crest of Pennard Hill (Old Welsh for high hill).

At Pennard Hill Farm, join a metalled road and follow it left to a junction. Turn right and then left down a narrow, unmetalled lane. Turn left when the

12.3 BRUTON TO EAST PENNARD

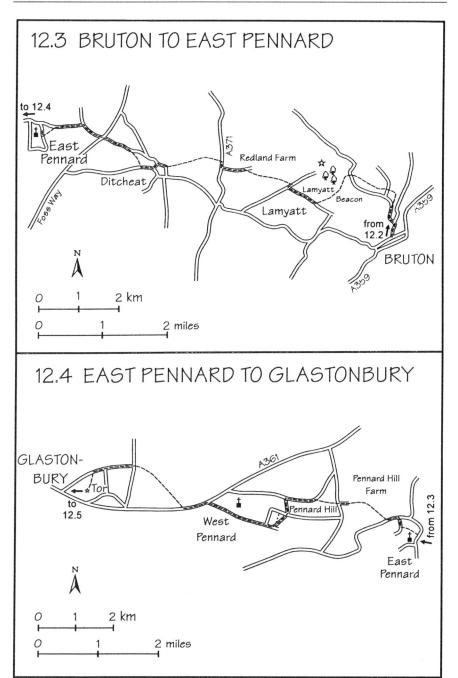

12.4 EAST PENNARD TO GLASTONBURY

lane meets a metalled road and left at the next junction. At the following junction turn right. Follow the road until it turns sharp right. The path is through a gate and downhill through the field. Bear right, across to the opposite corner, and pass a track on the right. Go through a second field to the road. Turn right and follow the road to West Pennard.

Continue through the village to the main Shepton to Glastonbury Road. On reaching it, turn left to Havyatt. Just beyond the road to Baltonsborough there is a signpost to a footpath to the right. Follow the path, emerging onto flat levels crisscrossed with electric fencing (insulated gateways are provided at necessary points). Cross to the stile to the right of an ancient earth bank – Ponters Ball; this embankment has a ditch on the east side, suggesting that if its purpose was defensive it was built by the inhabitants of Glastonbury to block access along the causeway from Shepton. It may have been built by the British inhabitants of Glastonbury in the post-Roman period as defensive work against the Saxons or other Britons. Other theories point to an Iron Age or even a medieval origin and a purpose of delineating the boundary of the abbey estates.

There is a fine prospect of the 'Isle of Avalon' and Glastonbury Tor. The present levels would have been underwater in the Dark Ages and medieval times. Havyatt may have been some kind of port since the name means 'harbour gate' and there are local stories that Ponters Ball was used by the Abbots of Glastonbury as a jetty.

Continue across a field to a concrete road. Continue diagonally left across the next field to a new waymarked stile. The diagonal route across the next field may be obstructed by planting, in which case cross the stile and turn left along the edge of the field, and then turn right on emerging into pasture. Cross to Norwood Park Farm. The path passes around north of the farm and emerges through the driveway of the house onto a lane. Cross the lane and ascend a steep lane over Stony Down, which leads to the foot of Glastonbury Tor.

Stage 4: Glastonbury to South Cadbury 628 252 – 20 miles

There are stiff climbs onto the Tor and the Poldens. Otherwise it is walking on the level through a mixture of arable and pastoral landscape. Waymarking is good through Glastonbury, variable elsewhere. Footpaths are occasionally obstructed by planting. Shops, hotels, pubs and restaurants are at Glastonbury and Street. There are pubs at Keinton Mandeville, Babcary, South Cadbury and Barton St David.

From the foot of the tor a steep, signposted path leads to the summit. From the top of the tor there is a fine prospect of the Somerset Levels. In prehistoric or Roman times one would have looked out on a vast expanse of water interrupted by occasional islands that now stand out as hills, such as the Poldens. On the top of the tor is the tower of St Michael – all that remains of a 13th-century church. The dedication to St Michael, the angel who fought and defeated the devil, suggests the tor was a pagan cult centre. Excavations on the tor have revealed fifth to seventh-century remains – possibly a Celtic hermitage.

By the Norman Conquest Glastonbury Abbey was second only to Westminster Abbey in wealth. Its fame rested on its claim to great antiquity, making it the oldest Christian foundation in Britain. In the Middle Ages evidence of this early monastery existed in the form of a famous wattle church that survived until the great abbey fire of 1184 (now the site of the Lady Chapel). Monks convinced the Norman historian, William of Malmesbury, that this definitely dated back to a Christian mission of AD166, and possibly to a mission sent out by the apostle Philip in the first century. Later, this first century mission came to be accepted as fact and identified with St Joseph of Arimathea, the man responsible for arranging Christ's burial.

Another of Glastonbury's claims was as a great centre of the Celtic Church before St Augustine's mission to Kent in AD597. Several scholars have argued for the existence of a monastery here earlier than the Saxon conquest. In post-Roman times Glastonbury lay close to the routes travelled by the Celtic saints between Ireland, South Wales, the British kingdom of Dumnonia and Brittany. The abbey also had close association with many of the pillars of Celtic Christianity – including St Patrick (claimed as the abbey's founder), St David, St Columba and St Brigid.

The Celtic connection brought with it tales of King Arthur and the holy grail. Arthur was originally the legendary British hero who led a rearguard action against the Saxons. His story became entwined around the legends of the grail – originally some Celtic pre-Christian symbol, later identified with the chalice of the Last Supper. And how could the chalice have reached Britain except through St Joseph of Arimathea? The Arthurian connection was confirmed with the 'discovery' in the Abbey grounds in 1191 of two bodies, said to be of Arthur and Guinevere. It was a Welshman, Gerald of Wales, who, in his account of the exhumation, made the connection between Glastonbury and the Isle of Avalon – the mystic isle of the dead of Welsh legends.

The vitality and inventiveness of Glastonbury legends lives on. Legends of Arthur and the grail have become enmeshed with speculation about ley lines, the Druids, and celestial zodiacs. So thirteen hundred years or more after the foundation of the abbey, Glastonbury still carries with it the atmosphere of a medieval pilgrimage centre – attracting to itself healers, practitioners of esoteric cults and 'new age' religion and traders in the exotic, as well as tourists coming for salvation or just to stare.

Take the path down the spine of the tor towards the town. Note the terraces on the hillside. These have been taken to be relics of Celtic or medieval farming, but one theory asserts that they comprise a man-made labyrinth cut out of the hillside some three thousand years ago as part of a penitential rite. Such labyrinths were found in ancient Egypt and Crete. Local tradition held that the tor is hollow and comprises the entrance to the underworld. The path descends to the road. Chalice Well and its peaceful gardens are on the right. Late tradition identifies Chalice Well as the spot where Joseph of Arimathea hid the grail. The spring flows through ironstone, which gives its waters a red tinge. In the 18th century it was famous for its healing qualities, particularly for asthma.

Turn left at the next junction, and at the next major junction go straight on. The road climbs to the summit of Wearyall Hill. A gate leads onto hillside. The Glastonbury Thorn is along a path to the left. Wearyall Hill is where St Joseph is supposed to have rested on his journey and stuck his staff into the ground,

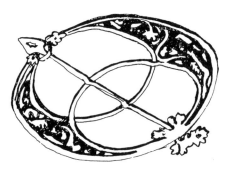

The Chalice Well symbol

whereupon it immediately burst into flower. The old thorn tree was cut down by the Puritans in the 17th century, but cuttings were taken. The present tree dates from the early 19th century. It flowers in early January. Looking west over the present industrial estate, by the Brue river are meadows once known as St Brides Fields because of the association of the local chapel with St Brigid. The area would have been natural landfall for pilgrims coming from Ireland. The chapel also features as the Chapel Adventurous in Arthurian legends.

Return to the road, turn right out of the gate, and descend the hill. Turn right at the junction and look for a waymarked entrance to fields on the left. Cross the fields and follow waymarks to an iron bridge over a weir. Half a mile downstream is Pomparles Bridge – the Arthurian Pons Perilis where Arthur, mortally wounded after the Battle of Cammlann, threw his sword into the water before being ferried across to Avalon.

After crossing the iron bridge turn right and walk along the river bank for about 400 metres. Turn left and cross the fields to a road. Turn right to follow the road to the church at Street, which has the air of a 19th-century industrial town, but has very ancient origins. Originally known as Lantakoy – the settlement of St Cai, an otherwise unknown Celtic saint – it is one of the few Somerset settlements that preserved a Celtic place name after the Saxon conquests. The circular churchyard is usually a sign of very early foundation, and possible pre-Christian religious use. In the middle ages the church was associated with St Gildas the Wise, the historian of Britain's decline and defeat, who is supposed to have retired from Glastonbury to found a church by a river nearby.

From the church follow the road past Strode College to Somerton Road. Turn left. After about three-quarters of a mile turn right along Portway. Look for the footpath sign on your left. Cross the fields to a lane. Turn right and then left. Continue along the road until you reach Middle Brooks. Turn right and continue for 400 metres to Gooselade on the left. Turn into the close, which leads to a path crossing a field. The path emerges onto a road. Turn right and then left along a path which climbs onto the Poldens.

At the top of the hill turn left. Proceed for slightly more than 400 metres and you will reach a crossroads. Take the narrow metalled lane immediately to your right. Pass Ivy Thorn Manor. Continue until the road turns sharp right into the Somerset Levels. At this point turn left, following the waymarking into a field. Turn right over a stile, and then left over the next waymarked stile on to a lane which leads to a metalled road that goes to the village of Dundon.

Go straight across the crossroads and follow the road around the village. The road passes around an Iron Age hill fort. After one mile turn right on to the

Somerton Road, and after about 300 metres turn left, following the footpath sign to Bunch Wood. The paths through Bunch Wood and Great Breach Wood are not waymarked. When the path enters the wood, follow the track straight ahead; it soon bears right and meets a track climbing from the right. Turn left and follow a track leading to a small clearing. Look for some wooden steps on the left which take the path up a steep incline. It emerges on a track running left-right. Turn right, and after 10 metres look to the left for steps entering the wood. Climb the steps to a track joining from the left. Turn right and soon join more steps, which take the path onto a wooded plateau. Turn right along the path, and after about 20 metres turn left along a grassy track. After 100 metres the track meets a slightly better defined forest track from the right. Turn left and keep on this track as it bears right, with other tracks joining from the left.

The track passes a marble obelisk commemorating the death of the son of a local rector in a shooting accident in the mid-19th century. About 300 metres past the monument the track crosses a substantial forest track, and after a further 400 metres the path leaves the wood and continues in a field along the wood's edge. When the corner of field is reached, turn left along the field boundary. The path passes farm building to emerge onto the Poldens Ridge road. Cross the road and enter a field through a white gate. The footpath crosses the field diagonally right to a white gate which is clearly visible. It may be obstructed by planting in summer, in which case turn right along the Poldens ridgeway and take the next road left, signed to Butleigh.

Where the path emerges onto Butleigh Road, cross over and follow the road marked to Higher Hill Farm. Follow the road down to a crossroads, where you turn right and walk along the road to a lodge gate. Take the track straight ahead to Kingsweston House and church. Cross a cattle grid and turn left off a roadway by farm buildings. There are cottages on the right. The footpath crosses a field, which may be obstructed by planting. The path meets a track from the right. Carry on along this track, which soon turns left and becomes overgrown but passable. Continue until the track emerges into a field. Cross the field diagonally left to join a track on the far side which leads down to Barton St David.

Turn right by the church. Just beyond the church is a track way to the right. Follow it to a stile and enter a meadow. Cross the meadow diagonally to the far corner. This path emerges onto a metalled road. Turn right here and follow the road to a T-junction at Keinton Mandeville.

Turn right and then immediately left to take a footpath signed to Coombe Lane. Follow the hedge left to the second gap. Then look right for a stile and footbridge leading over a ditch to the next field. Take this and follow the path to a road, then turn left. Follow the road past houses to its end, and then turn right under a railway bridge. Beyond the bridge follow a footpath signposted to the Fosse Way. Turn right at the end and go to the end of an overgrown track. Take the stile left into a field. Cross to the field gate opposite, then follow the hedge on the right to the edge of the field. Cross to the next field by a stile and follow the path to a gate diagonally opposite which leads onto Fosse Way.

Cross Fosse Way and follow the road to Babcary. Pass the church and turn right at the pub. After just over half a mile, take the road left leading to Little

Stuert House. To the left of the house is an entrance to a bridleway, which can be muddy. After one mile the bridleway is crossed by a track from the left. Turn right and follow the track for about 200 yards to where it enters a field. Look left for a small gap in the hedge, leading to a stile giving access to a field. Note the waymark arrow indicating the footpath along the edge of the field. Follow the field's edge round to the left to the field entrance (no gate) and cross into the next field. Carry straight on, following the field boundary on the left. to a concrete bridge over a ditch. Turn left – **do not cross the ditch.** At the next waymark point go straight on, joining a track which veers right. When the track turns right into the next field go straight on (follow the waymark). At the end of the field, turn right over a ditch and then left, following waymarking around the field's edges. Look out for a wooden bridge to the left which takes the path across the next field to a stile and bridge. Once over the bridge, turn left. After half a mile the path meets a trackway. Follow trackway to the A303.

Cross the **very busy** A303 to a signed footpath, which after three-quarters of a mile reaches Queen Camel. When the path emerges on to a narrow road, turn left. Cross the A359 and follow the marked footpath opposite to Western Bamflyde. Cross the field diagonally to your left. Cross into the next field and follow the field's boundary on the left. Cross a railway line and go through the next field to the road. Turn right and take the next right. At the next junction follow signs to Little Weston. Just beyond the next junction is a Leyland Trail sign to the left. Cadbury Castle is on the right. Follow the field boundary left and waymark signs to South Cadbury.

Cadbury Castle shows signs of occupation going back 4,500 years to Neolithic times. The huge hill fort was constructed about 600BC, and became a stronghold of the Durotriges who controlled Dorset and South Somerset. It fell to the Romans in AD70, after which it was abandoned but it may have contained a Roman temple from the third century. Re-fortified in the post-Roman period, it probably became the centre of British rule in this part of the Britain, guarding the southern flank of Selwood. It was probably abandoned for a time after the Saxon conquests, but reoccupied and substantially re-fortified by Ethelred the Unready, who may have minted coins here. John Leyland was told during his journey through Somerset in the 1540s that Cadbury was the site of King Arthur's Camelot. By the entrance to the fort is a well known as Arthur's Well.

Looking Ahead: One can argue a good case for a higher or lower route west from Somerset. The choice is yours: to go over the Somerset Levels to the Quantocks and Exmoor, or to go south to the countryside that was once the Kingdom of Wessex. Both routes end some way short of the Dartmoor section which follows them. However, the existence of well-signed walking routes such as the Two Moors Way and the South West Coast Path mean that the walking can be continuous. There are plans to have the walking line between the Axe crossing and Hound Tor ready for the summer of 1999. Details of the outline Celtic Way route, which runs behind to South-West coast over to Woodbury then through the low hills surrounding Dartmoor, can be found in Appendix 2.

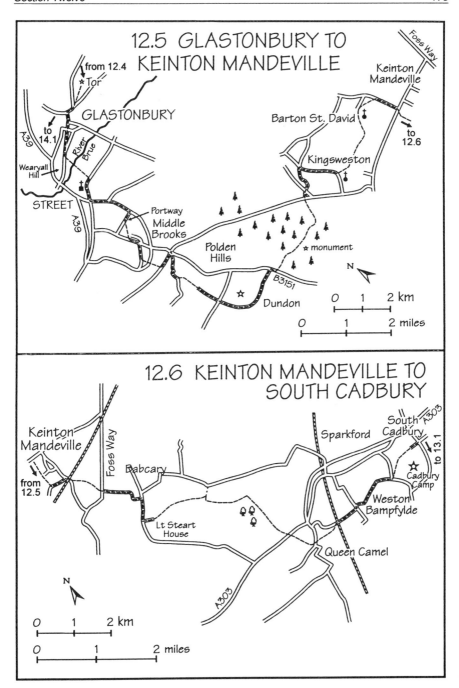

12.5 GLASTONBURY TO KEINTON MANDEVILLE

from 12.4

★ Tor

GLASTONBURY

to 14.1

A39

River Brue

Wearyall Hill

STREET

A39

Portway
Middle
Brooks

Polden
Hills

Dundon

B3151

Barton St. David

Kingsweston

Keinton Mandeville

Foss Way

to 12.6

★ monument

N

0   1   2 km

0   1   2 miles

12.6 KEINTON MANDEVILLE TO SOUTH CADBURY

Keinton
Mandeville

Foss Way

from 12.5

Babcary

Lt Steart
House

Sparkford

South
Cadbury

A303

to 13.1

☆ Cadbury
Camp

Weston
Bampfylde

Queen Camel

A303

N

0   1   2 km

0   1   2 miles

Section Thirteen
The Hill Forts of Wessex:
Cadbury Castle to the Axe Crossing
71 miles

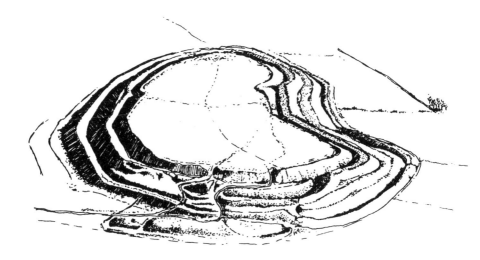

Maiden Castle, near Dorchester

David Williamson

As a water engineer in Somerset and Dorset for 30 years David Williamson got to know the landscape and geology well; the highways and byways were part of daily travelling and a knowledge of the history and the footpaths came exploring the two counties over that time and in the years since. After retirement he enjoyed the countryside even more when not involved in water supply development and emergency work overseas. Much of this is on behalf of Water Aid, to whom any royalties for this portion of the book will be donated.

Stages:

1. Cadbury to Sherborne – 7 miles
2. Sherborne to Cerne Abbas – 12½ miles
3. Cerne Abbas to Dorchester – 8 miles
4. Dorchester to Eggardon Hill – 14½ miles

5. Eggardon Hill to Pilsden Pen – 13 miles

6. Pilsdon Pen to the Axe Crossing – 16½ miles

Maps: Landrangers 183, 194 and 193. Pathfinder Sheets: ST 60/70, SY 60/70, ST 61/71, ST 62/72, ST 49/59, SY49/59, SY 29/39, SY 49/59 and ST 40/50. Outdoor Leisure 15 – Purbeck and Dorset.

Highlights: Cadbury Hill, the Beacon, the ridge path, Cerne Abbas Giant, Maiden Castle, Eggardon Hill, Lambert's Castle, Coney Castle, Pilsdon Pen and the coastal path.

Starting Point: South Cadbury Car Park (632 253).

Public Transport: Rail Enquiries – 0117 929 4255, Wilts and Dorset Bus Company – 01722 336855, Badgerline Buses – 01225 464446, Dorchester Coach Ways – 01305 262992, Dorchester Station – 01305 264423.

Additional Information: Almost all the villages along this section have pubs which will supply a meal, and the majority will offer accommodation. The route runs through the small towns of Sherborne and Dorchester, both having all facilities, through the village of Cerne Abbas and close by Beaminster, a cheerful small town. Once the coast is reached food and accommodation are plentiful. There are youth hostels at Beer – 01297 20296, Litton Cheney – 01308 482340.

Tourist Information: South Somerset – 01935 71279, West Dorset – 01305 267992

Introduction

The region generally known as Wessex, covering the areas of Wiltshire, Dorset and Somerset, has a concentration of hill forts, and all are worth a visit. The route takes in the Dorset area in five sections. From Cadbury Hill to the ancient town of Sherborne, then on to Cerne Abbas and its famous giant. The next section goes to Dorchester, with both Iron Age and Roman remains. From Dorchester we go along the ridges to Eggardon Hill, and finally through very rural Dorset to Pilsdon Pen.

An alternative route from Cadbury Hill to Ham Hill is waymarked as the Leland Trail, a route planned by the King's Geographer in 1547. From Ham Hill to Wayford, a few miles north of Pilsdon Pen, the route is waymarked as the Liberty Trail, which is based on the stories of people from the villages along the way who walked to Lyme Regis to join Monmouth for his uprising in 1685.

From Wayford the main route can be rejoined at Pilsdon Pen by following footpaths southwards through Drimpton.

Stage 1: Cadbury Castle to Sherborne – 7 miles

On this stage there are many splendid vantage points. As we leave Cadbury Castle and South Cadbury behind and go up on to the ridges the views are magnificent, particularly looking back to see the extent of the fort on Cadbury Hill. From the Beacon and Corton Hill there are views over much of South Somerset. Seven Wells Down is the source of the River Yeo, and as we follow the ridge of Poyntington Hill, the river follows the valley below. Poyntington and Oborne

Wessex fields

villages can be seen in the valley, and the Dorset hills towards the coast can be seen in the distance.

In Sherborne the information centre will provide all the details needed, ranging from leaflets on the town's wonderful history, to where to eat or stay. Sherborne is an old town, the abbey dates from AD705 and was rebuilt in the 12th and 15th centuries. The school alongside probably dates from as early as the abbey, but it certainly existed in the 11th century and had a royal charter in 1550. The old almshouses are situated by the entrance to the abbey. The castle which is now ruined was built in the 12th century and destroyed in the Civil War, but the present castle, on the other side of the river, was built by Sir Walter Raleigh in 1594 and is open to the public in the summer.

For this stage you will need to choose from the following maps: Landranger 183 or Pathfinder Sheets ST 61/71 and ST 62/72.

The road south from the village of South Cadbury passes the inn and church to a car park (632 253), a suitable start for the walk. Just after a small road joins from the left, follow the waymarked footpath over the stile on the left and across the field and stream. The path is marked as it runs straight along the side of the field before turning sharply to the right towards Whitcombe Mill. Pass through the farmyard and rejoin the road.

Turn left along the road and immediately turn left, walking up the hill. At the top, as the road levels out, double back on a footpath to the right and continue across the fields to the trig point on the Beacon. The views of Cadbury Hill and all around are quite magnificent. Turning back almost in the direction of

13.1 SOUTH CADBURY TO SHERBORNE

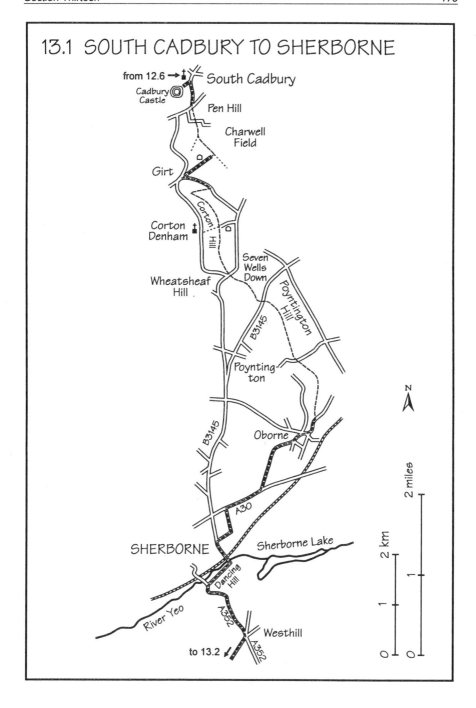

approach, follow the ridge footpath for over a mile, until you come out on a track. Turn right and go straight through the farmyard then follow the footpath alongside the hedge. This steadily descends until coming out on the road (640 218).

Turn left and shortly join another road bearing left up the hill. After about 80 metres, a bridleway is clearly marked on the right. Follow the signs across the fields and to a little bridge over the embryo River Yeo. Continue to the road. Cross straight over the Sherborne to Wincanton road (B 3145) in a no-man's land between the county signs for Somerset and Dorset, and follow the bridleway up the hillside on to the ridge. The footpath then follows the ridge for some two miles before coming out on a country lane. Continue along the lane for 400 metres, and then take a stoned track sharply to the right and go down into Oborne (655 187).

Turn left in the village, and then right to go past the church. Follow a track along the side of the hill to come out on the A30 at the edge of Sherborne. Here turn right and follow the main road until the sign to the town and information centre points us to the left. The town centre with all its amenities is only about half a mile away.

Stage 2: Sherborne to Cerne Abbas — 12½ miles

Leaving man's contribution to the townscape of Sherborne behind, the walk goes through the heart of rural Dorset, where the scenery is determined by the geology beneath. The climb out of Sherborne takes us on to the limestone ridge, where much of the ground is covered with natural and planted forestry. From here the walk is through agricultural land on the Oxford clay, but the background view here from left to right is the chalk ridge on to which we have to climb. Once on the ridge we have more fine views before our next special site comes into sight, and the path drops into the Cerne valley.

The village of Lillington has no facilities except a telephone and a post box, and the little church there is usually locked. Leigh has a shop, a bakery, the Carpenter's Arms, which is a good stopping place for refreshments, and all the facilities of a small rural community. St Nicholas's Church at Hilfield, all on its own by the roadside, is one of the smallest churches in the country. It dates from the fifteenth century, but was much restored in 1848. It is worth a visit just to see the bench ends. The Friary of St Francis, on the hillside at Hilfield, is the base for the Anglican friars, who mainly work in London and Liverpool but also in Tanzania. The chapel there is always open, they have a shop and there is always a welcome.

The picnic area on the Batcombe ridge gives fine views back across the two counties and shows how steep the hill up from the friary has been. We then arrive at the wonderful village of Cerne Abbas. For the present-day traveller Cerne Abbas has most things: three good pubs, at least three tea shops, accommodation and much to see. Historically, the abbey church dates from AD987, and the village and its history have grown from that beginning. The remains of the old abbey can be found at the top of Abbey Street. To visit these you pass the church and wonderful old buildings. On a weekend in June the gardens of the village are open, giving an opportunity to see the old buildings close up.

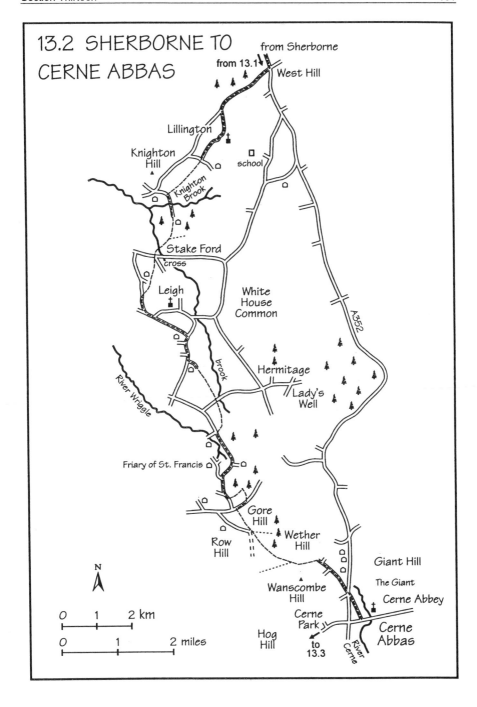

13.2 SHERBORNE TO CERNE ABBAS

from 13.1

from Sherborne

West Hill

Lillington

Knighton Hill

school

Knighton Brook

Stake Ford

cross

Leigh

White House Common

A352

brook

Hermitage

River Wriggle

Lady's Well

Friary of St. Francis

Gore Hill

Wether Hill

Row Hill

Giant Hill

The Giant

Wanscombe Hill

Cerne Abbey

N

Cerne Park

Cerne Abbas

0   1   2 km

Hog Hill

to 13.3

River Cerne

0   1   2 miles

On the hillside above the village, as we have seen from across the valley, is the Cerne Giant. The figure is cut into the chalk and measures 55 metres (180ft) from head to heel. Its origins are unknown, but there is little doubt that it dates from at least 2000 years ago, and possibly from Bronze Age times. The first records are only from the 1760s, but it was probably about then that the trenches were re-excavated. Its connection with pagan fertility rites and later with the abbey make its history even more interesting.

For this stage you will need Landrangers 183 and 194 or Pathfinder Sheets ST 60/70 and ST 61/71.

Our starting point is Sherborne Station (641 162). From here, cross the level crossing, go up the hill and cross the road. The footpath almost opposite rises through the woods and past the playing fields. Continue up the hill, and at the top of the wood fork right to come out at the junction of the A3030 and A352.

Cross the junction and proceed along the country lane signed to Lillington and Knighton. This quiet and little-used road passes through Honeycombe Wood. After a mile, fork left through the village of Lillington. After the vilage the road turns sharply to the right, but we go straight on along the track. After 200 metres take the waymarked footpath on the right to head across the fields. There are three fields to cross and the route is waymarked. There is often a crop in these fields, but the line of the footpath is always clear.

Coming out of the fields onto the farm road, go left and down the hill to Whitfield Farm. Pass through the farm yard, admiring the large herd of goats, and continue along the concrete farm track. After about 400 metres, adjacent the cattle trough, bear right across the field to the old gate into the wood. The footpath follows a clearing through the wood. Watch out for jays in the wood and you may see deer eyeing you from the wood anywhere along the walk. Having crossed a grassy field, we come out at the road.

Turn right, and in a few metres turn left along the road towards Leigh. After 200 metres take the grassy track to the right and follow the waymark signs across the fields to Leigh. In the village turn left, and then fork right along the country road (614 085). On reaching the road to Batcombe, turn right. After half a mile take the drove to the left. Continue to follow the footpath then cross the next road and go through the field to the road leading to Hilfield. Turning left along this road brings you to a road junction. One hundred metres to the left is the parish church of Hilfield, set in the field with no modern village, but a scene of peace and tranquillity.

Our route takes us the other way at the junction, along the road to the Friary of St Francis. Take time to pause here, to visit the Friary, its church, or even to attend one of the services held there regularly during each day. There is also a shop and a garden to visit. You will appreciate any rest you take here as the narrow road rises steeply up to Batcombe Ridge. An alternative is to branch to the left on one of the marked paths and follow it up the hillside, through the bluebell woods, to the picnic area (634 039).

If you follow the steeper route, a turn to the left at the top will bring you into the same picnic area, where the panoramic plaque shows the hills and features of Somerset. Information boards give the details of the local flora and fauna.

Opposite the top of the hill the footpath continues southwards along the ridge. After joining the Wessex Ridgeway for one hundred metres, fork left towards Cerne Abbas. Again there are magnificent views over the valley, and the outline of the Cerne Giant will come into view. The footpath will bring you to the information boards about the giant and its history in the lay-by near the village, on the A352 (662 016).

Stage Three: Cerne Abbas to Dorchester – 8 miles

Leaving Cerne Abbas, the walk also leaves the valley and follows the ridge between the Sydling and Cerne valleys before dropping steadily into the Frome valley at Grimstone. The route then follows the country road along the valley to Dorchester. Some of this road is along the route of the Roman road from Dorchester to Ilchester and passes the clearly visible outline of the Roman aqueduct which supplied the ancient town with water. The Iron Age fort at Poundbury is passed on the left on the outskirts of the town.

Dorchester is full of history. It is the Casterbridge of Hardy's novels and full of places he refers to in the books. The Bloody Assize was held here in 1685, following the Monmouth rebellion, and was presided over by Judge Jeffreys. In Roman times Durnovaria was an important city and its long, well-documented history is displayed in the museum.

The Poundbury Camp is not the only evidence of the ancient history of the Dorchester area: the Maumbury Rings are situated adjacent to the Weymouth road, just south of the market. These ancient earthworks were constructed about 2000BC, but their purpose is still unclear. They were certainly used by the Romans as an amphitheatre and they remain a fine sight. The main site of ancient interest is Maiden Castle, some two miles south of the town and dating from the same period as Maumbury Rings. The site extends for over a kilometre and was extensively excavated in the 1930s.

There is no place for refreshment on the route of the walk from Cerne Abbas to Dorchester so set off well prepared. However, Dorchester has all you will want. A good first call is the Information Office in Trinity Street, where you can obtain town guides, accommodation lists and locations of the eating houses.

Landranger 194 or Pathfinders ST 60/70 and SY 60/70 will be needed for this stage.

From the village of Cerne Abbas, cross the A352 and follow the road signed to Sydling St Nicholas up the hill to rejoin the footpath along the ridge (647 002). The path is clearly signed. Just over the ridge and turning left or southwards, the footpath continues for four miles until it joins the main Yeovil to Dorchester road (A37) at Grimstone. Cross this road, taking the road to Winterbourne Abbas, and then cross the River Frome (642 937). Shortly, turn left and follow the narrow road through the trees to Bradford Peverell and on into Dorchester.

Stage 4: Dorchester to Eggardon Hill – 14½ miles

Maiden Castle, one of the oldest and largest sites of interest in the area, is only two miles into this section of the walk. It can be taken as a walk out from Dorchester or as the first place of interest on the walk. Excavations show that the

13.3 CERNE ABBAS
TO DORCHESTER

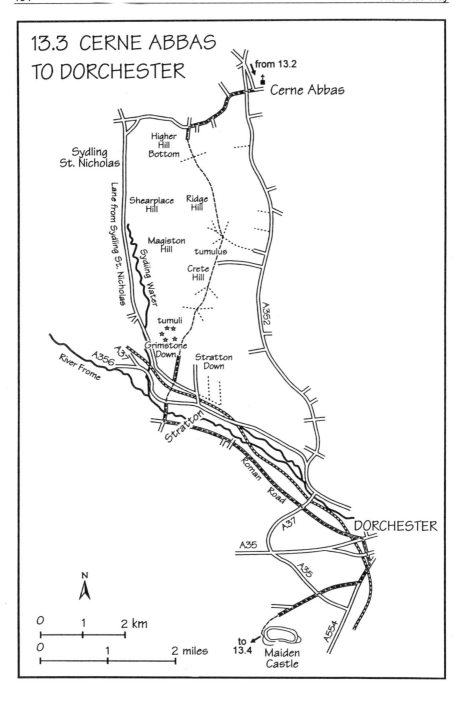

13.4 MAIDEN CASTLE TO EGGARDON HILL

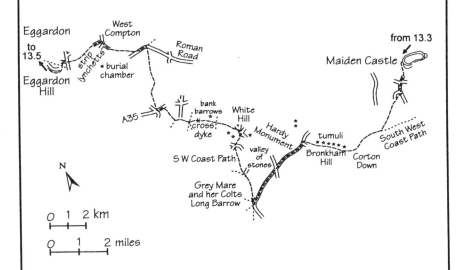

13.5 EGGARDON HILL TO PILSDON PEN

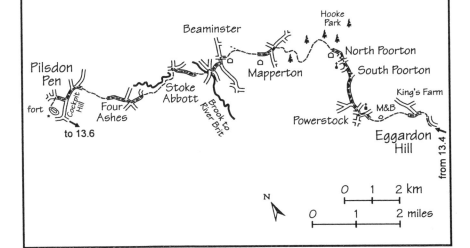

earliest habitation here was a late Stone Age village, and a huge bank burrow was constructed shortly afterwards. The triple-ditched ramparts encircling the entire perimeter were constructed during the Iron Age, and probably not completed until 200 to 100BC. This was the place of the last stand of the Durotiges tribe against the Romans, who then built their new town nearby. The Romano-British temple, which can still be seen, was probably not built until AD300.

The walk then crosses on to the ridge, with fine views over the coastline. The Hardy monument at which it emerges commemorates the Hardy who served with Nelson at Trafalgar. (The Hardy of literary fame has his monument at the top of the High Street in Dorchester.) Again, the views from here are truly magnificent, possibly one of the best coast panoramas in the country. It may be advisable to stock up with refreshment from the ever-present sellers here as there is little in the miles ahead.

A possible diversion from the walk at Hardy's Monument is to take the footpath to the south-west for about a mile, to the Hellstone. This is a Neolithic dolman at the entrance to a chambered long barrow which was 'restored' in the 1860s. From here the walk follows one ridge before crossing to another, further inland, and going on to Eggardon Hill.

There is no shop or village of any size along this 14-mile section. A diversion into Martinstown, between Maiden Castle and the Hardy monument, rather than going along the ridge will offer most facilities. Alternatively, continue through Little Bredy and Long Bredy to Litton Cheneys; the country roads will then lead back inland to Eggardon Hill. Although this is soft walking along the ridges, it is **very exposed to gales off the sea.** Be prepared for a change of weather and have the necessary equipment with you.

For this stage, choose your maps from the following: Landranger 194, Pathfinders SY 48/49 and SY 60/70 or Outdoor Leisure 15 – Purbeck and Dorset.

Take the Weymouth road southwards out of Dorchester, and shortly after Maumbury Ring and the railway bridge, fork right along Maiden Castle Road. This road and footpath brings you to the western end of Maiden Castle itself (665 887). Allow some time to explore this huge hill fort.

Continue along the footpath and drop into the valley, joining a country lane and turning right. Bear left at the fork and keep ahead at the junction with the main road. In about 100 metres bear right on a bridleway signed to Friar Waddon, passing through Ashton Farm. This bridleway will join the coastal footpath on the ridge, where we turn right towards Hardy's monument. This ridge footpath eventually comes out on the road just below the monument, which is approached by turning left (616 877).

Continue along the road, past the monument and on to the crossroads. Go straight on and take the stile on the right after 80 metres. The footpath follows the fence down into the valley. Our route then turns right up the road. Keeping left at a junction, the road then comes out at a T-junction with another road. Take the footpath straight in front and continue along another ridge until finally dropping down onto the A35. This is **a very dangerous** place to cross due to the speed of the traffic (570 913). Make the crossing and take the farm access road to the right after 150 metres. Where the tarmacked tracks fork, take the grassy footpath straight on down the hill and up the other side, eventually coming out on the old Roman road.

Turn left and either follow the road or the footpath just inside the field. An alternative here is to follow the road all the way to Eggardon Hill or to drop into the valley at the tiny village of West Compton and climb back up on to the ridge at Eggardon Hill. The footpath leading to the right from the ridge may be covered with crops, but just beyond the highest point on this part of the road, a track leads to the right down to the village. Go through the village, and at the road junction cross straight over towards Eggardon Hill Farm. Follow the track and footpath back onto the ridge.

At the road junction (547 946) cross straight over, and in 80 metres take the footpath across the field towards the ancient fort. Turn right at the footpath junction and go onto the site of Eggardon hill fort.

Stage 5: Eggardon Hill to Pilsdon Pen – 13 miles

The walk from Eggardon to Pilsdon Pen crosses the remotest parts of rural Dorset, at one place passing Loscombe, originally Lost Combe. Most of the section passes through wooded valleys well away from the beaten track, and to meet a fellow rambler will be an event. Parnham House is well worth a visit, not only for the house itself but to see the wonderful woodworking workshops and their output of modern furniture.

The small villages of Nettlecombe and Powerstock, towards the beginning of the section, have good pubs with food and accommodation. A short diversion from the route will lead to Beaminster, which has a plentiful supply of shops, pubs and accommodation. In Stoke Abbott the village hostelry has both food and accommodation. A diversion from Stoke Abbott will take you to Broadwindsor, which has a shop and several pubs.

Landrangers 193 and 194 or Pathfinders ST 49/59 and SY49/59 are required for this stage.

Continue along the top of Eggardon Hill, within the old earthworks, and out along the spur to the north-west. Scramble down the hillside, following the fence. You will finally come out on a track, where you should turn left and follow the farm track down the hill.

Where the track bears left, follow the footpath straight on. Cross the old railway line and come out at the end of the road at Castle Mill Farm. (A detour here through the village will quickly bring you to the Marquis of Lorne and refreshments or accommodation.) The footpath crosses the little bridge by the farm and follows the valley to Powerstock. At the road, turn right up the hill and into the village (518 962). In Powerstock, The Three Horseshoes will again offer refreshment and accommodation. In the centre of the village, opposite the church, turn half-left and follow the unsigned, narrow 'road' to South and then North Poorton (520 982).

In the village, keep straight on when the main road turns right. Turn left to go past the church, and keep straight on through the farmyard. Bear right and after a few metres go through the gate on the left, keeping to the left-hand hedge line. Go through the next gate and across or round the field, then over an old iron gate and down into the valley. Go through the gate in the bottom left-hand corner and follow the footpath, slowly dropping down the valley. After almost a mile, on approaching an open field, turn very sharp right through the gate and drop down to cross the river. Follow the track by an overgrown cottage to a footpath junction by an old oak tree (505 988). Continue straight on up the valley ahead. The path turns to the left after a gateway, and continues in the valley bottom to come out through a gate and on to a track by an old keeper's cottage.

Go 30 metres up the track and take the footpath sharp left. Cross the field to the road. Turn left at the road, and then right along the track at the Posie Tree of 'Ring a ring of roses' fame. Follow along the track and footpath until reaching the coppice. Here the path to the left takes you down a sunken footpath and through the old farmyard of Coombe Down Farm to the main Bridport to Beaminster road (477 002). **Alternatively**, keep straight on at the coppice, where the route turns left, and another sunken footpath will bring you almost into Beaminster town. To rejoin the main route, either follow the road towards Bridport as far as the entrance to Parnham House, or take the riverside footpath from opposite the police station.

Turn right along the road for a few metres, and then left down the drive to Parnham House. Cross the river and turn sharp left through the woods. Following the Jubilee Way signs, cross the stile out of the wood, turn half left and cross the field to the lane. Cross the lane and follow the footpath across the field running slightly downhill to come to a gate at the bottom. Go over the ditch and down to the stream. Bear right, ignoring the first bridge to go over the second bridge. Cross the steeply rising field ahead, passing a lone tree on the right to a gate in the far corner. Follow the overgrown track and shortly turn right into Long Barrow Lane, leading towards Stoke Abbot.

At the Bridport road turn right. Make to the right to get into Long Barrow Lane, leading towards Stoke Abbott. A footpath to the left cuts across to the village. Accommodation is available in the village and the New Inn offers both refreshment and accommodation.

Turn left in the village and follow the road up to Four Ash cross roads (440 003). Turn right, and in 200 metres take the farm road to the left. In another 200 metres you have the alternative of taking the footpath to the right up and over Leweston Hill, or following the track and footpath along the level around the base of the hill. Both will come out on the road from Broadwindsor to Birdsmoorgate. Turn left along the road and take the first road on the right running below Pilsdon Pen. After 500 metres, take the steep footpath on the left up to the top of the Pen (412 012).

Stage 6: Pilsdon Pen to the River Axe – 16½ miles

The first section, from Pilsdon Pen to Lambert's Castle, crosses the top of Marshwood Vale. The footpaths here are not walker-friendly, there are **very few footpath signs**, crops, mainly hay, cover the footpaths and there is plenty of **mud** even after little rain. Walking details have been especially carefully written for this section. The alternative route via Birdsmoorgate and Marshwood is available, but the road is narrow and the traffic always in a hurry.

13.6 PILSDON PEN TO CHARMOUTH AND SOUTH WEST COAST PATH

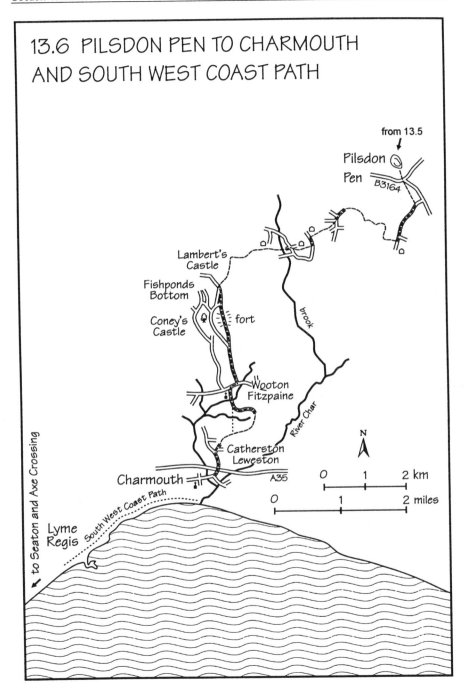

From Lambert's Castle and the smaller Coney Castle, the route leads to the sea at Charmouth and follows the coastal footpath through Lyme Regis to cross the River Axe at Seaton. Little is known about the large hill fort Lambert's Castle, covering 40 hectares (100 acres), or the smaller Coney's Castle, although the National Trust boards at each give some idea. On the sea front at Charmouth, an old sail loft has been converted into a Heritage Coastline Centre that has plenty of interesting information. Both Charmouth and Lyme Regis offer a range of accommodation, small shops both for gifts and supplies and the usual selection of hostelries.

Choose Landranger 193 or Pathfinders SY 29/39, SY 49/59 and ST 40/50 for this stage.

From 412 012, drop down the southern end of Pilsdon Pen, cross the road and take the road just to the left signed to Pilsdon. Continue down the hill for about 200 metres then take the footpath on the right between the house and tennis court. Cross the lawn, go down the steps and follow the lower fence round to the left. Enter the field by the footpath sign and follow the hedge. Go through the gate on the right and down across the field to a gate in the bottom corner. Turn right along the road for about 350 metres and then turn right up a track, just after the vehicle repair garage (413 997). At the top of the track turn right and go over the gate to follow a grassy track, coming out in front of Revelshay Farm. Turn left and follow the farm track. Just before the stream crossing, go through a gate on the right and cross the field, leaving by a gate in the opposite hedge. Keep on towards the bottom of the field and cross a stile. Another field and stile follow. Pass the building on the left and go through the gate, passing in front of Bettiscombe Manor. Follow the track back to Bettiscombe village, joining the road adjacent to the village hall.

Opposite the village hall (399 000), go through the gate to the left of the farm track. Go straight across the field and down the bank to cross the stream on a single sleeper bridge. Cross the field to a stile just to the right of an oak tree and continue across the field into an old farmyard, which has now been taken over by a woodturner. Follow the farm track to a left-hand bend, and just around the corner, enter a field by a stile on the right. Go straight across and pass the farm buildings on the left. Walk through the gate and down the track, to cross the road at Higher Sminhay Farm (388 992).

Just to the left, go up the bank and over the stile. Bear left, go through the gate in the bottom left-hand corner and then on to another gate in the corner. Cross the stream adjacent to the track and keep to the right, following the fence. Go through the gate into a wood and follow the track. Jump the stream and continue up a wet and muddy track to the farm. Follow the track for about 70 metres then go through a gate on the right and straight up the field to a gate leading on to the road. This is a good place to stop and admire the view behind, across Marshwood Vale to Pilsdon, Leweston, Eggardon and even Portland. Turn right along the road for 80 metres and then double back through a gate on the left. From here, go straight up the hillside or follow the path gently up the hill on to Lambert's Castle (373 990).

Work your way to the southern tip of this large site, and then go down the steep footpath to the road. Go straight ahead to the crossroads, under the over-head power lines, and straight ahead up the hill. The car park for Coney Castle is on the left after about 600 metres. The road passes through the centre of the fort, but at the informative National Trust notice board follow the footpath to the left around the fort, either in the ditch or just within the fort. This then re-joins the road at the southern end of Coney's Castle (372 973).

Follow the road down the hill for about 500 metres, until just after the entrance to Great Coombe Farm. The footpath is on the right, waymarked for both the Liberty Trail and the Wessex Ridgeway. Follow this footpath across the fields to join the road again at Wootton Fitzpaine.

Turn right over the bridge, left at the junction in the village and then fork left at the memorial clock. About 80 metres beyond the last house, go through the kissing gate on the right into the field. Follow this footpath through the valley to Charmouth, passing under the bypass road. Cross the main road in the village and proceed down the road to the sea (364 930).

The coastal footpath running westwards is signed from the seafront and climbs the cliffs. Follow the signs, coming out on the road into Lyme Regis. Go into the town, along the front to the Cob, and continue towards the bowling green (335 916). Here the coastal footpath sign will lead steeply up the hillside. Our route then follows the well-signed footpath. It is **a strenuous seven miles**, most of it through a nature reserve, rich in fossils, plants and birds. A landslip in 1839 brought eight million tons of rock down, leaving a chasm through which the path winds to the River Axe at Axmouth (252 900).

Looking Ahead: The Celtic Way ends here and resumes on Dartmoor. There is a continuation of hill forts right up to the edge of Dartmoor, and our proposed route runs between these: Blackberry Castle to Woodbury Castle, then a crossing of the River Exe below Exeter and on across the hills to Dartmoor. For the present, Axemouth to Hound Tor on Dartmoor is best walked by keeping on the South West Coastal Footpath to Teignmouth, and then following the Templer Way from there to the heart of Dartmoor at Widecombe, where it is possible to connect with the Celtic Way. For those of you interested in the link between Axemouth and Hound Tor, the proposed route (which has not yet been walked or tested, only surveyed) can be found in Appendix Two. The Dartmoor section contains two exciting and challenging moor crossings. Read the guidance carefully before making your choice of routes.

Section Fourteen
The Exmoor Option: Glastonbury to Exmoor

63 miles

Local wildlife

Peter Johnson

Peter Johnson has been a keen walker all his life and is a leader for one of the well-known walking holiday companies. As well as enjoying all kinds of walking in the Somerset and Bristol area, he feels very much at home in the Black Mountains and Brecon Beacons. He combines his walking with an interest in the history of our landscape. This has led him to projects such as retracing the route described by the 17th century map-maker John Ogilby, or following the process of land reclamation in his own area.

Stages:

1. Glastonbury to Burrow Mump (Burrowbridge) – 15 miles
2. Burrowbridge to Beacon Hill – 18 miles
3. Beacon Hill to Dunster – 15 miles
4. Dunster to Withypool via Dunkery Beacon – 15 miles

Maps: Landrangers 182 (Weston-super-Mare) and 181 (Minehead)

Highlights: Burrow Mump, Quantock Hills, Beacon Hill, Trendle Ring, St Decumen's Church, Dunster, Bat's Castle, Dunkery Beacon and Withypool.

Starting Point: Glastonbury Abbey (501 387).

Accommodation: The TICs will have full details, but there are youth hostels at Crowcombe – 01984 667249, Holford – 01722 337494, Minehead – 01643 702595 – (though this is more easily reached from Grabbist Hill than from Minehead itself) and Exford – 01643 831650 – which lies directly on the route of the Celtic Way.

Tourist Information: Glastonbury – 01458 832954, Bridgwater 01278 427652, Minehead – 01643 702624.

Introduction

This section follows a great loop from Glastonbury and its wetland environs to the Severn Estuary, which we survey from the heights of the Quantock Hills and Exmoor. The Celtic Way then joins the Two Moors Way to head south for Dartmoor and the South West. The walking varies from open moorland to well-defined footpaths and bridleways. Some of the field sections are not well signposted at present. The directions are written with this in mind. Road-walking has been kept to a minimum.

The theme of the way is well represented in this section. The origins of Glastonbury are shrouded in myth, legend and plain wishful thinking, but the seaboard of Somerset provides plenty of evidence of the Celtic past. In addition to a scatter of Bronze Age barrows of an earlier period, there are Iron Age settlements at Trendle Ring on the Quantocks and Bat's Castle near Dunster. The existence of the Celtic Church can be seen in a number of dedications to early saints – Decuman at Watchet, Caradoc at Carhampton, and Dubricius and Bridget at nearby Porlock and Brean.

A number of place names derive from the pre-Saxon language which was to survive for so much longer in Wales and Cornwall: amongst them Quantocks ('cantuc' meaning rim or circle) and Minehead ('mynydd' meaning hill). Look from these vantage points across to Wales and back over Steep Holm and Flat Holm, which sit in the water like giant stepping stones. It then becomes easy to view the estuary less as a barrier and more as a shared resource, for it once was a busy waterway providing a basis for a community of interest. Water rivalled land transport until comparatively recent times, and trade flourished across the Severn Estuary.

As well as the Celtic connection, the route has much to interest the walker, including fine medieval buildings, a diversity of wildlife, intriguing remains from our industrial past, and, of course, occasional stops for cream teas and cider! I wish you very happy walking.

For the Two Moors Way, linking Withypool to Grimspound on Dartmoor, you may find the guide book helpful, although you can follow it on Landrangers 181 and 191.

Stage 1: Glastonbury to Burrow Mump (Burrowbridge) – 15 miles

It is time to leave Glastonbury. Turn your back to the entrance to the abbey and head west down Benedict Street, which lies opposite and slightly to the right. Continue for about 800 metres, until you reach a brick wall. Turn right along a footpath and almost immediately cross a busy road at the crossing. Continue west for 100 metres, and at the end bear slightly right to a mini-roundabout. Cross the bridge and take Porchestall Drove out into the flat, open country of the Somerset Levels. Continue for slightly more than half a mile along this little-used metalled road, until you reach a T-junction immediately after crossing the River Brue.

Glastonbury Abbey was one of the main movers in beginning the process of draining the Somerset Levels in the early middle ages. Rivers such as the Brue have been altered and straightened to such an extent that their original course is uncertain.

Turn left (south), then shortly right along a track towards Cradlebridge Farm. Leaving all the farm buildings on your right, continue in a straight line, with the rhyne (drainage ditch) on your right. Two gates bar the path – cross using the stile on the left one and continue with the rhyne still on your right. Pass flooded peat workings on your left, and then on both sides until you reach the road. Turn left (south) and follow the road for about half a mile. On higher ground to the right a substantial-looking farm comes into view. Continue a little farther until an impressive drive, newly planted with trees, is reached. Follow this drive, which cuts back right at an acute angle to the road (north-west) to Sharpham Park Farm. Leaving all the buildings on your left, follow the drive round past the dairy and into a farm track which is hedged on both sides. Near the crest of the hill, go through into a field on the left and continue with the hedge on your right down to a T-junction.

Cross the road and continue north-west along a narrow lane. After a little more than one mile, you reach Ashcott. Cross the busy A39 by the post office, and continue west-south-west along Pedwell Lane to a T-junction. Turn left down the hill, and in about 100 metres turn right along a public footpath just past The Rookery. Keep a stone wall on your right and then continue in a generally westerly direction, first between double hedges and then with a hedge on your right. Cross the stile by the water trough, and then the ramshackle stile in the hedge (take care!). Bear slightly left to a gate into the lane.

Turn left down the lane and shortly before the descent becomes steeper, cross a stile on the right in a narrow gap in the hedge (public footpath). Continue heading west with a hedge on your right. At the next field boundary there is a stile some 20 metres to the left of a gate. Cross this and then a footbridge over a ditch. Follow the footpath along the left-hand edge of the fields until, af-

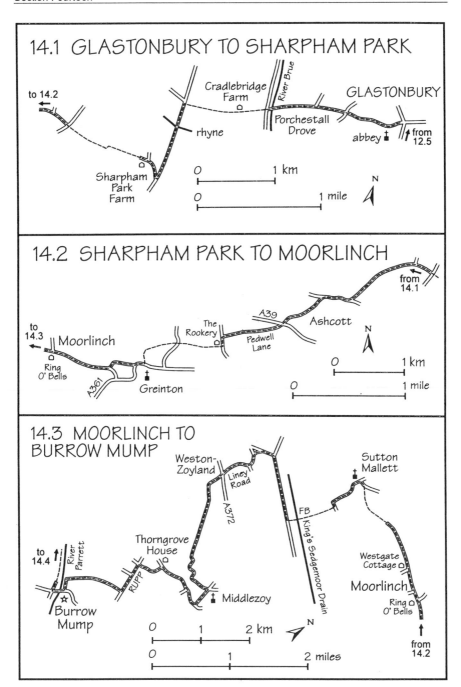

14.1 GLASTONBURY TO SHARPHAM PARK

to 14.2

Cradlebridge Farm

River Brue

GLASTONBURY

rhyne

Porchestall Drove

abbey

from 12.5

Sharpham Park Farm

0   1 km

0   1 mile

N

14.2 SHARPHAM PARK TO MOORLINCH

from 14.1

to 14.3

Moorlinch

The Rookery

A39

Ashcott

Pedwell Lane

N

Ring O' Bells

A361

Greinton

0   1 km

0   1 mile

14.3 MOORLINCH TO BURROW MUMP

Weston-Zoyland

Liney Road

A372

Sutton Mallett

FB

King's Sedgemoor Drain

Thorngrove House

RUPP

River Parrett

to 14.4

Burrow Mump

Middlezoy

Westgate Cottage

Moorlinch

Ring O' Bells

from 14.2

0   1   2 km

0   1   2 miles

N

196   The Celtic Way

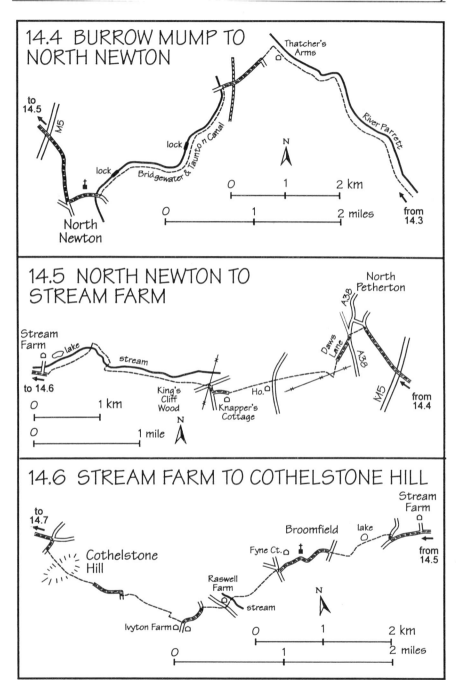

14.4 BURROW MUMP TO NORTH NEWTON

14.5 NORTH NEWTON TO STREAM FARM

14.6 STREAM FARM TO COTHELSTONE HILL

14.7 COTHELSTONE HILL TO CROWCOMBE GATE

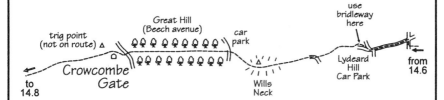

trig point
(not on route) △

Great Hill
(Beech avenue)

car
park

use
bridleway
here

Lydeard
Hill
Car Park

from
14.6

Crowcombe
Gate

to
14.8

Wills
Neck

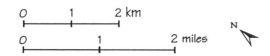

0   1   2 km

0   1   2 miles

N

14.8 CROWCOMBE GATE TO WILLITON

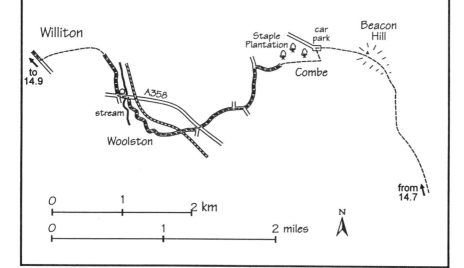

Williton

Staple
Plantation

car
park

Beacon
Hill

to
14.9

Combe

A358

stream

Woolston

from
14.7

0   1   2 km

0   1   2 miles

N

ter a gate, the field opens out on the left. Shortly Turn left on a field track, and aim to come out on the road to the right of Greinton church.

Turn right along the road, and continue straight ahead at a left bend. You are now on a minor road signposted to Moorlynch. Follow the road round to the left, then turn shortly right, again signposted to Moorlynch. Follow this road into the village of Moorlynch (400 366).

At the Ring O'Bells in Moorlynch, take the minor road straight ahead past the telephone box. After 200 metres continue straight ahead down a track, leaving Westgate Cottage on your left. Follow this track for just over a mile as it rises then contours westwards, emerging on the road leading into Sutton Mallett. Turn left at the church, following the road through the village, past Godfrey's Farm on the right and down the lane. At the bottom of the hill go left, and then shortly turn right (south) along the drove. Continue for 800 metres in this general direction, crossing a couple of minor footbridges, until you reach the substantial pedestrian footbridge crossing King's Sedgemoor Drain.

Continue across the field for 200 metres, then go through a gate and emerge on Sedgemoor Drove. Turn right (north-west) and follow the drove in a straight line for three-quarters of a mile. Turn left (south-west) at the point where the drove changes direction and follows the rhyne to the right. This track leads to the village of Westonzoyland. After 500 metres fork left, aiming for a red-brick house.

A short detour to the right leads to the battlefield of Sedgemoor, where in 1685 the rebellion of Monmouth was brought to an end, to be followed by the infamous Bloody Assizes of Judge Jeffreys, still something of a folk memory in the West Country.

Turn left and follow Liney Road round the edge of the village to the main road (A372). Cross the road and follow a farm track for two miles, initially south then south-west, finally reaching the church at Middlezoy on a metalled road after a series of left and right bends. Go down Church Road, passing the church on your left, and at a T-junction at the bottom turn right (noting the thatched cottages and post office stores to your left).

Follow the road west out of the village, and after about half a mile, at Thorngrove House, take the road left. Follow the road, which is not signposted, round a left turn at Wayside Cottage, then where it turns right after a further 200 metres, continue down the drove (signposted RUPP). After about 400 metres and the sixth transverse rhyne on the left, turn right (south-west) down the first drove to appear. Continue to the end and turn left into Burrowbridge (357 302).

Burrow Mump restates the theme of Glastonbury Tor. Though less grand, it is perhaps more in tune with its landscape, rising as an almost perfect cone above the total flatness of the moors. The church of St Michael is only an incomplete reconstruction, but the site must have been used as a refuge from the waters ever since humans first began exploring the Levels.

Stage 2: Burrowbridge to Beacon Hill – 18 miles

At Burrowbridge turn right, cross the River Parrett and turn right along the road signposted to Moorland. The road soon comes close to the river bank. At this point join the River Parrett Trail and follow the river bank for about two and a half miles. Shortly after the Thatcher's Arms the trail leaves the river (sign-posted) and heads south-west. Follow this bearing, first along a footpath, then a lane. Cross the railway and arrive at the Bridgwater and Taunton Canal. Origi-nally conceived as part of an uncompleted plan to link Exeter and Bristol, the canal is now an attractive leisure amenity.

Turn left and follow south along the towpath on the eastern bank of the ca-nal. About 400 metres beyond the second lock (King's Lock), turn right over the swing-bridge (there is a notice advertising the Harvest Moon). Follow the road past the church and into the village of North Newton.

From North Newton, turn right at the school and walk along the road, cross-ing the M5 (296 319). Continue over the motorway into North Petherton. The road enters the built-up area and forks left. Immediately take a well-worn foot-path left (south-west), emerging past playing fields on the main A38. Turn left and find Daws Lane on the other side of the road, just after the bus stop and postbox set in the wall. Follow the lane south-west past houses on the left. At the end of the lane cross a stile and continue with the hedge on your right. Cross a stile and pass under power lines as you join a vehicle track.. Shortly turn right on a vehicle track with the hedge on your right. Pass under the power lines again and where the track turns left, continue straight ahead across a field. Head towards a gate which is visible to the right of a red-brick house opposite. Cross the road at the gate and enter the field opposite (through the farm gate, not up the drive).

Continue in the same direction with the hedge on your left. Go over a metal farm gate and cross the field, aiming for the gate to the right of a stand of trees. Cross the gate and aim for the top left corner of the field. At this point you go through an opening on the left to join a farm track continuing in the same direc-tion. Go past Knapper's Cottage and continue until you meet a minor road.

Turn right along the minor road, and then in about 150 metres turn left at a T-junction. Turn immediately right down a signposted public footpath into King's Cliff Wood. Hold this generally westerly line down through the wood, joining a forest track at the bottom. Continue left until the track abruptly ends and then take the footpath going in the same direction. Bear right at a path junc-tion, go through a metal gate and shortly cross the stream. Follow the stream north-west until you reach a small, ivy-covered, ruined building. At this point cross the stream again and head south-west up the hill with the hedge on your right. Follow the track as it levels out. On the other side of the valley is Stream Farm, identified by its small fishing lake. Join the lane coming from this farm and continue straight ahead down the lane (242 319).

The lane from Stream Farm eventually joins a road. Turn right and after a short uphill stretch of about a hundred metres, go up the wooden steps on your left to join a public footpath. Follow the left-hand edge of the field. Cross the gate into the next field and go immediately left into the field with a stream at the bottom. Follow the top edge of the field, making eventually for a stile at the bot-tom of the field near a small lake. Cross the stile and a small bridge across a stream. Continue with the lake on your right, crossing a further small bridge. Follow the footpath signs over a stile and into the wood.

14.9 WILLITON TO HOME FARM

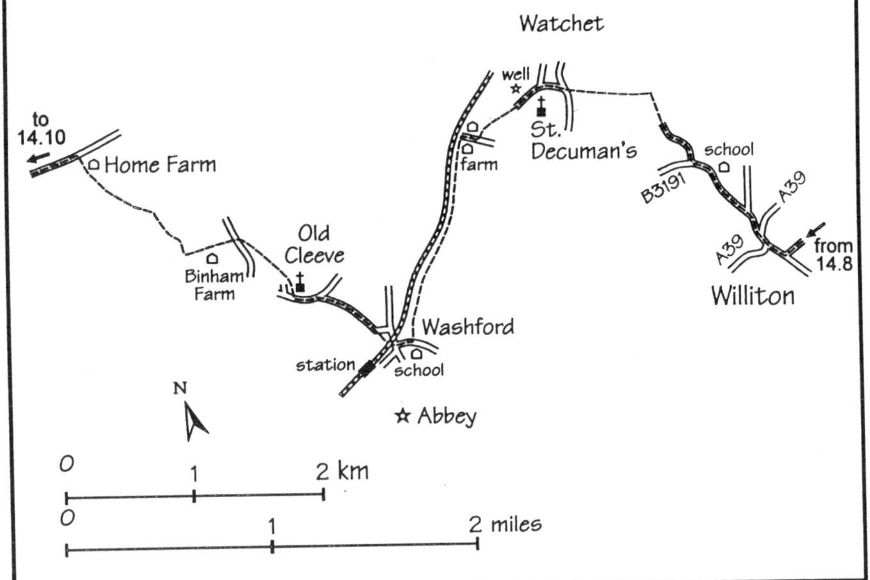
Watchet
well
St.
Decuman's
farm
school
B3191
A39
A39
from
14.8
Williton
to
14.10
Home Farm
Old
Cleeve
Binham
Farm
Washford
station
school
Abbey
N
0
1
2 km
0
1
2 miles

14.10 HOME FARM TO DUNSTER

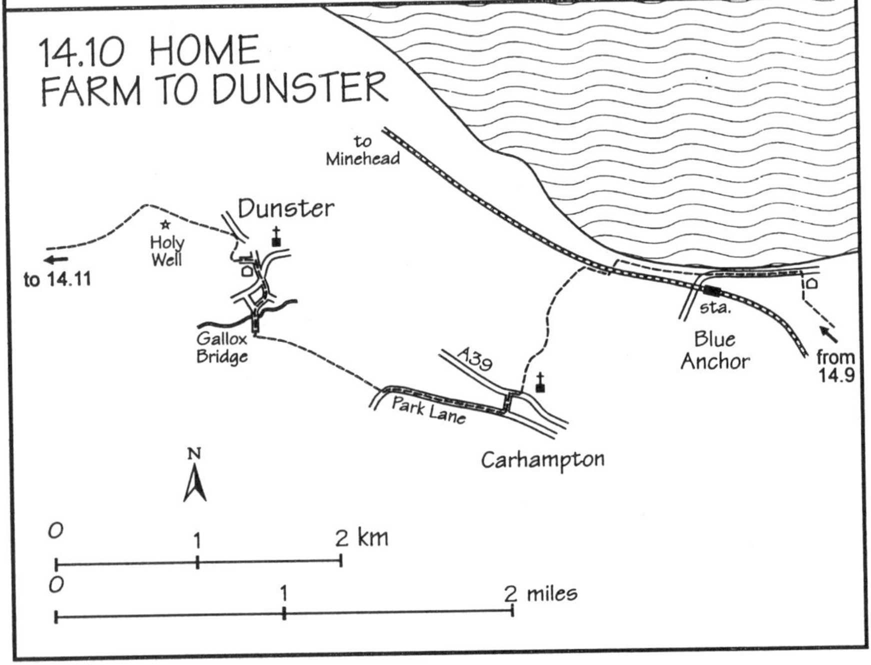
to
Minehead
Dunster
Holy
Well
to 14.11
Gallox
Bridge
A39
Park Lane
Carhampton
sta.
Blue
Anchor
from
14.9
N
0
1
2 km
0
1
2 miles

After 300 metres in the wood you will meet a track crossing the stream from the left. Follow this track uphill to the right until you emerge on a road. Turn left along the road and soon you will enter the village of Broomfield. Continue past the entrance to Fyne Court (National Trust), and at T-junction turn right.

Fyne Court is now occupied by Somerset Wildlife Trust, which has devised some excellent displays and nature trails. There is also a wide range of publications and leaflets of local interest.

The road soon bends left, and almost immediately a footpath leads off to the left just before a telephone box. Follow this path, and when it forks in about 400 metres go right. Joining a lane, you continue down to cross a ford and emerge on a road at Raswell House. Cross the road at this point and take the track opposite which leads up to a lane to Ivyton Farm. Opposite a barn a track on the right (public footpath – red flash) leads up across a field.

At the first field boundary go through the hedge and turn immediately right, following a track along the left-hand edge of the field boundary. Enter another field and continue along the hedge to the next field boundary. Go left, with a hedge on your left. Shortly after entering the next field, bear right along a track making towards the top of the hill. Follow the track through a gap in the hedge then bear right to the far right corner of the field. Cross the bank to a track (Ball Lane), which you follow right then left through woodland, following blue bridleway markers for 600 metres. Emerging from woodland you encounter solid wooden fences with warning notices about Exmoor ponies. Leave the track and head right into the open. Follow the permitted bridleway leading along the right edge of the wire fence, and then fork right up Cothelstone Hill, following a public footpath sign (yellow flash).

From the top of Cothelstone Hill, find a narrow footpath continuing over the top of the hill, descending gently and then more steeply through trees and bracken. Cross a stile at the bottom to enter more mature woodland and follow the track until you emerge on the road just to the left of a crossroads (189 331). Walk up the road opposite, signposted to Bagborough, continuing straight ahead where the main road bends to the left, until you reach the Lydeard Hill car park. (Take advantage of the bridleway on the right as the road becomes very narrow.)

From Lydeard Hill car park, cross the stile and head for Wills Neck, the highest point on the Quantocks, which you can go over or skirt round, bearing towards the right until you reach the south-eastern end of a long avenue of beech trees. With wonderful views in all directions and enticing stream-cut combes, the Quantocks offer both a well-defined, enjoyable ridge walk and an invitation to linger and explore. Follow this avenue, which is the National Trust property of Great Hill, until you reach a metalled road. Cross the road, bearing right, and at Crowcombe Gate Lodge (149 377), bear left. Continue on the same general bearing, keeping to the high ground, until you reach the trig. point of Beacon Hill.

Stage 3: Beacon Hill to Dunster – 15 miles

From Beacon Hill, make for the car park visible just before Staple Plantation in the middle distance, (west if visibility is limited!) From the top left corner of the

car park, do not enter the plantation, but go down some wooden steps and follow the path down into beautiful Weacombe Combe. Follow the path right
along the bottom of the combe. At the bottom go through a gate and come out on
the road at Combe Cottage. Continue down the lane and turn left at the T-
junction at the bottom. Follow this road for a little more than half a mile, until
you reach the main A358. Cross this road and almost immediately a minor
road, continuing straight ahead in the direction of Woolston. Cross the railway,
go through the village and after a further half a mile reach the A358 again. This
time turn left along the main road and cross a stream. Just past the garage, turn
right down a narrow, metalled lane. This leads through farm buildings to a
well-used footpath across several fields and stiles, coming out finally at Williton, on the A358 opposite the Wyndham Arms (078 408).

Turn right into Williton, and eventually leave on the B3191 to Watchet.
Look out for the school on the right. Shortly afterwards cross a stream, and then
in about 100 metres take the minor road going up to the right. This eventually
turns into a footpath leading to the outskirts of Watchet. Just before reaching
the houses, turn left up the side of a field (signposted 'Parsonage'). Follow this
path over several stiles and pass Parsonage Farm on your left. Cross the main
road and go down Brendon Road to reach St Decuman's Church.

Detour to Watchet by turning right down a tarmacked path past a brick
chimney. Watchet has a surprising little harbour which is a reminder of the
former importance of sea transport around the estuary.

To continue the walk, take the path straight ahead, leaving the church on
your left. You soon come to a gate leading to St Decuman's Well. Having taken
the few extra steps to visit the well, continue down the path across fields. Turn
right over a stile (signposted to Old Mineral Line), pass through Kentsford
Farm, linger (but not for too long!) by the weir and shortly you will reach a level
crossing. Do not cross but turn left and follow the path which runs parallel to
the line. This brings you out in Washford, opposite the school. Turn right along
the lane and shortly arrive at a T-junction.

For Cleeve Abbey (English Heritage) and an excellent impression of monastic life, turn left. For Washford Station and a fascinating collection of railway
memorabilia in the Somerset and Dorset Railway Museum, continue along the
footpath opposite.

To continue the walk, turn right under the railway bridge and go up the
steps immediately opposite. The path soon joins a road at the top which you
follow left (signposted Old Cleeve). At Old Cleeve, enter the churchyard on
your right and follow the path around the tower, leaving again by the far corner.
The footpath continues through the woods (signposted Blue Anchor). Soon
you go up some steps and bear left across a field to emerge on a road. Cross this
road and go down the right-hand lane opposite, which leads to Binham Farm.
The path goes to the right of the farm house and through a field to the far corner.
Join a concrete track leading away from the farm, and in about 50 metres go
through a hedge opening on the right. Bear right across the field (there is a small
footpath sign for confirmation on the telegraph pole). Follow the path beside
the brook all the way to Home Farm at Blue Anchor (029 434).

Turn left and head along the seafront. When the road turns inland to Blue Anchor station, just continue along the shoreline. After 800 metres of walking along the shingle the path crosses the railway line in the direction of Carhampton. Continue along the shoreline for about three miles if you want to detour via Minehead, terminus of both the West Somerset Railway and the South West Coast Path.

Otherwise, bear right across the first field then keep on the same bearing to the top left corner of the next field. Signposts will then lead you into Carhampton, where you come out by the church. This church is dedicated to St John, but at one time Carhampton had two churches. The other was dedicated to St Carantoc, another colourful saint who is associated in legend with early Welsh evangelism. Unfortunately, its site is not known for certain.

Turn right along the main road, and then shortly left down High Street. At the bottom is a T-junction where you turn right along Park Lane. Follow this road, which eventually turns into a rough track, as far as Carhampton Gate. Here you follow the footpath signs through fields to Dunster.

Enter Dunster by Gallox Bridge. Just after a small car park, turn right along Mill Gardens and turn left at the end into Mill Lane, which brings you into the top of the village. Dunster is very much on the tourist trail but don't let that put you off! Visit the Yarn Market, the castle, the mill or, at the very least, one of its many tea houses.

Stage 4: Dunster to Withypool via Dunkery Beacon – 15 miles

Opposite the entrance to Dunster Castle (National Trust) turn left up St George's Street. Immediately past the school, turn left along a metalled lane (signposted Grabbist Hill and Minehead). Turn right by the allotments into a short residential road, at the end of which a track leads up to the left (signposted Conduit Lane and Grabbist Hill). Follow this path, which can, indeed, be a bit of a conduit at times. The explanation appears in due course – another Holy Well on the left (985 438).

Shortly past the well, go through a gate and follow the path to the left. Keep to this path, generally heading westerly, for about two and a half miles, gradually rising over Grabbist Hill and Knowle Hill. There are fine views towards Minehead on the right and Bat's Castle on the left. Eventually the top of the hill is reached. You may hunt for the trig. point in vain, but a four-way signpost directs you to Wootton Courtenay through a gap in the trees to a parallel path on your left. Ensuring that your views are landward rather than seaward, continue to the very top of the hill and you shortly reach a fork. Go left here, and in 200 metres left again on a minor track. Soon you re-cross the major track and follow the footpath signposted to Wootton Courtenay. In 100 metres watch out for a not very obvious path which dives left and downwards through woodland to Wootton Courtenay. Turn right along the lane into the village. Continue through the village until you reach a three-pronged fork (935 434).

At the three-pronged fork, bear left along a road signposted Brockwell and Ford. You are likely to have been aware of Dunkery Beacon for some time now, and via a cattlegrid you soon reach its foot (National Trust). Now simply follow the bridleway leading to the cairn on the summit, 350 metres or over 1000 feet above. Exmoor expands on the feeling of wilderness which the Quantocks merely hint at. Open, treeless moors with heather, ponies and red deer. **Take care on these sections if the mist is down.**

From Dunkery Beacon (891 416), depart on the opposite side of the cairn. Take the left-hand of two paths leading below the next cairns, on a bearing slightly south of west. Following this path you eventually arrive at a road junction. Follow left (signposted Exford). The left turning at the next crossroads is signposted 'Bridleway Exford', and 200 metres along here a signpost directs you through a gate on the right. Exford is just over a mile away in the valley below.

From Exford, pass the post office on the green, cross the main road and go through the car park to the far end. A footpath (signposted Withypool) leads off through the fields and, joining a lane, leads right over a bridge into Court Farm. Turn left and continue through a field gate. The bridleway is well marked and switchbacks its way through field and woodland edge until it emerges through a gate on open land, with fine views left back to Dunkery Beacon. Pass through another gate and swing right through bracken to the top of Road Hill. Continue over the brow, round the right-hand edge of a combe. Bear left by a lone hedgerow beech and continue working left to the top of the next combe. Here the path forks and you leave the combe bearing right to reach the road (signposted Withypool). Cross the road and follow the permissive path down into Withypool (846 355).

At Withypool you join the Two Moors Way by crossing the river bridge and heading south. This route is marked on Landrangers 181 and 191. The destination is Grimspound on Dartmoor (700 809), at which point we rejoin the Celtic Way.

Looking Ahead: *The Celtic Way ends at this point and resumes at Grimspound, where it connects to the Dartmoor crossing starting at Hound Tor. Walking from Withypool to Grimspound is best done on the Two Moors Way.*

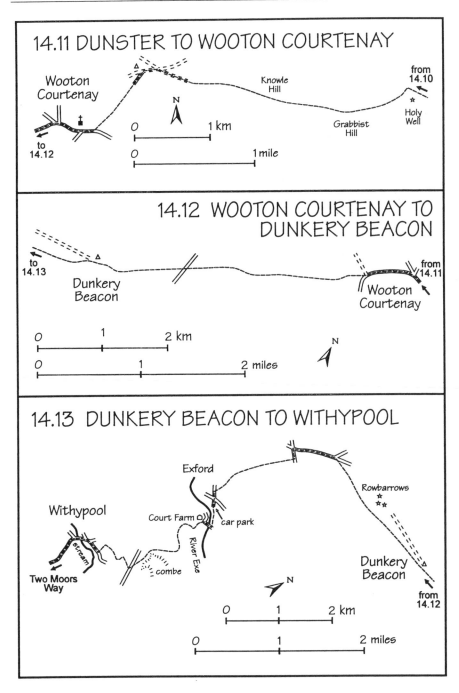

Section Fifteen
Dartmoor Crossing:
Hound Tor to Tavistock
27½ miles

Dennis Waters

Dennis Waters was born in Birmingham. At the age of 4 he moved with his parents to Reading, Berkshire. In 1978 he married Deborah and they had two children Steven and Serena and in 1987 moved to sleepy Teignmouth, Devon. Dennis works for the Royal Mail in Exeter and is also a member of the Territorial Army.

NOTE: two Dartmoor Crossing routes are described. Both begin at Hound Tor and end at Tavistock. Factors such as weather, experience, equipment and moorcraft should be taken into account when making a choice. The Lich Path is the more demanding route and should not be undertaken lightly.

Stages:

1. Connection from Grimspound to Hound Tor for walkers on the Two Moor's Way

2. Hound Tor to Bellever – 7½ miles

Lich Path Option – 20 miles

3. Bellever to Brent Tor – 14 miles

4. Brent Tor to Tavistock – 6 miles

Princetown Tracks Option – 20 miles

5. Bellever to Princetown – 7½ miles

6. Princetown to Walkhampton car park – 5½ miles

7. Walkhampton car park to Tavistock centre – 7 miles

Maps: Landrangers 191, 201; Outdoor Leisure Map 28. A compass is needed.

Highlights: Hound Tor, the medieval village, Bonehill Farm, Widecombe in the Moor and Bellever clapper bridge will be seen whichever route you choose.

Lich Path – Powder Mills, River Tavy and Brent Tor.

Princetown Tracks – Dunnabridge Pound, Dart and Swinscombe valleys, ancient tracks (pack horse route, the Jobbers' Road, monastic route) and Kistvaen (Bronze Age cremation chamber).

Starting Point: Hound Tor (743 790)

Transport: Buses are infrequent but it is possible to reach all the moorland towns by bus. The nearest railway stations are Newton Abbot and Okehampton. British Rail, Plymouth – 01752 221300, Devon Bus Enquiries – 01392 382800.

Accommodation: Youth Hostels at Bellever, 01822 880227; Plymouth, 01752 562189; Okehampton, 01837 53916.

Tourist Information: Bovey Tracey – 01626 832047, Newton Abbot – 01626 367494, Postbridge – 01822 880272, Tavistock – 01822 612938, Princetown High Moorland Visitors Centre – 01822 890414.

Dartmoor – a few warnings

Before beginning this section , a few words of warning must be given. Dartmoor is a wild, open place and is beautiful because of it, but care must be taken. If you are thinking of walking this route, it is important to remember the following.

•You must have adequate walking equipment: proper walking boots or stout shoes, waterproof clothing, a compass and a map are basic necessities.

•You must watch for changes in the weather such as mists that can shroud you and give you no views or idea of where to go next (hence the compass).

•Take particular care crossing streams, bogs and mires – there is not always a bridge, and after rain or a thaw a slight detour may be necessary.

•Dartmoor is used for military training with live ammunition. Part of one of the routes goes across Merrivale range and if the army are using it, you will have to take a detour. **Red flags fly when firing**, just above Powder Mills on Beardown Tor, but find out before setting out on this section. Ask at Youth Hostels, post offices and tourist information offices in the area, or phone **01752 501478**.

Introduction

Dartmoor is a National Park and forty per cent of it is Duchy of Cornwall estate land. It covers 365 square miles and is roughly circular, with several thriving market towns at its edge and its more recent historical centre at Princetown. Lydford and Widecombe and the ecclesiastical centres abutting the moor at Tavistock and Buckfast have, however, also influenced its management in the past.

Moorland is a special type of landscape. Different interest groups will stress varying aspects of the moor's character: the beauty and attractions; the need for safety and careful management. One cannot write about Dartmoor without drawing attention to both, and especially to its bogs and mists, and the ease with which walkers can lose their bearings and very easily become lost and helpless. This short section is one of the most challenging on the Celtic Way. A useful comparison to illustrate the moor's boggy character is to compare it to a watery basin with a raised rim. There are tales – not always apocryphal – of escaping Dartmoor prisoners getting lost for days and then giving themselves up to captivity with relief because the fears and dangers experienced outside on the moor were worse than those inside the prison. Do not underestimate the moor.

Apart from its beauty and its dangers, two features stand out about Dartmoor: age, and usage. Despite an inhospitable landscape, it has been thoroughly utilised from the earliest times and the evidence remains. The Dartmoor Crossing is filled with prehistoric remains: stone rows and circles; burial mounds; hut circles and field boundaries; clapper bridges and milestones. For 5000 years people have made their lives on Dartmoor, and when walking either route we cannot help but be reminded of them. The abundance of old tracks criss-crossing the moor show us the uses people made of the area: drovers, monks, jobbers, tinners, mariners, quarrymen and kings. It is not fanciful to feel that when you walk one of their tracks that something of them and the communities they served lives on. One of the most famous cross-moorland routes is described below, the Lich Path (or Lych Way). This was the route – also known as the Way of the Dead – taken by the funeral cortege to Lydford Church. For further information on these ancient routes I recommend Eric Hemery's *Walking Dartmoor's Ancient Tracks*.

Dartmoor, like Wordsworth's daffodils, flashes upon the inward eye long after the walking is over. While we are on the moor, we are a part of the moor – and something of the moor comes away with the walker afterwards.

Stage 1: Grimspound to Hound Tor Connection – for those arriving on the Two Moors' Way

Grimspound was built around the mid-Bronze Age and consists of 24 huts enclosed inside a walled area of approximately 145 by 170 metres. It is situated between Hookney and Hameldown Tor at about 500 metres above sea level. It had its own water supply, which still runs through the northern edge, called Grims lake.

To join the Dartmoor section of the Celtic Way, leave the Two Moors' Way at

Grimspound and follow the track heading east. After 500 metres, when coming to a choice of two tracks take the right-hand one. This track bears around to the right and heads down into the valley for a mile to reach a minor road to the left of Natsworthy Manor. Cross the road and continue on the track until coming to another road at Kitty Jay's Grave. Kitty Jay was a poor workhouse girl who was said to have been seduced by the son of her employer. In despair she killed herself, and because she was a suicide she was buried where three parishes met, so no-one had the responsibility for her. This is one of the most intriguing mysteries of the moor because there are always fresh flowers on her grave and no-one knows who places them there.

Leave Jay's Grave and cross the road, walking on the track for half a mile until meeting the next minor road. Turn right to follow the road to the car park at the junction, with Hound Tor in view just ahead.

Stage 2: Hound Tor to Bellever −7½ miles

Hound Tor car park, our starting point, usually has an ice cream van – the Hound of the Basketmeals! From the car park, head directly up the hill to Hound Tor, and head through the middle of and over the tor. Hound Tor is one of the most striking tors on Dartmoor and can be very crowded in the summer. It is reputedly the tor that inspired Arthur Conan Doyle in 1902 to write *The Hound of the Baskervilles*.

Next go along the track on a heading of 115 degrees, down the hill to the medieval village. There are 11 buildings: eight houses and three barns which were used for storing corn. The date for these dwellings is about middle Bronze Age, about 1000BC. After visiting the village, head for the right of Greator Rock on a heading of 190 degrees.

When you are on the right of the rocks, head towards a gate at about 200 degrees on a good, grassy path. Carry on through the gate and follow the path signposted to Bonehill Down, passing some interesting horse jumps and obstacles. On approaching a gate opening in a wall, go through and head on 270 degrees, passing further horse obstacles and another footpath sign. I did this part of the walk in May, and this area was a glorious carpet of thousands of bluebells. When you reach the road go through the gate and turn left, following the road over a cattle grid.

After crossing the cattle grid, take the track on the right across Bonehill Down. Follow this track until you come to the road by Bonehill Rocks, **making sure that you don't go left before the track runs to the road as this area is very boggy.** Turn right and follow this road down past some lovely old farm buildings, you will then come to a T-junction at the bottom of the hill.

Turn right and follow the road into the village of Widecombe in the Moor. Take time to have a look around Widecombe, and perhaps have a famous Devonshire cream tea. Widecombe is known by most people, and every September the famous Widecombe Fair takes over the whole village. There are toilets, two car parks, the old inn, the Rugglestone Inn, some gift shops, a lovely church (the cathedral of the moor) and two cafés. At the church house there is also a National Trust information centre with details of accommodation in the area.

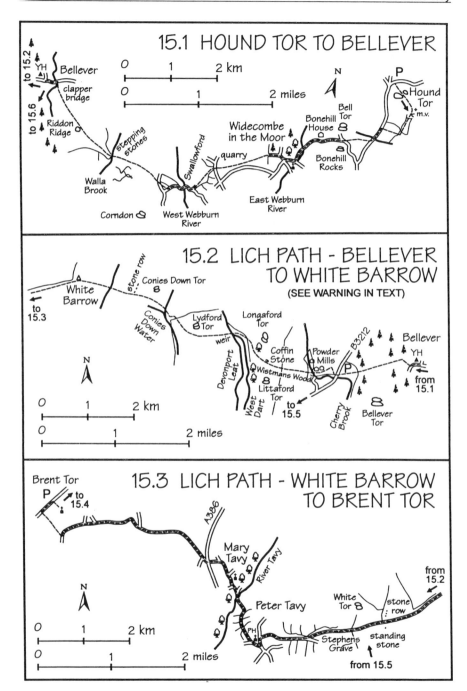

15.1 HOUND TOR TO BELLEVER

15.2 LICH PATH - BELLEVER TO WHITE BARROW
(SEE WARNING IN TEXT)

15.3 LICH PATH - WHITE BARROW TO BRENT TOR

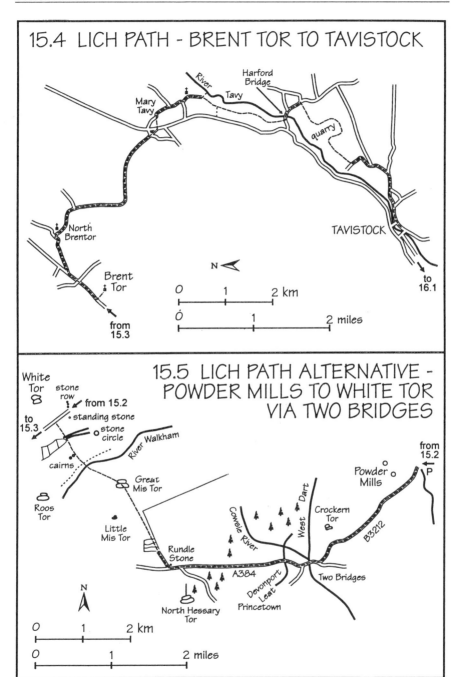

15.4 LICH PATH - BRENT TOR TO TAVISTOCK

Harford Bridge

River Tavy

Mary Tavy

quarry

North Brentor

TAVISTOCK

Brent Tor

N

0   1   2 km

0   1   2 miles

from 15.3

to 16.1

15.5 LICH PATH ALTERNATIVE - POWDER MILLS TO WHITE TOR VIA TWO BRIDGES

White Tor

stone row

from 15.2

to 15.3

standing stone

stone circle

River Walkham

cairns

Great Mis Tor

Roos Tor

Little Mis Tor

Rundle Stone

A384

North Hessary Tor

Princetown

Devonport Leat

Cowsic River

West Dart

Crockern Tor

Powder Mills

Two Bridges

B3212

from 15.2

P

N

0   1   2 km

0   1   2 miles

There are plenty of bed and breakfasts in the area so this is an ideal place to stop off for the night.

Walk through the village and take the road off on the right. Follow it for about 100 metres, until you meet a track on the left signposted to Grimspound via Hameldown. Follow this track, which can be **a bit rugged** in places, until you are out on the open moor again. Cross the moor on a heading of 230 degrees to an old quarry, which is now just a parking place for a few cars. I am not sure what was quarried here, but the ridge of Hameldown had many mines and quarries including arsenic, which was mined in many parts of the moor. Cross the road and follow the wall on the left heading west and eventually coming to a large gate. Go through the gate and enter the track and then take a right turn when you reach the road.

Follow the road, going past the farms of East and West Shallowford and up to the open moor again at (690 754). Take the track that skirts Corndon on a heading of 310, going up and then down the other side to the stepping stones over the Walla Brook at (675 758). These stepping stones are very large and usually well above the water, but when there has been a lot of rain you may end up with **wet feet**! Cross the stones and follow the track by the wall, and then follow the track up to the top of Riddon Ridge.

Follow the ridge and drop down the other side to the clapper bridge at Bellever. This clapper bridge was used until 1809, when the new bridge was built to allow heavier traffic to cross the river. The clapper bridge has now no central part.

Bellever youth hostel (655 744) is just up the hill from this bridge and is another ideal stopping place for the night. Youth hostels are perfect for walkers, offering inexpensive accommodation and good home-cooked meals. There are also some woodland walks available from here, and Postbridge is only about a mile away with the best clapper bridge on Dartmoor.

Bellever to Tavistock Options – Lich Path and Princetown Tracks

From here you need to make a choice based on your moorcraft: consider walking experience, map-reading ability, and the weather. Information will be needed about military use of the range at Merrivale if you are considering the Lich Path – ring 01752 501478. Information is also available at the Youth Hostel. The Lich Path is a Dartmoor crossing only for experienced walkers with some knowledge of Dartmoor.

The Lich Path

This route was known as the Way of the Dead because it was the route along which coffins were carried for burial at Lydford. It is a **challenging route** with some **difficult crossings of boggy ground**, and requires confident and tested way-finding skills. It crosses the army range at Merrivale so firing times need to be checked before a decision is made. It is stunningly beautiful and peaceful walking on the right day, but, as well as the other safety provisos, is **best done on a temperate, clear day when the forecast is settled**. Weather forecasts can be checked at the High Moorland Centre – 01822 890414, or the Postbridge TIC close to the start of the path – 01822 880272. If you plan to do this crossing, make sure you **inform someone** of the details of your walking.

Stage 3: Lich Path Option – Bellever to Brent Tor – 14 miles

This stage starts at Bellever clapper bridge (658 773). Follow the road up past the youth hostel and carry on in the same direction, signposted to Huccaby Cots, Dunnabridge Pound and Upper Cherrybrook Bridge. Follow this track up through a big gate and into the trees. Stay on this track through some very large trees, which at times make it almost seem as though it is dark. Then go through a clearing with a superb view of Bellever Tor on your left and Princetown ahead, with its radio mast on North Hessary Tor above the town. Carry on in the same direction until you come down to a small car park by the main road (635 771).

See the later alternative route in the case of live firing by the armed forces. The proper route of the Lich path (if there is no live firing) is to cross over the road and to climb over the stile entering the moor. **Warning: the route is supposed to go straight towards the chimney but it is very boggy in this area and you will have to skirt carefully around to the right.**

On reaching the Powder Mills, cross the track and walk through two gates followed by a metal gate, heading towards Littaford Tor on 280 degrees. Powder Mills was once a gunpowder factory which employed more than 100 people; it produced a highly explosive black powder and its position in the middle of nowhere was perfect. The high chimneys that you can see were used to carry away fumes and sparks.

Take the track just to the right of Littaford, which is not very prominent and is difficult to follow (just head towards the right of the clitter). Climb over the ladder stile and proceed over the brow of the hill until you come across a large flat rock (which is a good resting place). This is known as the coffin stone, it was a resting place for the funeral party that used the Lich Path on its way to Lydford. The views at this point are pure Dartmoor, and as far as the eye can see it is open moor and very rugged but very beautiful. I have been walking on Dartmoor for about 12 years now and I still cannot believe the beauty of the ruggedness and the changes in the scenery, with different views and colours depending on weather and light.

Keep walking in the same direction into the valley towards Wistmans Wood. Wistmans Wood is one of the only areas that is left of the original Dartmoor forest, it is an ancient wood of stunted oaks covered in moss and growing amongst boulders.

Keep above the wood and bear right, following a track between two groups of trees. You must then follow the wall until reaching a ladder stile. Climb over the ladder stile and then cross the West Dart river (the best part to cross is by the weir of the Devonport Leat (607 781)). The Devonport Leat was opened in 1793 to supply water for the Plymouth docks. It is 27 miles long and starts its life at this weir and now finishes at Burrator reservoir.

Head west uphill over the brow and below Lydford Tor (599 782). At this point you can get a good view of the notorious Dartmoor Prison, built originally for and by prisoners in the Napoleonic wars. Because of its position it is not so easy to escape. With the wild moors all around, prisoners have been known to escape and end up walking back into Princetown days later.

The route now goes on a heading of 310 and over a stile in the wall. Follow the wall to the left and head for the Cowsic river. Continue to follow this gully up to the left and then go on a heading of 280. According to the map, there is a stone row at this point but I have never found it, so don't worry if you can't see any stones as I have been told they are small and overgrown now. Keep going in the same direction over White Barrow (566 794) then bear left and follow the track by the wall going downhill. Follow this track all the way into the small and pretty village of Peter Tavy, passing a stone row, a standing stone (damaged in the Second World War), White Tor on your right and Stephen's grave.

Enter Peter Tavy and head for the church of St Peter. Walk down the track behind the church – it is signposted to the Peter Tavy Inn. Walk past the inn and after about 100 metres, take the bridlepath on the right, signposted to Mary Tavy. The track narrows, with lovely views and the sound of the Tavy on the left.

Walk through the gate and head for the church, descending down to the Tavy and crossing using the new wooden footbridge. After rain the water thunders down under this bridge on its way to Tavistock, and it's worth a few moments of relaxation at this point. After crossing the bridge, go through the gate on the right and follow the path up through the woods until you reach a road. Follow the road past Mary Tavy Power Station and some pretty cottages and into the village of Mary Tavy. Pass St Mary's Church and on reaching a road junction bear right, signposted towards Horndon. Walk past the primary school and follow the road signposted to Tavistock and Okehampton. Proceed over the bridge and climb up the hill, taking the bridlepath on the left by Glebe Cottage. Continue on this path until you reach the main road.

Cross the road with care as this is the main Okehampton to Tavistock road (A386) and go along the Brentor road. Walk straight on at the crossroads. After passing over a cattle grid (there is now a great view of Brentor church), carry on up the hill and drop down the other side. As you start to go around a right bend, take the road down to the left with a no through road sign. The road becomes a track and crosses over a disused railway and then a river bridge. Keep on this track and climb up through the trees. On reaching a junction, turn left and follow this on to a proper metalled road, passing a road and a bridlepath at Crosstrees. Walk around the bend and take the bridlepath on the right. Go through a gate and follow the hedge/fence on your left to the end of the field. Go through the gate and turn right to follow the road until you reach the entrance to Brentor church on your right. The car park on your left at this point has some toilets. It is well worth the climb up to the church for its superb views over the moor.

This is a perfect end to this stage, St Michael de Rupe Church is perched on top of Brentor (471 804), which is a volcanic outcrop. It was built in 1140 and means 'of the rock'. (Don't forget to sign the visitors book!)

Alternative route from Powder Mills to the track below White Tor – 9miles

If the military range is in use, follow this route. After leaving the car park at Higher Cherrybrook Bridge (635 771), turn left and walk down the main road towards Princetown. Keep on the grass verge. It is two miles to Two Bridges and this part must be taken with great care. Just before Two Bridges there is a tor on the right called Crockern Tor (616 757). This tor is famous for its history as it is nearly central to the stannary towns of Chagford, Plymouth, Ashburton and Tavistock. It was chosen for the place for the Tinners' Parliament. At one time Dartmoor was one of Europe's richest areas for this ore, and because of this the tinners were allowed to establish their own parliament. They had their own laws and people were sent to Lydford gaol if they broke any laws or refused to turn up when summoned by the stannary parliament. This parliament sat from about 1494 until 1796, when tin supplies started to dwindle.

At Two Bridges, just past Crockern Tor on the right, there is a car park. In the summer there is usually an ice cream van. The Two Bridges hotel has a bar selling cream teas, meals and has rooms on offer.

Carry on in the same direction and then bear right towards Tavistock and follow this road for another two miles until you come to Rundlestone (574 750). Instead of bearing right just past Two Bridges, you can make a detour into Princetown. The small village is overpowered by the prison, however, there are also public houses, cafés, shops, toilets and a visitors centre with lots to offer in the way of Dartmoor history, including an information centre. The Plume of Feathers has a camping field and rooms in its camping barn, and offers food, alcohol and entertainment some evenings. If you visit Princetown, to get to Rundlestone you walk past the prison, church and the new prison museum. Carry along this road out of the village and when you get to the road junction, turn left and you are at Rundlestone.

At Rundlestone, you take the track on the right, signposted to Great Mis Tor. This tor used to be on the military range, but was taken out of it a couple of years ago. After Great Mis Tor, take a bearing of 300 degrees, keeping just outside the firing range. **Warning: red and white poles show the range boundary.** Head down towards the River Walkham and up the other side towards the cairn at (548 777). Now head towards White Tor on about 330 degrees, skirting the walls and taking care around the boggy area. You must then climb up the other side and pick up the track which you back on course for Peter Tavy. If it has been very wet this area can be unpleasant and another route available is to walk down towards Roos Tor and then pick up the track going through the fields at (528 768). Follow the track down into Peter Tavy, where you can pick up the Lich Path as described in the latter part of Stage 3.

Stage 4: Brentor to Tavistock – 6 miles

After visiting Brentor church, go back to the road and turn right. Then take the second right into the village of North Brentor. Follow the road to the right past the church. Continue along this road around and into Mary Tavy. There is a bus service along this road into Tavistock if you prefer.

Cross the road and take the track opposite. Continue on this and then follow the lane passing the school and church. At the end of the road take the footpath on your right to a footbridge, then climb to a right-hand bend. Go over the stile on your left, and follow the wall on the right uphill to a gate. Carry on through another gate and then a stile. Go over the stile and continue with the hedge on your right, descending to a gate which you have to go through. After this, look out for a gap in the wall on the other side of the field. This is your next objective, then make for a sturdy stone stile.

Go across the next field to a gap in the hedge, then to a gate next to a tree on the right of the buildings. Go through the gate and walk along the track to the lane, turn left and cross the River Tavy by using Harford Bridge. Turn right at the next junction and right at the crossroads. Go up over the hill and down the other side to reach the main Princetown road. Turn right and continue down to the main Okehampton road, where you turn left into Tavistock.

The Princetown Tracks Option – Bellever to Tavistock – 19 miles

Princetown Tracks is a semi-circular route. It is possible to break the journey in Princetown or the Yelverton/Burrator area. An overnight stay in Princetown or the Yelverton area is possible. There are many good walking tracks around Princetown. The town – in reality no bigger than a village - is at the heart of the moors. Like the Lich Path, this Dartmoor route also starts from Bellever youth hostel. From there it moves south, then curves westward to Princetown. It continues on old walking tracks and over or alongside several tors into the centre of Tavistock. The walking is varied and quite energetic, but it is possible to leave the route if bad weather or tiredness make this necessary. Walking on the old tracks and the river valleys **can be exposed and gruelling**, even when the weather is unremarkable elsewhere. There is little to protect from the sweep of a cold wind or squall on parts of the route, so **go equipped for all eventualities**.

Stage 5: Bellever to Princetown – 7½ miles

From Bellever youth hostel (655 773), leave the hostel complex and go back east to the forest walk car park on your right and turn right on the track heading south signposted to "Laughter Hole". Follow this forest track past the car park through the gate and head uphill. As you can see from the map, there are four hut circles adjacent to the area. These are the circular remains of prehistoric dwellings and they proliferate throughout the moor.

When the track comes into a clearing take the track signposted "Laughter Hole Farm". Ignore any tracks and carry on going ahead through the next gate and onto a green lane with walled fields on both sides. You come to the buildings of Laughter Hole Farm (658 758), go past these and through the next gate. When you are around this area keep your eyes out for some Roe Deer. I spotted two grazing just above the farm the last time I walked it. You continue on the right hand track signposted "country road B3357 at Huccaby Cottage", this track goes uphill to another gate which leads to the open moor. The track that you now need to follow is signposted "Dunnabridge Pound", this is a good firm track with extensive views out over the valley of the East Dart River and Riddon Ridge on your left and on your right you will see Laughter Tor. As you carry on along this track on your right you will see on this side of the wall a stone row and on the other side of the wall a large standing stone. Also as you start dropping down towards Dunnabridge you will have a good view of Bellever Tor also on your right and behind you. When you go through the next gate you are entering the "Brownberry Newtake", which is part of the "Dartmoor Pony Society Moorland scheme", here you may see pure Dartmoor ponies which the society are reintroducing and trying to bring back to the moor instead of the interbred horses of all shapes and sizes you see on the moor at the moment.

You will approach the farm buildings associated with Dunnabridge Farm. The path passes to the left of these and comes out by a distinctive circular stone wall which is the old pound which, as its name suggests, was used to keep the beasts of those who had transgressed against local grazing agreements in some way. Come out to the Dartmeet road and walk uphill over the cattle grid until you have passed the field on the left after the pound.

Diversion to use after persistent heavy rain

Warning: the following route involves crossing stepping stones which may be difficult to use if the river is in full spate. If you are walking after excessive rain and you suspect that the river may be running high, consider the alternative below. Follow the Dartmeet road for about a mile then turn right to Huccaby Bridge. This is a lengthy diversion, but you can rejoin the Sherberton Track after crossing Hucccaby Bridge by following the road up the hill, and round to the right to Sherberton.

Continuation of route

At Dunnabridge, join the road and turn left. Follow this over a cattle grid and then leave the roadside by a small track on the right to go down into the valley. Follow the stone wall until you come to the gate and signpost (Sherberton Bridge Fm via Stepping Stones). Follow the path downhill through the gaps in the walls, there are also some blue dots to help.

You are now following the West Dart river and will pass the remains of a footbridge. Follow the path along the riverside – which is very beautiful to some stepping stones. These cross the West Dart and you then follow the River Swincombe. Follow this to a second set of stepping stones. Cross these and follow the path to a gate. Go through this and take a sharp right out of the valley and up to Sherberton Farm (645 734). Take the main track through and out of the complex, and take the track west on a bearing of 253 across the moor, ignoring a path off to Little Sherberton on the right.

Continue on the open moorland track for about one mile. At a field wall the bearing changes to 215 as the track turns more south-westerly. Keep going in this direction until you come to a major moorland junction of tracks. Take the path going straight on, signposted Whiteworks, and follow the blue marker posts to a gate and another signpost. Take the right path, signposted Princetown, on a bearing of 283 to another gate. Go through the gate and follow a really good path with the Princetown aerial in view for 99 per cent of the time.

After about one and a quarter miles, as the track starts rising after crossing Cholake Head, you will come to a kistvaen, marked on the map as a cairn circle.

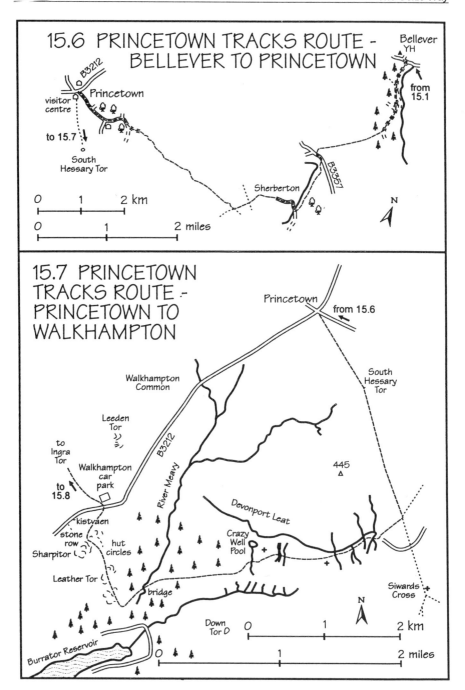

15.6 PRINCETOWN TRACKS ROUTE - BELLEVER TO PRINCETOWN

15.7 PRINCETOWN TRACKS ROUTE - PRINCETOWN TO WALKHAMPTON

15.8 PRINCETOWN TRACKS ROUTE - WALKHAMPTON TO OAKLEY

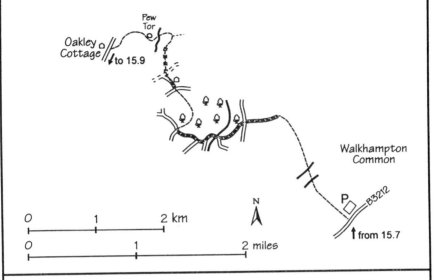

15.9 PRINCETOWN TRACKS ROUTE - OAKLEY TO TAVISTOCK

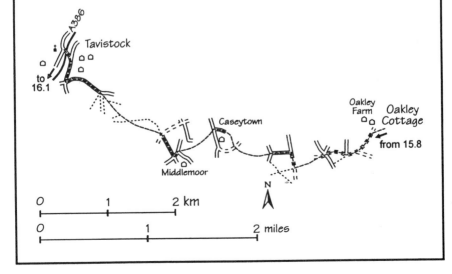

This is the Crock 'o Gold. You will see it on the left-hand side. It looks like a mini-stone circle. Perhaps the name is some reference to a folk memory of buried items from the Bronze Age cremation site, or is of some other significance.

Continue on the track, enjoying the views over the east moorland area. On a clear day you can see at least 20 tors to the north and east. You will come to a junction of tracks, the left-hand one is marked for Peat Cot but our route carries straight on down past the house on the right called Bullpark, over the Devonport Leat and on up the hill alongside a plantation, passing Tor Royal. This was built in 1798 by Thomas Tyrwhitt, who was the brains behind Dartmoor prison and the rise of Princetown. Take the metalled road past the Tor Royal buildings and follow it uphill for a mile, passing South Hessary House on your left and North Plantation on your right. The lane comes out in the centre of Princetown by the small building which houses both the local chapel and the church of St Michael and All Angels.

This is a good point to take a break. Princetown became the administrative centre for the moor in the 19th century. It is now famous for its prison, but there is more to the place than this. There is the High Moorland Centre with the usual tourist assistance plus a wealth of information about the moor. There is a gift shop, earth mysteries centre, café with sofas and coal fire, and two inns which offer a wide range of services, including bunk-house accommodation in the case of the Plume of Feathers.

Stage 6: Princetown to Walkhampton car park — 5½ miles

There is some ascent involved in this stage, as well as moorland walking. If bad weather or fatigue necessitate cutting the walking short this can be done at Leather Tor by going to Burrator and Yelverton.

Take the track from the centre of Princetown running from behind the Railway Inn and Plume of Feathers car parks. This is the Jobbers' Road – a medieval track used by travelling wool workers to move between Tavistock and Buckfastleigh. It was also used as the route for bringing prisoners on foot to Princetown from Ivybridge Station in the last century.

Follow the track with the wall to the left of you for three-quarters of a mile. This leads along a fine track to South Hessary Tor (597 724) with views over the moor to the walking ahead. Continue along the track after passing South Hessary Tor, following a line of water company boundary stones and a good wall. When the wall goes off to the left, continue straight on until just after a boundary stone that is in the middle of the track. Here you come to a crossroads of tracks (602 708). (Although seeming miles from everyday life, there is a road not far to the left running parallel with you.) Turn right. The track you have now joined moves gently downhill. There is a track to the left after 350 metres. Ignore this and continue to Older Bridge. The Devonport Leat runs close to the path for about 700 metres before going off to the right. To the south is a wayside cross, one of several on the monastic route used as a waymarker. We are above the Newleycombe valley. Continue on the track, passing disused tin workings, and look out for the cross at Crazywell Pool (583 704) on the hill to the north-west. The pool is well worth a short diversion. There is a lovely view from the

Crazywell Cross (Barrator in distance) - Photo by Dennis Waters

cross over to Burrator Reservoir, opened in 1898 to supply the city of Plymouth with water.

Rejoin the track, which is easy enough to find just below to the right. Follow the track into the forest and at a split of tracks turn right, then left signposted Leather Tor Farm. On reaching a stream, take the track over Leather Tor Bridge, signposted Leather Tor Farm again. Follow it until it comes out of the forest and onto the boulder-strewn side of Leather Tor.

Take the path directly by the fence and follow this until you come to the Devonport Leat again. Cross at the clapper bridge and follow the wall around to the right around the tor. Then head for the left of Sharpitor as this will reward you with superb views over Burrator, Plymouth and the sea.

On reaching the saddle you will see the main Yelverton/Princetown road, plus two car parks below you. Aim for the nearest of the two. If you prefer, go first to the summit of Sharpitor, then follow the path straight down to the road. You will come upon a stone row (if you can find it), unimpressive now, but in such a location perhaps an indication of the grave of someone important once. There is another stone row across the road on the common. Cross the road to the nearest car park on Walkhampton Common.

Stage 7: Walkhampton car park to Tavistock centre – 6 miles

If you like ponies, you will love this section as there are hundreds of them. From the first (southernmost)car park, take the track leading out of it and follow it downhill. On the horizon, to the west, if you had not noticed it before, stands the amazing landmark of Brentor, looking uncannily like Glastonbury

Tor. After two-thirds of a mile the track cross the Princetown railway, now disused, and used by cyclists and walkers. Now go through the gate and enter the more cultivated area around Routrundle.

Continue on the track and after 500 yards you pass another hut circle (again not easy to spot amongst all the boulders) and follow the edge of cultivated land, skirting Ingra Tor. Three hundred yards after the hut circle, the track bears sharp left and you come in sight of a metalled road at 550 724. At this point stop and take in the super view, on your right you can see Swell Tor Quarry and ahead of you on a heading of about 336 is Vixen Tor, where the nasty witch Vixana met her death by being pushed off the top by a noble moorman. Take the road for 300 yards to the next crossroads. Go straight over and downhill to Ward Bridge. After this follow the road uphill for 300 yards, noting the mossy walls and a peculiar cave on the right which is an old adit to a tin mine. Follow this to a cattle grid and take the very minor access road bearing right to the crossroads at Stoneycroft, this area is notorious for its woodpeckers and you can often hear them tapping away at the trees above. Take the track beside this large house and follow the footpaths through the fields eventually coming out by Gees Farm (536 728) and onto the road.

Take the minor road right for 100 yards then pick up the right-hand track again as it goes towards Pew Tor Cottage. Follow the track for 500 yards past Pew Tor Cottage and onto the Tor itself, this is a really nice tor with remnants of old quarrying in the way of some dressed stones inscribed "SSP" which was for Sampford Spiney Parish, there is also a rock-basin on the most northerly of the tor, this is a depression formed by a small stone being rubbed around by wind or water in a groove and eventually over thousands of years being enlarged into a saucer shaped pool.

After exploring the top, follow the track down on a westerly heading from Pew Tor. There are several, but they all come together at the point you want by Oakley Cottage (523 732). Take the track south-west, and follow it for 500 yards to a junction of minor roads. Go right toward Reddicliffe Farm and then take the second path on the left through the bracken to pass the farm. You are on Plasterdown and paths proliferate. If you follow the wall of the farm to the corner and then take a track on a bearing of 290, cross a road and keep in the same direction you will come to Downhouse at 512 729.

The stile to the start of the footpath to Casey town is in the trees and marked with a yellow dot. This track runs for just over a mile to Caseytown, following yellow dots and footpath signs to where you join a minor road. Turn right and take this for 400 yards passing a bend to the left and a track off to the right until you come to a junction where the road and tacks converge. Look for the track to the left between the two roads. Follow this across Whitchurch Down and head for and past a reservoir which is the building on the top of the down (an enclosed water tower) on a bearing of about 310 (watch out for golf balls). It is worth going to the top and sitting for a while on the benches that are placed around the building just for the views of the area you have just walked and Tavistock where the Tavistock Town Walk in the centre of this busy and historic town. The next section of the walk – the Land's End Trail – leaves from the Tavistock church in the High Street.

Postscript: Dartmoor is a fabulous place with plenty of history and interest for everyone. With this route I have tried to take in as much as possible of what it has to offer. I hope you get as much enjoyment from Dartmoor as I do – with its wild open moors, past industries, villages and wildlife – all on view for everyone to enjoy for free. Dartmoor has plenty of accommodation and eating and drinking places, too many to list.

Looking Ahead: *The next section of the walk is the Land's End Trail, compiled by members of Cornish Ramblers who have prepared a route along the spine of Cornwall which we shall be following from Tavistock to Trencrom Hill. Then Alexandra Pratt takes over the walking directions for the end of our long journey through Western Britain with her route around the extremity of the peninsula which ends at St Michael's Mount.*

Section Sixteen
Land's End Trail: Tavistock to Trencrom Hill
111 miles

The Cheesewring, Bodmin Moor

The Land's End Trail Team

This section was written by members of the Ramblers Association in Cornwall who have allowed us to incorporate their route description into this guide. They are preparing a route from Land's End to Avebury which follows the spine route up the peninsula. The format of the walking details is different in the following section only. We have incorporated the Land's End Trail team's details in their original form. As in other sections, you will need the accompanying Ordnance Survey maps.

Stages:

1. Tamar Valley Stage – Tavistock to Stoke Climsland – 12 miles
2. Caradon Hill Stage – Stoke Climsland to Caradon Hill (Henwood) – 7 miles
3. East Moor Stage – Henwood to Jamaica Inn (Bolventor) – 8 miles
4. Brown Willy Stage – Bolventor to St Breward – 8 miles
5. Camel Valley – St Breward to Dunmere Bridge – 10 miles
6. Saints' Way Stage – Dunmere Bridge to Tregonetha – 8 miles
7. Castle an Dinas Stage – Tregonetha to Mitchell – 12 miles
8. Windfarm Stage – Mitchell to Chiverton Cross – 12 miles
9. Carn Brea Stage – Chiverton Cross to Beacon – 12 miles
10. Clowance Stage – Beacon to Leedstown – 13 miles
11. Hayle River Stage – Leedstown to St Erth – 7 miles
12. Trencom Stage – St Erth to Trencom Hill – 2 miles

Maps: The appropriate OS maps for the stages you are going to walk.

Starting Point: Tavistock (482 745)

Transport: Western National Buses – 01209 719988

Youth Hostels: Plymouth – Belmont House – 01752 562189, Tintagel – 01840 770334, Golant, Fowey – 01726 833507, Perranporth – 01872 573812 and Penzance – Castle Horneck – 01736 62666.

Tourist Information: Fowey – 01726 833616, Plymouth – 01752 264849 and Penzance – 01736 62207

Introduction

Last summer, while planning the spine route through Cornwall, we became aware – through Brian Stringer – of the Land's End Trail team who have been working on a route from Land's End to Avebury. Our volunteers for the West of England were already underway by then, and we decided to stick with our routes through Devon and Somerset. However, the work of the Land's End Trail team through Cornwall was so close to the route we had envisaged that Brian Stringer, who has been a great source of information about groups working in Cornwall, liaised with the team. The outcome is that, with their permission, we are incorporating their route through Cornwall as far as Trencom, near Hayle, with appropriate and grateful acknowledgeme. We hope that the royalty they receive for this section will be helpful in their work.

Below are the 12 stages of the Land's End Trail route through Cornwall. It is not yet published, though I am told that it is planned for 1998. For anyone who would like more information about the Land's End Trail, we will pass on all enquiries.

The aims of the Land's End Trail team, and, therefore, the content and style of the following sections are quite different from those of the Celtic Way Project. In a very short space the team cover more than 100 miles of walking – a prodigious achievement in itself! There is, of necessity, less descriptive text than is generally to be found in the other Celtic Way routes, and **it is vitally important that you pay close attention to the section maps and your OS maps.**

One final point: we had intended that Tintagel should be a part of the route through Cornwall. If you would like to include this intriguing place in your walking, it is possible to do so by walking along the Camel Trail and the South West Coast Path.

Stage1: Tamar Valley Stage – Tavistock to Stoke Climsland – 12 miles

From Tavistock church, walk along the High Street to the beginning of Rocky Hill on the right. Go up the hill past Rubber and Plastics, then across Watts Road and on to the old Launceston Road. Turn left on to St Maryhaye Road. Go right on to the main road, then left at the footpath sign.

In the next section you will need to keep count! Cross over three stone stiles, then three wooden and two metal gates as you continue. To reassure you that you are on the correct route, you pass Downhouse Farm after one mile, and later Stilesweek. After the second metal gate, go on to a track then turn left at the road. Follow the road to Three Oaks. Next turn right and then left, down a minor road to Blanchdown Wood, which you reach in about two miles. The road ends and becomes a track.

Continue alongside the stream on your right until the track bears left to the River Tamar. Turn right along the river bank to a bridge over a stream, and follow the permissive path uphill to Capel Tor and on to a road. Turn left to Lamerhoe Lodge, which you reach in about four miles, and find a footpath on the right. Head for a stile in the top left-hand corner of the field. There is now one more stile and a short track to bring you to the road.

Turn right on to the road, then find a footpath on the left, leading down to Horsebridge. From Horsebridge, go over the packhorse bridge (dated 1437) and into Cornwall. Follow the track and immediately turn left at a gate with a green, permissive path signpost. Follow this path alongside the River Tamar for one mile, until you get to the end of the second stream. Turn right then left, along a track to Luckett village.

Turn right in the village. You are walking uphill and will pass Rose Cottage. Turn left at the junction to walk along a level road, passing Court House on the left. After 100 metres, turn right up a track and proceed for about 200 metres to Treoviston Farm. Here, go left to a corrugated shed and walk 35 metres to a wooden stile. Take care, there is barbed wire on the stile! Follow the left hedge to a metal gate in the corner. From here, head for a wooden fence, then go slightly right of the white building, over a wooden stile to a wooden gate and Higher Trowes Farm.

Go across the road – there is a footpath sign directing you over a metal gate. Follow the right-hand hedge uphill (an engine house is visible to the east, on your left). Head for the top corner of the field and a metal gate. Turn right along the road, go past Sunnymead to a T-junction. Turn left to Stoke Climsland.

Stage 2: Caradon Hill Stage – Stoke Climsland to Caradon Hill – 7 miles

Our starting point is opposite Stoke Climsland church, where you take a lane (signed). This turns into a footpath, going downhill to a stream. The path then goes uphill to Duchy Home Farm. Here, go straight on past the yellow building in the yard, and follow a track uphill to a wooden gate on the left. Go through the gate and follow the wall, **taking care not to wander into the quarry!**

When you reach a stone, step stile, go over it into a field. Follow the right-hand hedge to another stone stile, then a wooden stile. Next go half-right to a stile leading on to the road. Turn left along the road, passing Burraton Cottages. Cross the A388 (**beware traffic!**). Continue straight on along an unclassified road which becomes a track. Follow the track around a double bend (right and left) to the B3257. Turn right for half a mile along the road, and find a white track on the left. This track has two bends to the left and ends at a gate into a field. Follow the left-hand hedge to Treven Farm. There is a track to the right of the farm which leads to the road.

Turn right along the road and continue for 75 metres. Find a gate in the hedge on your left. Now follow the hedge on the right to a gate. Through the gate, follow the hedge on the left to the far hedge, then go right to a gate which leads to the road. Turn right for Linkinhorne. Go past the inn to a T-junction and bear right (signed Plushabridge, Rilla Mill). Continue to another T-junction, and go right for a few metres to a sign on the left directing you across the field to a metal gate. Cross the field, aiming for a big tree, and go through the metal gate. Follow the left-hand hedge to a 5-feet drop. Find the steps to the stream. Continue through Patrieda Barton Drive. Turn left on the drive and proceed to a short lane on the right. Go through a wooden gate and walk diagonally uphill to a hedge. Follow the hedge on the left to a road. Cross this road and follow the hedge on the left to another road.

Turn left on to the road then follow a road on the right to Rillaton. Turn right, walk for 50 metres then turn left to Starbridge. Follow the road past Lower Lake Farm – the road keeps bending left – you continue along the road to North Darley. Cross the B3254, go up a track and over a wooden stile to Darley Wood. Follow the yellow waymarks to Henwood. Turn left into the village, then fork right past the yellow Methodist chapel.

Stage 3: East Moor Stage – Henwood to Jamaica Inn – 8 miles

From Henwood village, take the road leading to Sharptor. Take the right-hand fork into the village, where the road bends left then right. It then becomes a track – signed to Wardbrook Farm. Keep left here. Go through a wooden gate in the farmyard and then follow a disused railway line. The trackbed makes a good path about three metres wide. Keep a metal fence on your left for nearly a mile. Go through a gate, and at the third wooden gate cross a small stream. Bear half-left to Withybrook.

Go across a stepping stone, through a wooden gate followed by a metal gate, and then up the embankment to a level track. Turn right and proceed for 250 metres to a wooden gate. Follow the track (**it may be very wet**) until it becomes

16.1 TAVISTOCK TO STOKE CLIMSLAND

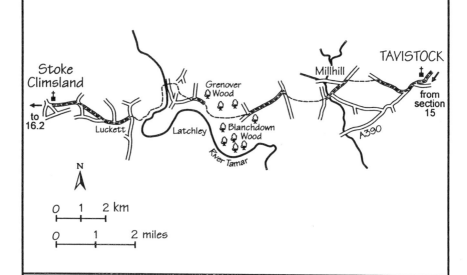

16.2 STOKE CLIMSLAND TO CARADON

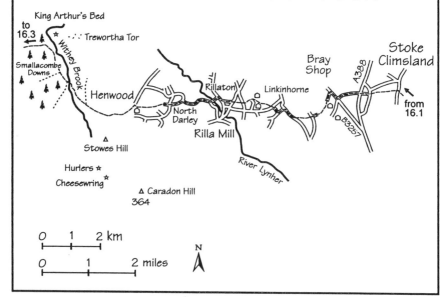

16.3 CARADON TO MERRY MEETING AND CAMEL TRAIL

16.4 CAMEL TRAIL TO BLACK CROSS

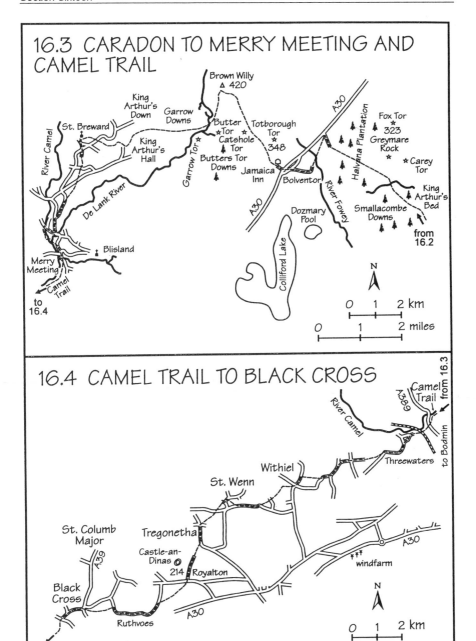

a level track (another disused railway line). This passes through a wooded area (Smallcombe Downs) for one mile. When you reach an open area on the right, find a wooden gate. Follow the track down to Rushyford Gate through a small field.

After the ford, head uphill in a north-westerly, half-left direction. As the hill levels out, Halvana Plantation, a conifer wood, appears ahead. Tracks can be found leading to a gate into the woods (208 773). Once you are in the woods, follow the track to a metal gate leading into a lane, ignoring the tracks to the left and right. Follow the lane to a road (the old A30) and continue to Webbs Down. This is partly open moorland and is walkable in all directions. There are sheep tracks and vehicle tracks. Try to find a vehicle track bearing north-west. In the woods, some areas are being felled and **directions are difficult**. Try to keep heading in a north-westerly direction through the woods.

Follow the track to the old A30 (Webbs Down). The new A30 bypass is ahead. Turn left. Ignore the first stile, which has a green footpath sign, and go to the second stile, which can be seen just ahead. Follow the yellow waymarks across four fields, over five stiles and across stepping stones down to the new bridge over the River Fowey. Go up a track through Dryworks Farm, and turn right along the road to Bolventor. This path is very well waymarked. Bolventor is a small hamlet – but access and parking here are very good.

Stage 4: Brown Willy Stage – Jamaica Inn, Bolventor to St Breward – 8 miles

In Bolventor, car parking is available at Jamaica Inn (184 767) for those joining the route here. There is no direct access to the other side of the new road at Bolventor except by turning right downhill for 200 metres, and then turning left under the new A30. Turn right at the next road then left towards Bolventor Church. Continue uphill for 350 metres, to a footpath sign on the right. Go over the stile and across the field to a stone stile. Here, follow the left-hand hedge downhill to a gap. Keep following the hedge until it ends, then follow a waymark and stone wall, also on the left. This will lead you to a stile where you join a track.

Cross a stream on your way to Dairywell Hill Farm. At the farm, follow the waymark and, keeping to the right of the farm building, follow the track as it leads uphill. Continue uphill along the track to Tolborough Tor, on your right. Ignoring a cross track, keep straight on. After 450 metres the track ends.

This is now open moorland but your path is obvious. Following the hedge on your left, bear slightly left and continue heading north. Continue to follow the hedge. Brown Willy is in view straight ahead. Soon the path gets better on the left side of the hedge and is distinct. Keep following the path to a metal gate. From here follow the left-hand fence, with Catshole Tor on your left.

Continue north, following a hedge where the fence crosses a path. **The stile here is difficult.** After the stile, cross over a wall and walk along the left-hand side. The path may be **boggy**. After one and a half miles, you come to a wire fence, which joins to our fence! Here go over the wooden stile on your left, which has a Nature Conservancy Council notice. From the stile head west, following a small track to the summit of Brown Willy.

From the summit, head in a southerly direction along the ridge. The path is easy – follow the waymarks with black arrows to Garrow Farm, and then along the track to the west. A track to the left leads over a stile and into a small plantation. Next go over a stile and on to open moor.

Follow the hedge on your right. Keep straight on when the wall ends, following the waymarks to King Arthur's Hall direct to another corner of the fence. Follow the path, with the fence on your left. After three fields the footpath goes to the left. Follow the right-hand hedge to Lower Candra Farm. Walk through the yard to a gate leading to open moor. Head in a south-westerly direction towards a farm on the left. Find a good vehicle track and head right to Irish Farm. Go downhill, diagonally across fields to a gap into a boggy area. Go over two stiles and a footbridge. Follow the right-hand hedge to Palmers Farm, where a gate leads you to a track and then on to a road. Cross the road. A footpath sign now leads you to follow the right-hand hedge to a stile. Follow the hedge on your left, then turn left over a stile. Follow the footpath to a track to St Breward Church (097 774).

Stage 5: Camel Valley – St Breward to Dunmere Bridge – 10 miles

There is car parking in St Breward, next to the church and pub (097 774). Follow the road to the left, past the last public house, then turn left and right to Ryelands. The road, which is right in front of houses, goes to Lower Penquite, then along a footpath and over stiles to Higher Penquite. Turn right along the road, then left along an old lane after 50 metres. You then walk across a short stretch of open moor to the road, where you turn left to Penvorder Cottages. Walk along the front of the cottages to find a gate, then go across a small playing field. Head left to an ornate iron gate, then take a granite stile into fields.

Follow the right-hand hedge to a wire fence with a wooden stile. Once across this, follow the fence on your left to a gate into the lane at Lower Lank Farm. Follow the lane to a road, then head south to Penpont (waymarked). After three-quarters of a mile there is a T-junction, turn right then right again to Poley's Bridge. Find the entrance to the Camel Trail in the car park on the left. The Camel Trail is a footpath/cycle track along the route of an old railway line. It is, therefore, a level and wide track, much **frequented by cyclists**. The route is easy to follow as it progresses through a wooded area, following the River Camel for most of the way.

Continuing on the Camel Trail, you will come across attractive pools along the river, including Weir Pool. At the north side of Dunmere Bridge, avoid crossing the busy A389 by taking the unsigned track to the left opposite the house at the side of the track. This emerges on the Bodmin spur of the Camel Trail. Turn left to go to Bodmin or turn right to go under the A389 and up the access track to an official Camel Trail car park at the rear of the public house. The most pleasant route to Bodmin for walkers from the north is by the ancient packhorse track. This begins to climb to the left, just before the unsigned track mentioned above. The packhorse track is not signed or waymarked. When this track joins the Bodmin spur, turn left. Bodmin has all the usual facilities of a county town.

16.5 BLACK CROSS TO CALLESTICK

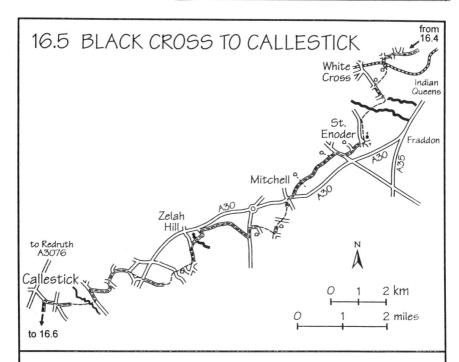

16.6 CALLESTICK TO SCORRIER

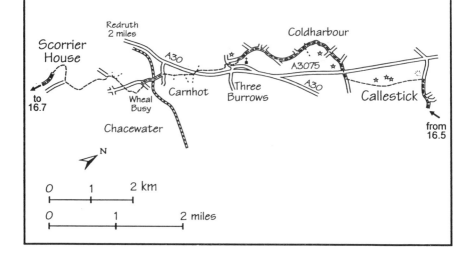

16.7 SCORRIER TO CARN ARTHEN

16.8 CARN ARTHEN TO CLOWANCE WOOD

Stage 6: Saints Way Stage – Dunmere Bridge to Tregonetha – 8 miles

For walkers joining the route at the beginning of this stage, there is free car parking in the official Camel Trail car park behind the public house (036 671). Take the gated exit at the bottom of the car park and turn left, emerging after 100 metres on to the Camel Trail, where you turn left. Continue to the information board, and take the left fork (the Camel Trail goes right). Walk under the bridge and follow the river to a footbridge across a stream. Go over a wooden stile on to a track, which you follow uphill to the road. Turn right to Nanstallon.

Walk on, from the school bus shelter on the left to a white house (Three Waters) on the right. At the T-junction, follow the road to the right, over a bridge and down a metalled road to crossroads. Here, turn left (Tremore). Follow the road for 200 metres. Take the track on the right and follow this in a westerly direction for one and a half miles. At the road turn right then left, downhill to Cork Farm. At the gate, continue along the track to a small footbridge. Turn left along the road to a T-junction. Take the right fork, signposted Withal, and follow the road to a T-junction with a track (to Lawellen Farm).

From the metal gate, follow the left-hand hedge to a wooden gate. Follow yellow waymarkers through the wood to another gate, and then go around the left-hand hedge to the end of the field. You will reach a track. To confirm that you are in the correct place, there should be a big shed on your right. Turn left along the track, to Whitehay Farm and then to the road. Here, turn left to climb a long, steep hill, and then turn right into Withiel.

At the church, take the track on the right (Saints Way waymark). After 50 metres the Saints Way goes right, but our route is straight on, up a stony track which narrows and winds to the left. Follow this to a gate into a field. Follow the right-hand hedge to a gap and metal gate. Walk up a metalled lane to Lanjrew Farm. Proceed through the farm and follow a track downhill to a fork. Keeping right at the fork, follow the track to a metal gate into a field. Ignore other metal gates on the right, as you follow the left-hand hedge and track to yet another metal gate. Keep following this track to join the road. Turn right and follow the road to Prince Park.

Go over the packhorse bridge to Demelza Mill. Continue uphill past Rostigan Farm on the left and a signpost to St Wenn. After three-quarters of a mile the road levels and bends to the right. On the right is a stone stile, the footpath goes diagonally right to the buildings on the skyline. Go over a stile then follow the left-hand hedge to the corner of the field. Follow the school buildings, looking for a granite stile. Turn left and go past the school to St Wenn church.

Follow the road slightly downhill for about 130 metres, to a large gate on the right. On the left of the gate there is a stile. Follow the right-hand hedge to another stone stile, then head diagonally left. About half-way across, look for your next stile. Go over the stile and across a narrow road. There is another stile, and then you head to the right-hand corner of the field, where there is a junction of barbed wire. Go through the stile and then head down over the sloping field towards a stile about three-quarters of the distance along the hedge. Once through the stile, head to a gate then diagonally to a gate in the right-hand corner. Turn right, go through a gate and follow the wooded track to the hamlet of Tregonetha.

Stage 7: Castle an Dinas Stage – Tregonetha to Mitchell – 12 miles

Car parking is available at Tregonetha Green (9956/638). Follow the B3274 southwards for a quarter of a mile to a series of roadside curve signs. Between the sixth and seventh signs, turn right. Head for the conifer trees on the skyline, south-westwards. At the conifers, the path joins a track (trees to the left). A gate leads to a track which bears slightly left. Follow the track to Castle Farm, and beyond to the road. The hill on the right is Castle-an-Dinas.

Cross the road and walk along the track to Royalton Farm. Follow the track through a gate and on to a wooden stile. Keep straight ahead. Follow the footpath and stiles in a south-westerly direction (by Blackacre Riding Stables). Turn left at the road, which bears south-west to a T-junction. Go right here and follow the road, turning left at Mons Tenement into the hamlet of Ruthvoes. Keep along the road to a T-junction, where you turn right. Walk along the road for a quarter of a mile to the farm entrance on the left to Treliver Farm. Turn left and right at the farm buildings, then follow the muddy track to a fairly new stile. Go over this and follow the right-hand hedge to a gate. Keep ahead to a wooden stile and steps to the road. Continue straight ahead to the road to Black Cross.

Go across the road and under a new bridge. Follow the road uphill to the A392 on the left, avoiding the left-hand turn to Carworgie. Find the track to Tresithney Farm and turn right. Go along the track until it enters a field. Head for two oak trees on the farm hedge. Go through the hedge – heading south-westerly to the right-hand corner of the field, where you go through a gap to the track leading to Barton Lane. Turn left and head downhill for half a mile. Where the road enters trees, find the footpath on the right (no sign).

After a short distance in the woods, the path turns right across the stream. After half a mile the path re-crosses the stream and then it follows a hedge on the right into a field. Go straight ahead with the hedge on the right until a road is reached through a gate by Troan Farm. Turn left into the farmyard, find a metal gate into a field then follow the right-hand hedge straight ahead to St Enoder Church. The gate on the track by the church leads to a road. Turn right, then at the T-junction turn left. Take the next right and keep to the road for three-quarters of a mile. Cross the A3058 and continue along the road for more than a mile, to the signpost to Carvynick (a quarter of a mile). When the road reaches the roundabout on the A3076, turn left. Go over the A30 into Mitchell.

Stage 8: Windfarm Stage – Mitchell to Chiverton Cross – 12 miles

There is car parking at the Plume and Feathers (860 545). The footpath starts near to Rose Terrace (no sign). The path runs uphill between two hedges and ends at a wooden kissing gate into a field. Follow the path to a bungalow, a small wooden kissing-gate, then across the road to Hendra House. Go down the track to Hendra Farm. At the end of the third field the path runs right at a metal gate. Follow the left-hand hedge until the end of the field. Go through the old gate and follow the track to a stream. Continue ahead under overhead electric wires, following the left-hand hedge to a double wooden gate. Go up the track to Trewaters bungalow, then to the A3076. Turn left then right after 150 metres, signposted Ennis

Follow the road for one mile to a T-junction, where you turn left. After 100 metres the road turns right to Ventonteague Farm. Keep along the road to a T-junction, and turn left. Find a footpath sign below a power-cable, turn right and follow the left hedge to small lane and gate. Go over a stile and through the farmyard to Trefonick Farm. Turn right for 25 metres to a metal gate on the left. Follow the overhead electric cable, with the hedge on the left, over stepping stones to the corner of the field. Follow the left-hand hedge until it goes round a corner, then take a well-trodden footpath to a hedge and stone stile. Turn right down the road to Trerice.

Look for the signpost on the left, go over the stile and follow the left-hand hedge to the bottom of the third field. Turn right to find the yellow waymark and the footbridge over the River Allen. Continue along the muddy track, past Tolgroggon, to the bridge over the Zelah bypass. Go across the old A30 to find a green lane. When this joins the road, turn right then left at the crossroads.

Heading towards Little Callestock, cross a stream, go uphill to a T-junction then turn left. After five metres, turn right along a stony track, passing Chiverton Moor Mine. Continue along the track then turn left at the road. Proceed downhill, then find a large wooden gate. Continue downhill through the gate to cross the field to its corner. Cross the stream and go through a small gate into a field. Keep ahead due west to Old Callestick Mine. The path goes through scrubland, then bears slightly right to a wooden gate. Heading diagonally right, walk around the left-hand hedge to the beginning of a track. Follow this **very muddy** track for a quarter of a mile to Callestick. Turn right to a T-junction, then go left uphill along the road to Callestick Veor. Turn left, passing through Higher Callestick Farm. Follow the track to the B3284, turn right for 50 metres to the A3075. Cross this to continue along the verge of the B3284 then go left along the minor road to Chiverton Cross via Silverwell.

Stage 9: Carn Brea Stage – Chiverton Cross to Beacon – 12 miles

There is car parking on the verges in the vicinity of Chiverton Cross (746 468). The Land's End Trail route is to the left of the church. The track is parallel to the A30 for some distance. It leads to a farm and chapel, left over the A30 then right down the road. The track continues straight on then bears left past corrugated buildings. You pass Carnhot House, go over a stream to the road then go straight across to a minor road. Over the railway bridge, continue along the road to a red telephone box. Turn left then right after 50 metres. Go right along the track to the old engineering works and follow it to the main road, the old A390.

Passing Westfield bungalow, turn left then right along a track to Killifreth. Go straight on over a stone stile into Unity Wood, following the right-hand hedge. When the path joins another, turn right and follow the path until it curves left, then right. At the end of wood, the path bears right and follows a fence to a track, this leads to the B3298. Turn right, continue on the road for a quarter of a mile then look for a footpath sign on the left. Follow the track under a bridge. The path becomes a road.

At a T-junction turn right (Pink Moors) to Vogue. At the next T-junction turn right past the Star Inn. At a fork take the left-hand road, signed Gwennap Pit. Walk uphill to the third track then turn right to the summit of Carn Marth. Turn left, go downhill along a track which becomes a road, Carn Marth Lane, and leads to the A393. Go straight across, past the telephone box and circular reservoir on left. At the road junction turn right along a track. Follow this track to the B3297. Go straight across to the road opposite and find a footpath on the left after 100 metres. Keep on this track across a field to a stile, and then go straight on along the track. Find a path on your right going downhill to Carnkie.

Fork left at the Methodist chapel, then take a signposted road/track leading to the summit of Carn Brea and the monument. Follow footpaths through rock to the west, along the ridge. The path leads on to a track. Go straight across, past a house on the left. The path is narrow and runs between two hedges, then turns left and right around a conservatory on to the road. Turn right. go down the road for 75metres then find a track on the left, which leads over a stile and across a field towards a farm. Go through a gate on to a farm track at Carn Arthen. Proceed down the track to a road. At a T-junction turn right, down to the stream at Brea Adit. Go straight across and uphill along the track, left and right, into Beacon Village.

Stage 10: Clowance Stage – Beacon to Leedstown – 13 miles

If you are joining the trail at this stage, there is car parking near the Pendarves Arms (655 394). Walk down the Tolcarne road. The road goes right (Knave-go-by) but you carry straight on to Tolcarne Farm. Follow the path down to a stream, over a stile and uphill along the right-hand hedge. Halfway along the second field, find a stone stile into another field. The path is diagonally left across the corner of the field to two granite posts. A stile leads on to the road. Go across the road, and down to Treslothan church.

Turn left at the well, past a house dated 1845. Follow the right-hand hedge to Treslothan Wood, then to the road at Higher Carwynnen Farm. Go down the road to the right. Follow the winding road to a stream. Turn left along a track to Higher Bodrivial. The path goes round the back of a house, then through four stone stiles and one wooden one at the end of a green lane.

Go across three fields to where another path joins, then head to the corner. Follow the right-hand hedge to a wooden stile, go across a track over a stile then head due south across fields to the road at Prospect Farm. Turn left, walk for 25 metres then go right, through two fields, using the gaps to track straight across. Continue on the same line through 10 fields (don't lose count!) and over 12 stiles, past Newton Round Farmhouse on the right. Follow the left-hand hedge to the B3280. Go straight across and down a lane, keeping the hedge on your left.

Keep the same line as you head across fields towards Crowan Church. The last few metres are down a short, narrow path to the left of the church and into the car park. Head in a north-westerly direction over a disused railway bridge and into a field. Following the right-hand hedge, go over a cattle grid into a field. Go over a granite grid as you continue on the same line to the B3303. There is a stile here with a sign. Go across the road and look for a blue right-of-

way sign leading across Clowance Time Share grounds. Follow the tarmacked drive through a wooded area and into a field at a stile. Follow the right-
hand hedge as it leads slightly left. Go through the gate and follow the track,
with woods on your right. The track bears right and left and follows the wood to
a wooden gate. From here, head to the corner of the field, and follow the left-
hand hedge to the gate to Clowance Wood Farm. Go across the road and past
greenhouses on the left to a gate. Turn right and then left after 50 metres along a
signposted track which leads through several gates to a bridleway. This joins a
road, and you should keep straight on. At a right-hand bend, bear left and follow the track across moorland to a gap, passing a metal fence as the track takes
you to a minor road. Turn right down the road, passing a bungalow (Southerly).
Continue straight on to a crossroads on the B3302. Leedstown is reached in a
quarter of a mile.

Stage 11: Hayle River Stage – Leedstown to St Erth – 7 miles

Car parking is available at Leedstown (607 341). Go across the B3302 and along
the farm lane to Polglase Farm. Keep to the left of the farm buildings as you go
through the gate (**beware of the pit**). Continue along the right-hand hedge to
stepping stones over a wall under a fallen tree. Turn left along a track, passing a
white cottage (gate) on the way to the B3280. Turn right, walk for a quarter of a
mile then find the path just after the primary school on the left. Follow the path,
left and right and straight on, then bend sharp left to Carsize Farm.

Follow the track bending to the right into old mine workings. Turn sharp
left on the track and head for a metal gate. Keep heading south-west over a stile
in the hedge. Turn left and right – follow the path to a stile leading on to a road
(follow the left-hand hedge if necessary). This is Conker Road – cross it and follow the metalled track which leads into a field. Go through the farm downhill,
then slightly right and immediately left to a stone stile. Once over this, go
straight across the field to a hedge and look for stepping stones over a wall.

Follow the left-hand hedge to a wooden, yellow marker post. Go over a
hump into the wooded area, looking for an old shed on the right. Head through
Kerthen Wood farmyard to a track. Go straight across the track then through
two fields, following the right-hand hedge. Bear right to look for a wooden stile
in the corner. Follow the right-hand hedge to another wooden stile in the corner, go over this to a track. Follow the track to a field, head north-west into another field and to a wooden stile. Past the stile, follow the left-hand hedge to a
minor road (Bosworgy Road).

Turn left and follow the road to a T-junction (Gurlyn Hill). Turn right, go
across the stream (Countess Bridge Lane) and along the road to a farmhouse on
the left. Turn left along a track and go through a galvanized gate to follow the
right-hand hedge to stepping stones over a wall. Your route is now straight on
to Trennack Farm. Here, go over a stile, through a narrow gap between a shed
and a farm building and walk down granite steps (signed). Turn left. Next go
down a slight incline then turn right down a **very muddy** track to a fork (561
332). Go through a wooden gate to a narrow footpath to Trennack Mill. Turn
left, and cross a bridge (blue marker post) over the River Hayle. Turn right along
the river bank to St Erth church.

16.9 CLOWANCE WOOD TO ST. ERTH

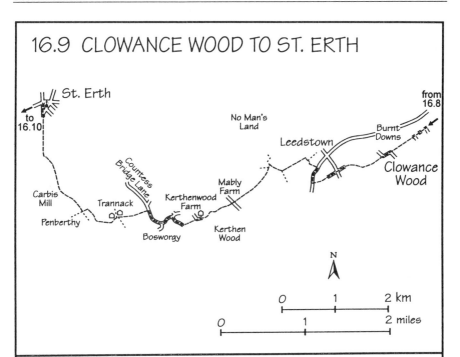

16.10 ST. ERTH TO TRENCROM FORT

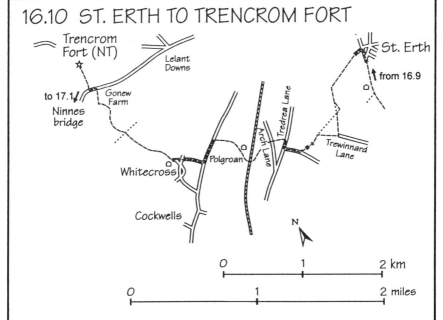

Stage 12: Trencrom Stage – St Erth to Trencrom Hill – 2 miles

Cross the bridge and go past toilets to the path on the left by a white house. Follow it across two fields to Tredrea Manor. Turn left and the track bends to the right before joining a metalled road. Go to a T-junction and turn right. At the next T-junction, turn right then left on to a footpath. Cross a lane to a wider track, which leads into a field. Bear left to a railway crossing. Go up the lane and through Polgrean Farm to the A30. Turn left to Whitecross School, then go right up the lane to Collorian. From here, continue straight on to the foot of Trencom Hill.

Looking Ahead: The walking directions from here begin at Trencom hill fort.

Again, we acknowledge the use of material prepared by the Land's End Trail Team and wish them well in their project to complete a long-distance walking route from Land's End to Avebury.

Section Seventeen
The Penwith Round – a circular route around Penwith and a linear route to St Michael's Mount

37 miles

St Michael's Mount

Alexandra Pratt

Alexandra Pratt is a graduate of Sussex University and is a relatively recent arrival in Cornwall. She has worked as a tour guide in the area and has completed this section on Penwith and has her own book of walks (Discovery Walks in Cornwall) in the far tip of Cornwall which is published this year, also by Sigma. She has had articles published on Cornish antiquities in Cornish World.

Stages:

Trencrom Hill to St Michael's Mount – 5 miles

Mousehole to Treen – 7 miles

Treen to Crows-An-Wra – 8½ miles

Crows-An-Wra to Cape Cornwall – 6 miles

Cape Cornwall to Penzance – 11 miles

Maps: Landranger 203, OS Explorer 7 (Land's End)

Highlights: Linear route – Trencrom Fort, Ninnesbridge chapel, Ludgvan church and St Michael's Mount. Circuit route – Castallack Round, The Pipers, Merry Maidens stone circle, Tregiffian barrow, Boskenna Cross, Treryn Dinas cliff castle, St Buryan, Boscawen-un stone circle, Sancreed church and crosses, Chapel Downs holy well, Sancreed Beacon, Carn Euny settlement, Brane barrow, Crows-An-Wra, Chapel Carn Brea, Nanjulian Cove, Carn Gloose, Cape Cornwall, Tregeseal stone circle, Chun Castle and Quoit, Bosullow Trehyllys settlement, Bodrifty settlement, Mulfra Quoit and settlement, Gulval, Penzance.

Starting Point: Trencrom Hill (518 363)

Additional Information: St Michael's Mount (National Trust Office) – 01736 710507

Transport: Western National Bus Company – 01209 719988

Accommodation: Youth hostels – Castle Horneck, Penzance – 01736 362666, fax 01736 362663; Land's End, St Just In Penwith – 01736 788437, fax 01736 787337.

Tourist Information: Penzance – 01736 362207

Introduction

From high, lonely moors, to gentle, wooded valleys to dramatic seascapes, Penwith provides a suitably timeless and startlingly beautiful backdrop for the wealth of antiquities held in this, the last stronghold of the Celts. This walk aims to include as many of these as possible. Several of the sites are very significant historically and still in use as centres for ritual today.

The route detailed in this section starts from Trencrom Hill and runs down to Mounts Bay. From here, the route is circular around Penwith, going first to Treen on the southern coast, across to Cape Cornwall in the far west, then back to Penzance. Each of the sections comprises a day's walking of up to seven hours, and concludes in areas where accommodation is available. The maps are intended for use with the appropriate OS map and a compass.

Stage 1: Trencrom Hill to St Michael's Mount – 5 miles

This is an easy walk which most people should be able to complete in about three hours. There is a car park on the south-west corner of the hill, and accommodation is available in Carbis Bay, two miles to the north.

This part of the route follows the pilgrim path St Michael's Way, which is part of the European Ways of St James, all of which lead to the cathedral in San-

17.1 TRENCROM FORT TO MOUNTS BAY

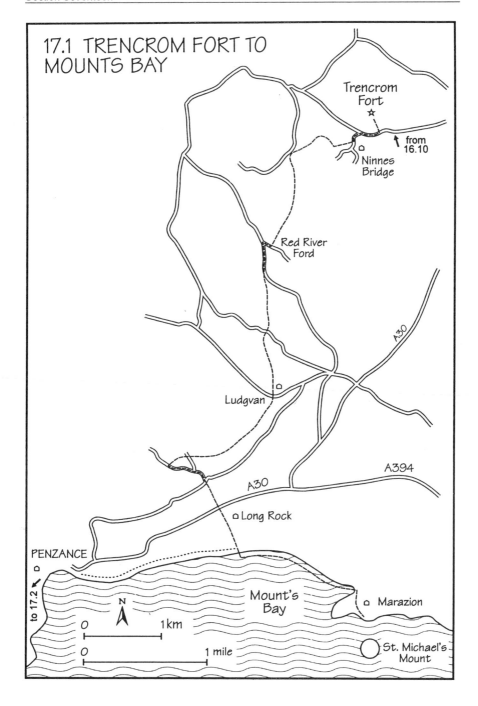

Trencrom
Fort
☆

from
16.10

Ninnes
Bridge

Red River
Ford

A30

Ludgvan

A394

A30

□ Long Rock

PENZANCE

to 17.2

Mount's
Bay

□ Marazion

N

0   1km

0   1 mile

St. Michael's
Mount

tiago de Compostela, Spain. St Michael's Way begins in St Ives, but the Celtic Way joins it at the summit of Trencrom Hill, where the last section ended. The summit of the hill is crowned by an Iron Age hill fort, which was possibly in use as late as the 8th or 9th century. The shape of the fort is still clearly visible as parts of the single rampart remain, as do the foundations of round houses inside. Like all such places in the far west, its history is interwoven with legends of 'spriggans', possibly a folk memory of the Beaker People, who lived here during the Bronze Age and were short and powerfully built.

From Trencrom, the views are breathtaking and stretch from sea to sea, including Mount's Bay, the conclusion of this section. To start the walk, descend the hill to the south-west corner and turn right on to the road. After about 200 metres, take the first turning on the left down to Ninnesbridge. The path turns right in front of the cottages, past the chapel which is now converted. This is one of the many chapels founded by John Wesley in the 18th century. His headquarters were not far away in St Ives.

Go over the wooden stile and follow the yellow waymarks across the fields to Trembethow Farm. In the farmyard, go left at the marker in front of the barn. Swinging right, cross two fields, a sunken lane and three more fields before walking downhill through some gorse to the road. Turn right and cross the Red River Ford, then follow the road uphill. Take the hairpin bend to the left at the junction. One hundred metres past Boskennal Farm there is a stile on the right. Cross this into fields which look down to the Mount. Follow the clearly marked way downhill and cross the stream, then climb uphill. Head for the pylon and enter the road via a granite stile. Turn left along the road for about 200 metres, then turn right between buildings, following the signs to a footbridge. Continue straight up the valley and eventually on to the track which leads into Ludgvan.

The church in Ludgvan is Norman, although there was probably a Celtic chapel here before the arrival of William the Conqueror's half-brother, Robert of Mortain. It is through the church that this tiny village can claim one of its several famous connections. For fifty years the rector was a Dr William Borlase, a famous antiquary and naturalist, who wrote extensively about Cornwall in the 18th century, including his most famous work *Antiquities Historical and Monumental Of The County of Cornwall* (1754).

Take the road opposite the church and at the first turning on the left, continue straight on to Tregarthen. About 500 metres past here, cross the track into a field, then turn left on to the lane. Continue down this lane for approximately half a mile (**taking care not to go left up the private track** crossed earlier). You eventually emerge at a T-junction. Follow the sign straight on across fields down to Long Rock, crossing the A30. The path emerges on another branch of St Michael's Way, which runs along the edge of the sand from Marazion and the Mount to Penzance. To visit St Michael's Mount, turn left. There is plenty of accommodation available if Marazion is preferred to Penzance.

Around the bay from the Mount is Penzance, a pleasant and elegant town with sub-tropical gardens and a large harbour presided over by St Mary's Church. Chapel Street in particular is worth a stroll, as it is home to the Egyptian House and the original home of Maria Branwell, mother of the Brontë sisters.

There are several significant historic sites in the Penzance area. The most notable of these is, of course, St Michael's Mount. Located just offshore from Marazion, Cornwall's oldest town, it was probably named after Mont Saint Michel in Brittany. This link has existed since the Bronze Age, or even earlier as precious metalwork was exported from here to Brittany and the Mediterranean. It is almost certainly the port of Ictis mentioned by Greek explorers, Pytheas and Diodorus around the third century BC. Its present name means 'ancient rock in a wood' in Cornish: reference perhaps, to the legend of Lyonesse, a lost land which was said to have stretched from the Lizard Peninsula to the Isles of Scilly. This mythical land was engulfed by the sea, leaving only one survivor, who escaped on a white horse. This tale may not be as far-fetched as it may appear as the fossilised remains of a sunken forest and Stone Age axes have been found on the sea bed of the bay.

The earliest visible remains, however, are of a Benedictine chapel and two Saxon crosses, with the castle dating to the fourteenth century, although not appropriated by the Crown for another two hundred years. The harbour can be visited all year, but the opening days of the castle should be checked in advance. Access is via the causeway, or by ferry (depending on the tide).

Interestingly, Penzance also lays claim to both the largest and the smallest Iron Age hill forts in the area. The former is called Lescudjack and is sited at the top of Castle Road, just above the train station. Measuring 160 metres from east to west, it is now badly neglected and obscured by a concrete wall, although part of the five-metre (16ft) rampart can still be seen.

In contrast to the above, Lesingey Round, meaning 'hedged stronghold', is just 80 metres (260ft) in diameter, although the clearly visible rampart reaches almost four metres (12ft) in height. It has yet to be excavated and is appropriately covered in trees. Situated on a hill above the youth hostel, access is frustratingly difficult, as there is no direct footpath and visitors must go round by road, then take the track marked 'Lesingey'.

Stage 2: Mousehole to Treen – 7 miles

The terrain on this stage is moderate to difficult and includes some steep stretches of coastal path. It will take about four hours to complete. Long term car parking may be a problem in Mousehole, but our starting point is a short bus ride from Penzance station. Pronounced locally as 'Mouzel', this is reputed to be the prettiest fishing village in Cornwall. The pilchard fishing around which the village grew died out fifty years ago, although Mousehole is still a working harbour. Outside the harbour walls lies Merlin's Rock, which features in a prophecy made by the seer himself:

'There shall land on the Rock Of Merlin
Those That Shall Burn Paul, Penzance And Newlyn'

Astonishingly, this is exactly what happened in 1595, when the Spanish invaded and burnt all but the manor house (now the Keigwin Arms) to the ground. The area is also famous as the resting place, a mile inland at Paul, of Dolly Pentreath, the last native Cornish speaker, who died in 1777. Despite the decline of fishing, life and the sea are still closely interwoven in the far west. In

1981 the local life boat, *Solomon Browne*, was lost with all hands whilst trying to rescue a coaster. Even in the modern age, life can be lost to the vagaries of the ocean.

Leave Mousehole via the footpath marked clearly on the south side of the chapel. This leads straight uphill to a lane. Go left for a few metres, then take the path on the right, which forms a hairpin, and go through the iron gate into farmland. From here, follow the footpath through the fields past Halwyn Farm (the stiles are well maintained and fairly easy to spot). Don't forget to look back as the views of Mousehole and across the bay to the Mount are magnificent. On reaching the lane turn right, then left at the T-junction. This lane goes to Castallack and the footpath follows the same route, but on the other side of the hedge. It is clearly marked.

At Castallack, go past the large, modern barn on the right and a gable end, before turning right through the wooden gate, to go past the house and down the grassy lane. This is very probably a very old path as it leads to Castallack Round. Look out for a narrow path through the grass on the right after the lane has become a path. The Round is a circular field, with parts of the wall remaining up to almost two metres high. Just to the north-west of this and a little further along the path are the remains of a hut circle. To the west by a few metres (again, follow the little paths) is a Bronze Age standing stone, just under two metres in height. On returning to the main path, it widens once again and winds downhill into the almost perfect valley of Lamorna. There are also some excellent views, inland this time, from this part of the path.

The lane emerges on to the B3315. Turn left and follow it as it climbs a hill. This ancient hamlet is Trewoofe. There are several legends in this area which link the once powerful Lovelis family with the Devil, who is usually portrayed as riding a black horse. The Rosemerryn fogou (now on private property, ask at the house at the end of the first track on the right after Trewoofe for permission to view it) is still said to be haunted by Squire Lovelis's tormented spirit. On an equally cheerful note, the next hill leads to a place of slaughter, otherwise known as Boleigh, which was the site of the last battle between the Cornish and English in AD935, completing King Athelstan's conquest of the West.

Once over the hill, the Pipers can clearly be seen. They are set back a little from the road, but are easily accessed. The tallest of the two is four and a half metres (15ft) high, the other four metres. Thought to be Bronze Age in origin (when this area was densely populated), they may have acted as wayside markers or territorial boundary stones. They may also simply be part of a system of outlying monuments connected to the Merry Maidens stone circle, which lies four hundred metres to the south-west. To reach this, follow the first footpath sign for the circle at the bend in the road and go across a field. This is a very well known and often visited site (perhaps because of its location). The nineteen stones form a true circle, 26 metres in diameter, which was probably used for public ceremonies and rituals. The legend of the schoolgirls caught dancing on a Sunday and turned to stone along with their musicians (the Pipers), probably dates from as late as the 18th century, though is possibly of pagan origin.

Leave the circle through the wooden stile in the far corner and turn left

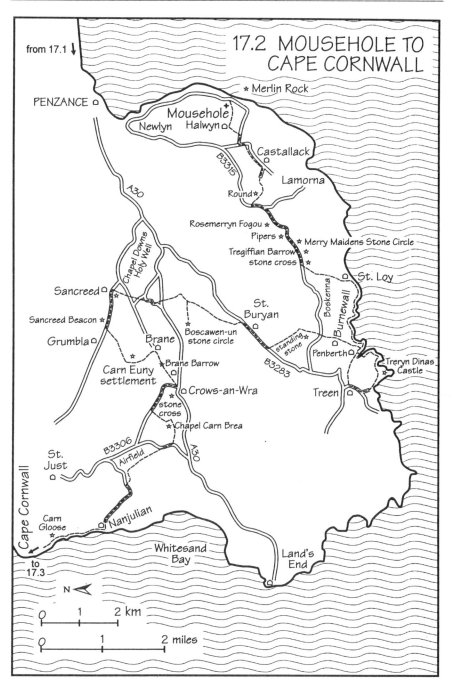

17.2 MOUSEHOLE TO CAPE CORNWALL

from 17.1

PENZANCE

★ Merlin Rock

Mousehole
Newlyn   Halwyn

Castallack

B3315

A30

Round ★

Lamorna

Rosemerryn Fogou ★

Pipers ★   ★ Merry Maidens Stone Circle

Tregiffian Barrow ★ ★

stone cross ★

St. Loy

Chapel Downs
Holy Well

Sancreed

St.
Buryan

Boskenna

Burnewall

Sancreed Beacon ★

Grumbla   Brane

Boscawen-un
stone circle

standing
stone

Penberth

Treryn Dinas
Castle

B3283

Carn Euny
settlement

★ Brane Barrow

Crows-an-Wra

Treen

stone
cross

Chapel Carn Brea

B3306

Airfield

A30

St.
Just

Carn
Gloose

Nanjulian

Whitesand
Bay

Land's
End

Cape Cornwall

to
17.3

N

0   1   2 km

0   1   2 miles

down the road. A few metres further on is Tregiffian barrow, a Neolithic chambered tomb, which was first excavated by the aforementioned Dr Borlase in 1871. It is about four metres long, but amazingly, the road goes over part of it, despite the fact it is a national monument. When it was excavated an unusual carved stone was found (now replaced by a replica) and on the floor were bones, charcoal and some urns containing human remains.

Continuing along the road, the Way passes the Boskenna Cross, unusually mounted on a roller, millstone and cider press, decorated with a Christ figure and wheel cross. In the hedge directly to its left is a standing stone, and on the right is a stile into a field. The path across the field emerges on the lane down to Boskenna itself. Walk through the hamlet and where the road swings to the right, continue downhill into the woods and the pretty hamlet of St Loy, which claims to be the sunniest village in England.

From here follow the yellow acorn markers of the South West Coastal Path in a stunning walk along the cliffs to the picturesque fishing village of Penberth. Continue along the path, up the cliffs on the other side of the harbour to the promontory with the famous Logan's Rock perched perilously at the very top. This area is the site of an Iron Age cliff castle called Treryn Dinas, now owned by the National Trust. Ramparts and ditches up to 300 metres long and seven metres high can still be seen. Many legends surround this site involving witches and 'small people'. The castle is also said to have belonged to King Arthur at some point, and a cave beneath the rock is supposed to hold Merlin, imprisoned within it forever by magic.

To find the village of Treen, turn right at the National Trust obelisk and follow the well-worn path inland across the fields. It takes 10 to 15 minutes, and as a reward there is one of the cosiest little pubs in Cornwall waiting. There is accommodation available at the campsite next to the village.

Stage 3: Treen to Crows-An-Wra — 8½ miles

This stage should take about five hours to walk on easy to moderate terrain. It is mostly farmland walking on good paths, with a short but **strenuous** coastal section. Treen can be reached on the B3315 or there is a bus from Penzance.

Turn right out of Treen village, then take a sharp right and follow the lane for half a mile to Penberth. Take the coastal path up the cliff on the left side of the harbour, but leave it at the second fork, going inland. This path curves to the right and becomes a wide track, passing through Burnewhall Farm. Cross the B3315, following the footpath sign over the stile and into a field with good views to the north. Keep to the right and go through the gate into the next field, which contains a standing stone. Follow the line of stiles, keeping St Buryan Church spire in view. The path leads onto a lane. Turn left and follow this until it joins the B3283 just outside the village.

St Buryan has played an important role for centuries, not least because its 30-metre (92ft) spire can be seen for miles around (providing a useful orientation point for walkers!) It was an important monastic site as early as the 10th century, as confirmed by Athelstan's charter. The churchyard still shows the raised oval outline of an early Christian cemetery enclosure and a 9th-century cross. Nearby is thought to be the battle site where Arthur fought off the Danes who had landed on Gwynver Beach (Whitesands Bay).

To continue on the route, take the B3283 past the church until the public footpath sign on the edge of the village. Follow this across the fields, past Pridden Farm, and head north-east, crossing a stream, until the path joins a wider, hedged path. Take a sharp left and continue until it emerges at Boscowen-un stone circle. This is the most complete and possibly the most significant circle in West Penwith. It certainly has an atmosphere which is missing from more touristic sites. Each of the stones are granite, except one which is pure quartz. The central heel stone leans towards two stone slabs, possibly cists which lie on the outside of the circle. It was in use up to the Dark Ages as a site of the Gorsedd of the Island of Britain. The Druid Henry Jenner revived this in 1928 and the the Gorsedd is now held annually at different sites around Cornwall, including Boscawen-un.

Retrace the path and continue past Boscawen Farm, where it becomes a track, passing a standing stone in the hedge on the left. Cross the A30 and follow the public footpath signs to Sancreed, through the tiny hamlet of Tregonbris, crossing and re-crossing country lanes.

Sancreed itself has two of the best late Dark Age stone crosses in Cornwall, both of which are in the churchyard. The one on the south porch in inscribed with the sculptor's own name 'Runho' and the shaft has double knotwork. The other cross is inscribed 'INCX X' with designs on all four sides, including a vase and flower.

Many churches in Cornwall are built on or near to the cells of early saints or hermits. These in turn had been located by holy wells, which often have a Christian superstructure, but pre-Christian powers. Chapel Downs holy well is a good example of this. A few minutes walk from the village (follow the signs opposite the church, passing the concrete hut), there is a tiny, ruined chapel next to it and a modern cross. The tree overhanging the well is adorned with rags and other offerings. This is an ancient custom used to invoke the well's healing and prophetic powers.

Retrace the path to the church and turn left, then left again, uphill to Sancreed Beacon. At the summit, on the right, there is a wooden gate to the beacon. At 560 feet (172 metres), this offers some of the best views in West Cornwall, rivalled only by Chapel Carn Brea. The beacon is owned by Cornwall Heritage Trust and is a nature reserve, as well as the site of a Bronze Age settlement. The outline of the settlement can still be seen, as can the remains of a field system and a burial mound.

Five minutes further down the road there is a left turn on to a bridleway, just before Grumbla. Follow this until it forms a T-junction with a wider track. Turn left and follow the signs for Carn Euny. Occupied periodically throughout the Iron Age, Carn Euny has an excellent mixture of round and courtyard houses. However, its most notable feature is the 20 metre (60ft) long fogou (meaning cave in Cornish), or souterrain. Comparable to those in Brittany, it has a side passage leading to an intact circular chamber containing a mysterious flue-less fireplace. It is still unclear as to what the fogous were used for. Opinion is divided between their role being for religious purposes, as a cold storage, or as a refuge from raiders.

From this point, the two campsites of Crows-an-Wra and Treave offer a choice of accommodation. Crows-an-Wra means 'Witch's Hill', and it was named after a hermit who lived in the chapel on Carn Brea, and was accused of being a sorcerer by the Dean of St Buryan. The route through Crows-an-Wra follows the track through the hamlet of Brane, turning right at the T-junction and then following the first footpath on the right, which is clearly defined and easy to walk. This passes the magnificent Brane Barrow, a well-preserved Scillonian chamber from the Neolithic period which is sic metres (20ft) in diameter and 7 feet tall. The barrow is on private land, but can be seen from the footpath, which is itself part of an ancient route stretching from Land's End to Penzance. The Crows-An-Wra campsite is just over a stream on the left hand side, and Treave is a little way along the A30, on the left.

Stage 4: Crows-An-Wra to Cape Cornwall – 6 miles

This takes about four hours of coastal, farmland and moorland walking over moderate terrain. To reach the starting point by car, take the A30 to Crows-An-Wra, where there is no official parking. Alternatively, take the Sennen Cove bus from Penzance.

We begin with a stiff climb up to Chapel Carn Brea (not to be confused with Carn Brea near Redruth), the first and last hill in England (and one of the highest in West Cornwall). Take the right turn at the Crows-An-Wra cross and go up the lane to the car park on the left. The path to the top is at the far end of the car park, through a kissing gate. The views from the summit are stunning, stretching in every direction and taking in the huge expanse of the Atlantic, the hills and moorland to the north, and away to the east, the massive white satellite dishes at Goonhilly Earth Station on the Lizard Peninsula can just be seen on a clear day. Also at the summit are the remains of two Bronze Age barrows and a medieval chapel. It is the site of the first in a chain of bonfires to be lit across Cornwall on Midsummer's Eve as members of the St Just Old Cornwall Society sing and pray in Cornish whilst sacrificing herbs and flowers to the sun god.

From the summit, take the path on the left downhill and go through a wooden gate to the end of a walled path which skirts the base of the hill. Turn right along the hedge line towards Kerrow Farm,0 then go left down the lane to the B3306. Go right up the road for a short distance, then turn left at Brea. Go through the courtyard to the back of the buildings, where there is a yellow arrow on the right. Follow similar arrows across farmland, though Brea Vean to the airfield. Keep to the left until the path joins the lane to the coast. This ends at Nanjulian. The driveway to the house is private, except for the footpath, which goes right in front of the buildings and leads to the cove of the same name. Turn right on to the coastal path proper and enjoy the stunning views. The large sandy bay which comes into view from the Cape when facing Land's End is Gwynver Beach, where the Danes who fought Arthur landed.

The path eventually joins a small tarmac road. Continue down this, along the coast (for the route back into the small town of St Just, turn right). An old tin mine should come into view. The Bronze Age barrow of Carn Gloose (otherwise known as Ballowall) is just past this on the left side of the road. It would have been an enclosed chamber up to 10 feet tall, surrounded by cists. Now only the stones remain. It is fairly intact, however, including the strange T-shaped pit in the centre. It is appropriate, perhaps, that such a remote and desolate spot should be full of stories of 'small people' dancing in the moonlight. Fanciful in the daylight maybe, but this walker saw it in thick mist at twilight!

Stage 5: Cape Cornwall to Penzance – 11 miles

This stage will take about six and a half hours to walk over moderate, mostly moorland, terrain. There is car parking at St Just and Cape Cornwall, or a bus from Penzance to St Just.

This section of the path covers a wild and ancient landscape with only the occasional farm or minor road to betray the existence of the 20th century. Indeed, much of this section follows the ancient 'Old St Ives Road', a trade route dating from the Neolithic period. However, in practical terms this does present difficulties for the walker. The **remoteness of the path** means that there is **no accommodation en route**, so unless one is lucky enough to stumble across a seasonal B&B, there is little choice other than to stagger on to the end. **I also suggest that the OS Explorer 7 map is essential, as is a compass.**

One of 'The Pipers' - Photo provided by Alex Pratt

From the car park at Cape Cornwall, take the South West Coastal Path towards Pendeen. As the path swings inland, follow the line of the valley until you emerge at a small group of houses by a stream. Cross this and take the path uphill, turning 90 degrees to the right at the second track. Continue down this until it comes to the B3306. Cross the road and walk down Truthwall Lane, which is marked by a camping sign. At the end of the road, turn left up No Go By Hill and take the first right, known as Kenthyon Lane. This is part of the 'Old St Ives Road' which then crosses Carnyorth Common, so follow the yellow arrows to just after the lake, then turn left and it's about 25 metres to Tregeseal stone circle.

This remote yet fairly complete circle is the sole survivor of a pair. The nineteen stones stand to a height of 1.5 metres (5ft), although there is no central stone. A few hundred metres to the north-east are the ruins of two chambered tombs, and there are several holed stones hidden in the gorse-covered common. Take the path at the north-east corner of the circle and head for the stile to the right of the imposing mass of rock known as Carn Kenidjack. This area is said to be haunted by the Devil on a black horse, and anyone wandering near the carn at night or in fog needs to cross the stile in order to escape his grasp. Once safely past the carn, turn right on to a track, which swings round to the left and joins the B3318. Directly opposite is a small area for parking cars and the start of a well-trodden permissive path (not marked on maps) which leads directly uphill to Chun Quoit. This part of Woon Gumpus Common is haunted by a 'spriggan' who is, by all accounts, extremely unpleasant and not to be confused with the more helpful 'small people', whose dislike of being seen at their good work is recorded in the old rhyme:

'Piskey fine and piskey gay,
Piskey will now fly away.'

The quoit itself is very well preserved. Although it was originally part of a barrow 11 metres (35ft) in diameter, the capstone still rests on all four uprights which have supported it since 3000BC. There is a burial chamber inside, but this was found to be empty on discovery in 1871. A few hundred metres to the east is Chun Castle, which was built around 200BC. Evidence of both tin and iron smelting have been found, dating from the same period as inside the castle walls, supporting the claim that the county has been trading in these riches since before the time of Christ. Indeed, even the metalwork in King Solomon's temple is said to have originated from Cornwall. Chun's importance to this trade is suggested by its defences, which include ditches, walls and a clever staggered entrance which can still be seen. It is thought to have been occupied as late as AD500 – thereby being in use for almost a thousand years.

From Chun Castle, the path follows the ancient way more closely, passing the Bosullow Trehyllys settlement (not yet excavated). Finding the way can initially be quite difficult. Look for a small path through the gorse north-east from the walls of the castle (roughly opposite the gate posts). After a few metres there is a stone marked with a yellow arrow pointing downhill, and passing the settlement on the right. Visits are by appointment only (call Penzance 261402 in advance), but worthwhile as this Romano-British village contains three courtyard houses and several round houses. The remains of a field system can also be seen. The track can easily be seen between the stone walls, but may become choked with bracken in high summer.

At the road, turn right and walk past the phone box at Bosullow, then left at the path signposted for Men–An-Tol. These peculiar stones date from the Bronze Age and have defeated all attempts to discover their true purpose. Legend suggests that the middle stone, which has a 51cm hole, has a curative effect on those who crawl through the hole widdershins, and in addition will act as an oracle if two brass pins are crossed on the top. The name itself gives us few clues, simply meaning 'stone of the hole'. Another mysterious stone is the Men Scyfa, located a few hundred metres from Men An Tol in a field on the left of the

17.3 CAPE CORNWALL TO PENZANCE

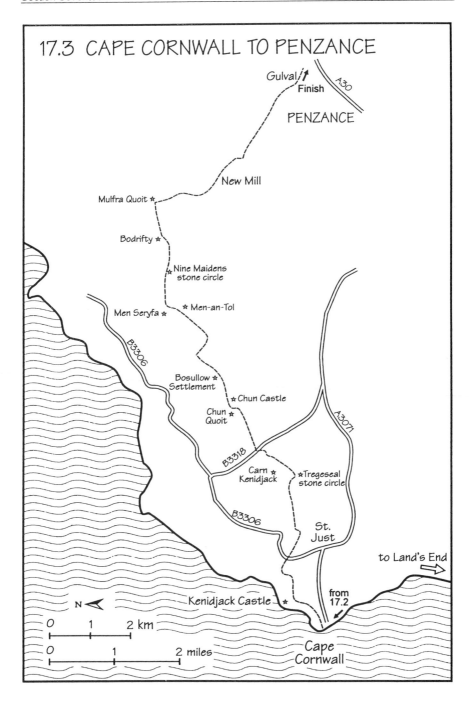

original path. The Latin inscription is to Rialobran, a young Dark Age warrior who died defending his land against a usurper.

The end of the lane is marked by the four parishes stone, and the path emerges on high, windswept moorland – about as different as is possible from the soft, wooded valleys on the southern side of Penwith, just a few short miles away. Ignore the yellow arrows and continue up the ridge, heading south-east towards the Nine Maidens stone circle on the left side of the path. Do not confuse this with a group of barrows and their ring of retaining stones a few metres before the Nine Maidens, on the right of the path. Nine Maidens is a true circle dating from the Bronze Age, with unusually high stones of up to two metres, although only eight remain upright. This ridge has several other monuments, including a cist and a standing stone.

From here, **it is very easy to lose the path.** Go east downhill, parallel with the hedge line on the left. The base of the hill is crossed by a track. Join this and turn right, until it comes to a T-junction. Go left through the gate, then right over the stile to Bodrifty Iron Age settlement. This site, though not as impressive as Carn Euny, was excavated in 1950 and revealed Bronze Age pottery and various other household objects, although the remains, including a field system and round houses, date from the Iron Age. Take the path from the south-east corner of the site and follow it around the base of Mulfra Hill, before swinging left to the summit and Mulfra Quoit.

A Neolithic tomb similar to Chun, Mulfra has not stood the test of time so well – the absence of the fourth upright has caused the capstone to slip and it now stands at an angle. However, it is an impressive 11 metres across and almost two metres high. There are several barrows on the northern side of the summit, although they are not easy to distinguish. Although the quoit may be reason enough to climb the hill, the stunning views to both coasts, including St Michael's Mount, are an added incentive.

Leave the summit by the path going south. As it becomes a sunken lane, look to the right for Mulfra Vean Courtyard House settlement, which has the remains of three houses dating from the late Iron Age. Once through the hamlet of Mulfra, the lane is paved. Turn left at the T-junction, then right at Newmill. Continue down the road until reaching the footpath marked on the left through the woods, then follow this uphill through Boscobba and Polkinghorn to Rosemorran. From here it is easier to follow the lane down into Gulval, where a good pint might be an appropriate reward for any survivors!

Looking Ahead: *The Celtic Way route through Western Britain ends at the end of the linear route, at St Michael's Mount. However, the following section gives details of the first stages of the route across to Brittany – Stonehenge to Winchester – with the intention of going over to Brittany from Portsmouth to St Malo and starting from Mont Saint Michel.*

Section Eighteen
Beginning the Link to Brittany: Stonehenge to Winchester

31½ miles

The Megalithic Ring of Stonehenge

Derek Prosser

Derek was born in Tywyn on the west coast of Wales in 1953. He moved to England in the mid-1960s, firstly to Oxfordshire and he now lives in Hampshire. He is married with two boys and a crazy little black dog. He recently completed a degree in History/Archaeology at King Alfred's College, Winchester.

Stages:

1. Stonehenge to Old Sarum – 8 miles
2. Old Sarum to Figsbury Ring – 5½miles
3. Figsbury Ring to King's Sombourne – 10 miles
4. King's Sombourne to Winchester – 8 miles

Maps: Landranger 184 and 185

Highlights: Stonehenge, Old Sarum, Figsburv Rings, Danebury, Winchester and Butser Hill.

Starting Point: Stonehenge car park (123 422)

Transport: Rail stations at Salisbury, Winchester, Romsey and Andover. Bus enquiries – 0345 023067. Buses to Stonehenge from Devizes, Swindon and Salisbury. The bus route from Salisbury to Andover takes in Winchester, Stockbridge, King's Sombourne and Romsey.

Accommodation: Youth hostels at Winchester – The City Mill – 01962 853723 and Portsmouth – Wymering Manor – 01705 375661.

Tourist Information: Winchester – 01962 840500, Portsmouth – 01705 826722

Introduction

This section runs from Stonehenge to Winchester. It is the beginning of a future link to Brittany. Immediate plans are to improve the current route and establish it with signs. It would be rewarding to see extensions to the Celtic Way. However, all this is for the future.

For the present, we can walk this section towards the south coast and experience the hills and tracks which have always formed part of the link between Britain and France. The terrain is all of rolling chalkland downs and shallow river valleys. Depending on the weather, there should be no difficulties walking the route, though in wet conditions the chalk downlands **can be slippery** under foot.

The history and archaeology of southern Wiltshire and Hampshire is varied, well documented and is too large to be covered in any depth in this guide. Much of the area's archaeology is pre-Celtic, such as Stonehenge and many of the barrows. The Celtic legacy is most obvious in the hill forts which are on the route, though there again many are not included, simply because there are too many. Of the historical sites of the area, Old Sarum, Winchester and Portsmouth have well-recorded pasts which merit individual attention.

Stage 1: Stonehenge (123 422) to Old Sarum (138 326) – 8 miles

From the car park at Stonehenge, turn right along the A344 (west) for approximately 300 metres, then turn left down a byway and across the very busy A303. Once across the A303 it is only a short walk to the Normanton Down complex of Bronze Age barrows, where you turn left and, passing through the barrows, come to another byway. Here you will find an information board giving details of the barrows. Turn right and head towards the small village of Lake. The byway drops down into a pleasant, open valley.

Continue along the valley. At Springbottom Farm take the right fork in the byway, and carry on until just before reaching the first house, where you will find a path marker on your right. Follow the path across a small field and along the edge of the wood. Cross over the road and go straight on down to the River Avon. Follow the Avon downstream until eventually you reach a tarmacked road in Upper Woodford. Here you turn left, pass the pub, and left again over the bridge. Remain on this road, passing a telephone box on your right, until you come to a wooded hillside.

The footpath joins the road at the beginning of the woods (131 365), next to a house. Follow the path south towards Salterton, where you rejoin the road for a short distance, taking you to Salterton Farm. Take care to avoid the slurry pit at Salterton Farm. The overgrown footpath continues south, climbing to a small copse. Here it is well worth looking back for the scenic views of the valley.

There are a number of footpaths in this small copse. On entering the copse, turn left for a few metres and then right. The footpath continues on to Old Sarum, which is visible on the skyline in the distance. The footpath comes into the north-east corner of Old Sarum. At the farm you turn right, which takes you to the car park, toilets and Old Sarum itself.

The site of Old Sarum (Sorviodunem) dates from approximately 3000BC.

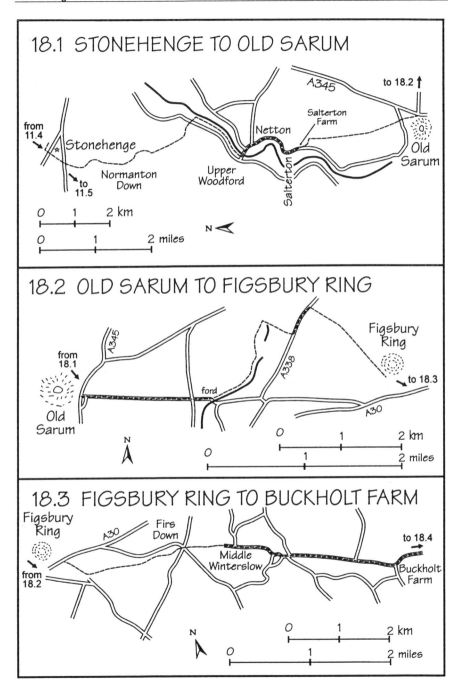

18.1 STONEHENGE TO OLD SARUM

to 18.2

A345

from 11.4

Stonehenge

Salterton Farm

Netton

Old Sarum

Normanton Down

Upper Woodford

Salterton

to 11.5

0   1   2 km

0   1   2 miles

N

18.2 OLD SARUM TO FIGSBURY RING

A345

from 18.1

Figsbury Ring

A338

Old Sarum

ford

to 18.3

A30

N

0   1   2 km

0   1   2 miles

18.3 FIGSBURY RING TO BUCKHOLT FARM

Figsbury Ring

A30

Firs Down

Middle Winterslow

to 18.4

Buckholt Farm

from 18.2

N

0   1   2 km

0   1   2 miles

This imposing site was occupied intermittently from 3000BC until Tudor times. The earthen banks were constructed to protect the people and their cattle. The outer bank dates from about 500BC, during the Iron Age. There was a settlement at Old Sarum during the Romano-British period, and a number of Roman roads radiated from the area. There is no evidence of Romano-British occupation of the site visible to the modem visitor.

During Anglo-Saxon times a battle was fought at Old Sarum (Searobyrg) and the Britons were defeated in AD552. The site was strengthened during the time of King Alfred to counter the Viking raiders. With the Norman conquest of 1066, Old Sarum's importance increased significantly. The local population was controlled from here, and this is where William the Conqueror disbanded his army in 1070. In 1075 it became a major religious site when it took over the diocese of Sherborne. A new cathedral was built soon after 1078. Soon after 1100, Bishop Roger had two palaces built at Old Sarum, one for himself and one for Henry 1. There followed a decline in the fortunes of old Sarum until 1540, when the site was no longer occupied.

Stage 2: Old Sarum (138 326) to Figsbury Ring (188 338) – 5½ miles

From the car park at Old Sarum, cross over the A345 and head for Ford. Continue along that road until you reach the river, where you turn left up the bridleway. Go through the gate and turn left, then right at the water treatment plant.

Follow the public footpath and go over the stile, past a single house on the left. Continue straight on. Carry on down the dirt track, then turn right over the river and on to the A338, where you turn left into village. Follow the main road past the church on your right, then turn right, following the sign for the Monarch Way Pass under the railway arch. Continue straight up the hill to Figsbury Ring, a fifth century BC hill fort.

Stage 3: Figsbury Ring (188 338) to King's Sombourne (361 309) – 10 miles

Setting out from the south-east corner of Figsbury Ring, follow the Monarch Way sign across the busy A30. Take the path up the hill, following the Monarch Way footpath due east through the woods. This path takes you just south of Firsdown. Continue along to the road junction, turn left and then right towards West Winterslow. After approximately 100 metres, turn left up a byway (Cobb Lane).

Follow the path uphill, past a Monarch Way sign, to woods. In the woods take the left fork, this is where the Celtic Way, Monarch Way and Clarendon Way join. Continue straight on up into Middle Winterslow, until you reach the road junction.

Go straight on at the road junction (a Roman road) and take the road in the direction of Gunville. Proceed straight ahead at another junction, down Middleton Road. Continue straight on where the road forks to the right, until you come to the common. Cut across the common heading east, passing the play area on your right.

Walk straight on at the metalled road for approximately 300 metres. At the

18.4 BUCKHOLT FARM TO HOPLANDS

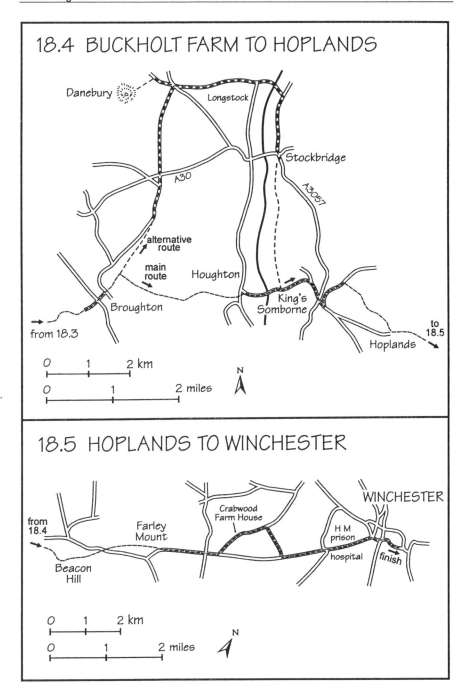

18.5 HOPLANDS TO WINCHESTER

road junction turn left then immediately right, following signs for Monarch/Clarendon Way. Continue along the lane until you reach Buckholt Farm, where temporary signs direct you around the back of the farm. Continue to follow the Clarendon Way sign, heading for Broughton. On your approach to Broughton village centre you have to turn right and then left towards The Greyhound pub.

You have a choice here: Broughton is the dividing point for the spur to Danebury. The main Celtic Way continues on to King's Sombourne. Both options continue straight along Rectory Lane. At the edge of the field the Clarendon/Celtic Ways turn right, the spur for Danebury goes almost straight across the field.

Option: Danebury Spur (324 371)

After crossing the field, you join a minor road. Turn right and continue until you reach the A30. Go straight across the A30, and follow the road for about one and a half miles. At the metalled road, turn left and continue for about 500 metres. This takes you on to the approach road for Danebury Ring.

The Iron Age hill fort of Danebury was constructed around 500BC. It is unusual in that large numbers of storage pits were found, many more than would be required by the estimated population of the area. The use of the site may have been that of storage or trading. It appears that occupation ended about 100BC. For those who are interested there are archaeological excavation reports compiled by Professor Barry Cunliffe available from the local libraries.

To return to the Celtic Way, retrace your steps down to the approach road and turn right, this brings you to a road junction. Take the second road on the left, which takes you east into the village of Longstock. In the village, turn left, walk for a short distance and then turn right. This road takes you over the River Test.

The Test Way passes down this valley and is signposted just before the A305. Turn south down the Test Way towards Stockbridge. Follow the Test Way signs along the outskirts of Stockbridge, straight across the first and second roundabouts. Follow the Test Way to its junction with the Clarendon/Celtic Ways.

Option: The Celtic Way from Broughton (311 332) to King's Sombourne (361 309)

At the end of Rectory Lane in Broughton, turn right and follow the Clarendon Way signs. This takes you along the back of the village. Follow the path through to Houghton, where you turn left and proceed for approximately 150 metres. Next turn right and go over the River Test. After crossing the River Test, the path crosses the Test Way, and **joins up with the Danebury Spur.**

From this junction, the Celtic Way goes east up the hill in the direction of King's Sombourne. Turn right at the first road junction, this takes you down into King's Sombourne village. Turn right on the A3057, go over the little river and continue until you come to the church.

Stage 4: King's Sombourne (361 309) to Winchester (485 294) – 8 miles

From the church at King's Sombourne, head north to the river. Here you turn right and follow the river upstream. About 600 metres upstream, the Clarendon/Celtic Way path is found on your right. Climb up the hill and down the other side, following the Clarendon Way signs. The path turns left and follows the course of a disused Roman road for a short distance, then veers through the woods to the right. There is a sharp left-hand turn which takes you back towards the Roman road, and another sharp right-hand turn taking you up a rather steep climb to Beacon Hill.

The pathway follows the top of the ridge and takes you past the Farley Mount Monument. The pathway then descends back in the direction of the Roman road, which you follow till you reach Crabwood House. Here you turn left through Crabwood Farm and go on to take the first turning right.

Continue until you come to a road junction, where you turn left and head down into Winchester city. When you reach the B3041 you turn right for a few metres, which brings you to a roundabout. This roundabout is on Romsey Road, Winchester. You turn left downhill with the hospital on your right and the prison on the left. You continue under the archway and straight down the High Street into the Broadway, where you will find King Alfred's statue.

Winchester was built on a crossing of the River Itchen, where ancient ridgeways met. With the coming of the Romans, Winchester (Venta Belgarum) became an important tribal centre, with classical Roman organisation and street plan. Later Venta Belgarum was allowed to build a town wall, as much a statement of its wealth and importance as defence.

After the departure of the Roman army, Winchester declined and did not regain any major importance until the late 9th century when the ancient kingdom of Wessex became pre-eminent in Anglo-Saxon England. The present cathedral was built by Bishop William of Wykeham in the 14th century and is one of the largest in the country. Near to the cathedral is Wolvesey Castle, scene of a battle in 1141, when Matilda's forces were defeated by those of King Stephen.

Today Winchester, although a small city, is the administrative centre for the county of Hampshire and contains many attractions for the inquisitive visitor. The statue of King Alfred the Great is the end of this part of the Celtic Way.

Appendix One

Below is an expansion on some of the ideas which have gone into the making of the Celtic Way Project

Curiosity

Most of what we create ends up like driftwood in the elements, but our fore-bears left a lasting legacy. In the absence of other records it must speak for them. It is not easy to understand the significance these ancient sites had for them and ignorance can pique our curiosity. While interpretation of documen-tary evidence about the past presents problems of authenticity and bias, lack of documentary evidence presents a different challenge. There is the space cre-ated by our unknowing which tempts us to rush in with our own world view. Places like Stonehenge and Glastonbury are prime examples of the way we deal with mysteries. We may approach the questions such places evoke in a forensic manner, or through the language of mysticism, or something in between the two. To ignore them is to dismiss a part of our reality. The places and the ques-tions exist.

So, the attitude motivating this project is that each generation needs to look at the evidence and remains of our prehistory and come to know it for them-selves. But it needs to be available for them to actually see, not only as tourists to a few famous centres, but as movers across the landscape to the great and lesser sites still remaining. Hence the Celtic Way route. What future genera-tions make of it will be up to them.

Towards an understanding of Celtic

Earlier researchers seem to have seen the prehistoric remains as evidence of waves of invasion. More recently the view has switched to one of relatively peaceful coexistence by different culture. The Celts were around in Britain for what is still the longest sustained period in our history. The first recognisably Celtic groups appeared in Britain well before the Romans. Today there are peo-ple who still consider themselves Celts, yet no one would define him or herself as Roman, or Norman. So the notion of being Celtic has some relevance today.

The prehistoric remains included on the route are usually defined as fol-lows: Stone Age, Bronze Age or Iron Age. The Stone Age – being the longest pe-riod – is usually subdivided into three: Old, Middle and New, i.e. Palaeolithic, Mesolithic, and Neolithic. The Iron Age – the most recent of the prehistoric pe-riods – often has two category names associated with it: La Tene and Hallstatt. The names reflect the sites where certain types of artefact were first found; their dissemination is now thought to be by trade rather than invasion. The La Tene artefacts were decorated in the way which has become known as Celtic. A help-ful work about the Celtic culture and legacy is Nora Chadwick's *The Celts*.

The Celts did not have literacy. Their learning and history were communi-cated orally. Caitlin Matthews, in her book *Elements of the Celtic Tradition*, writes of the long and intense learning period undertaken by those who were charged with maintaining and handing on the essence of the Celtic culture. Perhaps that this why so much of what we associate with the Celts has to do with myth, legend, song, story and poetry. Today, the student of prehistory is faced with a fascinating amalgam of archaeology and lore to sift through and interpret.

Stewardship

Groups are working with these ancient sites. The Chalice Well Trust in Glastonbury has been mentioned in Section Twelve. One in particular – Gatekeeper Trust – organises walks and talks around the ancient heritage sites, maintaining what is known and adding to it. An aim of the Celtic Way Project is to see more people walking the routes between these sites and experiencing something of their past. Another aim is for guided walking and temporary tented camps to assist this. The principles of stewardship are applicable anywhere on the planet and currently being applied by many groups and individuals. When we can walk to all the ancient sites on this shared and lovely planet we will be closer to our origins *and* our future.

Threads in the Tapestry

What do we know about the earliest inhabitants of this island? In the course of beginning the work on this project I came across a fascinating range of scholarship and speculation: Herodotus on the Hyperboreans; Nennius and Geoffrey of Monmouth on Arthur; the Welsh Triads and countless references to the several Merlin/Myrddin figures. I have read with interest the work by recent historians about the reverence of ore and ochre; for certain star groupings like the Plough/Great Bear (or Bear – Arth in Welsh), the elusive Pleiades; of George Borrow's fascination with the similarities between words from different cultures.

Dissemination theorists have made a case for certain ideas appearing in separate cultures, not by chance, but as indication of universal significance – knowledge once widespread and now lost, apart from in a few traces in sites and place names. The role of Christianity in incorporating ancient belief systems into its religious framework is familiar.

We can never know the full story of our ancient past. However, by walking the route we can come closer to it. Just as the stories of our ancestors were told in the lives they led and the marks they left on the land, the story of the Celtic Way will not be in the guide, but will be told by each individual who walks it and makes it real upon the landscape.

Appendix Two: The Woodbury Link

Prospective route details: Axe Crossing to Hound's Tor via Woodbury

The first part of this section runs gradually inland, taking in Branscombe, Blackbury Camp, then Sidford and on to Woodbury hill fort. It aims for the Topsham ferry crossing of the Exe (or the footbridge at Countess Wear). The second part of the section goes from Clapham, Doddiscombleigh, Great Leigh and Lustleigh to Hound's Tor. **There are no route details as no-one has walked it yet.** It seems likely that it will take at least two days to walk, with a natural break around the Exe crossing.

Maps: Landrangers 191 and 192

Beer to Blackbury Camp

From Beer youth hostel, using Landranger 192, go to the chapel and follow Leys Road round then take a turning into a track across the hill (224 893). Follow the track to a small plantation (213 890). Go right then take the path left, in the direction of the vicarage (207 887). Go through Branscombe village. Turn right, go uphill and take the footpath to Hole House (196 890). Go north on the lane and path past Rochenhaye and Elverway Farms (193 905). Cross the A3052 and take the path to Borcombe Farm (195 915). Go north to Blackbury Camp hill fort (188 924) and take the opportunity to explore the site.

Blackbury Camp to Woodbury Camp

Make for Sidbury by High (164 928) and Lower Sweetcombe Farms (158 920) or Harcombe Hill if better (168 914). At (137 917), by the inn, take the path west to Castle Hill. Go to Sidbury Castle fort (127 915) then take the footpath west to Beacon Hill (110 910). Follow the footpath to Harpford (091 903) then a footpath to Harpford Common (065 897). Take the track south to Hawkerland (057 889). Follow tracks to Woodbury Castle (033 874). (**Avoid Danger Area.**)

Woodbury to Clapham

Take the paths west to Woodbury, passing a campsite (020 875). Follow the minor road to Topsham and the ferry over the Exe (or the bridge at Countess Weir). Check ferry details in advance. Take the footpath from the ferry to Exminster (962 880). From Exminster, take the lane and footbridges over the A38 and A379 to Peamore House Hotel (918 878). Here take the footpath and lane to Clapham (898 870).

Clapham to Hound Tor

Go north-west on the lane to Dunchideock (visit the church) (884 878). Then go west along the lane to (870 878). **Change to Landranger 191.** From (870 878) go south-west on the lane to Doddiscombsleigh church (858 866). Go south on a lane, passing Great Leigh Farm (850 854). Descend into Lower Ashton, past the pub and to the River Teign. Cross the Teign by Spara Bridge, then cross the B3093. Take the lane going west (842 840) and after a short distance (400 metres?) take a track on the left (841 839). Go to Canonsteign Barton on a track (836 832). Then continue on the track to Shuttamoor (822 829).

On joining a lane, go left and follow it to crossroads. Go quick left then right (effectively going straight across) and follow the lane for approximately 600 metres (814 826). Take the track on the left at a bend (810 826), and follow this track to a lane and then to a car park (804 823). Here, take the lane heading north-west then follow the track past the reservoir to Bullaton Farm (802 820). The track becomes a footpath. Continue on this through woods. It comes out at the A382 at (795 817). Cross the road and continue on the footpath as it runs into Lustleigh village. Follow the lanes through Lustleigh, passing the inn and pub, and come out at the west of the village on a lane which becomes a path at (778 809).

Follow this path uphill to a fork. Go left and follow the path south to the River Bovey and a footbridge. Cross the bridge at (780 800). Continue on the path, now going north-west and meeting Becka Brook. The path goes through Hound Tor Woods to Becky Falls (760 800). Leave the path and enter a lane at the car park (758 800). At the lane's T-junction, go left. At the next fork go right, on a track through woods (757 800). Follow the track to a lane (755 794). Take the lane left. At a fork (745 794), go left to Hound Tor (743 790).

Suggestions for further reading.

The following books are just a small selection of those that have been helpful in providing background information for the guide but there are many others to suit all tastes:

General

Prehistoric Britain And Ireland Forde-Johnston,J. JM Dent 1976.

The Penguin Guide to Prehistoric England and Wales by James Dyer.

A Guide to the Prehistoric and Roman Monuments of England and Wales by Jacquetta Hawkes.

Mysterious Britain Janet and Colin Bird, published by Thorsons.

The Western Way. John and Caitlin Matthews. Published by Penguin. A guide to the Western mystery tradition

The Celts Nora Chadwick, published by Penguin

The Sun and the Serpent by Hamish Miller and Paul Broadhurst (Pendragon Press). An account of the exploration of the St. Michael Line.

The Elements of Celtic Christianity Anthony Duncan. Published by Elements Books Ltd. ISBN 1-85230-360-3

Original Blessing Matthew Fox. Bear and Co.

Reality Through the Looking Glass C.J.S. Clarke. Published by Floris Books.

The Orion Mystery Robert Bauval and Adrian Gilbert. Published by Mandarin.

The West:

The Jubilee Way, Northavon Section, published by the old Northavon District Council, obtainable from Tourist Information in Chipping Sodbury

The Cotswold Way, by Mark Richards, published by Reardon and Son; ISBN 1 873877 10 2

Avebury and Stonehenge – the greatest stone circles in the world – by Michael Pitts, printed by Stones Print

The Wessex Ridgeway – The Rambler's Association, May 1988 (a 137-mile walk from Marlborough to Lyme Regis, linked to the Great Ridgeway which started at Holme in East Anglia, and incorporates the Pedlars Way, Icknield Way and Ridgeway Path).

Ancient Trackways of Wessex – H. W. Timberley and Edith Bell, Phoenix House, 1965. ISBN 0 946 643 008

A Guide to the Prehistoric Remains in Britain, Vol 1 : South and East .R. Wainwright (Constable) ISBN 0 09 460 320 0

The Archaeology of Somerset. M. Aston & I. Burrow Somerset County Council 1982

Somerset, the Complete Guide Robin Bush. The Dovecote Press, 1994.

The Somerset Landscape Michael Havinden. Hodder and Stoughton, 1981.

The Draining of the Somerset Levels M. Williams. Cambridge University Press 1970

Walking Dartmoor's Ancient Tracks by Eric Hemery. Published by Robert Hale Limited

St Michael's Way Cornwall County Council Countryside Access Section 1994.

Journey To The Stones Cooke, I. Men-An-Tol Studio 1987.

The Visitor's Guide To Cornwall Pope, R.T., MPC Hunter 1983.

Secrets Of The Holy Headland Pratt, A.J. 'Cornish World' Issue 13 1997.

Myths And Legends Rolleston, T.W. Celtic Senate 1994

The Folklore Of Cornwall Shaw,T & Deane, T Batsford 1979.

A History Of Cornwall Soulsby,I Phillimore & Co 1986.

The Principal Antiquities Of The Lands End District Thomas, A.C., Pool, P & Weatherhill, C. Cornwall Archeological Society 1980.

Mysteries In The Cornish Landscape Thomas,T Bossiney 1991.

Myths And Legends Of Cornwall Weatherhill C & Devereau,P Sigma 1994.

Cornovia Weatherhill, C Alison Hodge 1985.

Belerion Weatherhill, C Alison Hodge 1981.

Wales:

The Pembrokeshire Coastal Footpath Guide by Dennis R Kelsall.

Sacred Stones by Terry Jones, Gomer Press

The Journey through Wales/The Description of Wales by Giraldus Cambrensis. Penguin Classics

Roman Britain by I.A.Richmond. The Pelican History of England ISBN 0 14 02.0315X

Wales Before 1066 – A Guide by D. Gregory, Gwasg Carreg Gwalch ISBN 0-86381-177-5

When was Wales ? by Gwyn A. Williams Pelican Books ISBN 0-14-022569-7

Wild Wales by George Borrow Chapters XCVII to XCVIII

British Regional Geology (SouthWales) HMSO ISBN 0 11 881184 1

The Megalithic Monuments of Wales by W F Grimes

Idylls of the King by Alfred Tennyson. A focus on the part Caerleon plays in the Arthurian legend

Arthurian Caerleon, by Chris Barber published by Blorenge Press.

The Physicians of Myddfai translated by John Pugh a facsimile reprint giving ancient remedies and the legend of the Lady of the Lake. Published by Llanerch Publishers for the Welsh Mss. Society.

A Book of Wales edited by D.M. and E.M. Lloyd. Published by Collins.

Arthur:

The Arthurian Tradition John Matthews. Published by Element Books Ltd.

Celtic Myth and Arthurian Romance Roger Sherman Loomis. Published by Constable.

The Landscape of King Arthur Geoffrey Ashe. Published by Webb and Bowers.

Mists of Avalon Marion Zimmer Bradley Ballantine Books. Fiction based on recent archaelogical findings.

The Secret Tradition in Arthurian Legend Gareth Knight published by The Aquarian press.

Lais Marie de France. Translated by G. S. Burgess and K Busby. Penguin Books. Songs from the Queen of Brittany of the legends of Arthur and Merlin.

The Mabinogion translated by Gwyn Jones and Thomas Jones. Published by Everyman.

Le Morte D'Arthur Thomas Malory. Published by University Books.

Passport Page

Use this page as a record of the sections of the Celtic Way that you complete. Specially-designed stickers are available at selected Tourist Information Centres along the route; in case of difficulty, please contact The Celtic Way Project (see overleaf).

Section 1	Section 2	Section 3
Section 4	Section 5	Section 6
Section 7	Section 8	Section 9
Section 10	Section 11	Section 12
Section 13	Section 14	Section 15
Section 16	Section 17	Section 18

Feed back Section

Please let us know details of the parts of the route you have walked and any comments or suggestions you wish to make. Send a copy of this page to: The Celtic Way Project, PO Box 111, Bridgend CF33 4YF.